500 Fat-Free Recipes

The Garden Variety Cookbook

The Pointe Book
(with Janice Barringer)

The Low-Cholesterol Olive Oil Cookbook
(with Barbara Earnest)

The Low-Cholesterol Oat Plan
(with Barbara Earnest)

500 Low-Fat Fruit and Vegetable Recipes

500 Low-Fat and Fat-Free Appetizers, Snacks, and Hors d'Oeuvres

500 (Practically) Fat-Free Pasta Recipes

500 More Fat-Free Recipes

500
(PRACTICALLY)
FAT-FREE
ONE-POT
RECIPES

500 (PRACTICALLY) FAT-FREE ONE-POT RECIPES

SARAH SCHLESINGER

Villard ❧ *New York*

Copyright © 1998 by Sarah Schlesinger

All rights reserved under International and Pan-American Copyright Conventions.
Published in the United States by Villard Books, a division of Random House, Inc.,
New York, and simultaneously in Canada by Random House of Canada Limited,
Toronto.

VILLARD BOOKS is a registered trademark of Random House, Inc.

Library of Congress Cataloging-in-Publication Data
Schlesinger, Sarah.
500 (practically) fat-free one-pot recipes / Sarah Schlesinger.
p.   cm.
Includes index.
ISBN 0-375-50114-2
1. Low-fat diet—Recipes. 2. Casserole cookery. I. Title.
RM237.7.S352 1998
641.5′638—dc21   98-16415

Random House website address: www.randomhouse.com
Printed in the United States of America on acid-free paper
2 4 6 8 9 7 5 3

Book design by Chris Welch

To Sam Gossage, the cocreator of this book, whose good heart is the source and center of everything

Special thanks to Robert Cornfield, Ruth Fecych, and the enthusiastic cooks and tasters who shared in the process of creating this book.

CONTENTS

❊

INTRODUCTION

ABOUT 500 (PRACTICALLY) FAT-FREE
▪ ONE-POT RECIPES ▪

The experience of gathering around a communal table, enjoying one an-other's company while sharing a heart- and soul-warming one-pot meal, is a joy that has been passed from generation to generation since the dawn of civ-ilization.

One-pot meals have always offered cooks the chance to create healthy, de-licious, economical meals with minimal cleanup. Today, they are a perfect culinary solution for a variety of contemporary concerns. One-pot meals are the ideal answer for cooks faced with less and less time to spend in the kitchen and increasing evidence of the need to address health and diet con-cerns. They are a freezable, easy-to-prepare, stressless, reheatable alternative to TV dinners and fast food. One-pot meals require only minimal cooking skills and little attention from the cook once they are in the pot.

This complete, practical resource is a cookbook for the way we cook now. It is a book to keep within easy reach on your kitchen countertop—not on a remote shelf for esoteric gourmet cookbooks whose recipes require a safari to retrieve the ingredients, hours of preparation, and a designer kitchen packed with special equipment. This down-to-earth collection of 500 delicious recipes with both traditional American and international roots addresses our need to keep meals simple, healthy, and light. With this book, the basic uten-sils and appliances, and minimal kitchen space, you can make wonderful, nu-tritious, affordable meals.

The recipes are streamlined for easy preparation, cooking, and cleanup. The ingredients are consistent with current guidelines for healthy eating. Each serving meets the FDA definition of "low-fat" with 3 grams of fat or less per serving. In addition to keeping fat intake low, the recipes feature vegetables and fruit, grains, and legumes to provide fiber, complex carbohydrates, vitamins, and minerals. A variety of salt-free seasonings are used to limit sodium intake.

One-pot cooking requires only a few appliances and utensils. When shopping, buy the best you can afford. Durability and reliability should be your primary concerns, since you'll be using the equipment for many years.

▪ POTS AND PANS ▪

Invest in high-quality cookware made of heavy-gauge materials that will quickly respond to changes in cooking temperature and equalize the flow of heat on the cooking surface. To determine the weight of a piece of cookware, look at the thickness of the walls and base, and rap it with your knuckles. You should hear a dull thud. The best choices are pots of anodized aluminum, enameled cast iron, stainless steel, and copper. Many brands of cookware combine several of these materials.

A Wonderful Basic All-Purpose Pot   The most important utensil you can own is a 4-quart nonstick Dutch oven with a removable ovenproof handle and a well-fitting, break-resistant, ovenproof glass lid. (Most glass lids are only ovenproof up to 350 degrees.) The pot should have a nonreactive surface and you should be able to move it from stovetop to oven to refrigerator. You can make most of the recipes in this book in such a pot.

You may wish to add the following:

Large Soup Pot   An 8- to 10-quart soup pot is useful for preparing large quantities. Soup pots should have heavy bottoms and well-fitting lids.

Saucepan   The most practical saucepan you will use is one that will hold 3 to 4 quarts. Saucepans should have straight sides and well-fitting lids.

Wok   Woks are wide, round-bottomed pans used extensively in Asian cooking. Woks can be used for stirfrying, steaming, braising, and stewing. Professional-weight woks made from carbon steel offer the best heat control. If you have an electric range, buy a flat-bottomed wok for even heat distribution. Gas ranges can use either a flat- or round-bottomed wok. Round-bottomed woks should be used with a ring stand placed narrow side up over a large burner.

Skillet   Skillets should be made of materials that conduct heat rapidly and evenly and that respond to changes in temperature. They should be of sufficient weight to prevent them from buckling or bending over time. Choose a 12-inch skillet with a nonstick finish, high sides, an ovenproof handle, and a well-fitting lid. Electric woks and skillets with nonstick finishes are also available.

Casserole Dishes   Flameproof casseroles in a variety of sizes (they range from 1½ quarts to 3 quarts) are useful for one-pot cooking. You can check the capacity of a casserole by measuring how much water it will hold.

Baking Pans   Baking pans may be made of ovenproof glass or stainless steel with a nonstick finish. The most useful size is 9 × 13 inches.

Expandable Metal Steamer Insert   A metal steamer insert will fit inside your Dutch oven or large saucepan. You can also use a bamboo steamer inside your wok.

▪ APPLIANCES ▪

Blender   Blenders are great for pureeing soups and sauces and chopping small amounts of food. The blender's tall, narrow container makes it ideal for liquids. When working with soup mixtures that have just been cooked, allow them to cool slightly before blending. Do not fill the container more than half full, cover the top with a dish towel or cloth before you put on the lid, and press down on the lid before turning on the motor. When blending hot liquid, increase the speed gradually to prevent it from splattering. If food gets caught on the blades, stop the machine. After the blades have come to a complete stop, use the handle of a spoon or a narrow spatula to dislodge food. If the mixture is too thick, add a bit of liquid. When ingredients are too heavy to allow the blades to move, try increasing the blender's speed. If this fails, divide the mixture into several batches.

Food Processor   A basic food processor with a large motor and bowl capacity that can chop, dice, slice, shred, and grind can significantly reduce the preparation time of one-pot meals. Blenders, however, are more efficient for pureeing soups. If your space or budget makes a food processor impractical, you can easily cook your way through this book without one.

▪ KITCHEN TOOLS ▪

Measuring Cups   You will need dry measuring cups (¼-cup, ⅓-cup, ½-cup, and 1-cup sizes) and liquid measuring cups (2- or 4-cup size). For dry measuring cups, metal is better than plastic, since plastic tends to become misshapen in the dishwasher.

Measuring Spoons You will need spoons in ⅛-, ¼-, ½-, and 1-teaspoon and 1-tablespoon measures.

Mixing Bowls You will need a set with flat bottoms in sizes ranging from 1½ to 8 quarts. Stainless-steel mixing bowls are a good choice.

Soup Ladle Look for a metal ladle with a 4- to 6-ounce bowl and 12- to 15-inch handle for serving soups and stews.

Long-Handled Spoons A collection of 12- to 15-inch long-handled wooden spoons, a long-handled slotted stainless-steel spoon, and a long-handled solid stainless-steel spoon are essential.

Spatulas Rigid wood spatulas are great for scraping the sides of pots and turning foods, while more flexible plastic or rubber spatulas are better for folding ingredients in curved bowls and removing pureed mixtures from blenders.

Knives A set of good sharp knives is a vital tool for any cook. Invest in knives with blades made of forged carbon or high-carbon stainless steel that resist stains and rust. The bottom end of the blade should be riveted to the handle. The most versatile is a broad, tapered 10-inch chef's knife for chopping, slicing, dicing, and mincing. A 6- to 8-inch utility knife is useful for cutting up small vegetables and herbs. A serrated knife makes cutting softer foods like bread and tomatoes a simple task. A small, short-bladed paring knife should be used to remove the skin of fruits and vegetables and cores. You will also need a sharpening steel and stone or an electrical knife sharpener.

Cutting Boards These can be made of wood or plastic. For sanitary purposes, have one board for fruit and vegetables and one (preferably wood) for poultry and fish. Use hot water and detergent to scrub boards after each use. Plastic boards can be washed in the dishwasher. Wooden boards can be cleaned with a mild solution of bleach and water or with lemon juice.

Cheesecloth A lightweight natural cotton cloth that will not flavor food or fall apart when wet can be used for straining liquids and for forming a packet for herbs and spices that can then be dropped into a soup pot. It is available in most supermarkets.

■ FOOD PREPARATION ■

■ Prepare and measure ingredients before you start to cook.

■ Keep in mind that the way ingredients are cut up affects not only their cooking time, but also the look and texture of the dish itself.

Chopped ingredients: Ingredients should be chopped in small pieces between ¼ inch and ½ inch square. If finely chopped pieces are called for, their size should not exceed ¼ inch. Chopped ingredients need not be absolutely even in size.

Diced ingredients: Diced ingredients should be cut into neat, even ¼-inch cubes.

Sliced ingredients: Thinly sliced ingredients should be sliced ⅛ inch thick. Coarsely sliced ingredients should be ¼ inch thick.

▪ If you put raw poultry or fish on a dish or counter surface, wash the surface with soap and water before using again.

▪ COOKING TECHNIQUES ▪

▪ Boiling, simmering, reducing, sautéing, and stirfrying are the cooking techniques most often used in preparing one-pot meals

Boiling   Cooking food in liquid that has been heated until bubbles break the surface. At sea level water boils at 212 degrees. A full rolling boil cannot be dissipated by stirring.

Simmering   Cooking food just enough for tiny bubbles to break the surface. Food simmers at about 185 degrees. If a soup boils too hard for too long, it will evaporate and burn. However, if a simmer is not maintained, the ingredients may not cook through in the allotted time. Simmering mixtures should be checked frequently, since they have a tendency to break into a boil as the temperature of stove and pot increases. If you can hear a simmering mixture bubbling, it is often an indication that the heat needs to be turned down.

Reducing   The process of boiling a liquid until at least half of the moisture evaporates. The concentrated liquid that remains has a more intense flavor and is thicker.

Sautéing   To cook food quickly in a small amount of stock, water, or oil. For the best results, be sure food you sauté is as dry as possible and heat the cooking liquid before adding the ingredients. Room-temperature foods brown faster and more evenly and absorb less liquid than cold foods. When sautéing, shake the pan often so the ingredients get evenly browned.

Stirfrying   Cooking small pieces of meat, seafood, or vegetables in a large pan over very high heat while constantly stirring. You can use a wok or large deep skillet that has enough room for you to rapidly stir and toss ingredients.

▪ SAFETY TIPS ▪

▪ To keep a pot from boiling over, give the steam an outlet by placing a toothpick between the pot and the cover. Do the same thing when baking a covered casserole.

▪ When stirring, be sure to reach down into the pot and redistribute the contents to prevent sticking and burning.

▪ To prevent burned hands, make sure oven mitts and potholders are dry before you handle a hot pot or pan.

▪ Before removing a pot or pan from the stove, make sure the burner is turned off.

▪ CLEANUP ▪

▪ Rest spoons and spatulas on a saucer or spoon rest to keep counters and stovetops clean.

▪ Clean up as you go. While your meal is cooking, wash utensils, cutting boards, and so forth. Soak the pot you used before you sit down to dinner.

▪ Scrubbing pots and pans will be an easier task if you wipe them out with paper towels before washing.

▪ Don't scour pots and pans with metal sponges and abrasive cooking materials. Use soft cleaners. Soak pots and pans before cleaning. Wash with soap and very hot water. Dry completely to prevent rust.

▪ If you end up with burned-on residue in a pot, scrape the area and add a few inches of water and 1 tablespoon of baking soda. Bring to a boil, cover, and continue to boil for 5 minutes. Remove from heat and let stand for 30 minutes.

▪ After using a wok, clean it well and dry it over a low burner.

▪ Before disassembling a blender for cleaning, make sure the blades have stopped running before removing the jar from the base. Don't let food dry on the blades; soak them in hot water if you can't clean them immediately. To clean your blender quickly, add a few drops of detergent to a container half filled with hot water. Turn on the blender for half a minute, then disassemble.

▪ STORAGE AND FREEZING ▪

▪ To save on cleanup time, store leftovers in the pot or casserole in which you cook them and reheat them in the same container whenever possible. Use refrigerated leftovers within 2 or 3 days.

▪ To prevent overcooking soup when you reheat it, reheat only the amount you expect to eat, rather than the whole pot.

▪ If you are going to freeze a dish, do not overcook it. Warming it up in the oven will continue the cooking process.

▪ To freeze one-pot dishes, first cool quickly and thoroughly. When filling freezer containers, leave an inch of space at the top to allow for expansion.

■ When warming up a frozen one-pot dish, check the seasoning during and after reheating, since some flavor is lost in freezing.

■ If you intend to freeze a baked casserole, before you begin, line a casserole dish with heavy-duty aluminum foil, leaving several inches of overhang on all sides. Fill with assembled ingredients. Bake, cool to room temperature, and freeze. Use the foil overhang to lift the frozen casserole from the container. Wrap in foil and seal the package airtight. Place in a freezer-proof plastic bag, label, and freeze. To thaw, remove the foil and place the frozen food back in the casserole in which it was baked. Defrost in the refrigerator overnight or place frozen in a 350-degree oven, doubling the original cooking time. Test by inserting a dinner knife into the center of the casserole for 10 seconds until the food is warmed through.

■ FINISHING TOUCHES ■

■ Serve soups, stews, and other one-pot meals in broad, shallow bowls. Serve thick, hearty dishes with knives and forks as well as spoons.

■ Any of the following garnishes can be added to one-pot entrées immediately before serving.

½ cup chopped spinach, kale, or other leafy vegetable sautéd in 2 tablespoons chicken broth or 1 tablespoon chicken broth and 1 tablespoon olive oil

Minced fresh chives, dill, coriander, chervil, parsley, rosemary, mint, fennel, scallions, or watercress

Diced or slivered carrots, turnip, potatoes, celery, red onion, red or green bell peppers, green beans, leeks, mushrooms, spinach, asparagus tips, artichoke hearts, or beets blanched or lightly browned in chicken broth or olive oil

Raw diced or slivered radishes, red or green bell peppers, carrots, celery, tomatoes, mushrooms, garlic, or cucumbers

Grated raw carrots, zucchini, jicama, beets, or onion

Popcorn

Slivered toasted almonds

Chopped hard-boiled egg white

Fat-free sour cream beaten with paprika to taste

Dollops of fat-free yogurt

Grated fat-free cheese

Sliced olives

Cooked rice or pasta

Lemon slices or lime slices

Minced lemon peel

■ To make croutons, cut whole-wheat, rye, French, or Italian bread into ½-inch squares. Place on baking sheets and bake in a 200-degree oven until

dry. Toss 3 cups dried bread cubes with 2 tablespoons olive oil and either 2 tablespoons fat-free Parmesan, ½ teaspoon paprika, 1 minced clove garlic, and
1 teaspoon minced onion; or 2 tablespoons olive oil, 2 minced cloves garlic,
½ teaspoon crumbled dried oregano, and ½ teaspoon ground black pepper; or
2 tablespoons olive oil, 1½ tablespoons lemon juice, 1 teaspoon freshly grated
lemon peel, and ½ teaspoon paprika. Brown in a 300-degree oven, stirring frequently.

▪ Serve whole-grain, French, Italian, or rye bread, rolls, crackers, or English
muffins.

▪ To create your own special toasted rounds, squares, and triangles, thinly
slice bread, remove crusts, and cut to the desired shape, allowing to dry for 1
day. Brush with olive oil and sprinkle with curry powder; a mixture of fat-free
Parmesan and paprika; poppy, caraway, or sesame seeds; minced fresh parsley;
or paprika. Bake in a 200-degree oven for 1 hour.

▪ THE ONE-POT PANTRY ▪

Here's an easy reference guide to the ingredients used in *500 (Practically) Fat-
Free One-Pot Recipes*.

Apple Juice Always buy unsweetened apple juice.

Apples When buying apples, look for ones that are free of bruises and
firm to the touch. If you are going to serve them raw, choose crisp, crunchy,
juicy apples, such as Granny Smith, Rome Beauty, or Gala. Store in a cool
place. Before putting them in the refrigerator, place in perforated plastic bags
or containers to keep them from drying out. Apple corers and apple cutters
make preparing apples easy. Since the flesh turns brown quickly, dip slices or
wedges in lemon juice mixed with water to preserve their color.

Apricots Choose apricots that look ripe and are on the firm side. They
should be smooth-skinned and blemish-free. Ripen them at room temperature, but refrigerate once ripe. When the fruit is soft to the touch, it is ready
to eat. Cut them in half and remove the pit. If you wish to remove the skin,
plunge them in boiling water for 30 seconds, then in cold water. Dried apricots are available year-round. They should be soft and tender when purchased. They store extremely well.

Arrowroot Arrowroot is a delicate thickener for sauces that has no flavor. It reaches its maximum thickening power before boiling and results in
very clear sauces. Two teaspoons arrowroot can replace 1 tablespoon cornstarch; 1½ teaspoons arrowroot can replace 1 tablespoon flour. Combine arrowroot with 2 tablespoons cold water before adding to sauce, then add
gradually. Arrowroot can be found on the spice rack in most supermarkets.

Artichoke Hearts Canned artichoke hearts are baby artichokes with tender leaves and bottoms in which the bristly choke is undeveloped and therefore edible. Buy only artichoke hearts packed in water. They can be stored unopened on a cool, dry pantry shelf for a year.

Asparagus   Select firm, straight green spears with closed, compact tips or buds. The optimum size for an asparagus stalk is ½ inch in diameter. Purchase spears of uniform thickness. Refrigerate uncovered spears and use them as soon as possible.

Baking Powder   Buy low-sodium double-acting baking powder. Don't expose baking powder to steam, humid air, wet spoons, or moisture. Store it in a tightly sealed container for no more than 6 months.

Bamboo Shoots   The tender-crisp, ivory-colored shoots of a particular, edible species of bamboo are cut as soon as they appear above ground. Canned shoots are available in most supermarkets.

Bananas   Bananas should be stored at room temperature until they are ripe. After ripening, they can be refrigerated for 3 or 4 days. Since bananas will discolor after cutting, dip pieces into a mixture of lemon juice and water to preserve color.

Barley   A hearty grain with a chewy texture and nutty taste, barley looks like rice and puffs up when cooked. The soluble fiber in barley is believed to be just as effective as that in oats for lowering cholesterol levels. Barley is commercially hulled to shorten the cooking time. Pearled barley is the most common variety.

Bean Sprouts   Sprouts are the infant plants that grow out of beans in a moist, warm environment. Look for moist and crisp-looking sprouts with a fresh scent. The shorter the tendrils, the younger and more tender the sprouts. Fresh sprouts will keep for 7 to 10 days in a plastic bag in the refrigerator. They should be kept moist, but don't allow a lot of free water to build up on the inside of the bag. Canned bean sprouts are also available.

Beans   Beans used in these recipes include *black beans, black-eyed peas, cannellini beans, chickpeas, Great Northern beans, kidney beans, red kidney beans, lima beans, navy beans, pinto beans, split peas,* and *wax beans.* Beans are high in fiber and low in fat. They are rich in protein and vitamins and contain no cholesterol. You can store cooked beans in the refrigerator for 1 week. They can be frozen in individual serving containers and quickly microwaved as needed. Slightly undercook beans you are planning to freeze.

Beets   Choose fresh beets that are firm and have smooth skins. When trimming off beet greens, leave 1 inch attached to prevent a loss of nutrients and color during cooking. Store in a plastic bag in the refrigerator for up to 3 weeks. Just before cooking, wash beets gently, taking care not to pierce the skin. Peel after cooking.

Bell Peppers (Green, Red, Yellow)   Buy plump, firm, brilliantly colored, well-shaped peppers with healthy-looking stems. Avoid those with soft spots, cracks, or soft stems. Refrigerate for up to several days in the crisper drawer. Red and yellow bell peppers will not keep as long as green peppers because of their high sugar content. When preparing bell peppers, halve them lengthwise. Remove seedy cores, stems, and white pith along ribs.

Blueberries When buying blueberries, avoid those that are very soft and show signs of mold or bruises. Use them within a day or two of purchase for best flavor. Look for firm, plump berries with a healthy color. Store in the refrigerator, unwashed in a shallow plastic container covered with paper towels. Use within several days. Gently wash blueberries in a strainer or colander before serving and pat dry, discarding any that have gone bad.

Bok Choy Look for bunches with firm, white stalks topped with crisp, green leaves. Bok choy should be refrigerated in an airtight container for 3 to 4 days.

Bread Breads used in these recipes include *bread crumbs, croutons, French bread, melba toast,* and *white bread.* Look for breads that have been prepared without added fat.

Broccoflower A cross between broccoli and cauliflower, broccoflower looks like a light green cauliflower. Shop for a firm head with compact florets and crisp, green leaves. Avoid any that are browning. It should be stored unwashed and tightly wrapped in the refrigerator for up to 5 days. Wash before using.

Broccoli Select unwrapped heads of broccoli that are firm, with tightly closed buds. The buds may show a bluish-purple cast but should not have opened to show yellow flowers. Store in a perforated plastic bag, or spray lightly with cold water and wrap in a damp cotton kitchen towel. Broccoli will keep for 2 or 3 days in the refrigerator.

Broth *Chicken Broth:* Look for low-sodium nonfat or reduced-fat canned chicken broth. If you cannot find nonfat canned chicken broth, pour a can of regular broth in a glass or plastic container and refrigerate overnight (or place in the freezer for 30 minutes) until fat congeals on the surface. Skim fat off before using.

Vegetable Broth: Commercially prepared nonfat vegetable broth can be found at your supermarket. You can also make vegetable broth from leftover raw and cooked vegetables. Strain it and freeze in an ice-cube tray for easy measuring.

Brussels Sprouts Choose brussels sprouts that have firm, tight heads. The core end should be clean and white. Sprouts that are small, green, and firm will taste best. Store unwashed in perforated plastic bags in the refrigerator for several days. Cut an "X" in the base of each sprout before cooking.

Bulgur Bulgur is made from whole-wheat kernels. The wheat kernels are parboiled, dried, and partially debranned, then cracked into coarse fragments to make bulgur.

Cabbage Cabbages should be heavy for their size, with crisp, fresh-looking leaves and no brown streaks or spots. Green cabbages should have deep green leaves. Red cabbage leaves should have no black edges. Wrap cabbage tightly in plastic bags and store in a refrigerator crisper for 4 to 7 days. Don't cut or shred cabbage until you are ready to use it. Discard old or wilted leaves, then cut in half and core.

Cantaloupe   A ripe melon should be firm but should give slightly when pressed at the stem end. Ripe cantaloupe should also have a fragrant, musky scent. Melons should be free of dents and bruises and should have dry rinds. If the melon is slightly unripe, store it at room temperature for 1 to 2 days. Refrigerate ripe melons and use within a few days.

Capers   Capers are the flower bud of a bush native to the Mediterranean and parts of Asia. They are picked, sun-dried, and pickled in a vinegar brine. Capers should be rinsed before using. Look for capers near olives in your supermarket or in the gourmet foods section.

Carrots   Shop for carrots that are small to medium in size, firm, and bright orange. Carrots can be sealed without their tops in perforated plastic bags in the refrigerator for several weeks. When preparing carrots, scrub and scrape the skin if it seems tough.

Cassava (Yuca)   Cassava is a root with tough brown skin and a crisp, white flesh. Cassava falls into two main categories—sweet and bitter. Bitter cassava is poisonous unless cooked. Cassava can be found in Caribbean and Latin American markets and can be stored in the refrigerator for up to 4 days.

Catfish   Catfish have a tough, inedible skin that must be removed before cooking. The flesh is firm, low in fat, and mild in flavor.

Cauliflower   Look for firm, compact, white or ivory heads surrounded by tender, green leaves. Avoid brown spots. Wrap cauliflower in perforated plastic bags and store unwashed in the refrigerator for up to 1 week.

Cayenne Pepper   Cayenne is a small, thin, hot red pepper usually found in a ground version on supermarket spice racks.

Celery   Choose firm branches that are tightly formed. The leaves should be green and crisp. Store in a plastic bag in the refrigerator and leave ribs attached to the stalk. When ready to use, wash well and trim leaves and base. To revive limp celery, trim ends and place in a jar of water in the refrigerator until crisp.

Cheeses   Nonfat *cheddar cheese, cottage cheese, mozzarella cheese,* and *Parmesan cheese* are used in the recipes in this book. Most of these cheeses are made from skim milk.

Chicken   Buy skinless chicken parts or skin them yourself. Look for the government grading stamp within a shield on the package and buy Grade A chicken. Store in the coldest part of your refrigerator. If the chicken is packaged tightly in cellophane, loosely rewrap in wax paper. Store raw chicken in the refrigerator for up to 2 days, and cooked chicken for up to 3 days. Salmonella bacteria are present on most poultry, so raw chicken should be handled with care. Rinse it thoroughly before preparing. After cutting or working with chicken, thoroughly wash utensils, cutting tools, cutting board, and your hands.

Chutney Chutney is a spicy condiment that contains fruit, vinegar, sugar, and spices. It can range in texture from chunky to smooth and can range in degree of spiciness from mild to hot. *Mango chutney*, which is readily available in most supermarkets, is suggested in some of the recipes.

Clams in Their Shells When buying hard-shell clams, be sure the shells are tightly closed. Tap any slightly open shells. If they don't snap closed, the clam is dead and should be discarded. Store live clams for up to 2 days in a 40-degree refrigerator. Shucked clams should be plump and packaged in clam liquor. Store shucked clams in the refrigerator in their liquor for up to 4 days. Before steaming clams, scrub them thoroughly with a brush. Rinse several times. To steam, place ½ inch of water in the bottom of a steamer. Place clams on the steamer rack. Cover the pot and steam over medium heat for 5 to 10 minutes or just until clams open. Discard any unopened clams. Canned clams are also available.

Cocoa Cocoa is dry, powdered, unsweetened chocolate from which the cocoa butter (i.e., fat) has been removed. Cocoa can replace unsweetened chocolate in many recipes. Look for cocoa with 1 gram or less of fat per serving.

Cod A popular white, lean, firm saltwater fish with a mild flavor. It is available year-round.

Collard Greens Shop for crisp, green leaves with no evidence of yellowing, wilting, or insect damage. Store in the refrigerator in a plastic bag for 3 to 5 days.

Corn Choose ears with fresh, green husks and silk ends free from decay or worm injury. If the silk is brown and slightly dry, the corn is ripe. The ears should feel cool. The top of the cob should be round rather than pointed. The stem of fresh-picked corn is damp and pale green. After 24 hours, it turns opaque, chalky, and eventually brown. When you press a thumbnail into a kernel, it should spurt milk. To remove kernels from the cob, stand the cob vertically and run a sharp knife down around its length.

Cornmeal Cornmeal is ground yellow or white corn kernels. Yellow cornmeal has more vitamin A. Cornmeal can be used to make polenta, an Italian pudding or mush that can be eaten hot or cold with sauce and other ingredients sprinkled over it.

Cornstarch A dense, powdery "flour" obtained from the corn kernel, cornstarch is used as a thickening agent. You will find it with other flours in your supermarket.

Couscous A precooked cracked-wheat product that is an alternative to rice, couscous is made from white durum wheat from which the bran and germ have been removed. Once cooked, it has a very light, airy quality and a silky texture. Couscous can be found in the supermarket with other grains such as rice or in the imported food aisle.

Crabmeat Crabmeat is sold fresh, frozen, and canned. It may be in the form of cooked lump meat (whole pieces of the white body meat) or flaked meat (small bits of light and dark meat from the body and claws).

Cranberries Raw cranberries offer more nutritional benefits than processed ones. The best cranberries are plump, firm, and lustrous. Avoid dull, sticky berries. The bright red varieties are tarter than the smaller, dark berries. Because of their tartness, most cranberry preparations require a sweetener, although it can be honey or maple syrup rather than sugar. Usually ½ cup sweetener to 1 pound fresh berries is enough.

Cranberry Sauce Canned cranberry sauces are available year-round in the canned-fruit section of your supermarket.

Cucumbers Choose firm, seedless cucumbers with smooth, brightly colored skins; avoid those with soft spots. Store whole cucumbers unwashed in a plastic bag in the refrigerator for up to 10 days. Wash well just before using. Since cucumbers tend to "weep" when they are sliced, you may want to take steps to prevent their giving off moisture. If so, place them in a colander with a light sprinkling of salt, toss, and let stand for 30 minutes. Rinse with cold water to wash off salt. With the back of a wooden spoon, press out as much moisture as you can, then pat dry with paper towels.

Currants Shop for fresh currants that are plump and without hulls. Currants should be refrigerated in an airtight container for up to 4 days.

Curry Powder Curry powder is a blend of herbs and spices that varies according to the country of origin, but usually includes turmeric, cardamom, and cayenne. Varieties can differ in intensity and heat, so use carefully. Curry becomes stronger in a dish that is refrigerated and then reheated.

Egg Whites Our recipes call for egg whites but not egg yolks, which are extremely high in cholesterol. Two egg whites can be substituted for a whole egg. When buying commercial egg substitutes, be sure to check the labels for fat content. Buy brands with 1 gram of fat (or less) per serving. Eight ounces (1 cup) of a commercial egg substitute replaces 4 whole eggs and 8 egg whites. Two ounces (¼ cup) of egg substitute is equivalent to 1 medium egg.

Eggplants Look for plump, firm eggplants with very shiny skins that are free of soft spots. Bright green caps indicate freshness. Wrap in plastic wrap and store in the refrigerator for up to 2 days.

Fenugreek Fenugreek seeds add flavor to curry powders, spice blends, and teas. They are available whole or ground and should be stored in a dark, cool place for up to 6 months.

Five-Spice Powder A combination of cinnamon, cloves, fennel seeds, star anise, and Szechuan peppercorns, five-spice powder is available in Asian markets and most supermarkets.

Flounder Flounder is a large flatfish with fine texture and delicate flavor. It is available whole or in fillets.

Flours Use unbleached, all-purpose flour that contains no whitening agents. Unbleached flour has a creamy off-white color. All-purpose flour is a mixture of soft wheat and hard, high-gluten wheat.

Garam Masala *Garam masala* is the Indian term for "warm," and this blend of dry-roasted spices may include ground black pepper, cinnamon, cloves, coriander, cumin, cardamom, dried chiles, fennel, mace, and nutmeg. You can mix your own garam masala, or buy it in many supermarkets or Indian markets.

Garlic Buy fresh garlic, garlic packed without oil, and minced dried garlic. When buying fresh garlic, look for bulbs with large, firm cloves. Store garlic in a cool, dry place. Roast fresh garlic in its skin to bring the flavor out before adding to a dish instead of sautéing. Before adding minced garlic to a dish, try microwaving it with a bit of lemon juice for 30 seconds.

Gingerroot Fresh gingerroot, which adds a distinctive, spicy flavor to many dishes, can be found in the produce department of most supermarkets. Peel away the tan skin and slice the root, then mince or grate. You can freeze leftover gingerroot wrapped in plastic freezer wrap until ready to use. *Ground ginger* adds flavor to soups and curries as well as sweet dishes. It should not be used as a substitute for freshly grated gingerroot.

Grapes Buy grapes that are plump, full-colored, and firmly attached to their stems. Store grapes unwashed in a plastic bag in the refrigerator. Wash thoroughly and blot dry just before eating or using.

Green Beans Buy thin beans without bulges; the skin should not feel tough or leathery. Avoid limp or spotted beans. Look for beans with good color, plumpness, and a fresh-looking velvety coat. Refrigerate beans in perforated plastic bags in the vegetable crisper and use within a few days.

Green Chiles Canned green chiles can be found in the international foods section of your supermarket with other ingredients used in Mexican cooking.

Haddock Haddock, a lower-fat relative of cod, has a firm texture and mild flavor.

Halibut Halibut meat is low-fat, white, firm, and mild-flavored. Fresh and frozen halibut are marketed as fillets and steaks.

Herbs The recipes in this book frequently call for *basil, bay leaves, chervil, chives, cilantro, dill, marjoram, mint, oregano, parsley, rosemary, sage, savory, tarragon,* and *thyme.* While fresh herbs are *always* preferable to dried herbs in terms of flavor, they are not always easy to obtain. Therefore, with the exception of parsley, which is widely available, I have suggested using dried herbs in the recipes. Keep dried herbs tightly covered in an airtight container. Don't expose them to extremely high heat or intense light. They are best if used within 6 months to a year, so it is wise to date containers at the time you purchase or store them. To maximize the flavor of dried herbs, soak them for several minutes in a liquid you will be using in the recipe, such as stock, lemon juice, or vinegar. Crush dried herbs before using by rubbing them between your fingers. If you can find fresh herbs at your supermarket or greengrocer (or can grow your own), after buying or picking them, wash them and place them in a jar of water. Cover with a plastic bag and place them in the refrigerator. They will keep for up to 2 weeks. They must be thoroughly patted dry with paper towels before you chop them or they will stick to the knife and each other. Use 3 parts fresh herbs for 1 part dried.

Hoisin Sauce   Also called Peking sauce, hoisin sauce is a mixture of soybeans, garlic, chile peppers, and various spices. It will keep indefinitely in the refrigerator. It can be found in the international foods section of your supermarket and at Asian markets.

Hominy   Hominy is dried corn whose hull and germ have been removed with lye or soda. Hominy grits—ground hominy grains—are white and about the size of toast crumbs. They have a thick, chewy texture when cooked.

Honey   Honey is sweeter than granulated sugar and easier to digest. Its flavoring and sweetness vary, depending on what kind of nectar the bees were eating when they made the honey.

Honeydew Melons   A ripe honeydew should be firm, have a smooth depression at its stem end, and have a fragrant, musky scent at its blossom end. The melon should be free of dents and bruises and should have a dry rind. The flesh should feel velvety and somewhat sticky. The deeper the color of the flesh, the sweeter it will be. Refrigerate ripe melons and use within a few days.

Horseradish   Prepared horseradish is mixed with vinegar and packed in jars. You can store it in the refrigerator for 3 to 4 months, but it will lose pungency as it ages. Fresh horseradish is a woody-looking root with a fiery flavor. To use, scrub or peel, then grate it. It can be stored in the refrigerator for 3 weeks.

Hot Pepper Sauce   Tabasco-type sauces are very hot purees of red chiles, vinegar, and numerous seasonings. The fiercely hot peppers used in Tabasco sauce are often 20 times hotter than jalapeño peppers. Hot pepper sauce is bright red when fresh and will last up to a year at room temperature. When a bottle of hot pepper sauce turns brown, throw it out.

Jalapeño Peppers   Jalapeño peppers are usually green, but are sometimes red when ripe. They are small and blunt-tipped and range from hot to fiery. They will contribute less heat to a recipe if the seeds are removed. Be sure to wear protective gloves when handling pepper seeds and be careful to wash your hands immediately after handling them. Be especially careful not to touch your eyes.

Jams and Jellies   Buy all-fruit jams, jellies, and marmalades that are sugar-free and made with fruit and fruit juices only.

Kale   Shop for green, tender leaves. Avoid any that look yellow or limp. Leaves that are too large may be bitter. Wrap in perforated plastic bags and refrigerate for about 1 week. Rinse well before using to get rid of grit.

Ketchup   Shop for low-sodium ketchup.

Leeks   Leeks should have crisp, brightly colored stalks and an unblemished white portion. Avoid leeks with withered or yellow-spotted stalks. The smaller the leek, the more tender it will be. Refrigerate leeks in a plastic bag for up to 5 days. Before using, trim nodes and stalk ends. Slit leeks from top to bottom and wash thoroughly to remove all the dirt trapped between the layers.

Lemon Juice and Lime Juice Lemon and lime juices are most flavorful when they are freshly squeezed. Store fresh lemons and limes in the refrigerator, or if using within a few days, at room temperature.

Lemon Peel Either grate the peel of fresh lemons or buy grated lemon peel in the spice section of your supermarket.

Lentils Lentils are dried as soon as they are ripe and can be found in supermarkets. They should be stored in an airtight container at room temperature and will keep for a year.

Lettuce Choose heads that are crisp and free of blemishes. Leaves should be washed and either drained completely, dried in a salad spinner, or blotted with a paper towel to remove all traces of moisture. Never allow leaves to soak, because their minerals will leach out. Refrigerate washed and dried lettuce in an airtight plastic container for 3 to 5 days.

Lobster Whole lobsters and chunk lobster meat are sold precooked as well as raw. When buying cooked lobster, be certain that its tail is curled, indicating that it was alive when cooked. Frozen and canned lobster meat is also available. When buying live lobster, be sure to cook it the day it is purchased.

Mangoes Mangoes are oval-shaped and about the size of an apple. They have a greenish-yellow skin that blushes red all over when ripe. Inside, the orange-yellow fruit surrounds a large, slender, white seed. Shop for mangoes with reddish-yellow skin that seems fairly firm. Some mangoes turn yellow all over when they are ripe. They smell fragrant when ready to eat. Avoid very soft or bruised mangoes and green mangoes. A few brown spots on the skin are normal indicators of ripeness. Store firm mangoes at room temperature. When they are soft to the touch, they can be stored in the refrigerator for up to 1 week. Don't cut mangoes until ready to serve them. Peel mangoes with a sharp knife, then slice down on one side as close to the seed as possible. Repeat with the other side. Trim off any remaining flesh from around the seed. Zip off the skin as you would a banana.

Milk Buy fresh skim milk, nonfat buttermilk, and instant nonfat dry milk. *Evaporated skim milk* can give dishes much of the richness of cream with almost none of the fat. It is a heat-sterilized, concentrated skim milk with half the water removed. As a result, its consistency resembles that of whole milk. Once a can of evaporated skim milk has been opened, the contents should be tightly sealed, refrigerated, and used within 5 days.

Molasses Molasses consists of the plant juices pressed from sugarcane that are then purified and concentrated by boiling. You can store an opened jar of molasses on the shelf for 12 months.

Mushrooms Buy young, pale button mushrooms. Brush them and wipe them with a damp cloth or paper towel. Don't soak them in water. When serving them raw, sprinkle with lemon juice or white wine to preserve their color. Mushrooms that will be stuffed for appetizers can be steamed over boiling water for 1 or 2 minutes or served raw. Also called forest mushrooms, fresh and dried *shiitake mushrooms* can be found in the produce sections of many supermarkets. They are parasol-shaped, brownish-black, and have a light garlic aroma. They contain B vitamins and minerals. To reconstitute dry shiitake mushrooms, cover with hot water and soak for about 30 minutes, or until they are soft. Drain. Squeeze out excess water. Remove and discard stems.

Mussels Buy mussels with tightly closed shells or those that snap shut when tapped. Avoid those with broken shells, that feel unusually heavy, or that feel light and loose when shaken. Fresh mussels should be stored in the refrigerator and used within a day or two. Scrub off sand and dirt. Remove the beard with a knife and scrape any barnacles from the shell. To rinse the grit out of the shells, place mussels in a pot and cover with salted cold water. Add 1 tablespoon flour for each gallon of water in the bottom of the steamer. Place mussels on the steamer rack. Cover the pot, and steam over medium heat for 5 to 10 minutes or until they open, but no longer. Discard any unopened mussels.

Mustard Unopened mustard can be stored in a cool, dark place for 2 years. Opened mustard should be refrigerated.

Mustard Seeds Mustard seeds are sold whole, ground into powder, or processed further into prepared mustard.

Nectarines Nectarines should be uniform in shape with a creamy yellow skin and no green at the stem end. Choose fruit whose skin yields to gentle pressure. Dip cut nectarines in lemon juice mixed with water to preserve color.

Nuts Buy dry-roasted, unsalted nuts. Most nuts will keep for 1 month at room temperature and for 3 months in the refrigerator. They can also be frozen for 6 to 12 months. You do not need to thaw them before using.

Oats Buy old-fashioned rolled oats or quick oats. Avoid instant oat products.

Okra Choose firm, brightly colored pods under 4 inches long. Larger pods may be tough and fibrous. Avoid those that are dull in color, limp, or blemished. Okra should be refrigerated in a plastic bag for up to 3 days. You can also buy canned and frozen okra.

Olive Oil Buy mild, light-flavored olive oil for all-purpose use, and extra-virgin olive oil for salad dressings. *Olive Oil Cooking Spray:* Buy olive oil cooking spray to use on baking or sauté pans. You can also buy an inexpensive plastic spray bottle and fill it with olive oil or canola oil.

Olives Buy pitted green and black olives, and pimiento-stuffed olives. Be sure to rinse them well to get rid of salty brine before using.

Onion Flakes and Onion Powder Both contain ground dehydrated onion. They are available in supermarkets.

Onions Choose onions that are heavy for their size, with dry skins that show no signs of spotting or moistness. Avoid those with soft spots or discolored skins. Store in a cool, dry place with good air circulation for up to 3 months.

Orange Juice Concentrate Orange juice concentrate can be used to sweeten some dishes. It can be found in the frozen food section of your supermarket.

Oranges Look for firm, heavy fruit with smooth skin. Avoid oranges with cuts or discolored skin around the stem end. Store whole oranges in the crisper drawers of your refrigerator or in open containers on your refrigerator shelves. Don't put them in airtight plastic bags because mold develops quickly when air can't circulate.

Orzo Orzo is a tiny pasta that resembles elongated rice or barley.

Oysters Buy only live oysters in tightly closed shells or those that snap shut when tapped. The smaller the oyster (for its type), the younger and more tender it will be. Fresh, shucked oysters should be plump and uniform in size, have good color, smell fresh, and be packaged in clear oyster liquor. Live oysters should be packed in ice, covered with a damp towel, and refrigerated (larger shell down) for up to 3 days. Refrigerate shucked oysters in their liquor, and use within 2 days. As an alternative to shucking oysters, you can place them in a 400-degree oven for 5 to 7 minutes. Then drop them briefly into ice water. They should open easily.

Papayas Select papayas that are at least half yellow and yield to gentle pressure. Look for fruit with smooth, unwrinkled skin. Avoid very soft or bruised ones with a fermented aroma. Green papayas will ripen at home at room temperature away from sunlight in 3 or 4 days. They are ripe when they yield to pressure when squeezed gently. Refrigerate ripe fruit and use within a week. You can either spoon the fruit out of the skin or peel and slice the fruit thinly.

Parsnips Fresh parsnips are available year-round and at their peak during fall and winter. Choose small to medium, well-shaped roots; avoid limp, shriveled, or spotted parsnips. They can be refrigerated in a plastic bag for up to 2 weeks.

Pasta Dried whole-grain and/or white pasta in the shape of *bow ties, elbow macaroni, fettuccine, fusilli, linguini, small pasta shells, spaghetti,* and *vermicelli,* plus *kasha* and *eggless noodles,* are used in the recipes. Stored in a cool, dry place, dried pasta keeps indefinitely. If you use fresh pasta, be sure to store it in the refrigerator until ready to cook. It should be used within 2 or 3 days or according to the date on the package. It can also be frozen and thawed before cooking. Dried and fresh pasta are both made from flour and water or flour and eggs. If you are watching your cholesterol, avoid pasta made with whole eggs. There are a number of fresh and dried pastas made from flour and egg whites. Durum wheat, the hardest, or semolina, the coarsest grind of durum, makes the most flavorful and resilient pasta. Pasta made from softer flours tends to turn soggy quickly. For main-dish recipes, allow 2 ounces of pasta per person.

Cooking Tips: Pasta taste and texture can be improved by cooking only until it becomes "al dente," or edible, but firm. Since you should cook pasta without adding oil to the water, prevent it from sticking together by cooking it in a large volume of rapidly boiling water. You should use at least 4 quarts per pound of dried pasta. Leave the pot uncovered. When placing strands of pasta in the pot, hold the bunch at one end and dip the other end into the water, curling it into the pot as it softens. Fresh pasta cooks much more quickly than dried pasta. As soon as the water returns to a boil, test fresh pasta by cutting a piece in half. If it's not done, you will see a thin line of white in the center. Turn cooked pasta into a large colander and shake several times to drain.

Peaches   Look for very fragrant fruit that gives slightly to pressure. Refrigerate ripe peaches for up to 5 days and bring to room temperature before serving. To peel, blanch peaches in boiling water for 30 seconds, and then plunge them into ice water.

Peanut Butter   Buy reduced-fat peanut butter, available at supermarkets and health food stores.

Pears   Avoid pears with soft spots near the stem or bottom end, and those with heavy bruises. If pears are still firm, ripen them at room temperature or place in a brown paper bag with a ripe apple until pears are soft to the touch. Ripe pears yield to gentle pressure at the stem end. Store ripe pears in the refrigerator and use in a few days. To keep cut pears from discoloring, drop them into a mixture of water and lemon juice.

Peas   Look for a bright color in fresh peas and crisp flesh with pods that snap, not bend. Old peas look spotted and limp. Refrigerate unwashed peas in a plastic bag for 4 or 5 days. To shell garden peas, snap off the top of the pod and pull the string down the side, pushing open the side seam in the process. The peas will pop out. Although the pods of sugar snap peas can be eaten, you still need to string both sides by snapping off the tip and pulling downward on the strings. Most snow peas need only their stem tips removed.

Pimientos   Pimiento is a kind of large, heart-shaped, sweet red pepper that is often sliced and sold in jars.

Pineapple   Pineapple can be purchased fresh, canned, or frozen. Fresh pineapple should be slightly soft to the touch with a full, strong color and no sign of greening. The leaves should be green. Fresh pineapple should be stored tightly wrapped in the refrigerator for up to 3 days. Canned pineapple is available in its own juice or in sugar syrup.

Potatoes   Choose potatoes that are firm, well-shaped, and blemish-free. Avoid potatoes that are wrinkled, sprouted, or cracked. Store potatoes in a cool, dark, well-ventilated place for up to 2 weeks. New potatoes should be used within 3 days. Refrigerated potatoes become sweet and turn dark when cooked. Always drop peeled potatoes in water immediately after peeling to prevent discoloration.

Prunes   Prunes have become an important part of fat-free eating, since they can replace fat in baking. Prunes are very high in pectin, which forms a protective coating around the air in baked goods, giving the foods the volume and lift usually provided by fat. Pectin can also enhance and trap flavor. Prunes are high in sorbitol, a humectant that attracts and binds moisture. Butter and shortening keep food moist because they cannot evaporate. Prune puree serves the same purpose as shortening, keeping baked goods moist. You can either make your own prune puree from whole prunes, buy commercially prepared pureed prunes in the form of baby food, or buy prune butter, which is located in either the jam and jelly or baking section of your supermarket. To make your own puree from whole prunes, place 1 cup prunes and ¼ cup water in a food processor or blender and puree.

Pumpkin Puree   Canned pumpkin puree is widely available. If you want to puree your own pumpkin, you can either steam, boil, or microwave fresh pumpkin cut in 1½-inch cubes and puree cooked cubes in a blender. To steam fresh pumpkin, boil ¾ to 1 inch of water in a steamer and place pumpkin cubes in a steamer basket or colander and cover. Steam for 15 minutes or until tender. To boil, add pumpkin cubes to a large pot of rapidly boiling water. Pumpkin should cook in 8 to 12 minutes. To microwave, place pumpkin cubes in a covered dish and microwave on HIGH for 8 minutes.

Pumpkins   Look for eating or sugar pumpkins. They are usually smaller than the decorative ones and weigh less than 7 pounds. They should be bright orange and still have their stems attached to prevent spoilage. Store a pumpkin for 1 to 2 months in a dry spot with temperatures in the 50-to-55-degree range. Pumpkin chunks keep in the refrigerator in a perforated plastic bag for a week. If you're using the whole pumpkin, wash it well, cut a lid off the top, and scoop out the seeds and stringy pulp. If you want only the flesh, cut off the top and cut across the bottom so the pumpkin stands flat on the counter. Then cut the skin away, working your way around the pumpkin. Then simply halve the peeled pumpkin, scrape out the seeds, and proceed to use the pulp. Save the seeds to bake for a delicious snack.

Quinoa   A nutty, light-brown grain originally from Peru, quinoa is high in protein and fiber and has a sturdier texture and flavor than rice. It makes an excellent substitute for rice.

Raisins   Buy dark, seedless raisins.

Rice   Rice is classified by its size—long, medium, or short grain. Long-grain rice is 4 to 5 times longer than it is wide. Long-grain rice comes in both white and brown varieties that, when cooked, produce light, dry grains that separate easily. Fragrant East Indian *basmati rice* is a long-grain rice. Brown rice is the entire grain with only the inedible outer husk removed. The nutritious, high-fiber bran coating gives it a light tan color, nutlike flavor, and chewy texture. It takes slightly longer to cook than long-grain white rice. Either white or brown rice can be used in recipes in this book.

Saffron Saffron is the most expensive spice in the world, but a tiny amount goes a long way. It can be purchased in threads, which can be steeped in water to release their full flavor, or in powdered form.

Salmon Recipes in this book call for salmon fillets and smoked salmon (fresh salmon that has undergone a smoking process).

Salsa Salsas, spicy relishes made from chopped vegetables, can be found in the condiments aisle or in the international foods section of your supermarket. Some fresh-vegetable salsas are also displayed in the refrigerator case alongside fresh tortillas.

Sauerkraut Sauerkraut is a fermented mixture of cabbage, salt, and spices. It can be purchased at supermarkets in jars. Fresh sauerkraut is also sold in plastic bags in the refrigerated section of the supermarket.

Scallions Choose those with crisp, bright green tops and a firm, white bulb. Store, wrapped in a plastic bag, in the vegetable crisper of your refrigerator for up to 3 days.

Scallops Scallops should have a sweet smell and a fresh, moist sheen. Because they perish quickly, they're usually sold shucked. They should be refrigerated immediately after purchase and used within a day or two. Bay scallops average about 100 to a pound, and their meat is sweeter and more succulent than sea scallops, which average 1½ inches in diameter and about 30 to a pound. Though slightly chewier, the meat of sea scallops is still sweet and moist.

Seeds Buy raw, unsalted sesame and sunflower seeds.

Sesame Oil This oil, made from sesame seeds, can be found in the international foods section of your supermarket or at Asian markets. Light sesame oil is milder than dark sesame oil.

Shallots Shallots are a member of the onion family, and their skin color varies from pale brown to rose. Shop for dry-skinned shallots that are plump and firm with no sign of wrinkling or sprouting. Fresh shallots can be refrigerated for up to a week.

Shrimp Raw shrimp should smell of the sea, with no hint of ammonia. Cooked, shelled shrimp should look plump and succulent. Whether or not you devein shrimp is a matter of personal preference. Deveining small and medium shrimp is primarily cosmetic; however, in large shrimp, the intestinal vein may contain grit. There are usually 31 to 35 medium shrimp to a pound and 21 to 30 large shrimp to a pound. To cook fresh shrimp, drop them, unshelled, into boiling water, reduce the heat at once, and simmer for 3 to 4 minutes.

Snap Peas *See* Peas.

Snow Peas Choose bright, crisp-colored pods with small seeds. Refrigerate in a plastic bag for up to 3 days. To prepare snow peas, trim ends and remove strings. Blanch for 15 seconds in boiling water. Remove with a slotted spoon, plunge into ice water, drain, and pat dry.

Sour Cream   Buy nonfat or reduced-fat sour cream.

Soy Sauce   Light soy sauce contains 33% to 46% less sodium than regular soy sauce, with little or no difference in flavor. Store in the refrigerator.

Spices   Spices used in these recipes include *allspice, caraway seeds, cardamom, cayenne pepper, chili powder, cinnamon, cloves, coriander, cumin, curry powder, fennel seeds, garam masala, ground black pepper, nutmeg, paprika, sesame seeds, turmeric,* and *white pepper.* Keep dried spices tightly covered in an airtight container. Don't expose them to extremely high heat or intense light. Dried spices are best if used within 6 months to a year, so it is wise to date containers when you purchase or store them. During the summer months, store cayenne pepper, paprika, chili powder, and dried red pepper flakes in the refrigerator.

Spinach   Buy fresh-looking, dark-green spinach with crisp leaves and thin stalks. Refrigerate unwashed spinach wrapped in a cotton kitchen towel. Careful cleaning is essential, because spinach is very gritty. Dump unwashed spinach into a sink filled with warm water. Drain. Rinse leaves under cold running water until they are completely free of grit. To stem, fold leaves lengthwise and zip off the stems. Frozen spinach can be substituted for fresh in many of the recipes that call for chopped spinach.

String Beans   *See* Green Beans.

Sugar   Table sugar is sucrose, a highly refined product made from sugar beets or sugarcane. It is so refined that it is nearly 100% pure and almost indestructible. Brown sugar is a variation on granulated sugar and shares its very long shelf life. Brown sugar contains granulated sugar coated with refined, colored, molasses-flavored syrup. Light brown sugar has less molasses flavor than dark brown sugar. To soften brown sugar that has turned hard, place in a sealed plastic bag with half an apple overnight. Store granulated sugar in an airtight container at room temperature. Store brown sugar in an airtight plastic bag inside a glass jar. Sugar substitutes are not recommended in the recipes. If you choose to buy sugar substitutes, be aware of their particular chemical compositions and any health implications.

Summer Squash (Pattypan, Yellow)   Summer squash has soft seeds and thin, edible skin. Choose smaller squash with brightly colored skin. Because summer squash is extremely perishable, store in a plastic bag in the refrigerator for no more than 5 days.

Sweet Potatoes   Although sweet potatoes are thought of as tubers, they are actually the roots of trailing vines belonging to the morning glory family. Look for unblemished, firm sweet potatoes with no soft spots or bruises. Types labeled yams or Louisiana yams are sweet, moist-fleshed varieties. Store raw sweet potatoes in a humid, well-ventilated spot with temperatures between 55 and 58 degrees. Wash well before cooking. Always drop peeled sweet potatoes in water immediately after peeling to prevent discoloration.

Swiss Chard Swiss chard is a member of the beet family and has crinkly green leaves and silvery, celerylike stalks. Pick bunches with tender greens and crisp stalks. Wrap in a plastic bag and refrigerate for up to 3 days.

Tabasco Sauce *See* Hot Pepper Sauce.

Tofu Tofu is available in health food stores, Asian markets, and many supermarkets. It has a bland, slightly nutty taste and assumes the flavor of foods with which it is cooked. Extremely perishable, tofu should be covered with water that must be changed daily and refrigerated no more than a week.

Tomatillos Shop for firm tomatillos with dry, tight-fitting husks. They can be refrigerated in a paper bag for up to a month. Remove husk and wash before using.

Tomatoes When buying canned tomatoes, choose Italian plum tomatoes if possible. Store unopened canned tomato products on a cool, dry shelf for no more than 6 months. After opening, transfer tomatoes to clean, covered glass containers and refrigerate. They will keep for a week. They tend to take on a metallic flavor if left in their cans. Leftover *tomato paste* and *tomato sauce* can be frozen for up to 2 months in airtight containers. Drop leftover tomato paste by the tablespoonful on a sheet of wax paper and freeze. When frozen, place in a plastic freezer bag and store in the freezer until needed. When using fresh tomatoes, choose firm, ripe ones. Ripen fresh tomatoes by placing in a brown paper bag and leaving in indirect sun. To remove skins, dunk the tomatoes in boiling water for 10 seconds, then dip them in cold water for 10 seconds. With a paring knife, remove the stem and peel the skin off.

Sun-Dried Tomatoes: Buy dry-packed sun-dried tomatoes if possible. If you can only find them packed in oil, rinse them in boiling water before using.

Tortillas Tortillas are made from either corn or flour. Corn tortillas usually do not contain oil or shortening. Tortillas can be warmed in the microwave by wrapping them in a damp paper towel and microwaving for 1 minute on HIGH.

Tuna Buy canned white albacore tuna packed in water, not in oil. Cans labeled "solid" or "fancy" contain large pieces of fish; those marked "chunk" contain smaller pieces.

Turkey Buy low-fat turkey breast with a fat content under 7%. When buying smoked and roast turkey at your deli counter, ask for products that are at least 97% fat-free. Buy sliced, fresh roast turkey breast whenever available.

Turnips Turnips should be small and firm without any wrinkles, which indicate that the vegetable has lost moisture and will be spongy. Turnips deteriorate quickly, so don't store them for more than a week in the refrigerator. Separate roots and greens before refrigerating.

Vinegars Vinegars are very sour, acidic liquids fermented from a distilled alcohol, often wine or apple cider. Tightly capped vinegar keeps up to a year at room temperature, or until sediment appears at the bottom of the bottle.

Balsamic Vinegar: Balsamic vinegar adds an elegant, complex, sweet-and-sour flavor to food. It is aged in Italy in wooden casks for about 4 years with the skins from red wine grapes, which gives it a slight sweetness.

Cider Vinegar: Cider vinegar is made from apple cider.

Rice Wine Vinegar: Japanese and Chinese vinegars made from fermented rice are milder than most Western vinegars. They can be found in many supermarkets and in Asian markets.

Wine Vinegar: Buy red and white wine vinegars.

Water Chestnuts   The canned variety of water chestnut, which is round and woody and about the size of a cherry tomato, can be refrigerated, covered with liquid, for 1 week after opening.

Watermelon   When a watermelon is ripe, with the juice and flavor at their peak, it should sound dull, flat, and heavy when tapped. Also, check the underside of the watermelon, which was resting on the ground during the growing period. A pale yellow color indicates a ripe, flavorful melon, while a white or greenish color can indicate that the melon was picked too soon. A shriveled stem also is a sign of ripeness. When buying cut watermelon, look for moist, brightly colored flesh. Store whole watermelons at room temperature. Cut melons should be wrapped and refrigerated.

Wine   Brandy, *cognac, pernod, dark rum, light rum, saki, dry sherry, vermouth, red wine,* and *white wine* are used in some of the recipes. Nonalcoholic wines can be substituted if desired.

Winter Squash (Acorn, Butternut, Hubbard, Spaghetti)   Buy winter squash that is hard, heavy, and clean. Avoid squash that have cracks or soft or decayed spots. Store squash in a dry place with low humidity and temperatures between 50 and 55 degrees.

Worcestershire Sauce   A thin, dark, piquant sauce that is usually a blend of garlic, soy sauce, tamarind, onion, molasses, lime, anchovies, vinegar, and various seasonings.

Yogurt   Buy only nonfat plain yogurt with less than 1 gram of fat per serving.

Zucchini   Choose zucchini that are small and tender. The skins should be thin, free of bruises, and a vibrant green. They can be refrigerated in a plastic bag for up to 5 days.

▪ USING THE NUTRITIONAL ANALYSES ▪

The recipes in this book have been nutritionally analyzed using Nutritionist IV software, which used USDA handbooks as its primary sources.

A nutritional analysis is given for each recipe on a per-serving basis. This analysis includes calories; fat (in grams); cholesterol (in milligrams); protein (in grams); carbohydrates (in grams); dietary fiber (in grams); and sodium (in milligrams). Numbers in the analyses are rounded off to the nearest digit.

When a choice is offered within the list of ingredients, the primary ingredient is the one analyzed. Optional ingredients are not included in the analyses.

Due to inevitable variations in the ingredients you may select, nutritional analyses should be considered approximate.

If you are concerned about sodium intake, be sure to check the sodium counts on individual recipes, because some fat-free products have high sodium contents.

500
(PRACTICALLY)
FAT-FREE
ONE-POT
RECIPES

POULTRY
MAIN DISHES

Spicy Eggplant with Chicken • Paprika Chicken • Chicken
Cacciatore • Chicken Cameroon • Chicken with Seafood and
Green Peas • Chicken Fajitas • Hoisin Chicken • Chicken
Paella • Simple Chicken Supper • Spiced Chicken with
Vegetables • Chicken and Shrimp with Many Vegetables •
Chicken Tenderloins with Snow Peas, Jalapeño, and Pineapple •
Balsamic Chicken • Chicken and Zucchini • Spicy Chicken and
Broccoli • Chicken with Brussels Sprouts and Cauliflower •
Chicken Paprika with Cabbage • Chicken with Carrot and
Cauliflower • Chicken with Broccoli, Carrots, and Orange Slices
• Chicken with Corn and Zucchini • Chicken-Jalapeño Jumble •
Chicken with Leeks, Carrot, Cabbage, and Turnips • Chicken with
Mushrooms • Chicken with Okra • Chicken with Shiitake
Mushrooms • Chicken with Spinach • Curried Chicken with
Sweet Potatoes • Stirfried Chicken with Water Chestnuts, Bamboo
Shoots, and Almonds • Chicken Paprika with Tomatoes and Green
Peppers • Chicken with Yellow Pepper, Bok Choy, and Bamboo
Shoots • Chicken with Yellow Peppers and Sun-Dried Tomatoes •
Chicken with Apples and Cranberry Sauce • Chicken with
Apricots • Tropical Chicken and Mixed Vegetables •
Wine-Simmered Chicken with Dried Apricots • Chicken–Bell
Pepper Curry • Chicken Mandarin • Mango Chicken •

Chicken with Nectarines ▪ Chicken and Pineapple in Sherry-Ginger Sauce ▪ Chicken with Artichokes ▪ Chicken with Peaches ▪ Chicken with Pears and Apricots ▪ Apple-Cabbage-Chicken Casserole ▪ Wine-Baked Chicken and Vegetables ▪ Baked Chicken with Barley and Vegetables ▪ Baked Chicken and Brown Rice with Vegetables in Wine Sauce ▪ Chicken and Summer Squash Baked in Wine-Garlic Sauce ▪ Chicken, Turnip, and Tomato Bake ▪ Chicken-Vegetable Bake ▪ Baked Chicken with Bulgur ▪ Turkey–Pinto Bean Chili ▪ Turkey–Black Bean Chili ▪ Chicken-Broccoli Chili ▪ Red and White Chicken Chili ▪ Pineapple-Chicken Chili ▪ Chicken and Green Pepper Chili with Bulgur ▪ Microwave Chicken Chili ▪ Chicken and Chickpeas ▪ Chicken with Black-eyed Peas ▪ Chicken Caribe with Red Pepper and Black Beans ▪ Chicken, Beans, and Barley ▪ Chicken and Broccoli with Bulgur ▪ Spanish Rice with Chicken ▪ Chicken with Couscous and Cannellini Beans ▪ Chicken and Vegetable Fried Rice ▪ Chicken and Rice in Saffron Sauce ▪ Spiced Chicken, Chickpeas, and Couscous ▪ Turkey with Asparagus and Linguine ▪ Turkey-Pear Curry ▪ Turkey, Broccoli, and Cauliflower Stirfry ▪ Turkey and Yams in Orange-Raisin Sauce ▪ Turkey with Zucchini and Red Pepper ▪ Creole Turkey ▪ Turkey Tenderloins with Vegetables in Rosemary-Wine Sauce ▪ Turkey Picadillo ▪ Chicken with Eggplant and Summer Squash ▪ Chicken Chili with White Beans ▪ Chicken with Curried Fruit ▪ Turkey with Snow Peas ▪ Curried Chicken and Green Peas ▪ Chicken with Mushrooms and Celery ▪ Chicken-Tomato Curry ▪ Curried Chicken with Apple and Mushrooms ▪ Turkey with Fruit and Wine ▪ Stirfried Leftover Turkey

❈ *Spicy Eggplant with Chicken* ❈

PREPARATION TIME: *15 minutes* • COOKING TIME: *36 minutes* •
YIELD: *4 servings*

1½ cups low-sodium nonfat chicken
   broth
2 skinless boneless chicken breast tenderloins, about 4 ounces each,
   chopped
1 medium onion, sliced
1 cups diced eggplant (2-inch cubes)
2 cups nonfat plain yogurt

1 tablespoon low-sodium tomato
   paste
½ teaspoon ground ginger
½ teaspoon ground cloves
½ teaspoon ground cumin
¼ teaspoon ground black pepper
2 cups cooked rice

1. Heat ¼ cup broth in a large saucepan. Add chicken and sauté until no longer pink, about 8 minutes. Remove and set aside.
2. Heat another ¼ cup broth in the saucepan. Add onion and sauté until it begins to soften, about 4 minutes.
3. Add remaining broth, eggplant, yogurt, tomato paste, ginger, cloves, cumin, and black pepper. Return chicken to the saucepan and simmer until chicken is cooked through and eggplant is tender, about 20 minutes.
4. Serve over rice.

Calories Per Serving: 295
Fat: 1 g
Cholesterol: 38 mg
Protein: 26 g

Carbohydrates: 45 g
Dietary Fiber: 1 g
Sodium: 174 mg

❈ *Paprika Chicken* ❈

PREPARATION TIME: *20 minutes* • COOKING TIME: *45 minutes* •
YIELD: *6 servings*

1 cup low-sodium nonfat chicken
   broth
6 skinless boneless chicken breast tenderloins, about 4 ounces each,
   chopped
1 medium onion, chopped
1 clove garlic, minced

½ cup water
2 tablespoons paprika
¼ teaspoon ground black pepper
1 medium tomato, chopped
1 medium green bell pepper, cored
   and cut into thin strips
½ cup nonfat plain yogurt

1. Heat ¼ cup broth in a large saucepan. Add chicken and sauté until no longer pink, about 8 minutes. Remove chicken and set aside.
2. Heat another ¼ cup broth in the saucepan. Add onion and garlic, and sauté until onion begins to soften, about 3 minutes.
3. Return chicken to the saucepan. Add remaining broth, water, paprika, black pepper, tomato, and bell pepper. Bring mixture to a boil, reduce heat, cover, and simmer until chicken is cooked through, about 25 minutes.
4. Stir in yogurt, simmer to heat through, and serve.

Calories Per Serving: 171   Carbohydrates: 9 g
Fat: 1 g   Dietary Fiber: 1 g
Cholesterol: 70 mg   Sodium: 91 mg
Protein: 31 g

✖ *Chicken Cacciatore* ✖

PREPARATION TIME: *20 minutes* • COOKING TIME: *37 minutes* •
YIELD: *4 servings*

¾ cup low-sodium nonfat chicken broth

4 skinless boneless chicken breast tenderloins, about 4 ounces each

1 medium onion, chopped

3 cups sliced mushrooms

2 cloves garlic, minced

1 tablespoon all-purpose flour

¼ cup dry white wine

1 cup low-sodium canned tomatoes, drained and chopped

1 medium green bell pepper, cored and cut into thin strips

½ teaspoon dried oregano

½ teaspoon dried basil

½ teaspoon dried thyme

¼ teaspoon ground black pepper

2 cups cooked rice

2 tablespoons grated nonfat Parmesan

1. Heat ¼ cup broth in a large saucepan. Add chicken and sauté until no longer pink, about 8 minutes. Remove chicken and set aside.
2. Heat another ¼ cup broth in the saucepan. Add onion, mushrooms, and garlic. Sauté until onion begins to soften, about 3 minutes.
3. Add flour and stir until smooth. Stir in remaining broth and wine, and continue to cook and stir for 2 minutes. Add tomatoes, bell pepper, oregano, basil, thyme, black pepper, and chicken. Cover and simmer until chicken is cooked through, about 20 minutes.
4. Divide rice among individual plates, top with chicken, sprinkle with Parmesan, and serve.

Calories Per Serving: 338	Carbohydrates: 44 g
Fat: 2 g	Dietary Fiber: 2 g
Cholesterol: 73 mg	Sodium: 91 mg
Protein: 35 g	

❋ *Chicken Cameroon* ❋

PREPARATION TIME: *25 minutes plus 3 hours marinating time* •
COOKING TIME: *58 minutes* • YIELD: *8 servings*

1½ cups dry white wine
½ teaspoon ground black pepper
4 skinless boneless chicken breast ten-
    derloins, about 4 ounces each,
    chopped
¼ cup low-sodium nonfat chicken
    broth
4 medium tomatoes, chopped
3 cloves garlic, minced
2 medium onions, chopped

1 teaspoon dried basil
½ teaspoon dried thyme
¼ teaspoon cayenne pepper
1 cup diced potato
1½ cups scraped and sliced carrots
3 medium bananas, sliced
1 cup pitted prunes
½ cup sliced green olives
¾ teaspoon sugar

1. Mix wine and black pepper in a glass bowl. Add chicken, coat with the marinade, cover, and allow to stand in the refrigerator for 3 hours.
2. Heat broth in a large saucepan. Add chicken and sauté for 8 minutes, until chicken is no longer pink. Add reserved marinade, tomatoes, garlic, onions, basil, thyme, cayenne pepper, potato, and carrots. Bring to a boil, reduce heat, cover, and simmer for 30 minutes.
3. Stir in bananas, prunes, olives, and sugar, and simmer for 15 more minutes before serving.

Calories Per Serving: 265	Carbohydrates: 39 g
Fat: 2 g	Dietary Fiber: 6 g
Cholesterol: 35 mg	Sodium: 270 mg
Protein: 16 g	

❋ *Chicken with Seafood and Green Peas* ❋

PREPARATION TIME: *25 minutes* • COOKING TIME: *44 minutes* •
YIELD: *6 servings*

4¼ cups low-sodium nonfat chicken
  broth
2 cloves garlic, minced
⅔ cup uncooked white rice
4 skinless boneless chicken breast tenderloins, about 4 ounces each,
  chopped
2 medium carrots, scraped and
  sliced
2 medium onions, quartered
2 medium stalks celery, with leaves,
  chopped

½ teaspoon ground black pepper
¼ cup chopped pimiento
½ teaspoon dried oregano
¼ teaspoon dried saffron threads,
  crushed
1 cup fresh or frozen green peas
⅔ pound fresh medium shrimp, peeled
  and deveined
1½ cups canned clams, drained

1. Heat ¼ cup broth in a large saucepan. Add garlic and rice, and sauté until rice begins to brown, about 6 minutes.
2. Add remaining broth, chicken, carrots, onions, celery, black pepper, pimiento, oregano, and saffron. Bring to a boil, reduce heat, cover, and simmer for 15 minutes.
3. Add peas, shrimp, and clams. Return to a boil, reduce heat, cover, and simmer slowly for 15 minutes before serving.

Calories Per Serving: 223
Fat: 2 g
Cholesterol: 156 mg
Protein: 41 g

Carbohydrates: 10 g
Dietary Fiber: 2 g
Sodium: 305 mg

❈ Chicken Fajitas ❈

PREPARATION TIME: 15 minutes plus 2 hours marinating time   ▪
COOKING TIME: 17 minutes   ▪   YIELD: 6 servings

6 tablespoons low-sodium nonfat
  chicken broth
¼ cup lime juice
½ teaspoon ground cumin
⅛ teaspoon cayenne pepper
4 skinless boneless chicken breast tenderloins, about 4 ounces each, cut
  into thin strips
1 medium red bell pepper, cored and
  cut into thin strips

1 medium yellow bell pepper, cored
  and cut into thin strips
1 medium green bell pepper, cored
  and cut into thin strips
1 medium onion, thinly sliced
2 cloves garlic, minced
¼ teaspoon ground black pepper
6 8-inch corn tortillas, warmed

1. Combine 2 tablespoons broth, lime juice, cumin, and cayenne pepper in a glass bowl. Add chicken, coat with the marinade, cover, and allow to stand in the refrigerator for 2 hours.
2. Heat 2 tablespoons broth in a wok. Add chicken and stirfry until no longer pink, about 8 minutes. Remove and set aside.
3. Heat remaining broth in the wok. Add bell peppers, onion, and garlic, and stirfry until vegetables begin to soften, about 4 minutes. Return chicken to the wok, sprinkle with black pepper, and stir until all ingredients are heated through, about 1 more minute.
4. Serve with corn tortillas for wrapping.

Calories Per Serving: 154 Carbohydrates: 16 g
Fat: 1 g Dietary Fiber: 1 g
Cholesterol: 47 mg Sodium: 89 mg
Protein: 20 g

❋ *Hoisin Chicken* ❋

PREPARATION TIME: *15 minutes* • COOKING TIME: *17 minutes* •
YIELD: *4 servings*

1½ tablespoons cornstarch
¼ teaspoon ground black pepper
¼ pound fresh medium shrimp, peeled and deveined
2 skinless boneless chicken breast tenderloins, about 4 ounces each, chopped
¾ cup low-sodium nonfat chicken broth
2 scallions, sliced

1 medium red bell pepper, cored and chopped
1 tablespoon reduced-sodium soy sauce
2 tablespoons hoisin sauce
1 tablespoon brown sugar
1 clove garlic, minced
1 teaspoon minced fresh gingerroot
1 tablespoon cold water
2 cups cooked rice

1. Combine 1 tablespoon cornstarch and black pepper. Place shrimp and chicken in a separate bowl, sprinkle with the cornstarch mixture, and toss to coat.
2. Heat ¼ cup broth in a wok. Add shrimp and chicken, and stirfry until chicken is cooked through, about 8 minutes. Remove and set aside.
3. Heat 2 tablespoons broth in the wok. Add scallions and bell pepper, and stirfry for 1 minute. Add soy sauce, hoisin sauce, brown sugar, garlic, gingerroot, and remaining broth. Cook and stir for 1 minute. Return shrimp and chicken to the wok.

4. Dissolve remaining cornstarch in cold water and stir into the wok. Cook and stir until sauce boils and begins to thicken, about 2 minutes. Serve at once over rice.

Calories Per Serving: 254
Fat: 1 g
Cholesterol: 78 mg
Protein: 23 g

Carbohydrates: 36 g
Dietary Fiber: 0 g
Sodium: 518 mg

✳ *Chicken Paella* ✳

PREPARATION TIME: *20 minutes* · COOKING TIME: *43 minutes* ·
YIELD: *5 servings*

3 cups low-sodium nonfat chicken broth

3 skinless boneless chicken breast tenderloins, about 4 ounces each, cut into ½-inch cubes

1 medium onion, chopped

2 cloves garlic, minced

¼ teaspoon dried saffron threads, crushed

2 cups low-sodium canned tomatoes, crushed, juice reserved

2 cups water-packed canned artichoke hearts, drained

1 medium red bell pepper, cored and diced

1 medium green bell pepper, cored and diced

1 teaspoon dried thyme

½ teaspoon dried basil

⅛ teaspoon cayenne pepper

¼ teaspoon ground black pepper

1¼ cups uncooked white rice

½ pound fresh medium shrimp, peeled and deveined

1. Heat ¼ cup broth in a large pot. Add chicken and sauté until no longer pink, about 8 minutes. Remove chicken and set aside.
2. Heat another ¼ cup broth in the pot. Add onion and garlic, and sauté until onion is just tender, about 3 minutes. Add remaining broth, saffron, tomatoes with juice, artichoke hearts, bell peppers, thyme, basil, cayenne pepper, and black pepper. Return chicken to the pot.
3. Stir in rice, bring to a boil, and reduce heat. Cover and simmer until rice is almost tender, about 20 minutes. Add shrimp and continue to simmer until cooked through, about 4 minutes, before serving.

Calories Per Serving: 378
Fat: 2 g
Cholesterol: 105 mg
Protein: 35 g

Carbohydrates: 56 g
Dietary Fiber: 5 g
Sodium: 266 mg

❊ *Simple Chicken Supper* ❊

PREPARATION TIME: *25 minutes plus 5 minutes standing time* •
COOKING TIME: *44 minutes* • YIELD: *6 servings*

4¼ cups low-sodium nonfat chicken
   broth
3 skinless boneless chicken breast tenderloins, about 4 ounces each, cut
   into ½-inch cubes
1 medium onion, chopped
1 clove garlic, minced
1 medium stalk celery, sliced

1 medium green bell pepper, cored
   and chopped
2 medium carrots, scraped and sliced
4 medium red potatoes, chopped
½ cup uncooked white rice
½ teaspoon dried thyme
¼ teaspoon ground black pepper
1 cup fresh or thawed frozen green
   peas

1. Heat ¼ cup broth in a large saucepan. Add chicken and sauté until no
   longer pink, about 8 minutes. Add onion, garlic, celery, green pepper, and
   carrots, and continue to sauté until onion begins to soften, about 4 minutes.
2. Stir in remaining broth, potatoes, rice, thyme, and black pepper. Bring to
   a boil, reduce heat, cover, and simmer until rice is just tender and chicken
   is cooked through, about 25 minutes.
3. Remove from heat, stir in peas, and allow to stand for 5 minutes before
   serving.

Calories Per Serving: 287
Fat: 1 g
Cholesterol: 35 mg
Protein: 19 g

Carbohydrates: 48 g
Dietary Fiber: 4 g
Sodium: 281 mg

❊ *Spiced Chicken with Vegetables* ❊

PREPARATION TIME: *10 minutes* • COOKING TIME: *43 minutes* •
YIELD: *4 servings*

½ cup low-sodium nonfat chicken
   broth
4 skinless boneless chicken breast tenderloins, about 4 ounces each
2 medium green bell peppers, cored
   and chopped
4 scallions, sliced

1½ cups apricot nectar
2 tablespoons Dijon mustard
¼ cup water
1¾ cups uncooked white rice
1½ cups chopped green beans (½-inch
   lengths)
½ cup chopped dried apricots

1. Heat ¼ cup broth in a large saucepan. Add chicken and cook, turning several times, until no longer pink, about 8 minutes. Remove chicken and set aside.
2. Heat remaining broth in the saucepan. Add bell peppers and scallions, and sauté until peppers begin to soften, about 4 minutes.
3. Combine apricot nectar, mustard, and water, and add to the saucepan. Stir in rice, green beans, and dried apricots. Return chicken to the pan. Bring to a boil, reduce heat, cover, and simmer until chicken is cooked through and rice is tender, about 25 minutes.
4. Transfer to individual plates and serve.

Calories Per Serving: 562
Fat: 2 g
Cholesterol: 70 mg
Protein: 35 g

Carbohydrates: 100 g
Dietary Fiber: 3 g
Sodium: 252 mg

❊ *Chicken and Shrimp with Many Vegetables* ❊

PREPARATION TIME: *20 minutes* • COOKING TIME: *17 minutes* •
YIELD: *4 servings*

1 egg white
2½ tablespoons cornstarch
2 skinless boneless chicken breast tenderloins, about 4 ounces each, cut into thin strips
¼ pound fresh medium shrimp, peeled and deveined
1 tablespoon cold water
2 tablespoons dry sherry
2 tablespoons reduced-sodium soy sauce

1½ cups low-sodium nonfat chicken broth
½ teaspoon sugar
4 cups chopped broccoli
1 cup sliced canned water chestnuts, drained
¼ cup canned bamboo shoots, drained
1 cup shredded cabbage
1 cup sliced mushrooms
3 scallions, sliced
1 teaspoon grated fresh gingerroot

1. Combine egg white and 1½ tablespoons cornstarch in a bowl. In separate batches, add chicken, then shrimp, and toss gently to coat all ingredients.
2. Combine remaining cornstarch with cold water in a separate bowl. Add sherry, soy sauce, ½ cup broth, and sugar. Mix well and set aside.
3. Heat ¼ cup broth in a wok. Add chicken and stirfry until cooked through, about 5 minutes. Add shrimp and stirfry for 3 more minutes.

4. Heat 2 tablespoons broth in the wok. Add broccoli, water chestnuts, bamboo shoots, and cabbage. Stirfry until broccoli begins to soften, about 3 minutes. Remove vegetables from the wok and set aside.
5. Heat remaining broth in the wok. Add mushrooms, scallions, and gingerroot. Stirfry for 1 minute. Return chicken, shrimp, vegetables, and sauce to the wok, and cook and stir until sauce begins to thicken and all ingredients are heated through, about 2 minutes.

Calories Per Serving: 184 Carbohydrates: 17 g
Fat: 1 g Dietary Fiber: 4 g
Cholesterol: 78 mg Sodium: 426 mg
Protein: 27 g

❋ Chicken Tenderloins with Snow Peas, ❋ Jalapeño, and Pineapple

PREPARATION TIME: *20 minutes* • COOKING TIME: *55 minutes* •
YIELD: *4 servings*

½ cup low-sodium nonfat chicken broth
4 skinless boneless chicken breast tenderloins, about 4 ounces each
1 medium onion, chopped
4 scallions, sliced
2 cloves garlic, minced
1 jalapeño pepper, seeded and minced
1 cup low-sodium tomato sauce
1½ cups pineapple juice

1 cup juice-packed canned pineapple chunks, drained
½ cup snow peas
1 medium tomato, chopped
1 cup sliced mushrooms
½ teaspoon dried oregano
½ teaspoon dried thyme
1 bay leaf
¼ teaspoon ground black pepper
¼ cup chopped fresh parsley

1. Preheat oven to 350 degrees.
2. Heat ¼ cup broth in a flameproof 2-quart casserole. Add chicken and sauté until no longer pink, about 8 minutes. Remove chicken and set aside.
3. Heat remaining broth in the casserole. Add onion, scallions, garlic, and jalapeño pepper, and sauté until onion begins to soften, about 3 minutes.
4. Stir in tomato sauce, pineapple juice, pineapple chunks, snow peas, tomato, mushrooms, oregano, and thyme. Add bay leaf and black pepper. Return chicken to the casserole, cover, and bake until chicken is cooked through, about 40 minutes.

5. Remove bay leaf. Transfer chicken and vegetables to individual plates, garnish with parsley, and serve.

Calories Per Serving: 182
Fat: 1 g
Cholesterol: 47 mg
Protein: 21 g

Carbohydrates: 22 g
Dietary Fiber: 3 g
Sodium: 153 mg

❋ *Balsamic Chicken* ❋

PREPARATION TIME: *15 minutes* • COOKING TIME: *33 minutes* •
YIELD: *4 servings*

¾ cup low-sodium nonfat chicken
   broth
4 skinless boneless chicken breast tenderloins, about 4 ounces each
2 cups quartered small new potatoes
1 medium onion, chopped
2 cloves garlic, minced

2 leeks (white parts only), sliced
5 medium carrots, scraped and cut
   into thin strips
1 medium red bell pepper, cored and
   cut into thin strips
½ teaspoon ground black pepper
¼ cup balsamic vinegar

1. Heat ¼ cup broth in a large saucepan. Add chicken and sauté until no longer pink, about 8 minutes. Remove and set aside.
2. Add potatoes, onion, and garlic, and sauté until onion begins to soften, about 4 minutes. Add more broth if necessary.
3. Stir in remaining broth, leeks, carrots, and bell pepper. Bring to a boil, reduce heat, cover, and simmer for 15 minutes. Stir in black pepper and vinegar, and simmer for 1 more minute.
4. Transfer to individual plates and serve.

Calories Per Serving: 328
Fat: 2 g
Cholesterol: 70 mg
Protein: 32 g

Carbohydrates: 48 g
Dietary Fiber: 6 g
Sodium: 141 mg

❅ Chicken and Zucchini ❅

PREPARATION TIME: *15 minutes* • COOKING TIME: *22 minutes* •
YIELD: *4 servings*

1 tablespoon reduced-sodium soy
   sauce
1 tablespoon dry sherry
1 tablespoon cornstarch
2 teaspoons nonfat chicken bouillon
   powder
¼ teaspoon sugar
3 skinless boneless chicken breast tenderloins, about 4 ounces each,
   chopped
6 tablespoons low-sodium nonfat
   chicken broth

4 cups thinly sliced zucchini
4 scallions, sliced
1 medium red bell pepper, cored and
   cut into strips
1 cup sliced canned water chestnuts,
   drained
¾ cup water
¼ teaspoon ground black pepper
2 cups cooked rice

1. Combine soy sauce, sherry, cornstarch, bouillon powder, and sugar in a
   bowl. Add chicken, mix well, and set aside.
2. Heat 3 tablespoons broth in a wok. Add zucchini, scallions, and bell pepper, and stirfry until vegetables begin to soften, about 5 minutes. Remove
   from the wok and set aside.
3. Heat remaining broth in the wok. Add chicken mixture and stirfry until
   chicken is cooked through, about 8 minutes.
4. Add water chestnuts, water, and black pepper. Cook and stir for 2 minutes. Return vegetables to the wok and cook until all ingredients are
   heated through, about 2 minutes.
5. Serve over rice.

Calories Per Serving: 271
Fat: 1 g
Cholesterol: 53 mg
Protein: 25 g

Carbohydrates: 39 g
Dietary Fiber: 2 g
Sodium: 203 mg

❅ Spicy Chicken and Broccoli ❅

PREPARATION TIME: *20 minutes* • COOKING TIME: *47 minutes* •
YIELD: *5 servings*

1 cup low-sodium nonfat chicken
  broth
¾ cup low-sodium tomato paste
1 medium onion, chopped
2 cups chopped broccoli
1 medium green bell pepper, cored
  and diced
2 cloves garlic, minced
1 bay leaf
1 tablespoon lemon juice

1 teaspoon sugar
1 tablespoon dried basil
2 teaspoons Dijon mustard
¼ teaspoon ground black pepper
⅛ teaspoon hot pepper sauce
5 skinless boneless chicken breast tenderloins, about 4 ounces each,
  chopped
2 cups cooked rice

1. Combine broth and tomato paste in a large pot. Mix thoroughly. Add onion, broccoli, bell pepper, garlic, bay leaf, lemon juice, sugar, basil, mustard, black pepper, and hot pepper sauce.
2. Add chicken and simmer until cooked through, about 45 minutes. Remove bay leaf.
3. Serve over rice.

Calories Per Serving: 369
Fat: 2 g
Cholesterol: 70 mg
Protein: 34 g

Carbohydrates: 54 g
Dietary Fiber: 3 g
Sodium: 197 mg

❋ Chicken with Brussels Sprouts ❋ and Cauliflower

PREPARATION TIME: 15 minutes • COOKING TIME: 27 minutes •
YIELD: 4 servings

¾ cup low-sodium nonfat chicken
  broth
3 skinless boneless chicken breast tenderloins, about 4 ounces each, cut
  into thin strips
2 cloves garlic, minced
1 pound brussels sprouts
3 cups chopped cauliflower
2 medium stalks celery, sliced

1 medium green bell pepper, cored
  and chopped
3 tablespoons water
1 tablespoon cornstarch
2 tablespoons reduced-sodium soy
  sauce
2 tablespoons dry sherry
1 teaspoon minced fresh gingerroot
2 cups cooked rice

1. Heat 2 tablespoons broth in a wok. Add chicken and garlic. Stirfry until chicken is cooked through, about 8 minutes. Remove chicken and set aside.
2. Heat another 2 tablespoons broth in the wok. Add brussels sprouts, cauliflower, celery, and bell pepper, and stirfry for 5 minutes. Add water, cover, and steam until vegetables are just tender, about 3 minutes.
3. Combine remaining broth and cornstarch in a small bowl. Stir into the wok. Add soy sauce, sherry, and gingerroot. Bring to a boil and stir constantly until sauce begins to thicken, about 2 minutes. Return chicken to the wok, continuing to stir until all ingredients are heated through, about 2 minutes.
4. Serve over rice.

Calories Per Serving: 314
Fat: 2 g
Cholesterol: 51 mg
Protein: 29 g

Carbohydrates: 47 g
Dietary Fiber: 6 g
Sodium: 425 mg

❋ *Chicken Paprika with Cabbage* ❋

PREPARATION TIME: *20 minutes* • COOKING TIME: *47 minutes* •
YIELD: *4 servings*

¼ cup low-sodium nonfat chicken broth
4 skinless boneless chicken breast tenderloins, about 4 ounces each, chopped
¼ cup minced onion
1 teaspoon paprika

½ teaspoon ground turmeric
2 cloves garlic, minced
¼ teaspoon ground black pepper
4 cups shredded cabbage
1 cup nonfat plain yogurt
1 tablespoon brown sugar

1. Heat ¼ cup broth in a large saucepan. Add chicken and sauté until no longer pink, about 8 minutes.
2. Add onion, paprika, turmeric, garlic, black pepper, and ¼ cup broth. Cover and simmer until chicken is cooked through, about 20 minutes. Remove chicken and set aside.
3. Add cabbage, yogurt, brown sugar, and remaining broth to the saucepan. Cover and simmer, stirring occasionally, until cabbage is just tender, about 15 minutes.
4. Transfer cabbage mixture to a serving dish, top with chicken, and serve.

Calories Per Serving: 193
Fat: 1 g
Cholesterol: 71 mg
Protein: 32 g

Carbohydrates: 13 g
Dietary Fiber: 2 g
Sodium: 157 mg

❋ *Chicken with Carrot and Cauliflower* ❋

PREPARATION TIME: *20 minutes* • COOKING TIME: *43 minutes* •
YIELD: *6 servings*

4 skinless boneless chicken breast ten-
    derloins, *about 4 ounces each,*
    chopped
¼ teaspoon ground black pepper
2 cups low-sodium nonfat chicken
    broth
1 medium onion, chopped

2 tablespoons honey
1 tablespoon Dijon mustard
1 teaspoon curry powder
2 cups chopped cauliflower
1 medium carrot, scraped and sliced
3 cups cooked rice

1. Sprinkle chicken with black pepper. Heat ¼ cup broth in a large pot. Add
   chicken and sauté until no longer pink, about 8 minutes. Remove chicken
   and set aside.
2. Heat another ¼ cup broth in the pot. Add onion and sauté until it begins
   to soften, about 3 minutes.
3. Stir honey, mustard, and curry powder into onion. Return chicken to the
   pot. Add remaining broth, cauliflower, and carrot, and bring mixture to a
   boil. Reduce heat, cover, and simmer for 20 minutes. Remove the cover
   and continue to simmer until liquid is reduced by half, about 5 minutes.
4. Serve over rice.

Calories Per Serving: 280
Fat: 1 g
Cholesterol: 47 mg
Protein: 24 g

Carbohydrates: 43 g
Dietary Fiber: 1 g
Sodium: 162 mg

❋ *Chicken with Broccoli, Carrots,* ❋ *and Orange Slices*

PREPARATION TIME: *15 minutes* • COOKING TIME: *54 minutes* •
YIELD: *6 servings*

2 tablespoons all-purpose flour
¼ teaspoon ground cinnamon
4 skinless boneless chicken breast tenderloins, about 4 ounces each, chopped
¼ cup low-sodium nonfat chicken broth

1 medium onion, chopped
1 cup uncooked white rice
2 cups orange juice
6 medium carrots, scraped and sliced
4 cups chopped broccoli
1 medium orange, sliced

1. Combine flour and cinnamon. Dredge chicken in flour mixture.
2. Heat broth in a large saucepan. Add chicken and sauté until no longer pink, about 8 minutes. Cover and simmer for 10 minutes. Remove chicken and set aside.
3. Add onion and rice to the saucepan and sauté until onion begins to soften, about 3 minutes.
4. Stir in orange juice and carrots, and bring to a boil. Add chicken to the saucepan, reduce heat, cover, and simmer for 20 minutes.
5. Add broccoli and orange slices, and continue to simmer until broccoli and rice are just tender, about 7 minutes. Serve at once.

Calories Per Serving: 308
Fat: 1 g
Cholesterol: 47 mg
Protein: 24 g

Carbohydrates: 51 g
Dietary Fiber: 6 g
Sodium: 86 mg

❋ *Chicken with Corn and Zucchini* ❋

PREPARATION TIME: *15 minutes* • COOKING TIME: *28 minutes* •
YIELD: *7 servings*

5 skinless boneless chicken breast tenderloins, about 4 ounces each, chopped
1 teaspoon paprika
½ cup low-sodium nonfat chicken broth
1 teaspoon dried oregano
1 teaspoon chili powder

½ teaspoon ground cumin
3 medium tomatoes, cut into wedges
2 cloves garlic, minced
1 medium zucchini, thinly sliced
1 medium onion, chopped
2 cups fresh or thawed frozen corn kernels

1. Sprinkle chicken with paprika.
2. Heat broth in a large pot. Add chicken and simmer for 20 minutes.

3. Stir in remaining ingredients. Simmer until zucchini is tender-crisp and other ingredients are heated through, about 5 minutes. Add water or broth if needed.

Calories Per Serving: 152　　Carbohydrates: 15 g
Fat: 1 g　　Dietary Fiber: 2 g
Cholesterol: 50 mg　　Sodium: 49 mg
Protein: 22 g

❀ *Chicken-Jalapeño Jumble* ❀

PREPARATION TIME: *25 minutes*　•　COOKING TIME: *51 minutes*　•
YIELD: *8 servings*

4¼ cups low-sodium nonfat chicken broth
2 medium onions, diced
2 medium green bell peppers, cored and diced
4 cloves garlic, minced
1 jalapeño pepper, seeded and minced
3 medium stalks celery, sliced
3 cups fresh or low-sodium canned tomatoes, crushed, juice reserved

2 cups low-sodium tomato paste
¼ teaspoon ground black pepper
1 teaspoon brown sugar
1 tablespoon molasses
½ teaspoon hot pepper sauce
1 teaspoon dried thyme
3 tablespoons lemon juice
4 skinless boneless chicken breast tenderloins, about 4 ounces each
4 cups cooked rice

1. Heat ¼ cup broth in a large pot. Add onions, bell peppers, and garlic, and sauté until onions begin to soften, about 4 minutes.
2. Add remaining broth, jalapeño pepper, celery, tomatoes with juice, tomato paste, black pepper, brown sugar, molasses, hot pepper sauce, thyme, and lemon juice. Bring to a boil, reduce heat, and simmer for 15 minutes.
3. Add chicken and continue to simmer until cooked through, about 25 minutes.
4. Serve over rice.

Calories Per Serving: 295　　Carbohydrates: 50 g
Fat: 2 g　　Dietary Fiber: 4 g
Cholesterol: 35 mg　　Sodium: 303 mg
Protein: 20 g

❋ *Chicken with Leeks, Carrot, Cabbage,* ❋ *and Turnips*

PREPARATION TIME: *20 minutes* • COOKING TIME: *52 minutes* •
YIELD: *6 servings*

3¼ cups low-sodium nonfat chicken
   broth
6 skinless boneless chicken breast tenderloins, about 4 ounces each
3 leeks (white parts only), sliced
2 cloves garlic, minced
2 cups diced potatoes
4 medium stalks celery, sliced

1 teaspoon caraway seeds
1 teaspoon dried thyme
1 teaspoon ground white pepper
2 cups shredded cabbage
1 medium carrot, scraped and sliced
2 cups diced turnips
¼ cup chopped fresh parsley

1. Heat ¼ cup broth in a large saucepan. Add chicken and sauté until no longer pink, about 8 minutes. Remove and set aside.
2. Add leeks and garlic to the saucepan and sauté until leeks begin to soften, about 3 minutes. Add more broth if necessary. Stir in remaining broth, potatoes, and celery. Bring to a boil, reduce heat, and simmer for 15 minutes.
3. Return chicken to the saucepan. Stir in caraway seeds, thyme, white pepper, cabbage, carrot, and turnips, and continue to simmer until chicken is cooked through and vegetables are tender, about 20 minutes.
4. Transfer to individual bowls, garnish with parsley, and serve.

Calories Per Serving: 312
Fat: 2 g
Cholesterol: 70 mg
Protein: 31 g

Carbohydrates: 42 g
Dietary Fiber: 6 g
Sodium: 246 mg

❋ *Chicken with Mushrooms* ❋

PREPARATION TIME: *25 minutes* • COOKING TIME: *41 minutes* •
YIELD: *4 servings*

4½ cups low-sodium nonfat chicken broth

2 skinless boneless chicken breast tenderloins, about 4 ounces each, chopped

2 cups sliced white mushrooms

1 cup sliced shiitake mushrooms

1 medium onion, chopped

1 medium green bell pepper, cored and diced

4 cloves garlic, minced

3 cups low-sodium canned tomatoes, drained and chopped

4 scallions, chopped

2 teaspoons dried oregano

1 teaspoon paprika

1 teaspoon dried thyme

½ teaspoon ground black pepper

½ teaspoon cayenne pepper

2 cups cooked rice

2 tablespoons chopped fresh cilantro

1. Heat ¼ cup broth in a large saucepan. Add chicken and sauté until no longer pink, about 8 minutes. Remove chicken and set aside.
2. Heat another ¼ cup broth in the saucepan. Add all mushrooms, onion, bell pepper, and garlic, and sauté until onion begins to soften, about 4 minutes.
3. Return chicken to the saucepan. Add remaining broth, tomatoes, scallions, oregano, paprika, thyme, black pepper, and cayenne pepper. Bring to a boil, reduce heat, and simmer until chicken is cooked through, about 15 minutes. Stir in rice and continue to simmer until heated through, about 5 minutes.
4. Garnish with cilantro and serve.

Calories Per Serving: 269
Fat: 2 g
Cholesterol: 35 mg
Protein: 19 g

Carbohydrates: 41 g
Dietary Fiber: 3 g
Sodium: 376 mg

❋ Chicken with Okra ❋

PREPARATION TIME: 15 minutes • COOKING TIME: 57 minutes •
YIELD: 6 servings

6 skinless boneless chicken breast tenderloins, about 4 ounces each, chopped

¼ teaspoon ground black pepper

⅛ teaspoon cayenne pepper

½ cup low-sodium nonfat chicken broth

3 cups sliced okra (½-inch slices)

2 medium onions, chopped

2 cloves garlic, minced

¼ cup all-purpose flour

4 cups water

3 cups cooked rice

1. Sprinkle chicken with black pepper and cayenne pepper. Heat ¼ cup broth in a large pot. Add chicken and sauté until no longer pink, about 8 minutes. Remove chicken and set aside.
2. Heat remaining broth in the pot. Add okra, onions, and garlic. Stir in flour and cook, stirring frequently, over low heat for 20 minutes.
3. Add chicken and water. Bring to a boil, reduce heat, and simmer until chicken is cooked through and mixture begins to thicken, about 25 minutes.
4. Serve over rice.

Calories Per Serving: 299
Fat: 1 g
Cholesterol: 70 mg
Protein: 32 g

Carbohydrates: 39 g
Dietary Fiber: 2 g
Sodium: 80 mg

❀ *Chicken with Shiitake Mushrooms* ❀

PREPARATION TIME: *15 minutes plus 10 minutes marinating time* •
COOKING TIME: *49 minutes* • YIELD: *6 servings*

7 cups low-sodium nonfat chicken broth
¼ cup dry sherry
1 clove garlic, minced
4 skinless boneless chicken breast tenderloins, about 4 ounces each, chopped

1 medium onion, minced
¼ pound shiitake mushrooms, sliced
3 cups cooked rice
½ cup chopped fresh parsley

1. Combine ¼ cup broth with sherry and garlic in a glass bowl. Add chicken and marinate for 10 minutes.
2. Heat another ¼ cup broth in a large pot. Stir in chicken and sauté until no longer pink, about 8 minutes. Remove chicken and set aside.
3. Heat 2 tablespoons broth in the pot. Add onion and sauté until it begins to soften, about 2 minutes. Stir in remaining broth and mushrooms. Bring to a boil, reduce heat, and simmer for 10 minutes. Return chicken to the pot and continue to simmer for 15 more minutes.
4. Serve over rice, topped with parsley.

Calories Per Serving: 275
Fat: 1 g
Cholesterol: 47 mg
Protein: 22 g

Carbohydrates: 39 g
Dietary Fiber: 2 g
Sodium: 375 mg

⁕ *Chicken with Spinach* ⁕

PREPARATION TIME: *25 minutes* • COOKING TIME: *27 minutes* •
YIELD: *4 servings*

¼ cup low-sodium nonfat chicken
    broth
5 cloves garlic, minced
1 tablespoon ground coriander
3 cups water
1 medium onion, diced
2 skinless boneless chicken breast ten-
    derloins, about 4 ounces each,
    chopped

6 cups chopped fresh or thawed
    frozen spinach
¼ teaspoon ground black pepper
2 cups cooked rice
2 tablespoons chopped fresh parsley

1. Heat broth in a large saucepan. Add garlic and coriander, and sauté for 1
   minute.
2. Add water, onion, and chicken. Bring to a boil, reduce heat, and simmer
   until chicken is almost cooked through, about 15 minutes. Add spinach,
   black pepper, and rice. Return to a boil, reduce heat, and simmer until
   spinach is wilted and all ingredients are heated through, about 5 more
   minutes.
3. Transfer to individual bowls, garnish with parsley, and serve.

Calories Per Serving: 224
Fat: 1 g
Cholesterol: 35 mg
Protein: 19 g

Carbohydrates: 35 g
Dietary Fiber: 3 g
Sodium: 104 mg

⁕ *Curried Chicken with Sweet Potatoes* ⁕

PREPARATION TIME: *15 minutes* • COOKING TIME: *42 minutes* •
YIELD: *6 servings*

1½ cups low-sodium nonfat chicken
    broth
1 medium onion, chopped
2 medium stalks celery, sliced
2 cloves garlic, minced

4 skinless boneless chicken breast ten-
    derloins, about 4 ounces each,
    chopped
¼ teaspoon ground ginger
¼ teaspoon dried thyme

1 tablespoon curry powder
2 cups diced sweet potatoes
¾ cup cooked or low-sodium canned
   chickpeas, rinsed and drained

3 cups cooked rice
¼ cup nonfat plain yogurt

1. Heat ¼ cup broth in a large saucepan. Add onion, celery, and garlic, and sauté until onion begins to soften, about 4 minutes.
2. Add chicken and sauté until no longer pink, about 8 minutes.
3. Combine remaining broth, ginger, thyme, and curry powder. Mix well and add to the saucepan. Add sweet potatoes. Bring to a boil, reduce heat, cover, and simmer for 20 minutes.
4. Stir in chickpeas, cover, and simmer for 5 more minutes. Serve over rice, topped with yogurt.

Calories Per Serving: 366
Fat: 2 g
Cholesterol: 62 mg
Protein: 25 g

Carbohydrates: 62 g
Dietary Fiber: 6 g
Sodium: 195 mg

❀ *Stirfried Chicken with Water Chestnuts,* ❀ *Bamboo Shoots, and Almonds*

PREPARATION TIME: *20 minutes* • COOKING TIME: *22 minutes* •
YIELD: *4 servings*

2¼ cups low-sodium nonfat chicken
   broth
4 skinless boneless chicken breast tenderloins, about 4 ounces each,
   sliced
1 small onion, sliced
2 medium stalks celery, sliced
1 cup sliced canned water chestnuts,
   drained

½ cup canned bamboo shoots,
   drained
1 tablespoon reduced-sodium soy
   sauce
1 teaspoon sugar
2 tablespoons cornstarch
¼ cup cold water
1 tablespoon toasted almond slivers
2 cups cooked rice

1. Heat ¼ cup broth in a large saucepan or wok. Add chicken and sauté until no longer pink, about 8 minutes. Add onion and celery, and sauté for 4 more minutes.
2. Add water chestnuts, bamboo shoots, remaining broth, and soy sauce. Cover and simmer for 5 minutes.

3. Mix sugar, cornstarch, and cold water, and add to the saucepan. Cook, stirring constantly, until mixture begins to thicken, about 3 minutes.
4. Serve, topped with almonds, over rice.

Calories Per Serving: 317
Fat: 2 g
Cholesterol: 70 mg
Protein: 31 g

Carbohydrates: 39 g
Dietary Fiber: 2 g
Sodium: 380 mg

❋ Chicken Paprika with Tomatoes ❋ and Green Peppers

PREPARATION TIME: *20 minutes* • COOKING TIME: *45 minutes* •
YIELD: *6 servings*

½ cup low-sodium nonfat chicken
   broth
6 skinless boneless chicken breast tenderloins, about 4 ounces each,
   chopped
2 medium onions, chopped
2 cloves garlic, minced
½ cup water

2 tablespoons paprika
¼ teaspoon ground black pepper
2 medium tomatoes, chopped
2 medium green bell peppers, cored
   and cut into thin strips
1 cup nonfat plain yogurt
3 cups cooked rice

1. Heat ¼ cup broth in a large pot. Add chicken and sauté until no longer pink, about 8 minutes. Remove chicken and set aside.
2. Heat remaining broth in the pot. Add onions and garlic, and sauté until onions begin to soften, about 3 minutes. Add water, paprika, black pepper, tomatoes, and chicken. Bring to a boil, reduce heat, cover, and simmer for 20 minutes.
3. Add bell peppers, cover, and continue to simmer until chicken is cooked through, about 5 minutes.
4. Transfer chicken and vegetables to individual plates. Stir yogurt into liquid remaining in the pot. Heat through, spoon sauce over vegetables, and serve with rice.

Calories Per Serving: 295
Fat: 2 g
Cholesterol: 71 mg
Protein: 33 g

Carbohydrates: 37 g
Dietary Fiber: 1 g
Sodium: 103 mg

Chicken with Yellow Pepper, Bok Choy, and Bamboo Shoots

PREPARATION TIME: *25 minutes* ▪ COOKING TIME: *18 minutes* ▪ YIELD: *6 servings*

1 cup low-sodium nonfat chicken broth
¼ cup dry sherry
1 tablespoon reduced-sodium soy sauce
1 teaspoon sugar
½ teaspoon ground ginger
1 medium onion, thinly sliced
2 cloves garlic, minced
4 skinless boneless chicken breast tenderloins, about 4 ounces each, cut into ½-inch cubes
2 medium stalks bok choy, thinly sliced diagonally
2 medium stalks celery, thinly sliced diagonally
1 scallion, thinly sliced diagonally
1 medium yellow bell pepper, cored and cut into thin strips
2 cups snow peas
1 cup sliced canned bamboo shoots, drained
2 tablespoons cornstarch
2 tablespoons cold water
3 cups cooked rice

1. Combine ¾ cup broth, the sherry, soy sauce, sugar, and ginger in a small bowl. Set aside.
2. Heat remaining broth in a large saucepan or wok. Add onion and garlic, and sauté until onion begins to soften, about 3 minutes. Add chicken and sauté until chicken is no longer pink, about 8 minutes.
3. Stir in broth-sherry mixture, bok choy, celery, scallion, bell pepper, snow peas, and bamboo shoots. Cover tightly and steam until vegetables are just tender, about 3 minutes.
4. Mix cornstarch and cold water in a separate bowl and add to chicken. Stir until sauce begins to thicken, about 2 minutes.
5. Serve over rice.

Calories Per Serving: 261
Fat: 1 g
Cholesterol: 47 mg
Protein: 23 g
Carbohydrates: 38 g
Dietary Fiber: 3 g
Sodium: 175 mg

❈ Chicken with Yellow Peppers ❈ and Sun-Dried Tomatoes

PREPARATION TIME: *20 minutes* • COOKING TIME: *38 minutes* •
YIELD: *4 servings*

½ cup low-sodium nonfat chicken
  broth
4 skinless boneless chicken breast tenderloins, about 4 ounces each,
  chopped
1 medium onion, sliced
3 medium yellow bell peppers, cored
  and cut into thin strips
3 cloves garlic, minced

3 sun-dried tomatoes, soaked in hot
  water for 15 minutes, drained,
  and minced
1 bay leaf
1 tablespoon chopped fresh parsley
½ teaspoon dried rosemary
¼ teaspoon ground black pepper
1 cup water
½ cup red wine vinegar
2 cups cooked rice

1. Heat ¼ cup broth in a large saucepan. Add chicken and sauté until no
   longer pink, about 8 minutes. Remove chicken and set aside.
2. Heat remaining broth in the saucepan. Add onion, bell peppers, garlic,
   tomatoes, bay leaf, parsley, rosemary, and black pepper. Sauté until peppers begin to soften, about 5 minutes.
3. Return chicken to the saucepan. Add water and bring to a boil. Reduce
   heat, cover, and simmer for 15 minutes. Add vinegar, cover, and continue
   to simmer for 5 more minutes. Remove bay leaf.
4. Serve over rice.

Calories Per Serving: 312
Fat: 1 g
Cholesterol: 70 mg
Protein: 33 g

Carbohydrates: 43 g
Dietary Fiber: 2 g
Sodium: 88 mg

❈ Chicken with Apples and Cranberry Sauce ❈

PREPARATION TIME: *20 minutes* • COOKING TIME: *41 minutes* •
YIELD: *5 servings*

½ cup low-sodium nonfat chicken broth

5 skinless boneless chicken breast tenderloins, about 4 ounces each, cut into ½-inch cubes

1 medium onion, chopped

2 medium apples, peeled, cored, and chopped

1 cup cranberry sauce

½ cup seedless raisins

1 tablespoon cider vinegar

1 tablespoon brown sugar

¼ teaspoon ground black pepper

2 cups cooked rice

1. Heat ¼ cup broth in a large pot. Add chicken and sauté for 4 minutes. Add onion and continue to sauté until onion begins to soften and chicken is no longer pink, about 8 minutes.
2. Combine apples, cranberry sauce, raisins, vinegar, brown sugar, black pepper, and remaining broth in a separate bowl. Stir into the chicken.
3. Bring mixture to a boil, reduce heat, cover, and simmer until apples are soft and chicken is cooked through, about 25 minutes.
4. Serve over rice.

Calories Per Serving: 327
Fat: 1 g
Cholesterol: 60 mg
Protein: 27 g

Carbohydrates: 68 g
Dietary Fiber: 3 g
Sodium: 50 mg

❋ *Chicken with Apricots* ❋

PREPARATION TIME: *25 minutes* • COOKING TIME: *40 minutes* •
YIELD: *6 servings*

½ cup low-sodium nonfat chicken broth

6 skinless boneless chicken breast tenderloins, about 4 ounces each

2 cloves garlic, minced

2½ cups sliced juice-packed canned apricots, drained

1½ cups orange juice

3 tablespoons brown sugar

3 tablespoons white vinegar

1½ teaspoons ground nutmeg

1½ teaspoons dried basil

3 cups cooked rice

1. Heat ¼ cup broth in a large saucepan. Sauté chicken until no longer pink, about 8 minutes. Add broth as necessary. Remove chicken and set aside.
2. Combine remaining broth, garlic, apricots, orange juice, brown sugar, vinegar, nutmeg, and basil in the saucepan. Cover and simmer for 10 minutes.

3. Return chicken to the saucepan, cover, and simmer until chicken is cooked through, about 20 minutes.
4. Serve over rice.

Calories Per Serving: 330
Fat: 2 g
Cholesterol: 70 mg
Protein: 31 g

Carbohydrates: 47 g
Dietary Fiber: 2 g
Sodium: 76 mg

✳ *Tropical Chicken and Mixed Vegetables* ✳

PREPARATION TIME: *20 minutes* • COOKING TIME: *44 minutes* •
YIELD: *4 servings*

1 cup low-sodium nonfat chicken broth
2 skinless boneless chicken breast tenderloins, about 4 ounces each, chopped
½ cup sliced mushrooms
1 medium green bell pepper, cored and chopped
1 medium onion, chopped

1 cup juice-packed canned pineapple chunks, juice reserved
2 medium carrots, scraped and sliced
½ teaspoon dried basil
¼ teaspoon ground ginger
¼ teaspoon curry powder
1 tablespoon brown sugar
1 cup sliced canned water chestnuts, drained
2 cups cooked rice

1. Heat ¼ cup broth in a large saucepan. Add chicken and sauté until no longer pink, about 8 minutes. Remove chicken and set aside.
2. Heat another ¼ cup broth in the saucepan. Add mushrooms, bell pepper, and onion, and sauté until onion begins to soften, about 4 minutes. Remove vegetables and set aside.
3. Add remaining broth, reserved pineapple juice, carrots, basil, ginger, curry powder, and brown sugar to the saucepan. Return chicken to the saucepan. Bring to a boil, reduce heat, and simmer until carrots are just tender and chicken is cooked through, about 20 minutes.
4. Return mushrooms, bell pepper, and onion to the saucepan. Add pineapple chunks and water chestnuts and simmer to heat through, about 5 more minutes.
5. Serve over rice.

Calories Per Serving: 229
Fat: 1 g
Cholesterol: 0 mg
Protein: 6 g

Carbohydrates: 52 g
Dietary Fiber: 3 g
Sodium: 62 mg

❈ *Wine-Simmered Chicken* ❈ *with Dried Apricots*

PREPARATION TIME: *25 minutes* • COOKING TIME: *47 minutes* •
YIELD: *6 servings*

½ cup all-purpose flour
½ teaspoon ground black pepper
6 skinless boneless chicken breast tenderloins, about 4 ounces each,
  chopped
1½ cups low-sodium nonfat chicken
  broth
½ cup dry white wine
2 cups dried apricot halves, each cut
  in half

1½ teaspoons ground cinnamon
1 medium onion, chopped
2 cloves garlic, minced
½ teaspoon dried rosemary
½ teaspoon ground ginger
¼ teaspoon cayenne pepper
3 cups cooked rice
¼ cup chopped fresh parsley

1. Combine flour and black pepper. Dredge chicken in flour mixture.
2. Heat ¼ cup broth in a large saucepan. Add chicken and sauté until no longer pink, about 8 minutes. Remove chicken and set aside.
3. Add wine, apricots, and ½ teaspoon cinnamon to the saucepan and simmer for 3 minutes. Remove apricot mixture and set aside.
4. Heat another ¼ cup broth in the saucepan. Add onion, garlic, and rosemary, and sauté until onion begins to soften, about 3 minutes. Add remaining cinnamon and ginger, and sauté for 1 more minute.
5. Stir in remaining broth, cooking liquid from the apricots, and cayenne pepper. Return chicken and apricots to the saucepan, cover, and simmer until chicken is cooked through, about 20 minutes.
6. Serve over rice, topped with parsley.

Calories Per Serving: 335
Fat: 1 g
Cholesterol: 70 mg
Protein: 31 g

Carbohydrates: 47 g
Dietary Fiber: 2 g
Sodium: 158 mg

❈ *Chicken—Bell Pepper Curry* ❈

PREPARATION TIME: *25 minutes plus 1 hour marinating time* •
COOKING TIME: *25 minutes* • YIELD: *8 servings*

1 tablespoon reduced-sodium soy sauce
2 cloves garlic, minced
1 cup pineapple juice
6 skinless boneless chicken breast tenderloins, about 4 ounces each, cut into 1-inch cubes
¼ cup low-sodium nonfat chicken broth
2 cups low-sodium tomato juice
1 medium red bell pepper, cored and cut into thin strips
1 medium green bell pepper, cored and cut into thin strips
2 medium onions, chopped
2 teaspoons curry powder
2 teaspoons garam masala
2 teaspoons paprika
½ cup water
4 cups cooked rice

1. Combine soy sauce, garlic, and pineapple juice in a glass bowl. Add chicken and marinate for 1 hour in the refrigerator.
2. Heat broth in a large saucepan. Add chicken and marinade, and sauté until chicken is no longer pink, about 8 minutes. Add tomato juice, bell peppers, onions, curry powder, garam masala, paprika, and water. Bring to a boil, reduce heat, cover, and simmer until chicken is cooked through, about 15 minutes.
3. Serve over rice.

Calories Per Serving: 258
Fat: 1 g
Cholesterol: 53 mg
Protein: 24 g
Carbohydrates: 38 g
Dietary Fiber: 2 g
Sodium: 109 mg

Chicken Mandarin

PREPARATION TIME: *20 minutes* ▪ COOKING TIME: *18 minutes* ▪ YIELD: *4 servings*

¼ cup low-sodium nonfat chicken broth
3 skinless boneless chicken breast tenderloins, about 4 ounces each, chopped
2 leeks (white parts only), thinly sliced
2 scallions, sliced
¼ cup dry white wine
1 tablespoon minced fresh gingerroot
½ cup orange juice
1 tablespoon grated orange peel
1 tablespoon all-purpose flour
¼ teaspoon sugar
1 medium tomato, chopped
1 cup juice-packed canned mandarin oranges, juice reserved
¼ cup ground black pepper

1. Heat broth in a large saucepan. Add chicken, leeks, and scallions, and sauté until chicken is no longer pink, about 8 minutes. Remove chicken and set aside.
2. Whisk together wine, gingerroot, orange juice, orange peel, flour, and sugar in a small bowl.
3. Transfer wine mixture to the saucepan, add tomato, and bring to a boil. Reduce heat, and simmer, stirring constantly, for 3 minutes. Return chicken to the saucepan. Stir in mandarin oranges with juice, and black pepper, and simmer to heat through, about 3 minutes.
4. Serve at once on individual plates.

Calories Per Serving: 184	Carbohydrates: 20 g
Fat: 1 g	Dietary Fiber: 2 g
Cholesterol: 53 mg	Sodium: 60 mg
Protein: 22 g	

❈ *Mango Chicken* ❈

PREPARATION TIME: *15 minutes* • COOKING TIME: *19 minutes* •
YIELD: *4 servings*

¼ cup low-sodium nonfat chicken broth

3 skinless boneless chicken breast tenderloins, about 4 ounces each, cut into thin strips

2 medium stalks celery, sliced

4 scallions, sliced

1 medium red bell pepper, cored and cut into thin strips

1 medium yellow bell pepper, cored and cut into thin strips

1 medium mango, peeled, cored, and cut into thin strips

1 tablespoon reduced-sodium soy sauce

3 tablespoons lime juice

2 cups cooked rice

1. Heat 2 tablespoons broth in a large wok. Add chicken and stirfry until cooked through, about 8 minutes. Remove chicken and set aside.
2. Heat remaining broth in the wok. Add celery, scallions, and bell peppers, and stirfry until peppers begin to soften, about 4 minutes.
3. Stir in mango, soy sauce, lime juice, and chicken, and continue to stirfry until all ingredients are heated through, about 3 minutes.
4. Serve over rice.

Calories Per Serving: 278	Carbohydrates: 43 g
Fat: 1 g	Dietary Fiber: 3 g
Cholesterol: 53 mg	Sodium: 206 mg
Protein: 25 g	

❊ *Chicken with Nectarines* ❊

PREPARATION TIME: *15 minutes* • COOKING TIME: *18 minutes* •
YIELD: *5 servings*

¾ cup low-sodium nonfat chicken
   broth
3 skinless boneless chicken breast tenderloins, about 4 ounces each,
   chopped
1 medium onion, chopped
3 medium stalks celery, sliced

4 medium nectarines, pitted and
   sliced
1 clove garlic, minced
2½ teaspoons curry powder
2 tablespoons lemon juice
½ teaspoon sugar

1. Heat 2 tablespoons broth in a wok. Add chicken and stirfry until cooked
   through, about 5 minutes. Remove chicken and set aside.
2. Heat another 2 tablespoons broth in the wok. Add onion, celery, nectarines, and garlic. Stirfry until onion begins to soften, about 4 minutes.
3. Combine curry powder, remaining broth, lemon juice, and sugar. Add to
   the wok and stir for about 3 minutes.
4. Return chicken to the wok and continue to stir until all ingredients are
   heated through, about 2 minutes.

Calories Per Serving: 193
Fat: 2 g
Cholesterol: 53 mg
Protein: 24 g

Carbohydrates: 23 g
Dietary Fiber: 3 g
Sodium: 93 mg

❊ *Chicken and Pineapple in* ❊ *Sherry-Ginger Sauce*

PREPARATION TIME: *20 minutes* • COOKING TIME: *36 minutes* •
YIELD: *6 servings*

¾ cup low-sodium nonfat chicken
   broth
6 skinless boneless chicken breast tenderloins, about 4 ounces each,
   chopped
1 medium onion, finely chopped

1 medium green bell pepper, cored
   and chopped
1 cup juice-packed canned pineapple
   chunks, juice reserved
¼ cup dry sherry

1 tablespoon reduced-sodium soy
   sauce
1 tablespoon brown sugar
2 teaspoons rice vinegar

½ teaspoon ground ginger
¼ teaspoon ground black pepper
2½ cups cooked rice

1. Heat ¼ cup broth in a large pot. Add chicken and sauté until no longer pink, about 8 minutes.
2. Add onion and bell pepper, and sauté until onion begins to soften, about 3 minutes.
3. Combine pineapple chunks with juice, remaining broth, sherry, soy sauce, brown sugar, vinegar, ginger, and black pepper. Pour mixture over chicken. Bring to a boil, reduce heat, cover, and simmer until chicken is cooked through, about 20 minutes.
4. Serve over rice.

Calories Per Serving: 315
Fat: 1 g
Cholesterol: 70 mg
Protein: 31 g

Carbohydrates: 42 g
Dietary Fiber: 1 g
Sodium: 157 mg

❀ *Chicken with Artichokes* ❀

PREPARATION TIME: *20 minutes* • COOKING TIME: *35 minutes* •
YIELD: *5 servings*

¼ cup low-sodium nonfat chicken
   broth
5 skinless boneless chicken breast tenderloins, about 4 ounces each,
   chopped
4 small white onions, quartered
1½ cups water-packed canned artichoke hearts, drained

¼ cup water
2 tablespoons minced fresh parsley
1 teaspoon dried marjoram
¼ teaspoon ground black pepper
2 bay leaves
2 cups cooked rice

1. Heat broth in a large saucepan. Add chicken and sauté for 4 minutes. Add onions and sauté for 4 more minutes.
2. Add artichoke hearts and water. Stir to distribute evenly. Sprinkle parsley, marjoram, and black pepper over chicken. Add bay leaves, cover tightly, and simmer, basting frequently, until chicken is cooked through, about 25 minutes. Add more water if needed. Remove bay leaves.
3. Serve over rice.

Calories Per Serving: 269　　　Carbohydrates: 33 g
Fat: 1 g　　　　　　　　　　Dietary Fiber: 4 g
Cholesterol: 70 mg　　　　　　Sodium: 111 mg
Protein: 31 g

❈ *Chicken with Peaches* ❈

PREPARATION TIME: *20 minutes* • COOKING TIME: *39 minutes* •
YIELD: *4 servings*

4 skinless boneless chicken breast tenderloins, about 4 ounces each
¼ cup all-purpose flour
¼ cup low-sodium nonfat chicken
  broth
½ cup sugarless all-fruit peach jam
1 teaspoon grated lemon peel

1 tablespoon reduced-sodium soy
  sauce
2 cups sliced juice-packed canned
  peaches, juice reserved
1 medium green bell pepper, cored
  and chopped
2 cups cooked rice

1. Dredge chicken in flour. Heat broth in a large saucepan. Add chicken and
   sauté until no longer pink, about 8 minutes. Coat chicken with peach
   jam.
2. Combine lemon peel, soy sauce, and peach juice in a separate bowl, and
   add to chicken. Cover the saucepan and simmer, basting several times,
   until chicken is cooked through, about 20 minutes.
3. Add bell pepper and cook 5 more minutes. Add peaches to the chicken
   and heat through, about 4 minutes.
4. Serve over rice.

Calories Per Serving: 412　　　Carbohydrates: 68 g
Fat: 1 g　　　　　　　　　　Dietary Fiber: 2 g
Cholesterol: 70 mg　　　　　　Sodium: 202 mg
Protein: 31 g

❈ *Chicken with Pears and Apricots* ❈

PREPARATION TIME: *25 minutes* • COOKING TIME: *50 minutes* •
YIELD: *6 servings*

1 tablespoon all-purpose flour
1½ teaspoons curry powder

½ teaspoon paprika
½ teaspoon dried basil

½ teaspoon dried oregano

4 skinless boneless chicken breast ten-
    derloins, about 4 ounces each,
    chopped

¾ cup low-sodium nonfat chicken
    broth

1 medium onion, chopped

3 cloves garlic, minced

2 cups diced pears

1 tablespoon honey

1 cup seedless raisins

1 tablespoon lemon juice

1½ cups juice-packed canned apri-
    cots, chopped, juice reserved

2 cups cooked rice

1. Preheat oven to 350 degrees.
2. Combine flour, ½ teaspoon curry powder, the paprika, basil, and oregano. Place chicken and flour mixture in a paper bag and shake to coat chicken with flour mixture.
3. Heat ¼ cup broth in a flameproof 2-quart casserole. Add chicken and sauté until no longer pink, about 8 minutes. Remove chicken and set aside.
4. Heat another ¼ cup broth in the casserole. Add onion and garlic, and sauté until onion begins to soften, about 3 minutes. Stir in remaining broth, pears, remaining curry powder, honey, raisins, lemon juice, and apricots with juice. Cover and simmer, stirring occasionally, for 10 minutes.
5. Remove from heat, stir in rice, and return chicken to the casserole. Place the casserole in the oven and bake for 25 minutes. Serve at once.

Calories Per Serving: 327
Fat: 1 g
Cholesterol: 47 mg
Protein: 21 g

Carbohydrates: 60 g
Dietary Fiber: 3 g
Sodium: 50 mg

❊ Apple-Cabbage-Chicken Casserole ❊

PREPARATION TIME: 25 minutes • COOKING TIME: 40 minutes •
YIELD: 4 servings

¼ cup low-sodium nonfat chicken
    broth

4 skinless boneless chicken breast ten-
    derloins, about 4 ounces each

3 scallions, minced

3 cups shredded cabbage

2 medium apples, peeled, cored, and
    quartered

1 teaspoon grated fresh gingerroot

2 tablespoons molasses

½ cup water

1 tablespoon lemon juice

¼ teaspoon ground black pepper

1. Preheat oven to 375 degrees.
2. Heat 2 tablespoons broth in a flameproof 2-quart casserole. Add chicken and sauté until no longer pink, about 8 minutes. Remove chicken and set aside.
3. Heat remaining broth in the casserole. Add scallions and cabbage, and sauté for 3 minutes. Top with a layer of chicken, and then with a layer of apples.
4. Whisk together gingerroot, molasses, water, lemon juice, and black pepper in a separate bowl and pour over apples. Cover the casserole and bake until chicken is cooked through, about 25 minutes.
5. Remove from the oven and serve.

Calories Per Serving: 198	Carbohydrates: 20 g
Fat: 1 g	Dietary Fiber: 2 g
Cholesterol: 70 mg	Sodium: 63 mg
Protein: 28 g	

❋ *Wine-Baked Chicken and Vegetables* ❋

PREPARATION TIME: *15 minutes* • COOKING TIME: *60 minutes* •
YIELD: *6 servings*

1½ cups low-sodium nonfat chicken broth
6 skinless boneless chicken breast tenderloins, about 4 ounces each
½ teaspoon ground black pepper
½ cup canned mushrooms, drained
1 cup water-packed canned artichoke hearts, drained

1 cup canned bamboo shoots, drained
1 cup sliced canned water chestnuts, drained
1½ cups nonfat plain yogurt
½ cup dry white wine

1. Preheat oven to 350 degrees.
2. Heat ¼ cup broth in a flameproof 3-quart casserole. Add chicken, sprinkle with black pepper, and sauté until no longer pink, about 8 minutes.
3. Combine mushrooms, artichoke hearts, bamboo shoots, and water chestnuts, and add to the casserole. Combine yogurt and wine, and pour over vegetables. Cover and bake for 50 minutes.

Calories Per Serving: 188	Carbohydrates: 7 g
Fat: 1 g	Dietary Fiber: 1 g
Cholesterol: 70 mg	Sodium: 228 mg
Protein: 34 g	

❊ *Baked Chicken with Barley and Vegetables* ❊

PREPARATION TIME: *15 minutes*　•　COOKING TIME: *1 hour 22 minutes*　•
YIELD: *4 servings*

*3½ cups low-sodium nonfat chicken
broth*
*4 skinless boneless chicken breast ten-
derloins, about 4 ounces each,
chopped*
1 medium onion, chopped
2 medium stalks celery, chopped
*1 medium green bell pepper, cored
and chopped*

*1 medium yellow summer squash,
chopped*
1 cup pearl barley
½ teaspoon ground black pepper
*1 cup low-sodium canned tomatoes,
chopped, juice reserved*

1. Preheat oven to 350 degrees.
2. Heat ¼ cup broth in a flameproof 3-quart casserole. Add chicken and
   sauté until no longer pink, about 8 minutes. Remove chicken and set
   aside.
3. Heat another ¼ cup broth in the casserole. Add onion, celery, bell pepper,
   and squash, and sauté until vegetables begin to soften, about 5 minutes.
   Add barley and sauté for 1 more minute.
4. Add remaining broth. Bring to a boil, reduce heat, cover, and simmer for
   30 minutes.
5. Stir in chicken, black pepper, and tomatoes with juice. Cover and bake
   until chicken is cooked through, about 30 minutes.
6. Drain any excess liquid, transfer to individual plates, and serve at once.

Calories Per Serving: 345
Fat: 2 g
Cholesterol: 70 mg
Protein: 33 g

Carbohydrates: 46 g
Dietary Fiber: 10 g
Sodium: 331 mg

❊ *Baked Chicken and Brown Rice* ❊
with Vegetables in Wine Sauce

PREPARATION TIME: *15 minutes plus 10 minutes standing time*　•
COOKING TIME: *45 minutes*　•　YIELD: *6 servings*

Olive oil cooking spray
1 small zucchini, chopped
1 medium onion, chopped
1 medium red bell pepper, cored and
    chopped
1 cup low-sodium nonfat chicken
    broth
1 cup dry white wine
¼ cup chopped fresh parsley

½ teaspoon dried basil
1 bay leaf
½ teaspoon dried thyme
1 cup uncooked brown rice
1 cup low-sodium canned tomatoes,
    drained and chopped
6 skinless boneless chicken breast ten-
    derloins, about 4 ounces each,
    chopped

1. Preheat oven to 350 degrees. Lightly coat a 3-quart casserole with olive oil cooking spray.
2. Combine zucchini, onion, bell pepper, broth, wine, parsley, basil, bay leaf, and thyme in the casserole.
3. Stir in rice, tomatoes, and chicken. Cover tightly and bake until chicken is cooked through and rice is tender, about 45 minutes. Remove from the oven and allow to stand, covered, for 10 minutes.
4. Remove bay leaf and serve.

Calories Per Serving: 276
Fat: 1 g
Cholesterol: 70 mg
Protein: 31 g

Carbohydrates: 29 g
Dietary Fiber: 1 g
Sodium: 82 mg

❀ Chicken and Summer Squash Baked ❀ in Wine-Garlic Sauce

PREPARATION TIME: *15 minutes* • COOKING TIME: *47 minutes* •
YIELD: *6 servings*

6 skinless boneless chicken breast ten-
    derloins, about 4 ounces each
1 teaspoon paprika
¼ cup low-sodium nonfat chicken
    broth
40 cloves garlic, peeled and left whole
2 medium carrots, scraped and sliced

4 medium baking potatoes, cut into
    eighths
2 medium stalks celery, sliced
⅓ cup dry white wine
3 cups sliced zucchini
3 cups sliced yellow summer squash
¼ cup chopped fresh parsley

1. Preheat oven to 375 degrees. Sprinkle chicken with paprika.
2. Heat broth in a flameproof 3-quart casserole. Add chicken and sauté until no longer pink, about 5 minutes.

3. Add garlic cloves, carrots, potatoes, and celery. Pour wine over vegetables, cover, and bake for 25 minutes.
4. Add zucchini and squash, and return to the oven until squash is just tender and chicken is cooked through, about 15 more minutes.
5. Serve topped with parsley.

Calories Per Serving: 264
Fat: 2 g
Cholesterol: 50 mg
Protein: 22 g

Carbohydrates: 39 g
Dietary Fiber: 6 g
Sodium: 75 mg

❋ *Chicken, Turnip, and Tomato Bake* ❋

PREPARATION TIME: *20 minutes* ▪ COOKING TIME: *1 hour 10 minutes* ▪
YIELD: *6 servings*

Olive oil cooking spray
6 skinless boneless chicken breast tenderloins, about 4 ounces each
2 cups low-sodium canned tomatoes, crushed, juice reserved
1 medium onion, diced
2 cloves garlic, minced

1½ cups boiling water
6 turnips, diced
¾ cup uncooked white rice
1 tablespoon curry powder
2 teaspoons sugar
¼ teaspoon ground ginger
½ teaspoon ground black pepper

1. Preheat oven to 450 degrees. Lightly coat a 3-quart casserole with olive oil cooking spray.
2. Place chicken in the casserole, and bake for 10 minutes.
3. Reduce oven temperature to 375 degrees. Add tomatoes with juice, onion, garlic, water, turnips, rice, curry powder, sugar, ginger, and black pepper. Cover and bake, stirring occasionally, for 1 hour.

Calories Per Serving: 253
Fat: 2 g
Cholesterol: 70 mg
Protein: 30 g

Carbohydrates: 30 g
Dietary Fiber: 3 g
Sodium: 97 mg

❊ Chicken-Vegetable Bake ❊

PREPARATION TIME: *20 minutes* • COOKING TIME: *1 hour* • YIELD: *4 servings*

Olive oil cooking spray
2 teaspoons dried rosemary
2 tablespoons dried parsley
½ teaspoon ground black pepper
4 skinless boneless chicken breast tenderloins, about 4 ounces each
6 cloves garlic, minced

4 medium carrots, scraped and sliced
1 medium onion, sliced
3 cups diced potatoes
1 cup chopped green beans (1-inch lengths)
2 medium stalks celery, sliced
1 cup dry white wine

1. Preheat oven to 350 degrees. Lightly coat a 3-quart casserole with olive oil cooking spray.
2. Combine rosemary, parsley, and black pepper.
3. Arrange chicken on the bottom of the casserole. Sprinkle half the seasoning mixture over chicken. Add garlic, carrots, onion, potatoes, green beans, and celery. Sprinkle remaining seasoning mix over vegetables.
4. Pour wine over vegetables, cover, and bake until chicken is cooked through, about 1 hour.

Calories Per Serving: 388
Fat: 2 g
Cholesterol: 70 mg
Protein: 33 g

Carbohydrates: 53 g
Dietary Fiber: 6 g
Sodium: 98 mg

❊ Baked Chicken with Bulgur ❊

PREPARATION TIME: *15 minutes* • COOKING TIME: *1 hour 10 minutes* • YIELD: *4 servings*

2 cups low-sodium nonfat chicken broth
4 skinless boneless chicken breast tenderloins, about 4 ounces each, cut into ½-inch cubes
3½ cups low-sodium canned tomatoes, chopped, juice reserved

1 medium onion, chopped
3 cloves garlic, minced
3 tablespoons lemon juice
½ cup seedless raisins
½ teaspoon ground black pepper
½ cup ripe olives
2 cups bulgur

1. Preheat oven to 350 degrees.
2. Heat ¼ cup broth in a flameproof 3-quart casserole. Add chicken and sauté until no longer pink, about 8 minutes. Remove chicken and set aside.
3. Combine remaining broth, tomatoes with juice, onion, garlic, lemon juice, raisins, black pepper, olives, and bulgur in the casserole. Return chicken to the casserole, cover, and bake until chicken is cooked through, about 1 hour.

Calories Per Serving: 483
Fat: 3 g
Cholesterol: 70 mg
Protein: 39 g

Carbohydrates: 81 g
Dietary Fiber: 19 g
Sodium: 232 mg

❀ *Turkey–Pinto Bean Chili* ❀

PREPARATION TIME: *10 minutes* • COOKING TIME: *32 minutes* •
YIELD: *6 servings*

¼ cup low-sodium nonfat chicken broth
½ pound ground turkey breast
1 medium onion, chopped
2 cloves garlic, minced
1½ tablespoons chili powder
½ cup diced canned mild green chiles, drained

6 cups low-sodium canned tomatoes, crushed, juice reserved
4 cups low-sodium canned pinto beans, rinsed and drained
4 scallions, chopped

1. Heat broth in a large saucepan. Add turkey, onion, and garlic, and sauté until turkey is no longer pink, about 5 minutes.
2. Add chili powder, chiles, tomatoes with juice, and pinto beans. Bring to a simmer, cover, and cook, stirring occasionally, for 25 minutes.
3. Serve topped with scallions.

Calories Per Serving: 259
Fat: 2 g
Cholesterol: 23 mg
Protein: 22 g

Carbohydrates: 42 g
Dietary Fiber: 11 g
Sodium: 166 mg

❀ *Turkey–Black Bean Chili* ❀

PREPARATION TIME: *15 minutes* • COOKING TIME: *32 minutes* •
YIELD: *8 servings*

¼ cup low-sodium nonfat chicken
  broth
¾ pound ground turkey breast
2 medium onions, chopped
1 medium red bell pepper, cored and
  chopped
½ cup diced canned mild green chiles,
  drained
3 cloves garlic, minced

3½ cups low-sodium canned tomatoes, crushed, juice reserved
1½ cups low-sodium tomato paste
8 cups low-sodium canned black
  beans, rinsed and drained
1½ tablespoons chili powder
¾ teaspoon dried oregano
¼ teaspoon ground black pepper
2 scallions, minced

1. Heat broth in a large saucepan. Add turkey and sauté until no longer pink, about 5 minutes.
2. Add onions, bell pepper, chiles, garlic, tomatoes with juice, tomato paste, black beans, chili powder, oregano, and black pepper. Cover and simmer for 25 minutes.
3. Serve topped with scallions.

Calories Per Serving: 360
Fat: 2 g
Cholesterol: 26 mg
Protein: 29 g

Carbohydrates: 60 g
Dietary Fiber: 17 g
Sodium: 89 mg

❀ *Chicken-Broccoli Chili* ❀

PREPARATION TIME: *15 minutes* • COOKING TIME: *30 minutes* •
YIELD: *6 servings*

¼ cup low-sodium nonfat chicken
  broth
2 medium onions, chopped
3 cloves garlic, minced
2 medium green bell peppers, cored
  and chopped
1 medium red bell pepper, cored and
  chopped

3 skinless boneless chicken breast tenderloins, about 4 ounces each,
  chopped
2 cups low-sodium canned tomatoes,
  drained and chopped
2 cups low-sodium canned pinto
  beans, rinsed and drained
2 cups chopped broccoli

1 teaspoon chili powder
¼ teaspoon cayenne pepper

¼ cup chopped fresh parsley

1. Heat broth in a large skillet. Add onions, garlic, bell peppers, and chicken, and sauté until chicken is no longer pink, about 8 minutes.
2. Add tomatoes, pinto beans, broccoli, chili powder, and cayenne pepper. Bring to a boil, reduce heat, cover, and simmer until chicken is cooked through and vegetables are tender, about 20 minutes.
3. Serve topped with parsley.

Calories Per Serving: 189
Fat: 1 g
Cholesterol: 35 mg
Protein: 21 g

Carbohydrates: 25 g
Dietary Fiber: 7 g
Sodium: 64 mg

❀ *Red and White Chicken Chili* ❀

PREPARATION TIME: *10 minutes* • COOKING TIME: *27 minutes* •
YIELD: *6 servings*

6 tablespoons low-sodium nonfat chicken broth
3 skinless boneless chicken breast tenderloins, about 4 ounces each, chopped
1 medium onion, chopped
2 cloves garlic, minced
1½ tablespoons chili powder
2½ teaspoons ground cumin

3½ cups low-sodium canned tomatoes, drained and chopped
2 cups low-sodium pinto beans, rinsed and drained
2 cups low-sodium cannellini beans, rinsed and drained
¾ cup low-sodium tomato paste
3 tablespoons chopped scallions

1. Heat broth in a large saucepan. Add chicken, onion, and garlic, and sauté until chicken is no longer pink, about 8 minutes.
2. Stir in chili powder, cumin, tomatoes, pinto beans, cannellini beans, and tomato paste. Bring to a boil, reduce heat, and simmer until chicken is cooked through and all ingredients are heated through, about 12 minutes.
3. Serve topped with scallions.

Calories Per Serving: 285
Fat: 2 g
Cholesterol: 35 mg
Protein: 27 g

Carbohydrates: 43 g
Dietary Fiber: 12 g
Sodium: 90 mg

❊ *Pineapple-Chicken Chili* ❊

PREPARATION TIME: *15 minutes* • COOKING TIME: *39 minutes* •
YIELD: *5 servings*

6 tablespoons low-sodium nonfat
　chicken broth
3 skinless boneless chicken breast ten-
　derloins, about 4 ounces each,
　chopped
1 medium onion, chopped
1 medium red bell pepper, cored and
　chopped

2 cups orange juice
1½ cups uncooked white rice
1½ tablespoons chili powder
¼ teaspoon ground cinnamon
½ teaspoon ground black pepper
2½ cups juice-packed canned pineap-
　ple chunks, drained

1. Heat 4 tablespoons broth in a large saucepan. Add chicken and sauté until
   no longer pink, about 8 minutes. Remove and set aside.
2. Heat remaining broth in the saucepan. Add onion and bell pepper, and
   sauté until onion begins to soften, about 4 minutes.
3. Stir in orange juice and rice. Combine chili powder, cinnamon, and black
   pepper in a separate bowl. Stir half the mixture into the saucepan.
4. Add pineapple chunks. Place chicken on top of pineapple and sprinkle remaining chili powder mixture on chicken. Bring to a boil, reduce heat,
   cover, and simmer until chicken is cooked through and rice is tender,
   about 20 minutes.

Calories Per Serving: 359
Fat: 2 g
Cholesterol: 42 mg
Protein: 21 g

Carbohydrates: 64 g
Dietary Fiber: 2 g
Sodium: 75 mg

❊ *Chicken and Green Pepper Chili* ❊
with Bulgur

PREPARATION TIME: *20 minutes* • COOKING TIME: *37 minutes* •
YIELD: *5 servings*

¾ cup bulgur
1½ cups hot water
4 skinless boneless chicken breast ten-
　derloins, about 4 ounces each,
　chopped

¼ teaspoon ground black pepper
1½ cups low-sodium nonfat chicken
　broth
4 medium green bell peppers, cored
　and chopped

2 cloves garlic, minced
2 teaspoons chili powder

2 teaspoons paprika
¼ cup minced fresh parsley

1. Combine bulgur and hot water in a medium bowl. Set aside.
2. Sprinkle chicken with black pepper. Heat ¼ cup broth in a large saucepan or wok. Add chicken and sauté until no longer pink, about 8 minutes. Remove chicken and set aside.
3. Heat another ¼ cup broth in the saucepan. Add bell peppers and garlic, and sauté until peppers begin to soften, about 4 minutes.
4. Add remaining broth, chili powder, and paprika. Return chicken to the saucepan. Bring to a boil, reduce heat, cover, and simmer until chicken is cooked through, about 10 minutes.
5. Drain liquid from bulgur. Add bulgur to chicken. Return to a boil, reduce heat, and simmer, stirring frequently, until bulgur is just tender, about 8 minutes.
6. Serve topped with parsley.

Calories Per Serving: 262
Fat: 1 g
Cholesterol: 56 mg
Protein: 26 g

Carbohydrates: 38 g
Dietary Fiber: 5 g
Sodium: 208 mg

❀ *Microwave Chicken Chili* ❀

PREPARATION TIME: *15 minutes* • COOKING TIME: *26 minutes* •
YIELD: *4 servings*

1 tablespoon low-sodium nonfat chicken broth
1 medium onion, chopped
1 clove garlic, minced
3 skinless boneless chicken breast tenderloins, about 4 ounces each, minced
3½ cups low-sodium canned tomatoes, crushed, juice reserved

⅔ cup low-sodium tomato paste
1 cup diced canned mild green chiles, drained
4 cups low-sodium canned black beans, rinsed and drained
1 tablespoon chili powder
¾ teaspoon ground cumin
¾ teaspoon ground cinnamon
¼ cup chopped fresh parsley

1. Combine broth, onion, and garlic in a microwave-safe 3-quart casserole. Cook on HIGH, stirring once, for 4 minutes.
2. Add chicken and cook on HIGH for 7 more minutes.

3. Stir in tomatoes with juice, tomato paste, chiles, black beans, chili pow-der, cumin, and cinnamon. Return to the microwave and cook on HIGH, stirring once, for 15 more minutes.
4. Transfer to individual bowls, garnish with parsley, and serve.

Calories Per Serving: 287
Fat: 2 g
Cholesterol: 35 mg
Protein: 27 g

Carbohydrates: 44 g
Dietary Fiber: 12 g
Sodium: 245 mg

❀ *Chicken and Chickpeas* ❀

PREPARATION TIME: *20 minutes plus 15 minutes soaking time*　•
COOKING TIME: *1 hour*　•　YIELD: *4 servings*

¼ cup low-sodium nonfat chicken
　broth
4 skinless boneless chicken breast ten-
　derloins, about 4 ounces each,
　chopped
4 cloves garlic, minced
4 cups water
1 teaspoon dried saffron threads,
　crushed
1 tablespoon chopped fresh parsley

¼ teaspoon ground black pepper
1 cup uncooked white rice
1 cup chopped fresh or thawed frozen
　green beans (1-inch lengths)
3 sun-dried tomatoes, soaked in hot
　water for 15 minutes, drained,
　and minced
1½ cups cooked or low-sodium
　canned chickpeas, rinsed and
　drained

1. Heat broth in a large saucepan. Add chicken and garlic, and sauté until chicken is no longer pink, about 8 minutes.
2. Add water, saffron, parsley, and black pepper. Cover and simmer for 20 minutes. Remove chicken and set aside.
3. Bring liquid to a boil, stir in rice, and cook for 10 minutes. Add green beans and cook for 10 more minutes. Stir in tomatoes and chickpeas. Add chicken and simmer to heat through, about 5 minutes.
4. Drain any excess liquid and serve at once.

Calories Per Serving: 434
Fat: 2 g
Cholesterol: 70 mg
Protein: 38 g

Carbohydrates: 67 g
Dietary Fiber: 6 g
Sodium: 368 mg

❄ *Chicken with Black-eyed Peas* ❄

PREPARATION TIME: *20 minutes* • COOKING TIME: *40 minutes* •
YIELD: *4 servings*

¾ cup low-sodium nonfat chicken
  broth
4 skinless boneless chicken breast tenderloins, about 4 ounces each,
  chopped
1 medium onion, chopped
2 cups sliced mushrooms

½ teaspoon ground black pepper
1 teaspoon dried thyme
½ teaspoon dried marjoram
3 cups low-sodium canned black-eyed
  peas, rinsed and drained
1 medium tomato, chopped

1. Heat ¼ cup broth in a large pot. Add chicken and sauté until no longer
   pink, about 8 minutes. Remove chicken and set aside.
2. Heat another ¼ cup broth in the pot. Add onion and mushrooms, and
   sauté until onion begins to soften, about 3 minutes.
3. Stir in remaining broth, black pepper, thyme, marjoram, black-eyed peas,
   and chicken. Add tomato, cover, and simmer until chicken is cooked
   through, about 25 minutes.

Calories Per Serving: 359
Fat: 2 g
Cholesterol: 70 mg
Protein: 40 g

Carbohydrates: 45 g
Dietary Fiber: 8 g
Sodium: 135 mg

❄ *Chicken Caribe with Red Pepper* ❄ *and Black Beans*

PREPARATION TIME: *20 minutes* • COOKING TIME: *33 minutes* •
YIELD: *6 servings*

6 skinless boneless chicken breast tenderloins, about 4 ounces each, cut
  into ½-inch cubes
¼ teaspoon ground black pepper
1½ cups low-sodium nonfat chicken
  broth
1 medium onion, chopped
2 cloves garlic, minced
1 cup low-sodium tomato sauce

1 medium red bell pepper, cored and
  diced
½ teaspoon ground cinnamon
¼ teaspoon ground cloves
⅛ teaspoon cayenne pepper
2 cups low-sodium canned black
  beans, rinsed and drained
3 cups cooked rice

1. Sprinkle chicken with black pepper. Heat ¼ cup broth in a large saucepan. Add chicken and sauté until no longer pink, about 8 minutes. Remove chicken and set aside.
2. Heat another ¼ cup broth in the saucepan. Add onion and garlic, and sauté until onion begins to soften, about 3 minutes.
3. Stir in tomato sauce and remaining broth. Add bell pepper, cinnamon, cloves, and cayenne pepper. Bring to a boil, reduce heat, and simmer for 10 minutes.
4. Add chicken and beans, and continue to simmer until all ingredients are heated through and bell pepper is just tender, about 5 minutes.
5. Serve over rice.

Calories Per Serving: 383   Carbohydrates: 47 g
Fat: 2 g   Dietary Fiber: 5 g
Cholesterol: 70 mg   Sodium: 104 mg
Protein: 37 g

❊ *Chicken, Beans, and Barley* ❊

PREPARATION TIME: *20 minutes* • COOKING TIME: *50 minutes* •
YIELD: *8 servings*

4 skinless boneless chicken breast tenderloins, about 4 ounces each, cut
   into ½-inch cubes
4 cups low-sodium nonfat chicken
   broth
½ cup pearl barley
2 medium onions, chopped
½ teaspoon dried basil
½ teaspoon dried thyme

½ teaspoon ground black pepper
3 medium stalks celery, sliced
3 medium carrots, scraped and sliced
1 cup thawed frozen lima beans
2 medium tomatoes, chopped
2 cups low-sodium canned pinto
   beans, rinsed and drained
¾ cup fresh or thawed frozen green
   peas

1. Combine chicken and broth in a large saucepan. Bring to a boil, reduce heat, and simmer for 20 minutes.
2. Add barley, onions, basil, thyme, and black pepper, and simmer for 10 more minutes.
3. Stir in celery, carrots, and lima beans, and continue to simmer for 10 additional minutes.
4. Add tomatoes, pinto beans, and green peas, and cook until peas are done, about 5 minutes. Transfer to individual plates and serve.

Calories Per Serving: 226
Fat: 1 g
Cholesterol: 35 mg
Protein: 24 g

Carbohydrates: 30 g
Dietary Fiber: 9 g
Sodium: 144 mg

❊ *Chicken and Broccoli with Bulgur* ❊

PREPARATION TIME: *15 minutes*   •   COOKING TIME: *28 minutes*   •
YIELD: *4 servings*

¼ *cup low-sodium nonfat chicken
broth*
3 *skinless boneless chicken breast tenderloins, about 4 ounces each, cut
into ½-inch cubes*
1 *medium onion, chopped*
2 *cloves garlic, minced*
1 *cup sliced mushrooms*
3 *medium carrots, scraped and sliced*

2 *cups chopped broccoli*
2 *medium tomatoes, chopped*
½ *cup water*
½ *cup bulgur*
1 *teaspoon dried oregano*
1 *teaspoon dried basil*
¾ *teaspoon ground cumin*
½ *teaspoon ground black pepper*

1. Heat broth in a large skillet. Add chicken and sauté until no longer pink, about 8 minutes.
2. Add onion, garlic, mushrooms, carrots, broccoli, and tomatoes, stirring for 4 more minutes.
3. Stir in water, bulgur, oregano, basil, cumin, and black pepper. Bring to a boil, reduce heat, cover, and simmer until bulgur is tender, about 12 minutes.

Calories Per Serving: 221
Fat: 2 g
Cholesterol: 53 mg
Protein: 26 g

Carbohydrates: 28 g
Dietary Fiber: 8 g
Sodium: 86 mg

❊ *Spanish Rice with Chicken* ❊

PREPARATION TIME: *20 minutes*   •   COOKING TIME: *40 minutes*   •
YIELD: *6 servings*

2½ cups low-sodium nonfat chicken broth

3 skinless boneless chicken breast tenderloins, about 4 ounces each, chopped

2 medium onions, sliced

4 scallions, sliced

2 cloves garlic, minced

1 jalapeño pepper, seeded and minced

2 medium green bell peppers, cored and chopped

4 medium tomatoes, chopped

½ cup uncooked white rice

½ teaspoon dried oregano

½ teaspoon ground black pepper

1 bay leaf

¼ cup chopped fresh parsley

1. Heat 3 tablespoons broth in a large skillet. Add chicken and sauté until no longer pink, about 8 minutes.
2. Add onions, scallions, garlic, jalapeño pepper, and bell peppers, and continue to sauté until onions begin to soften, about 4 more minutes. Add tomatoes and simmer for 2 minutes.
3. Stir in remaining broth, rice, oregano, and black pepper. Add bay leaf, bring to a boil, reduce heat, cover, and simmer until rice is tender, about 20 minutes. Add small amounts of water if necessary. Remove bay leaf.
4. Serve topped with parsley.

Calories Per Serving: 160
Fat: 1 g
Cholesterol: 35 mg
Protein: 16 g

Carbohydrates: 22 g
Dietary Fiber: 2 g
Sodium: 128 mg

❈ Chicken with Couscous and ❈ Cannellini Beans

PREPARATION TIME: 15 minutes   •   COOKING TIME: 36 minutes   •
YIELD: 4 servings

6 tablespoons low-sodium nonfat chicken broth

4 skinless boneless chicken breast tenderloins, about 4 ounces each, cut into ½-inch cubes

1 medium onion, chopped

4 medium carrots, scraped and sliced

3 medium stalks celery, sliced

2 cloves garlic, minced

2 cups water

1 cup uncooked couscous

2 cups low-sodium canned cannellini beans, rinsed and drained

1 cup chopped artichoke hearts

2 tablespoons lime juice

½ teaspoon ground black pepper

1. Heat ¼ cup broth in a large saucepan. Add chicken and sauté until no longer pink, about 8 minutes. Remove chicken and set aside.
2. Heat remaining broth in the saucepan. Add onion, carrots, and celery, and sauté until onion begins to soften, about 4 minutes. Stir in remaining ingredients.
3. Return chicken to the saucepan. Bring to a boil, reduce heat, cover, and simmer until chicken is cooked through, about 20 minutes.

Calories Per Serving: 479
Fat: 2 g
Cholesterol: 70 mg
Protein: 43 g

Carbohydrates: 73 g
Dietary Fiber: 18 g
Sodium: 168 mg

❋ *Chicken and Vegetable Fried Rice* ❋

PREPARATION TIME: *20 minutes* • COOKING TIME: *44 minutes* •
YIELD: *6 servings*

3 cups water
3 tablespoons reduced-sodium soy sauce
⅛ teaspoon cayenne pepper
1 cup uncooked white rice
¼ cup low-sodium nonfat chicken broth
1 teaspoon sesame oil
2 skinless boneless chicken breast tenderloins, about 4 ounces each, chopped

4 cups thinly sliced bok choy
1 medium green bell pepper, cored and diced
2 scallions, thinly sliced
1 cup sliced canned water chestnuts, drained
2 teaspoons rice vinegar

1. Combine water, soy sauce, and cayenne pepper in a large pot. Bring to a boil. Stir in rice. Return to a boil, reduce heat, cover, and simmer until almost tender, about 15 minutes. Drain any excess liquid. Remove rice and set aside.
2. Heat broth and sesame oil in the pot. Add chicken and sauté until no longer pink, about 8 minutes. Add bok choy, bell pepper, and scallions, and sauté until pepper begins to soften, about 5 minutes. Add more broth if necessary.
3. Stir in rice, water chestnuts, and vinegar, and simmer until all ingredients are heated through, about 10 minutes.
4. Transfer to individual plates and serve immediately.

Calories Per Serving: 157
Fat: 1 g
Cholesterol: 23 mg
Protein: 23 g
Carbohydrates: 24 g
Dietary Fiber: 1 g
Sodium: 302 mg

Chicken and Rice in Saffron Sauce

PREPARATION TIME: *20 minutes* ▪ COOKING TIME: *35 minutes* ▪ YIELD: *7 servings*

2¾ cups low-sodium nonfat chicken broth
5 skinless boneless chicken breast tenderloins, about 4 ounces each, chopped
1 medium onion, chopped
2 cloves garlic, minced
½ cup dry sherry
2 medium yellow bell peppers, cored and chopped
¼ teaspoon dried saffron threads, crushed
¼ teaspoon ground black pepper
⅛ teaspoon cayenne pepper
1¼ cups uncooked white rice
1 cup fresh or thawed frozen green peas

1. Heat ¼ cup broth in a large pot. Add chicken and sauté until no longer pink, about 8 minutes. Remove chicken and set aside.
2. Heat another ¼ cup broth in the same pot. Add onion and garlic, and sauté until onion begins to soften, about 3 minutes.
3. Return chicken to the pot. Stir in remaining broth, sherry, bell peppers, saffron, black pepper, cayenne pepper, rice, and peas. Bring to a boil, reduce heat, cover, and simmer until rice is just tender, about 20 minutes. Serve immediately.

Calories Per Serving: 257
Fat: 1 g
Cholesterol: 50 mg
Protein: 26 g
Carbohydrates: 34 g
Dietary Fiber: 1 g
Sodium: 98 mg

Spiced Chicken, Chickpeas, and Couscous

PREPARATION TIME: *20 minutes plus 10 minutes standing time* ▪ COOKING TIME: *44 minutes* ▪ YIELD: *4 servings*

2 cups low-sodium nonfat chicken
   broth
4 skinless boneless chicken breast tenderloins, about 4 ounces each,
   chopped
1 medium onion, chopped
2 cloves garlic, minced
1 medium green bell pepper, cored
   and chopped
2 medium tomatoes, chopped
2 cups cooked or low-sodium canned
   chickpeas, rinsed and drained

½ cup seedless raisins
1 bay leaf
1½ teaspoons dried thyme
1 teaspoon ground cumin
¼ teaspoon ground allspice
⅛ teaspoon ground cloves
¼ teaspoon ground black pepper
1 cup uncooked couscous
¼ cup chopped fresh parsley

1. Heat ¼ cup broth in a large pot. Add chicken and sauté until no longer pink, about 8 minutes. Remove chicken and set aside.
2. Heat another ¼ cup broth in the pot. Add onion and garlic, and sauté until onion begins to soften, about 3 minutes.
3. Return chicken to the pot. Add remaining broth, bell pepper, tomatoes, chickpeas, raisins, bay leaf, thyme, cumin, allspice, cloves, and black pepper. Bring to a boil, reduce heat, cover, and simmer until chicken is tender, about 25 minutes. Remove bay leaf.
4. Stir in couscous. Bring to a boil, remove from heat, stir well, and allow to stand for 10 minutes.
5. Serve topped with parsley.

Calories Per Serving: 348
Fat: 2 g
Cholesterol: 47 mg
Protein: 30 g

Carbohydrates: 54 g
Dietary Fiber: 10 g
Sodium: 357 mg

❊ *Turkey with Asparagus and Linguine* ❊

PREPARATION TIME: *20 minutes* • COOKING TIME: *46 minutes* •
YIELD: *6 servings*

2¼ cups low-sodium nonfat chicken
broth
6 scallions, sliced
2 cloves garlic, minced
¼ teaspoon cayenne pepper
3 skinless boneless turkey breast tenderloins, about 4 ounces each,
chopped
⅓ cup boiling water

1 tablespoon all-purpose flour
½ cup dry white wine
½ teaspoon dried tarragon
2 medium stalks celery, sliced
1 teaspoon ground white pepper
2 ounces uncooked linguine, broken
into small pieces
4 cups chopped fresh asparagus spears
(1-inch lengths)

1. Heat ¼ cup broth in a large saucepan. Add scallions, garlic, and cayenne
   pepper, and sauté until scallions begin to soften, about 2 minutes.
2. Add turkey and continue to sauté until turkey is no longer pink, about 8
   minutes. Combine water and flour in a separate bowl. Whisk together
   flour mixture, wine, and remaining broth. Stir into the saucepan.
3. Add tarragon, celery, and white pepper. Bring to a boil, reduce heat, cover,
   and simmer for 15 minutes.
4. Stir in linguine, cover, and simmer for 5 minutes. Add asparagus and continue to simmer until tender, about 10 minutes.
5. Transfer to individual bowls and serve.

Calories Per Serving: 141
Fat: 1 g
Cholesterol: 35 mg
Protein: 17 g

Carbohydrates: 14 g
Dietary Fiber: 1 g
Sodium: 148 mg

❊ Turkey-Pear Curry ❊

PREPARATION TIME: 20 minutes ▪ COOKING TIME: 43 minutes ▪
YIELD: 4 servings

¼ cup low-sodium nonfat chicken
broth
1 medium onion, chopped
1 clove garlic, minced
4 skinless boneless turkey breast tenderloins, about 4 ounces each,
chopped
1 tablespoon curry powder

1 teaspoon paprika
½ teaspoon ground ginger
¼ teaspoon sugar
¼ teaspoon chili powder
¾ cup low-sodium tomato sauce
2 cups chopped pears
2 cups cooked rice

1. Heat broth in a large saucepan. Add onion and garlic, and sauté until onion begins to soften, about 3 minutes. Add turkey, curry powder, paprika, ginger, sugar, and chili powder, and sauté until turkey is no longer pink, about 8 more minutes.
2. Add tomato sauce and enough boiling water to cover ingredients. Cover the saucepan and simmer for 20 minutes. Add pears and simmer until tender, about 10 minutes.
3. Serve over rice on individual plates.

Calories Per Serving: 380
Fat: 2 g
Cholesterol: 70 mg
Protein: 32 g
Carbohydrates: 60 g
Dietary Fiber: 4 g
Sodium: 92 mg

Turkey, Broccoli, and Cauliflower Stirfry

PREPARATION TIME: *15 minutes* ▪ COOKING TIME: *23 minutes* ▪ YIELD: *4 servings*

1¼ cups low-sodium nonfat chicken broth
3 skinless boneless turkey breast tenderloins, about 4 ounces each, cut into thin strips
6 scallions, sliced
4 cups chopped broccoli
4 cups chopped cauliflower
1 medium carrot, scraped and sliced
3 tablespoons dry sherry
1 tablespoon reduced-sodium soy sauce
½ teaspoon ground black pepper
1½ tablespoons cornstarch

1. Heat ¼ cup broth in a large saucepan or wok. Add turkey and sauté until cooked through, about 8 minutes. Remove turkey and set aside.
2. Heat another 2 tablespoons broth in the saucepan. Add scallions, broccoli, cauliflower, and carrot. Sauté for 5 minutes.
3. Stir in remaining broth, sherry, soy sauce, black pepper, and cornstarch. Bring to a boil, reduce heat, and stir until sauce begins to thicken and vegetables are just tender, about 5 minutes.
4. Return turkey to saucepan, heat through, and serve immediately.

Calories Per Serving: 179
Fat: 1 g
Cholesterol: 53 mg
Protein: 26 g
Carbohydrates: 16 g
Dietary Fiber: 4 g
Sodium: 279 mg

❋ *Turkey and Yams in Orange-Raisin Sauce* ❋

PREPARATION TIME: *15 minutes* · COOKING TIME: *38 minutes* ·
YIELD: *4 servings*

3 tablespoons low-sodium nonfat
   chicken broth
4 skinless boneless turkey breast tenderloins, about 4 ounces each,
   chopped
1½ cups orange juice

¼ teaspoon ground cinnamon
⅛ teaspoon ground ginger
¼ teaspoon ground black pepper
2 medium yams, peeled and diced
½ cup seedless raisins
2 cups cooked rice

1. Heat broth in a large pot. Add turkey and sauté until no longer pink, about 8 minutes.
2. Combine orange juice, cinnamon, ginger, and black pepper in a separate bowl. Stir into the pot. Add yams and raisins. Bring mixture to a boil, reduce heat, cover, and simmer until yams are tender and turkey is cooked through, about 25 minutes.
3. Serve over rice.

Calories Per Serving: 417
Fat: 2 g
Cholesterol: 70 mg
Protein: 31 g

Carbohydrates: 70 g
Dietary Fiber: 3 g
Sodium: 68 mg

❋ *Turkey with Zucchini and Red Pepper* ❋

PREPARATION TIME: *15 minutes* · COOKING TIME: *29 minutes* ·
YIELD: *4 servings*

1 cup low-sodium nonfat chicken
   broth
3 skinless boneless turkey breast tenderloins, about 4 ounces each,
   chopped
1 medium onion, chopped
2 cloves garlic, minced
1 medium red bell pepper, cored and
   chopped

1 cup sliced zucchini
2 cups sliced mushrooms
2 medium stalks celery, sliced
2 medium carrots, scraped and sliced
½ teaspoon dried basil
½ teaspoon dried oregano
1 teaspoon paprika
½ teaspoon ground black pepper
¼ cup chopped fresh parsley

1. Heat ¼ cup broth in a large saucepan. Add turkey and sauté until no longer pink, about 8 minutes. Remove turkey and set aside.
2. Add another ¼ cup broth to the saucepan. Add onion, garlic, bell pepper, zucchini, mushrooms, celery, and carrots, and sauté until onion begins to soften, about 4 minutes.
3. Stir in remaining broth, basil, oregano, paprika, and black pepper. Return turkey to the saucepan, cover, and simmer until turkey is cooked through and vegetables are tender, about 10 minutes.
4. Transfer to individual bowls, garnish with parsley, and serve.

Calories Per Serving: 135	Carbohydrates: 10 g
Fat: 1 g	Dietary Fiber: 2 g
Cholesterol: 53 mg	Sodium: 85 mg
Protein: 22 g	

❋ *Creole Turkey* ❋

PREPARATION TIME: *20 minutes* • COOKING TIME: *38 minutes* •
YIELD: *5 servings*

1 teaspoon dried basil
1 teaspoon dried thyme
⅛ teaspoon cayenne pepper
4 skinless boneless turkey breast ten-
 derloins, about 4 ounces each, cut
 into ½-inch cubes
3 tablespoons low-sodium nonfat
 chicken broth
1 medium onion, finely chopped
1 medium yellow bell pepper, cored
 and chopped

2 medium celery stalks, sliced
2 cloves garlic, minced
2 cups low-sodium tomato sauce
1 cup low-sodium canned tomatoes,
 chopped, juice reserved
¼ cup chopped fresh parsley
2 tablespoons dry red wine
2 bay leaves
1 teaspoon ground marjoram
¼ teaspoon ground black pepper
2½ cups cooked rice

1. Combine basil, thyme, and cayenne pepper. Toss with the turkey.
2. Heat broth in a large saucepan. Add turkey and sauté until no longer pink, about 8 minutes.
3. Add onion, bell pepper, celery, and garlic, and sauté until the onion begins to soften, about 4 minutes.
4. Stir in tomato sauce, tomatoes with juice, parsley, wine, bay leaves, marjoram, and black pepper. Bring to a boil, reduce heat, cover, and simmer until turkey is cooked through and celery is tender, about 20 minutes. Remove bay leaves.
5. Serve over rice.

Calories Per Serving: 291
Fat: 1 g
Cholesterol: 56 mg
Protein: 27 g

Carbohydrates: 41 g
Dietary Fiber: 3 g
Sodium: 93 mg

❄ *Turkey Tenderloins with Vegetables* ❄ *in Rosemary-Wine Sauce*

PREPARATION TIME: *20 minutes* ▪ COOKING TIME: *34 minutes* ▪
YIELD: *4 servings*

6 tablespoons low-sodium nonfat
   chicken broth
4 skinless boneless turkey breast tenderloins, about 4 ounces each
1 medium onion, sliced
6 cups sliced mushrooms
3 medium carrots, scraped and sliced
3 cups chopped zucchini

2 cloves garlic, minced
2 medium tomatoes, chopped
½ teaspoon ground black pepper
¼ teaspoon dried rosemary
½ cup dry white wine
1 tablespoon lemon juice
2 cups cooked rice
¼ cup chopped fresh parsley

1. Heat 4 tablespoons broth in a large saucepan. Add turkey and sauté until no longer pink, about 8 minutes. Remove and set aside.
2. Heat remaining broth in the saucepan. Add onion, mushrooms, carrots, zucchini, and garlic, and sauté until onion begins to soften, about 4 minutes.
3. Add tomatoes, black pepper, rosemary, wine, and lemon juice. Return turkey to the saucepan. Bring to a boil, reduce heat, and simmer for 15 minutes.
4. Serve over rice, topped with parsley.

Calories Per Serving: 401
Fat: 2 g
Cholesterol: 70 mg
Protein: 35 g

Carbohydrates: 59 g
Dietary Fiber: 5 g
Sodium: 103 mg

❋ Turkey Picadillo ❋

PREPARATION TIME: *15 minutes* • COOKING TIME: *31 minutes* •
YIELD: *6 servings*

¼ cup low-sodium nonfat chicken
   broth
¾ pound ground turkey breast
1 clove garlic, minced
1 medium onion, chopped
1 medium green bell pepper, cored
   and chopped
2 cups low-sodium canned tomatoes,
   chopped, juice reserved
¾ cup low-sodium tomato paste

½ cup dry sherry
½ teaspoon ground cumin
½ teaspoon chili powder
¼ teaspoon dry mustard
¼ cup ground cinnamon
⅛ teaspoon ground cloves
½ teaspoon ground black pepper
1 tablespoon brown sugar
½ cup seedless raisins
3 cups cooked rice

1. Heat broth in a flameproof 3-quart casserole. Add turkey and sauté until
   no longer pink, about 8 minutes. Add garlic, onion, and bell pepper, and
   sauté until onion begins to soften, about 3 minutes.
2. Stir in tomatoes with juice, tomato paste, sherry, cumin, chili powder, dry
   mustard, cinnamon, cloves, black pepper, brown sugar, and raisins. Bring
   to a boil, reduce heat, and simmer for 15 minutes.
3. Serve over rice.

Calories Per Serving: 189
Fat: 1 g
Cholesterol: 47 mg
Protein: 21 g

Carbohydrates: 25 g
Dietary Fiber: 3 g
Sodium: 75 mg

❋ Chicken with Eggplant and Summer Squash ❋

PREPARATION TIME: *20 minutes* • COOKING TIME: *35 minutes* •
YIELD: *6 servings*

¼ cup low-sodium nonfat chicken
  broth
2 medium onions, chopped
2 cloves garlic, minced
5 cups chopped eggplant
2 medium red bell peppers, cored and
  chopped
5 cups chopped yellow summer
  squash
3 medium tomatoes, chopped

½ cup chopped fresh parsley
1 teaspoon dried basil
½ teaspoon ground black pepper
2 tablespoons low-sodium tomato
  paste
1 cup chopped cooked chicken breast
2 cups cooked rice
¼ cup shredded nonfat mozzarella

1. Heat broth in a large saucepan. Add onions, garlic, eggplant, and bell peppers, and sauté until onions begin to soften, about 5 minutes.
2. Add squash, tomatoes, parsley, and basil. Bring to a boil, reduce heat,
   cover, and simmer for 15 minutes.
3. Stir in black pepper, tomato paste, and cooked chicken, and simmer for 10
   minutes more.
4. Serve over rice, sprinkled with cheese.

Calories Per Serving: 173
Fat: 2 g
Cholesterol: 5 mg
Protein: 6 g

Carbohydrates: 34 g
Dietary Fiber: 3 g
Sodium: 55 mg

❋ Chicken Chili with White Beans ❋

PREPARATION TIME: 20 minutes ▪ COOKING TIME: 17 minutes ▪
YIELD: 6 servings

2¼ cups low-sodium nonfat chicken
  broth
2 medium onions, chopped
4 scallions, sliced
4 cloves garlic, minced
½ cup chopped canned mild green
  chiles, drained
2½ teaspoons chili powder
2½ teaspoons ground cumin
2 teaspoons dried oregano

4 cups low-sodium canned Great
  Northern beans, rinsed and
  drained
2 cups low-sodium canned tomatoes,
  chopped, juice reserved
2 skinless boneless chicken breast tenderloins, about 4 ounces each,
  cooked and chopped
1 cup chopped fresh parsley

1. Heat ¼ cup broth in a large saucepan. Add onions, scallions, and garlic, and sauté until onions begin to soften, about 3 minutes. Add chiles, chili powder, cumin, and oregano. Sauté for 4 more minutes.
2. Stir in remaining broth, beans, tomatoes with juice, cooked chicken, and ¾ cup parsley. Bring to a boil, reduce heat, and simmer to heat through, about 5 minutes.
3. Serve topped with remaining parsley.

Calories Per Serving: 251
Fat: 2 g
Cholesterol: 13 mg
Protein: 19 g

Carbohydrates: 41 g
Dietary Fiber: 11 g
Sodium: 251 mg

❇ *Chicken with Curried Fruit* ❇

PREPARATION TIME: *15 minutes* • COOKING TIME: *17 minutes* •
YIELD: *4 servings*

¼ cup orange juice
1 medium onion, chopped
1 clove garlic, minced
4 teaspoons curry powder
½ teaspoon chili powder
½ teaspoon ground cumin
⅓ cup all-purpose flour
*2 cups low-sodium nonfat chicken
   broth*

½ teaspoon ground black pepper
*3 skinless boneless chicken breast ten-
   derloins, about 4 ounces each,
   cooked and chopped*
3 cups watermelon balls
1 cup sliced mango
1 cup sliced canned peaches, drained

1. Heat orange juice in a large saucepan. Add onion, garlic, curry powder, chili powder, and cumin. Simmer, stirring constantly, until onion begins to soften, about 4 minutes.
2. Add flour and mix well. Stir in broth and black pepper. Bring to a boil, reduce heat, and simmer for 5 minutes.
3. Add cooked chicken, watermelon, mango, and peaches, and simmer to heat through, about 3 minutes.
4. Transfer to individual bowls and serve.

Calories Per Serving: 236
Fat: 2 g
Cholesterol: 53 mg
Protein: 27 g

Carbohydrates: 30 g
Dietary Fiber: 3 g
Sodium: 140 mg

❊ *Turkey with Snow Peas* ❊

PREPARATION TIME: *15 minutes* · COOKING TIME: *10 minutes* ·
YIELD: *4 servings*

1 cup juice-packed canned pineapple
   chunks, ½ cup juice reserved
1 tablespoon cornstarch
3 tablespoons cider vinegar
¼ cup honey
1 teaspoon Dijon mustard
2 teaspoons low-sodium tomato paste
¼ teaspoon cayenne pepper
¼ cup low-sodium nonfat chicken
   broth
1 tablespoon minced fresh gingerroot

1 medium onion, sliced
2 cloves garlic, minced
1 cup sliced mushrooms
1 medium green bell pepper, cored
   and cut into thin strips
3 skinless boneless turkey breast tenderloins, about 4 ounces each,
   cooked and chopped
1 cup snow peas
1 medium tomato, chopped
2 cups cooked rice

1. Combine reserved pineapple juice, cornstarch, vinegar, honey, mustard, tomato paste, and cayenne pepper, and set aside.
2. Heat broth in a large skillet or wok. Add gingerroot, onion, garlic, mushrooms, and bell pepper, and sauté until onion begins to soften, about 4 minutes.
3. Add pineapple juice mixture, pineapple chunks, cooked turkey, snow peas, and tomato. Cook and stir until sauce thickens and ingredients are heated through, about 4 minutes.
4. Serve over rice on individual plates.

Calories Per Serving: 365
Fat: 2 g
Cholesterol: 53 mg
Protein: 26 g

Carbohydrates: 64 g
Dietary Fiber: 3 g
Sodium: 117 mg

❊ *Curried Chicken and Green Peas* ❊

PREPARATION TIME: *10 minutes* · COOKING TIME: *15 minutes* ·
YIELD: *4 servings*

3 cups low-sodium nonfat chicken
   broth

1 tablespoon curry powder
2 cloves garlic, minced

3 skinless boneless chicken breast tenderloins, about 4 ounces each,
 cooked and chopped
1 medium yellow bell pepper, cored
 and chopped
1 medium stalk celery, sliced

1 tablespoon honey
¾ cup fresh or thawed frozen green
 peas
½ cup seedless raisins
2 cups cooked rice

1. Puree broth, curry powder, and garlic in a blender or food processor.
2. Place pureed mixture in a large saucepan and bring to a boil. Add chicken, bell pepper, and celery. Reduce heat and simmer for 10 minutes.
3. Stir in honey, peas, and raisins, and continue to simmer until vegetables are tender, about 5 minutes.
4. Serve over rice.

Calories Per Serving: 340
Fat: 1 g
Cholesterol: 53 mg
Protein: 29 g

Carbohydrates: 54 g
Dietary Fiber: 3 g
Sodium: 134 mg

❊ *Chicken with Mushrooms and Celery* ❊

PREPARATION TIME: *15 minutes* • COOKING TIME: *37 minutes* •
YIELD: *4 servings*

2¼ cups low-sodium nonfat chicken
 broth
1 medium onion, chopped
1 medium green bell pepper, cored
 and cut into thin strips
1 cup sliced mushrooms
2 medium stalks celery, sliced

1 cup uncooked white rice
¼ cup skim milk
¼ teaspoon ground black pepper
2 skinless boneless chicken breast tenderloins, about 4 ounces each,
 cooked and chopped

1. Heat ¼ cup broth in a large saucepan. Add onion, bell pepper, mushrooms, and celery, and sauté until onion begins to soften, about 4 minutes.
2. Stir in remaining broth and rice, and bring to a boil. Reduce heat, cover, and simmer for 15 minutes.
3. Add milk and black pepper, and continue to simmer until rice is just tender, about 10 more minutes.
4. Stir in cooked chicken and heat through, about 5 minutes.
5. Drain any excess liquid, transfer to individual plates, and serve.

Calories Per Serving: 273

Fat: 1 g

Cholesterol: 35 mg

Protein: 18 g

Carbohydrates: 44 g

Dietary Fiber: 2 g

Sodium: 213 mg

❊ *Chicken-Tomato Curry* ❊

PREPARATION TIME: *20 minutes* ▪ COOKING TIME: *26 minutes* ▪
YIELD: *4 servings*

*2 tablespoons low-sodium nonfat
  chicken broth*

1 medium onion, chopped

*1 medium red bell pepper, cored and
  chopped*

2 cloves garlic, minced

*2 skinless boneless chicken breast ten-
  derloins, about 4 ounces each,
  cooked and chopped*

½ teaspoon ground black pepper

1½ teaspoons curry powder

*3½ cups low-sodium canned toma-
  toes, chopped, ½ cup juice reserved*

¼ cup chopped fresh parsley

½ cup seedless raisins

2 cups cooked rice

1. Heat broth in a large saucepan. Add onion, bell pepper, and garlic, and
   sauté until onion begins to soften, about 4 minutes.
2. Add chicken, black pepper, curry powder, tomatoes with ½ cup juice, parsley, and raisins. Simmer for 20 minutes.
3. Serve over rice on individual plates.

Calories Per Serving: 286

Fat: 2 g

Cholesterol: 35 mg

Protein: 19 g

Carbohydrates: 51 g

Dietary Fiber: 5 g

Sodium: 111 mg

❊ *Curried Chicken with Apple* ❊
and Mushrooms

PREPARATION TIME: *15 minutes* ▪ COOKING TIME: *18 minutes* ▪
YIELD: *4 servings*

*1¼ cups low-sodium nonfat chicken
  broth*

*2 cups chopped cooked chicken
  breast*

3 cups sliced mushrooms
⅓ cup chopped onion
3 tablespoons all-purpose flour
1½ teaspoons curry powder
1 cup chopped apple

¼ cup chopped fresh parsley
¼ cup skim milk
1 cup water
2 cups cooked rice

1. Heat ¼ cup broth in a large saucepan. Add cooked chicken and sauté for 4 minutes.
2. Add mushrooms and onion. Sauté for 5 more minutes.
3. Stir in flour, remaining broth, curry powder, apple, parsley, milk, and water. Simmer, stirring constantly, until apple and vegetables are just tender, about 5 minutes.
4. Serve over rice.

Calories Per Serving: 256
Fat: 1 g
Cholesterol: 35 mg
Protein: 18 g

Carbohydrates: 41 g
Dietary Fiber: 2 g
Sodium: 127 mg

❋ *Turkey with Fruit and Wine* ❋

PREPARATION TIME: *15 minutes*   •   COOKING TIME: *41 minutes*   •
YIELD: *4 servings*

½ cup low-sodium nonfat chicken broth
4 skinless boneless turkey breast tenderloins, about 4 ounces each
¼ teaspoon dried rosemary
¼ teaspoon dried thyme
1 medium onion, chopped
1 medium green bell pepper, cored and chopped

3 medium carrots, scraped and sliced
½ cup dry red wine
½ cup chopped pitted prunes
½ cup chopped dried apricots
1 medium sweet potato, peeled and chopped
1 cup juice-packed canned pineapple chunks, drained
1 tablespoon brown sugar

1. Heat ¼ cup broth in a large saucepan. Add turkey, sprinkle with rosemary and thyme, and sauté until turkey is no longer pink, about 8 minutes. Remove and set aside.
2. Heat remaining broth in the saucepan. Add onion, bell pepper, and carrots, and sauté until onion begins to soften, about 4 minutes. Add wine, prunes, apricots, and sweet potato, cover, and simmer for 15 minutes.
3. Add pineapple chunks, sprinkle with brown sugar, and simmer for 10 more minutes.

Calories Per Serving: 329
Fat: 1 g
Cholesterol: 70 mg
Protein: 30 g

Carbohydrates: 50 g
Dietary Fiber: 5 g
Sodium: 109 mg

❋ Stirfried Leftover Turkey ❋

PREPARATION TIME: *15 minutes* • COOKING TIME: *13 minutes* •
YIELD: *4 servings*

*¼ cup low-sodium nonfat chicken
broth*
½ cup chopped scallions
*1 medium green bell pepper, cored
and diced*
2 cups chopped cooked turkey breast
1 tablespoon rice vinegar

1 tablespoon cornstarch
*2½ cups juice-packed canned pineap-
ple chunks, juice reserved*
2 tablespoons brown sugar
1 medium tomato, chopped
¼ teaspoon ground black pepper

1. Heat 2 tablespoons broth in a wok. Add scallions and bell pepper, and stir-fry until scallions begin to soften, about 2 minutes. Remove vegetables and set aside.
2. Heat remaining broth in the wok. Add cooked turkey and stirfry for 2 minutes.
3. In a separate bowl, combine vinegar, cornstarch, pineapple chunks with juice, and brown sugar. Add to the wok and cook, stirring constantly, until mixture boils and begins to thicken, about 2 minutes. Stir in scallion and bell pepper mixture. Cover and cook until all ingredients are heated through.
4. Stir in tomato, sprinkle with black pepper, and serve.

Calories Per Serving: 195
Fat: 1 g
Cholesterol: 53 mg
Protein: 22 g

Carbohydrates: 26 g
Dietary Fiber: 2 g
Sodium: 98 mg

SEAFOOD MAIN DISHES

Aegean Cod • Cod with Artichokes • Cod with Broccoli and Cauliflower • Lemon-Dill Cod and Vegetables • Sweet and Sour Cod • Cod with Okra and Zucchini • Cod and Shrimp with Hominy • Cod with Great Northern Beans and Bow-tie Pasta • Baked Flounder and Mushrooms • Flounder with Tomatoes and Orange • Baked Flounder with Green Pepper and Onion • Flounder with Spinach and Orzo • Flounder with Vegetables in Wine-Tomato Sauce • Haddock with Snow Peas and Potatoes • Simmered Haddock with Mixed Vegetables • Orange Roughy with Broccoli and Mushrooms • Red Snapper Baked with Tomatoes and Garlic • Peninsula Snapper Baked in Wine • Seafood Carnival • Sole with Asparagus • Tomato-Sole Casserole • Quick Sweet-and-Sour Tuna • Tuna and Peppers with Linguine • Tuna with Cucumber, Yellow Squash, and Rotelle • Easy Clam Pilaf • Crab-Vegetable Sauté • Potato-Tomato-Crab Curry • Jalapeño-Crab Delight • Crab and Shrimp Casserole • Eastern Shore Oyster Creole • Scallops and Broccoli • Orange-Pineapple-Scallop Stirfry • Scallops with Sugar Snap Peas and Corn • Stirfried Scallops • Basil-Tomato-Shrimp Pasta • Shrimp Gumbo •

Shrimp, Scallops, and Tricolor Peppers with Penne • Shrimp with
Green Peas and Chiles • Spicy Shrimp • Shrimp and Okra •
Pineapple-Shrimp Stirfry • Shrimp and Rice • Stirfried
Scallops with Tomato, Bell Pepper, and Mushrooms •
Shrimp-Vegetable Stirfry

❋ *Aegean Cod* ❋

PREPARATION TIME: *10 minutes* • COOKING TIME: *14 minutes* •
YIELD: *6 servings*

1 medium onion, chopped
1 medium green bell pepper, cored and chopped
1 medium red bell pepper, cored and chopped
2 cups chopped broccoli
3 medium tomatoes, chopped

1 teaspoon dried basil
½ teaspoon ground black pepper
1¼ cups orange juice
1 pound fresh cod fillet, cut into 1-inch cubes
¼ cup all-purpose flour

1. Combine onion, bell peppers, broccoli, tomatoes, basil, black pepper, and ¼ cup orange juice in a large saucepan. Bring to a boil.
2. Place fish on top of vegetables. Pour ½ cup orange juice over fish, cover, and simmer until fish flakes easily, about 7 minutes.
3. Remove fish to a warm platter and set aside. Combine remaining orange juice and flour in a separate bowl, and stir into the saucepan. Stir until liquid begins to thicken, about 4 minutes.
4. Spoon vegetables over fish and serve.

Calories Per Serving: 178
Fat: 1 g
Cholesterol: 49 mg
Protein: 24 g

Carbohydrates: 18 g
Dietary Fiber: 4 g
Sodium: 85 mg

❋ *Cod with Artichokes* ❋

PREPARATION TIME: *15 minutes* • COOKING TIME: *15 minutes* •
YIELD: *4 servings*

2 tablespoons low-sodium nonfat chicken broth
1½ cups sliced mushrooms
1 clove garlic, minced
3 medium tomatoes, chopped
½ teaspoon dried basil

⅛ teaspoon dried thyme
1 pound fresh cod fillet, cut into 1-inch cubes
1½ cups water-packed canned artichoke hearts, drained and chopped
½ teaspoon ground black pepper

1. Heat broth in a large skillet. Add mushrooms and garlic, and sauté for 4 minutes.

2. Add tomatoes, basil, thyme, fish, and artichokes. Cover and simmer for an additional 4 minutes.
3. Remove cover and continue to simmer until fish flakes easily, about 5 more minutes.
4. Sprinkle with black pepper and serve.

Calories Per Serving: 154
Fat: 2 g
Cholesterol: 53 mg
Protein: 23 g

Carbohydrates: 14 g
Dietary Fiber: 5 g
Sodium: 161 mg

❀ *Cod with Broccoli and Cauliflower* ❀

PREPARATION TIME: *15 minutes* • COOKING TIME: *24 minutes* •
YIELD: *4 servings*

¼ cup low-sodium nonfat chicken broth
1 medium leek (white part only), chopped
2 cups low-sodium canned tomatoes, chopped, juice reserved
1 cup chopped cauliflower

2 cups chopped broccoli
¼ cup orange juice
½ cup uncooked white rice
1 pound fresh cod fillets, about ¾ inch thick
¼ teaspoon ground black pepper
¼ cup chopped fresh parsley

1. Heat broth in a large saucepan. Add leek and sauté until just softening, about 3 minutes.
2. Add tomatoes with juice, cauliflower, broccoli, orange juice, and rice.
3. Arrange fish in a single layer on top of vegetables. Sprinkle with pepper. Bring to a boil, reduce heat, cover, and simmer, turning fish once, until fish flakes easily, about 15 minutes.
4. Serve topped with parsley.

Calories Per Serving: 285
Fat: 2 g
Cholesterol: 65 mg
Protein: 28 g

Carbohydrates: 42 g
Dietary Fiber: 6 g
Sodium: 132 mg

✵ *Lemon-Dill Cod and Vegetables* ✵

PREPARATION TIME: *20 minutes* • COOKING TIME: *20 minutes* •
YIELD: *6 servings*

Olive oil cooking spray
3 cups diced potatoes (½-inch cubes)
3 medium carrots, scraped and diced
1 medium onion, chopped
2 medium tomatoes, chopped
1 medium yellow bell pepper, cored and chopped
¼ cup chopped fresh parsley

1 teaspoon dried dill
2 cloves garlic, minced
¼ teaspoon ground black pepper
¾ cup low-sodium nonfat chicken broth
2 teaspoons lemon juice
½ pound fresh cod fillet

1. Lightly coat a large saucepan with olive oil cooking spray. Arrange potatoes in a layer on the bottom of the pan. Add a layer of carrots, followed by a layer of onion, a layer of tomatoes, and a layer of bell pepper.
2. Sprinkle the top with parsley, dill, garlic, and black pepper.
3. Combine broth and lemon juice in a separate bowl, and pour over vegetables. Lay cod, skin side down, on top of vegetables. Bring to a boil, reduce heat, cover, and simmer for 10 minutes.
4. Remove cover, and continue to simmer until fish is cooked through and liquid begins to thicken, about 10 more minutes.
5. Remove cod skin, break up fish, and return it to the saucepan. Gently toss to mix, transfer to individual plates, and serve.

Calories Per Serving: 217
Fat: 3 g
Cholesterol: 16 mg
Protein: 14 g

Carbohydrates: 35 g
Dietary Fiber: 4 g
Sodium: 85 mg

✵ *Sweet and Sour Cod* ✵

PREPARATION TIME: *20 minutes* • COOKING TIME: *21 minutes* •
YIELD: *6 servings*

1¼ cups orange juice
¼ cup vinegar
¼ cup brown sugar
3 tablespoons cornstarch
1 tablespoon reduced-sodium soy
  sauce
3 cloves garlic, minced
¼ cup low-sodium nonfat chicken
  broth
1 pound fresh cod fillet, cut into
  1-inch cubes

2½ cups juice-packed canned pineapple chunks, drained
1 cup sliced canned water chestnuts,
  drained
1 medium green bell pepper, cored
  and chopped
2 medium tomatoes, chopped
3 cups cooked rice

1. Combine orange juice, vinegar, brown sugar, cornstarch, soy sauce, and garlic, and set aside.
2. Heat broth in a large skillet. Add cod and sauté for 4 minutes. Pour in orange juice mixture and stir for 3 minutes. Remove fish and set aside.
3. Add pineapple chunks, water chestnuts, bell pepper, and tomatoes to the skillet, and cook until vegetables begin to soften, about 8 minutes. Return cod to the skillet and cook until fish flakes easily, about 4 more minutes.
4. Serve over rice.

Calories Per Serving: 348
Fat: 1 g
Cholesterol: 33 mg
Protein: 17 g

Carbohydrates: 68 g
Dietary Fiber: 2 g
Sodium: 154 mg

❊ Cod with Okra and Zucchini ❊

PREPARATION TIME: 15 minutes • COOKING TIME: 23 minutes •
YIELD: 4 servings

¼ cup low-sodium nonfat chicken
  broth
2 cups sliced okra
1 medium onion, thinly sliced
2 cloves garlic, minced
2 cups sliced zucchini
6 medium tomatoes, chopped

2 cups fresh or thawed frozen corn
  kernels
¼ teaspoon ground black pepper
¼ teaspoon dried red pepper flakes
1 pound fresh cod fillet, cut into
  1-inch cubes

1. Heat broth in a large saucepan. Add okra and sauté for 3 minutes. Add onion and garlic, and sauté until onion begins to soften, about 4 minutes.

2. Add zucchini and tomatoes, and stir for 5 more minutes. Stir in remaining ingredients and simmer until fish flakes easily, about 8 minutes.

Calories Per Serving: 246
Fat: 2 g
Cholesterol: 49 mg
Protein: 27 g

Carbohydrates: 35 g
Dietary Fiber: 6 g
Sodium: 100 mg

❋ *Cod and Shrimp with Hominy* ❋

PREPARATION TIME: *20 minutes* • COOKING TIME: *30 minutes* •
YIELD: *6 servings*

6¼ *cups low-sodium nonfat chicken broth*
1 *medium red onion, finely chopped*
4 *cloves garlic, minced*
4 *cups canned hominy, drained*
½ *cup chopped canned mild green chiles, drained*

½ *teaspoon ground cumin*
¼ *teaspoon cayenne pepper*
¾ *pound fresh cod fillet, cut into 1-inch cubes*
¾ *pound fresh medium shrimp, peeled and deveined*

1. Heat ¼ cup broth in a large saucepan. Add onion and garlic, and sauté until onion begins to soften, about 4 minutes.
2. Add remaining broth, hominy, chiles, cumin, and cayenne pepper. Bring to a boil, reduce heat, cover, and simmer for 10 minutes.
3. Add cod and simmer for 5 more minutes. Stir in shrimp and continue to simmer until fish flakes easily and shrimp have turned pink, about 3 more minutes.

Calories Per Serving: 231
Fat: 2 g
Cholesterol: 111 mg
Protein: 31 g

Carbohydrates: 19 g
Dietary Fiber: 2 g
Sodium: 518 mg

❋ *Cod with Great Northern Beans* ❋ *and Bow-tie Pasta*

PREPARATION TIME: *20 minutes* • COOKING TIME: *33 minutes* •
YIELD: *4 servings*

1 cup low-sodium nonfat chicken
   broth
2 scallions, minced
1 medium green bell pepper, cored
   and diced
1 clove garlic, minced
3 medium tomatoes, chopped
½ teaspoon dried basil
½ teaspoon dried thyme

¼ teaspoon dried oregano
2½ cups low-sodium canned Great
   Northern beans, rinsed and
   drained
½ teaspoon ground black pepper
½ pound fresh cod fillet, cut into
   1-inch cubes
3 cups cooked bow-tie pasta
¼ cup chopped fresh parsley

1. Heat ¼ cup broth in a large saucepan. Add scallions, bell pepper, and garlic, and sauté until scallions begin to soften, about 3 minutes.
2. Add remaining broth, tomatoes, basil, thyme, oregano, and beans, and simmer for 15 minutes. Stir in black pepper. Add cod and simmer until it flakes easily, about 7 minutes.
3. Add pasta and simmer to heat through, about 4 more minutes.
4. Serve topped with parsley.

Calories Per Serving: 209
Fat: 1 g
Cholesterol: 25 mg
Protein: 19 g

Carbohydrates: 30 g
Dietary Fiber: 8 g
Sodium: 118 mg

❊ Baked Flounder and Mushrooms ❊

PREPARATION TIME: 20 minutes • COOKING TIME: 20 minutes •
YIELD: 4 servings

Olive oil cooking spray
¼ cup chopped fresh parsley
1 cup sliced mushrooms
¼ teaspoon ground black pepper
3 cups low-sodium canned tomatoes,
   drained and chopped

4 fresh flounder fillets, about
   4 ounces each
3 cups cooked rice
3 tablespoons lemon juice

1. Preheat oven to 400 degrees.
2. Lightly coat a 2-quart casserole with olive oil cooking spray. Spread the parsley over the bottom of the casserole. Combine the mushrooms, black pepper, and tomatoes, and spoon half the mixture over the parsley.
3. Place the fish on the mushroom mixture and cover with the remaining mushroom mixture. Bake until the fish flakes easily, about 20 minutes.

4. Divide the rice among individual plates, place a fillet on each, and sprinkle with lemon juice. Spoon mushroom mixture over the fish and serve.

Calories Per Serving: 358
Fat: 3 g
Cholesterol: 77 mg
Protein: 33 g

Carbohydrates: 50 g
Dietary Fiber: 2 g
Sodium: 146 mg

❋ *Flounder with Tomatoes and Orange* ❋

PREPARATION TIME: *20 minutes* • COOKING TIME: *46 minutes* •
YIELD: *4 servings*

¼ cup low-sodium nonfat chicken
   broth
1 medium onion, chopped
2 cloves garlic, minced
1 cup diced zucchini
2 cups low-sodium canned tomatoes,
   crushed, juice reserved
1½ teaspoons chili powder

½ teaspoon dried basil
¼ teaspoon ground cumin
¼ teaspoon ground black pepper
4 fresh flounder fillets, about
   4 ounces each
⅓ cup orange juice
1 tablespoon minced orange peel
¼ cup chopped fresh parsley

1. Preheat oven to 350 degrees.
2. Heat broth in a flameproof 2-quart casserole. Add onion and garlic, and sauté until onion begins to soften, about 4 minutes.
3. Add zucchini, tomatoes with juice, chili powder, basil, cumin, and black pepper. Simmer until liquid begins to thicken, about 20 minutes. Remove tomato mixture and set aside.
4. Arrange fillets in a single layer in the casserole. Combine tomato mixture, orange juice, and orange peel, and pour over fish. Bake until flounder flakes easily, about 20 minutes.
5. Place fillets on individual plates, top with sauce and parsley, and serve.

Calories Per Serving: 196
Fat: 2 g
Cholesterol: 79 mg
Protein: 30 g

Carbohydrates: 14 g
Dietary Fiber: 3 g
Sodium: 167 mg

❋ Baked Flounder with Green Pepper ❋ and Onion

PREPARATION TIME: *15 minutes* • COOKING TIME: *30 minutes* •
YIELD: *4 servings*

1 medium onion, quartered
1 medium green bell pepper, cored
  and chopped
3 medium tomatoes, chopped
1 cup low-sodium tomato juice

1 cup sliced mushrooms
1 teaspoon lemon juice
¼ teaspoon ground black pepper
1½ pounds fresh flounder fillet

1. Preheat oven to 375 degrees.
2. Combine onion, bell pepper, tomatoes, tomato juice, mushrooms, lemon juice, and black pepper in a flameproof 2-quart casserole. Simmer for 5 minutes.
3. Place flounder in the casserole. Cover with sauce and bake, basting several times, until fish flakes easily, about 25 minutes.

Calories Per Serving: 188
Fat: 2 g
Cholesterol: 74 mg
Protein: 32 g

Carbohydrates: 11 g
Dietary Fiber: 3 g
Sodium: 108 mg

❋ Flounder with Spinach and Orzo ❋

PREPARATION TIME: *15 minutes* • COOKING TIME: *24 minutes* •
YIELD: *4 servings*

¼ cup low-sodium nonfat chicken
  broth
4 scallions, sliced
2 cups chopped fresh spinach
2 medium tomatoes, chopped
1 clove garlic, minced

1½ cups water
2 tablespoons lemon juice
1 cup uncooked orzo
½ teaspoon ground black pepper
1 pound fresh flounder fillets, about
  ¾ inch thick

1. Heat broth in a large saucepan. Add scallions and sauté for 2 minutes. Add spinach, half the tomatoes, and the garlic. Sauté until spinach is limp, about 4 minutes.

2. Stir in remaining tomatoes, water, 1 tablespoon lemon juice, the orzo, and black pepper. Arrange flounder in a single layer on top of vegetable mixture and sprinkle with remaining lemon juice.
3. Bring to a boil, reduce heat, cover, and simmer until fish flakes easily and orzo is tender, about 12 minutes.

Calories Per Serving: 219
Fat: 1 g
Cholesterol: 49 mg
Protein: 26 g

Carbohydrates: 25 g
Dietary Fiber: 1 g
Sodium: 113 mg

❀ *Flounder with Vegetables in* ❀ *Wine-Tomato Sauce*

PREPARATION TIME: *20 minutes* • COOKING TIME: *49 minutes* •
YIELD: *4 servings*

¼ cup dry white wine
1 medium onion, chopped
3 cloves garlic, minced
1 medium green bell pepper, cored
  and cut into thin strips
2 medium carrots, scraped and sliced
3 medium stalks celery, sliced
3 cups diced potatoes
1 cup low-sodium tomato sauce

3 medium tomatoes, chopped
1½ tablespoons honey
½ teaspoon dried thyme
⅛ teaspoon cayenne pepper
1 bay leaf
¾ pound fresh flounder fillet, cut into
  1-inch cubes
¼ cup chopped fresh parsley

1. Heat wine in a large saucepan. Add onion and garlic, and sauté until onion begins to soften, about 4 minutes.
2. Add bell pepper, carrots, celery, potatoes, tomato sauce, tomatoes, honey, thyme, cayenne pepper, and bay leaf. Bring to a boil, reduce heat, cover, and simmer until potatoes are just tender, about 30 minutes.
3. Stir in flounder and continue to simmer until it is just cooked through, about 10 more minutes. Remove bay leaf.
4. Serve topped with parsley.

Calories Per Serving: 292
Fat: 2 g
Cholesterol: 58 mg
Protein: 25 g

Carbohydrates: 43 g
Dietary Fiber: 5 g
Sodium: 160 mg

❋ *Haddock with Snow Peas and Potatoes* ❋

PREPARATION TIME: *25 minutes* · COOKING TIME: *43 minutes* ·
YIELD: *6 servings*

1 cup low-sodium nonfat chicken
  broth
½ cup dry white wine
2 medium tomatoes, chopped
2 tablespoons chopped fresh parsley
1 teaspoon dried dill
1 medium onion, minced
2 cloves garlic, minced
1 jalapeño pepper, seeded and minced

2 medium stalks celery, diced
2 medium carrots, scraped and diced
2 medium potatoes, diced
1 pound fresh haddock fillet, cut into
  1-inch cubes
3 scallions, sliced
1½ cups fresh or thawed frozen snow
  peas, cut into thin strips
½ teaspoon ground black pepper

1. Combine broth, wine, tomatoes, parsley, dill, onion, garlic, and jalapeño pepper in a large saucepan. Bring to a boil, reduce heat, and simmer for 20 minutes.
2. Add celery, carrots, and potatoes, and simmer until potatoes are just tender, about 15 more minutes.
3. Stir in haddock, scallions, and snow peas. Cover and simmer until fish flakes easily, about 5 minutes. Stir in black pepper, transfer to individual bowls, and serve.

Calories Per Serving: 258
Fat: 1 g
Cholesterol: 33 mg
Protein: 19 g

Carbohydrates: 41 g
Dietary Fiber: 9 g
Sodium: 271 mg

❋ *Simmered Haddock with Mixed Vegetables* ❋

PREPARATION TIME: *15 minutes* · COOKING TIME: *33 minutes* ·
YIELD: *4 servings*

¼ cup low-sodium nonfat chicken
  broth
¼ cup minced onion
2 cloves garlic, minced
2 medium carrots, scraped and thinly
  sliced
1 cup sliced mushrooms

2 medium tomatoes, chopped
¼ cup chopped fresh parsley
½ teaspoon dried basil
½ teaspoon ground black pepper
2 tablespoons lemon juice
1 pound fresh haddock fillet

1. Combine broth, onion, garlic, carrots, mushrooms, tomatoes, parsley, basil, and black pepper in a large saucepan. Bring to a boil, reduce heat, and simmer for 15 minutes.
2. Stir in lemon juice. Add haddock, cover, and simmer until fish flakes easily, about 15 more minutes.

Calories Per Serving: 142
Fat: 1 g
Cholesterol: 65 mg
Protein: 23 g

Carbohydrates: 10 g
Dietary Fiber: 2 g
Sodium: 99 mg

❋ *Orange Roughy with Broccoli* ❋ *and Mushrooms*

PREPARATION TIME: *15 minutes* · COOKING TIME: *23 minutes* ·
YIELD: *4 servings*

¼ cup low-sodium nonfat chicken broth
1 medium onion, sliced
1 medium green bell pepper, cored and cut into thin strips
2 cups low-sodium canned tomatoes, drained and chopped
¼ cup water
¼ cup dry white wine

2 cups chopped broccoli
2 cups sliced mushrooms
½ teaspoon ground black pepper
2 cloves garlic, minced
½ teaspoon dried dill
½ teaspoon sugar
¾ pound fresh orange roughy fillet, cut into 1-inch cubes
2 cups cooked rice

1. Heat broth in a large saucepan. Add onion and bell pepper, and sauté until onion begins to soften, about 3 minutes.
2. Stir in tomatoes, water, wine, broccoli, mushrooms, black pepper, garlic, dill, and sugar.
3. Place orange roughy cubes on vegetables. Bring mixture to a boil, reduce heat, cover, and simmer until fish flakes easily, about 15 minutes.
4. Serve over rice on individual plates.

Calories Per Serving: 261
Fat: 1 g
Cholesterol: 37 mg
Protein: 21 g

Carbohydrates: 39 g
Dietary Fiber: 3 g
Sodium: 83 mg

❋ Red Snapper Baked with Tomatoes ❋ and Garlic

PREPARATION TIME: *20 minutes* ▪ COOKING TIME: *33 minutes* ▪
YIELD: *4 servings*

*½ cup low-sodium nonfat chicken
  broth*
½ cup chopped onion
4 cloves garlic, minced
3 medium stalks celery, sliced
*1 medium green bell pepper, cored
  and cut into thin strips*
1 cup diced zucchini
*2 cups low-sodium canned tomatoes,
  drained and chopped*

¾ teaspoon Worcestershire sauce
*2 tablespoons low-sodium tomato
  sauce*
½ teaspoon chili powder
1 lemon, thinly sliced
1 bay leaf
¼ teaspoon cayenne pepper
*4 fresh red snapper fillets, about
  4 ounces each*

1. Preheat oven to 350 degrees.
2. Heat ¼ cup broth in a flameproof 2-quart casserole. Add onion, garlic, celery, bell pepper, and zucchini, and sauté until onion begins to soften, about 4 minutes.
3. Add tomatoes, remaining broth, Worcestershire sauce, tomato sauce, chili powder, lemon, bay leaf, and cayenne pepper. Simmer for 5 minutes.
4. Place red snapper in the casserole and spoon vegetables over. Cover and bake until fish flakes easily, about 20 minutes. Remove bay leaf before serving.

Calories Per Serving: 169
Fat: 2 g
Cholesterol: 41 mg
Protein: 26 g

Carbohydrates: 13 g
Dietary Fiber: 2 g
Sodium: 161 mg

❋ Peninsula Snapper Baked in Wine ❋

PREPARATION TIME: *20 minutes* ▪ COOKING TIME: *26 minutes* ▪
YIELD: *4 servings*

*½ cup low-sodium nonfat chicken
  broth*

1 medium onion, chopped
1 cup sliced mushrooms

1 medium green bell pepper, cored
  and chopped
1 cup diced zucchini
2 cups diced potatoes
4 fresh red snapper fillets, about
  8 ounces each

½ cup low-sodium tomato sauce
¼ cup dry white wine
½ teaspoon dried oregano
½ teaspoon dried basil
½ teaspoon ground black pepper
¼ cup chopped fresh parsley

1. Preheat oven to 350 degrees.
2. Heat ¼ cup broth in a flameproof 2-quart casserole. Add onion, mush-rooms, bell pepper, zucchini, and potatoes, and sauté for 4 minutes.
3. Place snapper on vegetables. Combine remaining broth, tomato sauce, wine, oregano, basil, and black pepper, and pour over fish. Cover and bake until fillets flake easily, about 20 minutes.
4. Serve topped with parsley.

Calories Per Serving: 289
Fat: 2 g
Cholesterol: 41 mg
Protein: 27 g

Carbohydrates: 33 g
Dietary Fiber: 3 g
Sodium: 126 mg

❀ *Seafood Carnival* ❀

PREPARATION TIME: *20 minutes* • COOKING TIME: *1 hour 1 minute* •
YIELD: *6 servings*

¼ cup low-sodium nonfat chicken
  broth
1 medium onion, chopped
1 medium green bell pepper, cored
  and chopped
1 clove garlic, minced
¼ cup chopped canned mild green
  chiles, drained
3 cups low-sodium canned tomatoes,
  drained and chopped

½ teaspoon ground black pepper
1 pound fresh red snapper fillet, cut
  into 1-inch cubes
½ pound fresh medium shrimp, peeled
  and deveined
3 tablespoons lemon juice
3 cups cooked rice
¼ cup chopped fresh parsley

1. Heat broth in a large skillet. Add onion, bell pepper, and garlic, and sauté until onion begins to soften, about 4 minutes. Add chiles, tomatoes, and black pepper. Simmer until mixture begins to thicken, about 30 minutes.
2. Place snapper and shrimp on top of vegetables, drizzle with lemon juice, cover, and simmer until snapper flakes easily and shrimp have turned pink, about 15 minutes. Remove seafood and set aside.

3. Bring sauce to a boil and cook, stirring constantly, until thickened, about 5 minutes.
4. Serve seafood over rice, topped with sauce and sprinkled with parsley.

Calories Per Serving: 282   Carbohydrates: 37 g
Fat: 2 g   Dietary Fiber: 2 g
Cholesterol: 85 mg   Sodium: 135 mg
Protein: 27 g

❋ *Sole with Asparagus* ❋

PREPARATION TIME: *20 minutes*   •   COOKING TIME: *39 minutes*   •
YIELD: *6 servings*

2½ cups low-sodium nonfat chicken broth
1 medium onion, chopped
3 cloves garlic, minced
2 medium potatoes, diced
3 tablespoons lemon juice
1 teaspoon dried thyme
1 bay leaf

1½ cups water-packed canned artichoke hearts, drained and chopped
3 medium carrots, scraped and sliced
2 cups chopped fresh asparagus spears (1-inch lengths)
1 pound fresh sole fillet, cut into small pieces
½ teaspoon ground black pepper

1. Heat ¼ cup broth in a large saucepan. Add onion and garlic, and sauté until onion begins to soften, about 3 minutes.
2. Add remaining broth, potatoes, lemon juice, thyme, and bay leaf. Bring to a boil, reduce heat, and simmer for 15 minutes. Add artichoke hearts, carrots, and asparagus, and simmer for 10 more minutes. Remove bay leaf.
3. Add sole, cover, and simmer until fish flakes easily, about 5 minutes.
4. Season with black pepper, transfer to individual bowls, and serve.

Calories Per Serving: 186   Carbohydrates: 25 g
Fat: 1 g   Dietary Fiber: 4 g
Cholesterol: 33 mg   Sodium: 160 mg
Protein: 20 g

❀ *Tomato-Sole Casserole* ❀

PREPARATION TIME: *20 minutes* ▪ COOKING TIME: *27 minutes* ▪ YIELD: *4 servings*

½ cup low-sodium nonfat chicken broth
2 cups sliced mushrooms
2 medium tomatoes, chopped
2 cloves garlic, minced
2 cups chopped cauliflower
4 fresh sole fillets, about 4 ounces each
½ pound fresh medium shrimp, peeled and deveined
3 tablespoons lemon juice
¼ cup chopped fresh parsley

1. Preheat oven to 350 degrees.
2. Heat ¼ cup broth in a flameproof 3-quart casserole. Add mushrooms and sauté for 3 minutes.
3. Stir in remaining broth, tomatoes, garlic, and cauliflower, and simmer for 5 minutes.
4. Place fish fillets on top of vegetables. Arrange shrimp on fish, sprinkle with lemon juice, and bake until sole is cooked through and shrimp are pink, about 15 minutes.
5. Place seafood on individual plates, top with vegetables and parsley, and serve.

Calories Per Serving: 223
Fat: 3 g
Cholesterol: 163 mg
Protein: 40 g
Carbohydrates: 7 g
Dietary Fiber: 1 g
Sodium: 248 mg

❀ *Quick Sweet-and-Sour Tuna* ❀

PREPARATION TIME: *20 minutes* ▪ COOKING TIME: *17 minutes* ▪ YIELD: *2 servings*

¼ cup low-sodium nonfat chicken
   broth
1 medium onion, chopped
1 clove garlic, minced
2 tablespoons dry sherry
2 tablespoons low-sodium tomato
   paste
1 tablespoon brown sugar
1 tablespoon red wine vinegar
1 teaspoon reduced-sodium soy sauce
¼ teaspoon ground ginger

½ cup orange juice
1 cup juice-packed pineapple chunks,
   drained
1 medium green bell pepper, cored
   and chopped
1 medium tomato, chopped
½ small (3½-ounce) can water-
   packed solid white albacore tuna,
   drained and crumbled
1 cup cooked rice

1. Heat broth in a large skillet. Add onion and garlic, and sauté until onion
   begins to soften, about 3 minutes.
2. Whisk together sherry, tomato paste, brown sugar, vinegar, soy sauce, and
   ginger in a separate bowl. Stir into the onion. Add orange juice and cook,
   stirring, until mixture begins to bubble, about 2 minutes.
3. Add pineapple chunks and bell pepper, cover, and cook until pepper is just
   tender-crisp, about 7 minutes.
4. Stir in tomato and tuna, and heat through, about 3 minutes.
5. Serve over rice.

Calories Per Serving: 345
Fat: 2 g
Cholesterol: 18 mg
Protein: 16 g

Carbohydrates: 66 g
Dietary Fiber: 4 g
Sodium: 315 mg

❋ Tuna and Peppers with Linguine ❋

PREPARATION TIME: 10 minutes ▪ COOKING TIME: 22 minutes ▪
YIELD: 4 servings

2 quarts water
8 ounces fresh linguine
1 medium red bell pepper, cored and
   cut into thin strips
1 medium green bell pepper, cored
   and cut into thin strips
3 scallions, sliced
1 cup dry white wine

2 cloves garlic, minced
¾ teaspoon dried dill
2 teaspoons Dijon mustard
½ teaspoon ground black pepper
2 6-ounce cans water-packed solid
   white albacore tuna, drained and
   crumbled

1. Bring water to a rapid boil in a large saucepan. Add pasta and cook until just tender, about 3 minutes. Drain pasta well and return to the saucepan.
2. Stir in bell peppers, scallions, ¾ cup wine, and the garlic. Bring to a boil, reduce heat, cover, and simmer for 5 minutes.
3. Stir in remaining wine, dill, mustard, black pepper, and tuna. Simmer to heat through, about 2 minutes.
4. Transfer to individual plates and serve at once.

Calories Per Serving: 327
Fat: 2 g
Cholesterol: 18 mg
Protein: 19 g

Carbohydrates: 46 g
Dietary Fiber: 1 g
Sodium: 270 mg

❈ *Tuna with Cucumber, Yellow Squash,* ❈ *and Rotelle*

PREPARATION TIME: *10 minutes* • COOKING TIME: *17 minutes* •
YIELD: *4 servings*

2 quarts water
8 ounces uncooked rotelle
1 6-ounce can water-packed solid
white albacore tuna, drained and
crumbled
1 cup sliced cucumber
1 cup sliced yellow summer squash

1 medium tomato, chopped
1 cup nonfat plain yogurt
2 tablespoons red wine vinegar
2 tablespoons Dijon mustard
1 tablespoon dried dill
½ teaspoon ground black pepper

1. Bring water to a rapid boil in a large saucepan. Add pasta and cook until just tender, about 8 minutes. Drain and return to the saucepan.
2. Stir in tuna, cucumber, squash, and tomato.
3. Combine yogurt, vinegar, mustard, dill, and black pepper in a separate bowl, and pour over pasta.
4. Toss to combine all ingredients, transfer to individual plates, and serve.

Calories Per Serving: 321
Fat: 3 g
Cholesterol: 19 mg
Protein: 23 g

Carbohydrates: 51 g
Dietary Fiber: 1 g
Sodium: 316 mg

✳ *Easy Clam Pilaf* ✳

PREPARATION TIME: *20 minutes* • COOKING TIME: *35 minutes* •
YIELD: *4 servings*

*2¼ cups low-sodium nonfat chicken
  broth*
¼ cup minced onion
4 medium stalks celery, sliced
1 clove garlic, minced
½ teaspoon dried tarragon
½ teaspoon dried basil

¼ teaspoon ground black pepper
¼ cup chopped fresh parsley
1 cup uncooked white rice
2 cups canned minced clams, drained
*1 cup fresh or thawed frozen green
  peas*

1. Heat ¼ cup broth in a large skillet. Add onion, celery, and garlic, and sauté until celery begins to soften, about 4 minutes.
2. Stir in tarragon, basil, black pepper, parsley, and rice. Sauté for 3 more minutes.
3. Add remaining broth and bring to a boil. Reduce heat, cover, and simmer for 15 minutes. Add clams and peas, cover, and simmer until rice is tender and peas are done, about 7 minutes. Drain any excess liquid before serving.

Calories Per Serving: 346
Fat: 2 g
Cholesterol: 54 mg
Protein: 26 g

Carbohydrates: 51 g
Dietary Fiber: 2 g
Sodium: 291 mg

✳ *Crab-Vegetable Sauté* ✳

PREPARATION TIME: *20 minutes* • COOKING TIME: *13 minutes* •
YIELD: *4 servings*

*¼ cup low-sodium nonfat chicken
  broth*
2 medium stalks celery, sliced
1 medium carrot, scraped and sliced
1 cup sliced mushrooms
*1 medium green bell pepper, cored
  and chopped*
1 medium onion, sliced
2 cloves garlic, minced

*1 cup fresh cooked or shredded
  canned crabmeat*
*½ cup fresh or thawed frozen green
  peas*
⅓ cup water
¼ teaspoon dried dill
¼ teaspoon ground black pepper
2 cups cooked rice

1. Heat broth in a large saucepan. Add celery, carrot, mushrooms, bell pepper, onion, and garlic, and sauté until onion begins to soften, about 5 minutes.
2. Stir in crabmeat, peas, water, dill, and black pepper, and simmer for 4 minutes.
3. Toss with rice and serve.

Calories Per Serving: 201
Fat: 1 g
Cholesterol: 34 mg
Protein: 11 g

Carbohydrates: 36 g
Dietary Fiber: 2 g
Sodium: 121 mg

❋ *Potato-Tomato-Crab Curry* ❋

PREPARATION TIME: *20 minutes* • COOKING TIME: *35 minutes* •
YIELD: *6 servings*

1¼ cups low-sodium nonfat chicken broth
2 medium onions, sliced
2 cups sliced mushrooms
⅛ teaspoon ground ginger
1 teaspoon dried thyme
1 teaspoon dried marjoram
2 tablespoons chopped fresh parsley
1 teaspoon dried basil

1 teaspoon dried dill
½ teaspoon ground turmeric
2 cups chopped potatoes
3 medium tomatoes, chopped
2 teaspoons curry powder
2 cups fresh cooked or shredded canned crabmeat
1 tablespoon lemon juice
3 cups cooked rice

1. Heat ¼ cup broth in a large saucepan. Add onions, mushrooms, ginger, thyme, marjoram, parsley, basil, dill, and turmeric, and sauté until onions begin to soften, about 5 minutes.
2. Add remaining broth, potatoes, tomatoes, and curry powder. Bring to a boil, reduce heat, and simmer for 20 minutes.
3. Stir in crabmeat and lemon juice, and simmer to heat through, about 3 minutes.
4. Serve over rice.

Calories Per Serving: 280
Fat: 1 g
Cholesterol: 40 mg
Protein: 16 g

Carbohydrates: 51 g
Dietary Fiber: 3 g
Sodium: 199 mg

❊ *Jalapeño-Crab Delight* ❊

PREPARATION TIME: *20 minutes* ▪ COOKING TIME: *19 minutes* ▪
YIELD: *4 servings*

¼ cup low-sodium nonfat chicken
 broth
1 medium onion, finely chopped
4 cloves garlic, minced
1 medium green bell pepper, cored
 and chopped
2 jalapeño peppers, seeded and
 minced
4 medium tomatoes, chopped

3 tablespoons low-sodium tomato
 paste
¼ teaspoon ground black pepper
¼ teaspoon sugar
1 tablespoon lime juice
½ cup dry sherry
2 cups fresh cooked or shredded
 canned crabmeat
3 cups cooked rice
2 tablespoons chopped fresh parsley

1. Heat broth in a large saucepan. Add onion, garlic, bell pepper, and
   jalapeño peppers, and sauté until onion begins to soften, about 4 minutes.
2. Add tomatoes, tomato paste, black pepper, and sugar, and simmer, stirring
   occasionally, until mixture begins to thicken, about 10 minutes.
3. Stir in lime juice, sherry, and crabmeat. Cover and simmer very gently
   until crabmeat is heated through, about 3 minutes.
4. Serve over rice, topped with parsley.

Calories Per Serving: 135
Fat: 1 g
Cholesterol: 60 mg
Protein: 16 g

Carbohydrates: 15 g
Dietary Fiber: 3 g
Sodium: 471 mg

❊ *Crab and Shrimp Casserole* ❊

PREPARATION TIME: *15 minutes* ▪ COOKING TIME: *30 minutes* ▪
YIELD: *4 servings*

Olive oil cooking spray
1 medium green bell pepper, cored
 and chopped
1 medium red bell pepper, cored and
 chopped

2 medium stalks celery, sliced
1 medium onion, chopped
1 cup bread crumbs
1 cup fresh cooked or shredded
 canned crabmeat

½ pound fresh medium shrimp,
  peeled, deveined, and halved
½ teaspoon ground black pepper

1 teaspoon Worcestershire sauce
¾ cup nonfat plain yogurt
1 teaspoon reduced-sodium soy sauce

1. Preheat oven to 350 degrees. Lightly coat a 2-quart casserole with olive oil cooking spray.
2. Combine bell peppers, celery, onion, bread crumbs, crabmeat, and shrimp in a large bowl.
3. Mix together black pepper, Worcestershire sauce, yogurt, and soy sauce in a separate bowl.
4. Mix together yogurt mixture with seasoned shellfish, transfer to the prepared casserole, and bake for 30 minutes.

Calories Per Serving: 141
Fat: 1 g
Cholesterol: 93 mg
Protein: 18 g

Carbohydrates: 14 g
Dietary Fiber: 2 g
Sodium: 374 mg

❋ *Eastern Shore Oyster Creole* ❋

PREPARATION TIME: *20 minutes* • COOKING TIME: *33 minutes* •
YIELD: *6 servings*

4 cups low-sodium canned tomatoes,
  chopped, juice reserved
1 medium stalk celery, sliced
1 cup sliced mushrooms
1 medium green bell pepper, cored
  and diced
1 small onion, minced
¼ teaspoon hot pepper sauce

¼ teaspoon chili powder
¼ teaspoon dried tarragon
½ teaspoon ground black pepper
1 tablespoon lemon juice
2 cups shucked oysters, liquid
  reserved
½ teaspoon sugar
6 cups cooked rice

1. Combine tomatoes, celery, mushrooms, bell pepper, onion, hot pepper sauce, chili powder, tarragon, black pepper, and lemon juice in a large saucepan.
2. Mix reserved tomato juice and oyster liquid, add enough water to make 2 cups, and stir into the saucepan. Cover and simmer for 30 minutes.
3. Stir in oysters and sugar, and continue to simmer to heat through, about 3 minutes.
4. Serve over rice.

Calories Per Serving: 343

Fat: 3 g

Cholesterol: 45 mg

Protein: 12 g

Carbohydrates: 66 g

Dietary Fiber: 2 g

Sodium: 123 mg

❊ *Scallops and Broccoli* ❊

PREPARATION TIME: *15 minutes* • COOKING TIME: *20 minutes* •
YIELD: *5 servings*

¼ cup low-sodium nonfat chicken
  broth

1 medium onion, chopped

1 clove garlic, minced

1 medium green bell pepper, cored
  and diced

2 cups low-sodium canned tomatoes,
  chopped, juice reserved

½ cup dry sherry

1 bay leaf

1 teaspoon dried basil

2 cups chopped broccoli

¼ teaspoon ground black pepper

2 teaspoons cornstarch

¼ cup cold water

¾ pound fresh scallops

2½ cups cooked rice

1. Heat broth in a large saucepan. Add onion, garlic, and bell pepper. Sauté until onion begins to soften, about 4 minutes.
2. Stir in tomatoes with juice, sherry, bay leaf, basil, broccoli, and black pepper. Bring to a boil, reduce heat, cover, and simmer until broccoli begins to soften, about 4 minutes.
3. Mix cornstarch and cold water. Bring liquid in the saucepan to a boil. Stir in cornstarch mixture and cook, stirring constantly, until liquid begins to thicken, about 2 minutes.
4. Add scallops, reduce heat, cover, and simmer until scallops are opaque, about 3 minutes. Remove bay leaf.
5. Serve over rice on individual plates.

Calories Per Serving: 121

Fat: 1 g

Cholesterol: 22 mg

Protein: 14 g

Carbohydrates: 13 g

Dietary Fiber: 3 g

Sodium: 142 mg

❊ *Orange-Pineapple-Scallop Stirfry* ❊

PREPARATION TIME: *20 minutes* • COOKING TIME: *12 minutes* •
YIELD: *4 servings*

½ cup low-sodium nonfat chicken
　broth
1 scallion, minced
1 medium green bell pepper, cored
　and diced
1 medium onion, chopped
1 teaspoon minced fresh gingerroot
1 clove garlic, minced
2 cups fresh scallops, halved

1 cup fresh or canned pineapple
　chunks, drained
1 medium orange, peeled, sectioned,
　and chopped
2 tablespoons reduced-sodium soy
　sauce
1 tablespoon dry sherry
2 cups cooked rice

1. Heat ¼ cup broth in a wok. Add scallion, bell pepper, onion, gingerroot, and garlic, and stirfry for 1 minute.
2. Add scallops and stirfry until they are opaque, about 3 minutes. Remove scallops and set aside.
3. Heat remaining broth in the wok. Add pineapple chunks and orange, and stirfry for 2 minutes. Return scallops to the wok, stir in soy sauce and sherry, and heat through, about 2 minutes.
4. Serve over rice.

Calories Per Serving: 263
Fat: 1 g
Cholesterol: 22 mg
Protein: 15 g

Carbohydrates: 47 g
Dietary Fiber: 2 g
Sodium: 412 mg

❊ *Scallops with Sugar Snap Peas and Corn* ❊

PREPARATION TIME: *15 minutes* • COOKING TIME: *10 minutes* •
YIELD: *4 servings*

¼ cup low-sodium nonfat chicken
　broth
2 cloves garlic, minced
1 medium red bell pepper, cored and
　cut into thin strips
1 medium green bell pepper, cored
　and cut into thin strips

1 pound fresh scallops
1 teaspoon minced fresh gingerroot
½ teaspoon ground black pepper
2 cups sugar snap peas
1 cup fresh or thawed frozen corn
　kernels
2 tablespoons minced fresh chives

1. Heat broth in a large saucepan. Add garlic and bell peppers, and sauté for 3 minutes.
2. Add scallops, gingerroot, and black pepper, and sauté for 2 more minutes.
3. Add peas and corn kernels, cover, and simmer for 3 minutes.
4. Transfer to individual plates, garnish with chives, and serve.

Calories Per Serving: 210
Fat: 1 g
Cholesterol: 39 mg
Protein: 24 g

Carbohydrates: 28 g
Dietary Fiber: 4 g
Sodium: 195 mg

❊ *Stirfried Scallops* ❊

PREPARATION TIME: *10 minutes* • COOKING TIME: *11 minutes* •
YIELD: *4 servings*

1 tablespoon reduced-sodium soy sauce
1 tablespoon cornstarch
1 pound fresh scallops, halved
¼ cup low-sodium nonfat chicken broth
4 cups sliced mushrooms

1 medium red bell pepper, cored and cut into thin strips
1 cup snow peas
2 tablespoons water
½ teaspoon ground black pepper
2 cups cooked rice

1. Combine soy sauce and cornstarch in a bowl and mix well. Add scallops and toss to coat.
2. Heat 2 tablespoons broth in a large skillet. Stirfry scallops until they are opaque, about 3 minutes. Remove and set aside.
3. Heat remaining broth in the skillet. Add mushrooms, bell pepper, and snow peas. Stirfry until tender-crisp, about 2 minutes. Add water to the skillet. Return scallops, sprinkle with black pepper, and mix until just heated through, about 2 minutes.
4. Serve over rice on individual plates.

Calories Per Serving: 273
Fat: 2 g
Cholesterol: 37 mg
Protein: 25 g

Carbohydrates: 39 g
Dietary Fiber: 2 g
Sodium: 320 mg

❊ *Basil-Tomato-Shrimp Pasta* ❊

PREPARATION TIME: *15 minutes* • COOKING TIME: *3 minutes* •
YIELD: *4 servings*

8 quarts water
8 ounces fresh linguine
4 cups chopped broccoli
3 tablespoons white wine vinegar
1 teaspoon olive oil
¼ teaspoon ground black pepper

2 medium tomatoes, chopped
3 scallions, sliced
¼ pound fresh medium shrimp,
 cooked, peeled, and deveined
¼ cup chopped fresh basil
2 tablespoons grated nonfat Parmesan

1. Bring water to a boil in a large saucepan. Add linguine and broccoli, and cook until pasta is just tender, about 3 minutes. Drain well and transfer to a large bowl.
2. Combine vinegar, olive oil, and black pepper in a separate bowl, and pour over pasta and broccoli. Add tomatoes, scallions, shrimp, and basil, and toss well.
3. Serve topped with Parmesan.

Calories Per Serving: 301
Fat: 3 g
Cholesterol: 43 mg
Protein: 17 g

Carbohydrates: 54 g
Dietary Fiber: 7 g
Sodium: 98 mg

❊ *Shrimp Gumbo* ❊

PREPARATION TIME: *25 minutes* • COOKING TIME: *44 minutes* •
YIELD: *8 servings*

4¼ cups low-sodium nonfat chicken
  broth
2 medium onions, diced
1 medium green bell pepper, cored
  and diced
1 medium red bell pepper, cored and
  diced
4 cloves garlic, minced
1 jalapeño pepper, seeded and minced
3 medium stalks celery, sliced
4 cups fresh or low-sodium canned
  tomatoes, crushed

1 cup low-sodium tomato paste
¼ teaspoon ground black pepper
1 teaspoon brown sugar
1 tablespoon molasses
½ teaspoon hot pepper sauce
1 teaspoon dried thyme
2 bay leaves
3 tablespoons lemon juice
1 pound fresh medium shrimp, peeled
  and deveined
6 cups cooked rice
2 scallions, minced

1. Heat ¼ cup broth in a large pot. Add onions, bell peppers, and garlic, and
   sauté until onions begin to soften, about 4 minutes.
2. Add remaining broth, jalapeño pepper, celery, tomatoes, tomato paste,
   black pepper, brown sugar, molasses, hot pepper sauce, thyme, bay leaves,
   and lemon juice. Bring to a boil, reduce heat, and simmer for 30 minutes.
3. Add shrimp and continue to simmer until they turn pink, about 4 minutes. Remove bay leaves.
4. Serve over rice, topped with minced scallions.

Calories Per Serving: 332
Fat: 2 g
Cholesterol: 86 mg
Protein: 18 g

Carbohydrates: 59 g
Dietary Fiber: 3 g
Sodium: 355 mg

❋ Shrimp, Scallops, and Tricolor Peppers ❋ with Penne

PREPARATION TIME: *15 minutes* • COOKING TIME: *12 minutes* •
YIELD: *4 servings*

¾ cup low-sodium nonfat chicken
  broth
3 cups chopped zucchini
1 medium red bell pepper, cored and
  cut into thin strips
1 medium yellow bell pepper, cored
  and cut into thin strips

1 medium green bell pepper, cored
  and cut into thin strips
1 medium red onion, thinly sliced
2 tablespoons minced fresh parsley
½ cup bottled clam juice
⅓ cup skim milk
½ pound fresh scallops

*¼ pound fresh medium shrimp, peeled
  and deveined*

*⅛ teaspoon cayenne pepper
2 cups cooked penne*

1. Heat ¼ cup broth in a large saucepan. Add zucchini, bell peppers, and onion. Cover and simmer until vegetables just begin to soften, about 3 minutes.
2. Add remaining broth, parsley, clam juice, milk, and scallops. Cook, stirring occasionally, until scallops are opaque, about 3 minutes. Add shrimp and cook until they turn pink, about 4 minutes. Stir in cayenne pepper.
3. Serve over pasta.

Calories Per Serving: 249
Fat: 2 g
Cholesterol: 106 mg
Protein: 29 g

Carbohydrates: 28 g
Dietary Fiber: 3 g
Sodium: 386 mg

❋ *Shrimp with Green Peas and Chiles* ❋

PREPARATION TIME: *20 minutes* • COOKING TIME: *36 minutes* •
YIELD: *6 servings*

*2¼ cups low-sodium nonfat chicken
  broth*
2 cups uncooked white rice
1 medium onion, chopped
2 medium stalks celery, sliced
1 clove garlic, minced
*1 medium green bell pepper, cored
  and chopped*
*1½ cups low-sodium canned toma-
  toes, diced, juice reserved*

*½ cup chopped canned mild green
  chiles, drained*
*1 cup fresh or thawed frozen green
  peas*
*¾ pound fresh medium shrimp, peeled
  and deveined*
1 teaspoon ground cumin
½ teaspoon ground black pepper

1. Heat ¼ cup broth in a large saucepan. Add rice and cook, stirring, until rice begins to darken, about 4 minutes.
2. Add onion, celery, garlic, and bell pepper. Sauté until onion begins to soften, about 3 minutes.
3. Stir in tomatoes with juice, chiles, and remaining broth. Bring to a boil, reduce heat, cover, and simmer for 10 minutes.
4. Stir in peas, cover the saucepan, and simmer until rice is just tender, about 7 more minutes.
5. Add shrimp, cumin, and black pepper. Stir constantly until shrimp turn pink, about 3 minutes.

Calories Per Serving: 364	Carbohydrates: 63 g
Fat: 2 g	Dietary Fiber: 3 g
Cholesterol: 86 mg	Sodium: 188 mg
Protein: 22 g	

❋ *Spicy Shrimp* ❋

PREPARATION TIME: *20 minutes* • COOKING TIME: *7 minutes* •
YIELD: *6 servings*

½ cup low-sodium nonfat chicken broth
1 tablespoon oyster sauce
1 tablespoon reduced-sodium soy sauce
3 tablespoons dry white wine
1 tablespoon sugar
2 teaspoons cornstarch
1 tablespoon minced fresh gingerroot
4 cloves garlic, minced
1 jalapeño pepper, seeded and minced

2 scallions, sliced
1 teaspoon ground black pepper
1 medium red bell pepper, cored and diced
1 medium yellow bell pepper, cored and diced
2 cups snow peas
1 pound fresh medium shrimp, peeled and deveined
3 cups cooked rice

1. Whisk together ¼ cup broth, the oyster sauce, soy sauce, white wine, sugar, and cornstarch in a bowl, and set aside.
2. Heat remaining broth in a wok. Add gingerroot, garlic, jalapeño pepper, scallions, and black pepper, and stirfry for 1 minute.
3. Add bell peppers and snow peas, and stirfry for 1 minute. Add shrimp and continue to stirfry for 2 more minutes, until shrimp turn pink.
4. Gradually add sauce to the wok. Stir for 1 minute. Serve over rice.

Calories Per Serving: 266	Carbohydrates: 40 g
Fat: 2 g	Dietary Fiber: 2 g
Cholesterol: 116 mg	Sodium: 396 mg
Protein: 20 g	

❋ *Shrimp and Okra* ❋

PREPARATION TIME: *20 minutes* • COOKING TIME: *20 minutes* •
YIELD: *4 servings*

1 cup low-sodium nonfat chicken broth

4 cups sliced fresh or canned okra, drained

¼ cup chopped onion

3 cups diced eggplant

3 tablespoons grated fresh gingerroot

2 jalapeño peppers, seeded and minced

4 medium tomatoes, chopped

½ pound fresh medium shrimp, peeled and deveined

1. Heat broth in a large saucepan. Add okra and simmer for 4 minutes. Stir in onion and eggplant, and simmer for 4 more minutes. Add gingerroot, jalapeño peppers, and tomatoes, and simmer for 4 additional minutes.
2. Add shrimp and continue to simmer until they turn pink, about 5 minutes. Add water if necessary.

Calories Per Serving: 189
Fat: 2 g
Cholesterol: 86 mg
Protein: 18 g

Carbohydrates: 27 g
Dietary Fiber: 5 g
Sodium: 355 mg

❊ *Pineapple-Shrimp Stirfry* ❊

PREPARATION TIME: *20 minutes* • COOKING TIME: *9 minutes* •
YIELD: *4 servings*

½ cup low-sodium nonfat chicken broth

1 scallion, minced

1 teaspoon minced fresh gingerroot

1 medium green bell pepper, cored and diced

1 clove garlic, minced

¾ pound fresh medium shrimp, peeled and deveined

1 cup fresh or canned pineapple chunks, drained

1 medium orange, peeled, sectioned, and chopped

2 tablespoons reduced-sodium soy sauce

1 tablespoon dry sherry

2 cups cooked rice

1. Heat ¼ cup broth in a wok. Add scallion, gingerroot, bell pepper, and garlic, and stirfry for 1 minute.
2. Add shrimp and stirfry until they turn pink, about 3 minutes. Remove shrimp and set aside.
3. Heat remaining broth in the wok. Add pineapple chunks and orange, and stirfry for 2 minutes. Return shrimp to the wok, stir in soy sauce and sherry, and heat through, about 2 minutes.
4. Serve over rice.

Calories Per Serving: 285
Fat: 2 g
Cholesterol: 129 mg
Protein: 21 g

Carbohydrates: 45 g
Dietary Fiber: 2 g
Sodium: 429 mg

❈ *Shrimp and Rice* ❈

PREPARATION TIME: *20 minutes* ▪ COOKING TIME: *39 minutes* ▪
YIELD: *4 servings*

*2½ cups low-sodium nonfat chicken
    broth*
1 medium onion, chopped
2 cloves garlic, minced
2 medium stalks celery, sliced
1 medium carrot, scraped and diced
*1 medium green bell pepper, cored
    and chopped*
*2 cups low-sodium canned tomatoes,
    chopped, juice reserved*

1 bay leaf
1½ teaspoons dried thyme
¾ teaspoon chili powder
½ teaspoon paprika
¼ teaspoon ground black pepper
⅛ teaspoon cayenne pepper
1½ cups uncooked white rice
*½ pound fresh medium shrimp, peeled
    and deveined*

1. Heat ¼ cup broth in a large saucepan. Add onion and garlic, and sauté until onion begins to soften, about 3 minutes.
2. Add remaining broth, celery, carrot, bell pepper, tomatoes with juice, and bay leaf. Stir in thyme, chili powder, paprika, black pepper, and cayenne pepper. Bring to a boil, reduce heat, cover, and simmer for 10 minutes.
3. Stir in rice. Return to a boil, reduce heat, cover, and simmer for 10 more minutes. Add shrimp, cover, and simmer until rice is tender and shrimp have turned pink, about 10 minutes. Remove bay leaf.

Calories Per Serving: 241
Fat: 2 g
Cholesterol: 49 mg
Protein: 14 g

Carbohydrates: 42 g
Dietary Fiber: 4 g
Sodium: 131 mg

❊ *Stirfried Scallops with Tomato, Bell Pepper,* ❊ *and Mushrooms*

PREPARATION TIME: *20 minutes* • COOKING TIME: *20 minutes* •
YIELD: *4 servings*

¾ cup low-sodium nonfat chicken
  broth
1 scallion, minced
1 teaspoon minced fresh gingerroot
1 clove garlic, minced
2 cups fresh scallops, halved
1 medium tomato, diced
1 cup sliced mushrooms

1 medium green bell pepper, cored
  and diced
1 medium onion, sliced
2 tablespoons reduced-sodium soy
  sauce
1 tablespoon dry sherry
2 cups cooked rice

1. Heat ¼ cup broth in a wok. Add scallion, gingerroot, and garlic. Stirfry for
   1 minute.
2. Add scallops and stirfry until they are opaque, about 3 more minutes. Remove scallops and set aside.
3. Heat another ¼ cup broth in the wok. Add tomato, mushrooms, bell pepper, and onion, and stirfry for 2 minutes. Add remaining broth. Bring to a
   boil, reduce heat, cover, and simmer until vegetables are just tender-crisp,
   about 5 minutes.
4. Return scallops to the wok. Add soy sauce and sherry, and heat through,
   about 2 minutes.
5. Serve over rice.

Calories Per Serving: 216
Fat: 1 g
Cholesterol: 22 mg
Protein: 15 g

Carbohydrates: 34 g
Dietary Fiber: 1 g
Sodium: 432 mg

❊ *Shrimp-Vegetable Stirfry* ❊

PREPARATION TIME: *20 minutes* • COOKING TIME: *20 minutes* •
YIELD: *4 servings*

¾ cup low-sodium nonfat chicken
broth
1 scallion, minced
1 teaspoon minced fresh gingerroot
1 clove garlic, minced
¾ pound fresh medium shrimp, peeled
and deveined
1 cup diced zucchini

1 medium green bell pepper, cored
and diced
1 medium onion, sliced
2 tablespoons reduced-sodium soy
sauce
1 tablespoon dry sherry
2 cups cooked rice

1. Heat ¼ cup broth in a wok. Add scallion, gingerroot, and garlic. Stirfry for 1 minute.
2. Add shrimp and stirfry until they turn pink, about 3 more minutes. Remove shrimp and set aside.
3. Heat another ¼ cup broth in the wok. Add zucchini, bell pepper, and onion, and stirfry for 2 minutes. Add remaining broth. Bring to a boil, reduce heat, cover, and simmer until vegetables are just tender-crisp, about 5 minutes.
4. Return shrimp to the wok. Add soy sauce and sherry, and heat through, about 2 minutes.
5. Serve over rice.

Calories Per Serving: 120
Fat: 2 g
Cholesterol: 129 mg
Protein: 19 g

Carbohydrates: 6 g
Dietary Fiber: 1 g
Sodium: 447 mg

BEAN
MAIN DISHES

Pinto Beans and Winter Squash · Kidney Beans with Orzo
· Pinto Bean and Cheese Bake · Kidney Beans and Spinach ·
Pinto Beans and Rice with Six Vegetables · Pinto Beans and
Potatoes · Gingered Pinto Beans with Green Beans · Pinto
Beans, Apples, and Sweet Potatoes · Kidney Beans, Vegetables,
and Couscous · Red Beans and Pasta · Spinach and Chickpeas
with Couscous · Chickpeas and Cauliflower · Chickpeas with
Vegetables and Couscous · Lentils with Broccoli and Sweet
Potato · Lentils with Pumpkin · Three-Bean Chili · Bean,
Couscous, and Vegetable Casserole · Black Beans and Rice ·
Black Beans and Green Chiles · Baked Black Beans with Jalapeño
Pepper · Oven-Baked Black Bean Tortillas · Black Bean Chili
with Cornbread Crust · Layered Black Bean Casserole · Spicy
Baked Black Beans and Pineapple · Black Beans with Sweet
Potatoes · Black Beans with Squash and Zucchini · Black-eyed
Peas with Okra, Corn, and Tomatoes · Black-eyed Peas and Rice
· Baked Black-eyed Peas with Tomatoes and Mushrooms ·
Cannellini Beans with Cabbage · White Beans and Mushrooms in
Wine Sauce with Couscous · Bean-Pineapple Jumble ·
Cannellini Beans and Green Peas · White Beans and Spinach ·

Cannellini Beans with Garlic ▪ Stovetop Maple-Mustard Beans ▪ Great Northern Beans and Eggplant Bake ▪ Great Northern Beans with Zucchini, Sweet Potatoes, and Kale ▪ Orange-Dijon Cannellini Beans ▪ Navy Beans with Fruit and Vegetables ▪ White Beans and Apples ▪ Green Chile and Pinto Bean Casserole ▪ Simple Beans and Rice

✳ *Pinto Beans and Winter Squash* ✳

PREPARATION TIME: *20 minutes plus 10 minutes standing time* •
COOKING TIME: *29 minutes* • YIELD: *6 servings*

¼ cup low-sodium vegetable broth
1 medium onion, chopped
2 cloves garlic, minced
2 cups diced butternut squash
2½ teaspoons curry powder
½ teaspoon ground black pepper

¼ teaspoon ground cloves
3 cups water
1½ cups uncooked white rice
2 cups chopped fresh spinach
2 cups low-sodium canned pinto
    beans, rinsed and drained

1. Heat broth in a large pot. Add onion and garlic, and sauté until onion begins to soften, about 3 minutes.
2. Stir in squash, curry powder, black pepper, cloves, water, and rice. Bring to a boil, cover, and simmer for 15 minutes. Add spinach and beans, cover, and continue to simmer until rice is tender, about 5 minutes.
3. Remove from heat, stir gently, and allow to stand for 10 minutes before serving.

Calories Per Serving: 307
Fat: 1 g
Cholesterol: 0 mg
Protein: 10 g

Carbohydrates: 66 g
Dietary Fiber: 7 g
Sodium: 26 mg

✳ *Kidney Beans with Orzo* ✳

PREPARATION TIME: *20 minutes plus 5 minutes standing time* •
COOKING TIME: *1 hour 19 minutes* • YIELD: *7 servings*

8 cups water
1 medium onion, chopped
2 cloves garlic, minced
½ cup uncooked white rice
1 cup uncooked orzo
1 cup fresh, drained canned, or
    thawed frozen corn kernels
2 cups low-sodium canned kidney
    beans, rinsed and drained

½ cup chopped canned mild green
    chiles, drained
1½ teaspoons chili powder
¼ teaspoon ground black pepper
1 cup nonfat cottage cheese
½ cup grated nonfat cheddar
¼ cup chopped fresh parsley

1. Combine water, onion, garlic, and rice in a flameproof 3-quart casserole. Cover and bring to a boil. Reduce heat and simmer for 30 minutes.
2. Preheat oven to 375 degrees.
3. Add orzo. Return to a boil, reduce heat, cover, and simmer for 12 more minutes. Add corn and continue to simmer for 3 additional minutes. Remove from heat and allow to stand for 5 minutes.
4. Stir in kidney beans, chiles, chili powder, and black pepper. Cover and bake for 10 minutes. Stir in cottage cheese and cheddar, and bake until heated through, about 10 more minutes.
5. Serve topped with parsley.

Calories Per Serving: 234   Carbohydrates: 46 g
Fat: 1 g   Dietary Fiber: 6 g
Cholesterol: 2 mg   Sodium: 154 mg
Protein: 12 g

❇ *Pinto Bean and Cheese Bake* ❇

PREPARATION TIME: *25 minutes* • COOKING TIME: *43 minutes* •
YIELD: *8 servings*

¼ cup low-sodium nonfat chicken
   broth
1 medium onion, chopped
2 cloves garlic, minced
1 medium green bell pepper, cored
   and chopped
3 cups low-sodium tomato sauce
1½ teaspoons ground cumin

1 teaspoon chili powder
4 cups low-sodium canned pinto
   beans, rinsed and drained
8 6-inch corn tortillas
1 cup nonfat ricotta
1 cup shredded nonfat cheddar
½ cup nonfat plain yogurt
1 medium tomato, finely chopped

1. Preheat oven to 350 degrees.
2. Combine broth, onion, and garlic in a flameproof 3-quart casserole. Cook, stirring, until onion begins to soften, about 3 minutes. Add bell pepper, tomato sauce, cumin, and chili powder. Simmer for 5 minutes. Add beans and stir to mix well. Remove half the mixture and set aside.
3. Cover vegetables in the casserole with 4 tortillas. Spread ricotta and then remaining vegetables evenly on tortillas. Sprinkle with half the cheddar and top with remaining tortillas.
4. Cover the casserole and bake for 30 minutes.
5. Sprinkle remaining cheddar on top of the casserole, and bake, uncovered, until cheese begins to melt, about 5 minutes.
6. Serve topped with yogurt and chopped tomato.

Calories Per Serving: 266

Fat: 2 g

Cholesterol: 6 mg

Protein: 20 g

Carbohydrates: 46 g

Dietary Fiber: 8 g

Sodium: 363 mg

❊ *Kidney Beans and Spinach* ❊

PREPARATION TIME: *15 minutes* · COOKING TIME: *12 minutes* ·

YIELD: *4 servings*

¼ cup low-sodium nonfat chicken
   broth

1 tablespoon rice vinegar

1 cup diced yellow summer squash

1 medium red bell pepper, cored and
   cut into thin strips

¼ cup minced scallions

2 cups chopped fresh spinach

1 cup low-sodium canned dark red
   kidney beans, rinsed and drained

1 teaspoon dried basil

½ teaspoon ground black pepper

2 cups cooked rice

1. Heat broth and vinegar in a large saucepan. Add squash, bell pepper, and
   2 tablespoons scallions, and sauté for 4 minutes.
2. Add spinach, kidney beans, basil, and black pepper, and sauté until squash
   is just tender and all ingredients are heated through, about 6 minutes.
3. Serve over rice, sprinkled with remaining scallions.

Calories Per Serving: 198

Fat: 1 g

Cholesterol: 0 mg

Protein: 7 g

Carbohydrates: 41 g

Dietary Fiber: 5 g

Sodium: 45 mg

❊ *Pinto Beans and Rice with Six Vegetables* ❊

PREPARATION TIME: *25 minutes* · COOKING TIME: *48 minutes* ·

YIELD: *8 servings*

5¼ cups low-sodium nonfat chicken
   broth
3 cloves garlic, minced
1 medium onion, minced
1 medium green bell pepper, cored
   and diced
½ teaspoon cayenne pepper
¼ teaspoon ground black pepper
3 cups diced white potatoes

1 cup low-sodium canned tomatoes,
   drained and chopped
2 cups chopped fresh green beans
   (1-inch lengths)
3 cups low-sodium canned pinto
   beans, rinsed and drained
½ pound fresh asparagus spears, cut
   into 1-inch lengths
1 cup fresh or frozen green peas
2 cups uncooked white rice

1. Heat ¼ cup broth in a large saucepan. Add garlic, onion, and bell pepper, and sauté until onion begins to soften, about 5 minutes.
2. Add cayenne pepper, black pepper, potatoes, and tomatoes, and sauté for 5 more minutes.
3. Stir in remaining broth and bring to a boil. Add green beans. Reduce heat, cover, and simmer for 5 minutes. Stir in pinto beans, asparagus, peas, and rice. Return to a boil, reduce heat, cover, and simmer until rice is just tender, about 25 minutes.

Calories Per Serving: 356
Fat: 1 g
Cholesterol: 0 mg
Protein: 12 g

Carbohydrates: 77 g
Dietary Fiber: 7 g
Sodium: 40 mg

❀ *Pinto Beans and Potatoes* ❀

PREPARATION TIME: *20 minutes* • COOKING TIME: *35 minutes* •
YIELD: *6 servings*

2 tablespoons low-sodium tomato
   paste
2 tablespoons lemon juice
1 teaspoon ground cumin
1 teaspoon ground cinnamon
½ teaspoon ground coriander
¼ teaspoon ground cardamom
¼ teaspoon ground cloves
¼ teaspoon cayenne pepper

2¼ cups low-sodium nonfat chicken
   broth
3 cloves garlic, minced
1 tablespoon minced fresh gingerroot
4 cups low-sodium canned pinto
   beans, rinsed and drained
2½ cups diced potatoes
2 bay leaves
¼ teaspoon ground black pepper
½ cup nonfat plain yogurt

1. In a small bowl, whisk together tomato paste, lemon juice, cumin, cinnamon, coriander, cardamom, cloves, and cayenne pepper, and set aside.
2. Heat ¼ cup broth in a large saucepan. Add garlic and gingerroot, and sauté for 1 minute. Stir in tomato paste mixture, beans, potatoes, and bay leaves. Add remaining broth, bring to a boil, reduce heat, cover, and simmer, stirring frequently, until potatoes are just tender, about 30 minutes.
3. Remove bay leaves. Stir in black pepper, transfer to individual plates, top with yogurt, and serve.

Calories Per Serving: 268	Carbohydrates: 54 g
Fat: 1 g	Dietary Fiber: 10 g
Cholesterol: 0 mg	Sodium: 38 mg
Protein: 14 g	

❊ *Gingered Pinto Beans with Green Beans* ❊

PREPARATION TIME: *20 minutes*   •   COOKING TIME: *12 minutes*   •
YIELD: *6 servings*

¾ cup low-sodium nonfat chicken broth
1 tablespoon minced fresh gingerroot
½ teaspoon curry powder
½ teaspoon ground black pepper
2 medium onions, sliced
4 medium stalks celery, sliced
2 tablespoons reduced-sodium soy sauce
1 tablespoon cornstarch

3 cups low-sodium canned pinto beans, rinsed and drained
1 medium green bell pepper, cored and cut into thin strips
1½ cups chopped fresh green beans (1-inch lengths)
¼ cup chopped fresh parsley
3 medium tomatoes, chopped
3 cups cooked rice

1. Heat ¼ cup broth in a large saucepan. Add gingerroot, curry powder, and black pepper. Stir in onions and celery, and sauté until onions begin to soften, about 4 minutes.
2. In a separate bowl, combine soy sauce, cornstarch, and remaining broth. Mix well and stir into the saucepan. Add pinto beans, bell pepper, green beans, parsley, and tomatoes. Simmer until all ingredients are heated through, about 6 minutes.
3. Serve over rice.

Calories Per Serving: 288	Carbohydrates: 59 g
Fat: 1 g	Dietary Fiber: 9 g
Cholesterol: 0 mg	Sodium: 251 mg
Protein: 12 g	

❀ Pinto Beans, Apples, and Sweet Potatoes ❀

PREPARATION TIME: 16 minutes • COOKING TIME: 44 minutes •
YIELD: 8 servings

1¼ cups low-sodium nonfat chicken
  broth
1 cup chopped onion
2 medium green bell peppers, cored
  and chopped
2 cups low-sodium canned tomatoes,
  chopped, juice reserved
1 cup juice-packed canned pineapple
  chunks, drained

2 cups diced sweet potatoes
2 large tart apples, peeled, cored, and
  chopped
4 cups low-sodium canned pinto
  beans, rinsed and drained
2 teaspoons chili powder
1 teaspoon ground cumin
½ teaspoon ground cinnamon
½ teaspoon ground black pepper

1. Heat ¼ cup broth in a large saucepan. Add onion and bell peppers, and
   sauté until onion begins to soften, about 4 minutes.
2. Stir in remaining broth, tomatoes with juice, pineapple chunks, sweet
   potatoes, apples, beans, chili powder, cumin, cinnamon, and black pepper.
   Bring to a boil, reduce heat, cover, and simmer, stirring frequently, until
   potatoes are just tender, about 35 minutes.
3. Transfer to individual bowls and serve.

Calories Per Serving: 235
Fat: 1 g
Cholesterol: 0 mg
Protein: 10 g

Carbohydrates: 49 g
Dietary Fiber: 10 g
Sodium: 39 mg

❀ Kidney Beans, Vegetables, and Couscous ❀

PREPARATION TIME: 25 minutes plus 5 minutes standing time •
COOKING TIME: 32 minutes • YIELD: 6 servings

1¼ cups low-sodium nonfat chicken
  broth
1 medium onion, chopped
2 medium green bell peppers, cored
  and chopped
1 medium leek (white part only),
  chopped
3 cloves garlic, minced

2 medium carrots, scraped and sliced
1 medium parsnip, diced
1½ cups diced sweet potatoes
2 cups low-sodium canned tomatoes,
  chopped, juice reserved
2 cups low-sodium canned kidney
  beans, rinsed and drained
½ cup chopped dried apricots

½ cup seedless raisins
1 tablespoon honey
2 teaspoons ground cinnamon
½ teaspoon ground cumin

¼ teaspoon ground black pepper
1½ cups uncooked couscous
2¼ cups boiling water

1. Heat ¼ cup broth in a large saucepan. Add onion, bell peppers, leek, garlic, carrots, parsnip, and sweet potatoes. Simmer, stirring frequently, for 15 minutes.
2. Stir in remaining broth, tomatoes with juice, beans, dried apricots, raisins, honey, ½ teaspoon cinnamon, the cumin, and black pepper. Continue to simmer, stirring frequently, for 15 minutes.
3. In a separate bowl, combine remaining cinnamon and couscous. Pour boiling water over couscous, cover, and allow to stand for 5 minutes.
4. Arrange couscous on individual plates, spoon stew on top, and serve.

Calories Per Serving: 320
Fat: 1 g
Cholesterol: 0 mg
Protein: 9 g

Carbohydrates: 72 g
Dietary Fiber: 12 g
Sodium: 98 mg

❊ Red Beans and Pasta ❊

PREPARATION TIME: *20 minutes* • COOKING TIME: *15 minutes* •
YIELD: *4 servings*

¼ cup low-sodium nonfat chicken
    broth
1 medium onion, chopped
2 cloves garlic, minced
2½ cups low-sodium canned kidney
    beans, liquid reserved
1 cup low-sodium canned tomatoes,
    crushed, juice reserved

1 teaspoon ground cinnamon
¼ teaspoon cayenne pepper
¼ teaspoon dried thyme
1 cup cooked small pasta shells
¼ cup grated nonfat mozzarella
¼ cup minced onion

1. Heat broth in a large saucepan. Add chopped onion and garlic, and sauté until onion begins to soften, about 3 minutes.
2. Add beans with liquid, tomatoes with juice, cinnamon, cayenne pepper, thyme, and pasta. Simmer until all ingredients are heated through, about 10 minutes.
3. Transfer to individual bowls, stir 1 tablespoon mozzarella into each serving, top with minced onion, and serve.

Calories Per Serving: 328
Fat: 2 g
Cholesterol: 5 mg
Protein: 19 g

Carbohydrates: 61 g
Dietary Fiber: 5 g
Sodium: 248 mg

❈ *Spinach and Chickpeas with Couscous* ❈

PREPARATION TIME: *15 minutes plus 5 minutes standing time* •
COOKING TIME: *25 minutes* • YIELD: *4 servings*

2¼ cups low-sodium vegetable broth
½ cup chopped onion
2 cloves garlic, minced
2 teaspoons curry powder
6 cups chopped fresh spinach

2 cups cooked or low-sodium canned
   chickpeas, rinsed and drained
¼ teaspoon ground black pepper
2 cups boiling water
1 cup uncooked couscous

1. Heat ¼ cup broth in a large saucepan. Add onion, garlic, and curry powder, and sauté until onion begins to soften, about 4 minutes.
2. Add remaining broth and spinach. Bring to a boil, reduce heat, and simmer for 10 minutes. Stir in chickpeas and black pepper, and continue to simmer until spinach is tender and chickpeas are heated through, about 5 more minutes.
3. Pour boiling water over couscous, cover, and allow to stand for 5 minutes.
4. Divide couscous among separate bowls.
5. Serve spinach-chickpea mixture over couscous.

Calories Per Serving: 174
Fat: 1 g
Cholesterol: 0 mg
Protein: 10 g

Carbohydrates: 34 g
Dietary Fiber: 9 g
Sodium: 468 mg

❈ *Chickpeas and Cauliflower* ❈

PREPARATION TIME: *15 minutes* • COOKING TIME: *25 minutes* •
YIELD: *6 servings*

¾ cup low-sodium nonfat chicken
   broth
1 medium onion, chopped

3 cloves garlic, minced
1 teaspoon ground cumin
1 tablespoon curry powder

¼ teaspoon cayenne pepper
4 cups chopped cauliflower
2 cups low-sodium canned tomatoes,
  chopped, juice reserved

2 cups cooked or low-sodium canned
  chickpeas, rinsed and drained
1 cup fresh or frozen green peas
½ teaspoon ground black pepper

1. Heat ¼ cup broth in a large saucepan. Add onion, garlic, cumin, curry powder, and cayenne pepper, and sauté until onion begins to soften, about 3 minutes.
2. Stir in remaining broth and cauliflower, and bring to a boil. Reduce heat, cover, and simmer for 5 minutes.
3. Add tomatoes with juice, chickpeas, and green peas. Return to a boil, reduce heat, cover, and simmer until peas are done, about 12 minutes. Stir in black pepper and serve.

Calories Per Serving: 308
Fat: 1 g
Cholesterol: 0 mg
Protein: 9 g

Carbohydrates: 27 g
Dietary Fiber: 5 g
Sodium: 308 mg

❊ *Chickpeas with Vegetables and Couscous* ❊

PREPARATION TIME: *20 minutes plus 5 minutes standing time*   •
COOKING TIME: *20 minutes*   •   YIELD: *8 servings*

3 cups boiling water
1½ cups uncooked couscous
1½ teaspoons ground turmeric
¼ cup low-sodium nonfat chicken
  broth
2 medium onions, chopped
1 cup shredded cabbage
1 medium turnip, diced
2 cups sliced yellow summer squash

1 cup cooked or low-sodium canned
  chickpeas, rinsed and drained
2 cups chopped tomatoes
1 teaspoon minced fresh gingerroot
½ teaspoon ground cumin
½ teaspoon ground coriander
¼ teaspoon ground black pepper
1 cup seedless raisins

1. In a large bowl, pour boiling water over couscous. Stir in turmeric, cover, and allow to stand for 5 minutes.
2. Heat broth in a saucepan. Add onions and sauté until onions begin to soften, about 3 minutes.
3. Stir in cabbage, turnip, squash, chickpeas, tomatoes, gingerroot, cumin, coriander, and black pepper. Cover and simmer until turnip begins to soften, about 15 minutes.
4. Serve vegetables over couscous. Top with raisins.

Calories Per Serving: 212

Carbohydrates: 47 g

Fat: 1 g

Dietary Fiber: 8 g

Cholesterol: 0 mg

Sodium: 29 mg

Protein: 6 g

❋ *Lentils with Broccoli and Sweet Potato* ❋

PREPARATION TIME: *20 minutes plus 10 minutes standing time*　•
COOKING TIME: *59 minutes*　•　YIELD: *4 servings*

1 cup dried lentils, rinsed and drained
5 cups water
2 tablespoons low-sodium nonfat
　chicken broth
1 medium onion, diced
2 cloves garlic, minced
1 medium tomato, diced

2 teaspoons curry powder
¼ teaspoon cayenne pepper
¼ teaspoon ground turmeric
2 medium carrots, scraped and diced
1 medium sweet potato, diced
2 cups chopped broccoli

1. Combine lentils and water in a large saucepan. Bring to a boil, reduce heat, cover, and cook until lentils are just tender, about 30 minutes.
2. Remove lentils and 2 cups cooking liquid, and set aside.
3. Heat broth in the saucepan. Add onion and garlic, and sauté until onion begins to soften, about 3 minutes. Stir in tomato, curry powder, cayenne pepper, and turmeric, and sauté for 1 more minute.
4. Add carrots, sweet potato, and reserved lentils and cooking liquid. Bring to a boil, reduce heat, and simmer, stirring occasionally, for 15 minutes.
5. Remove from heat, stir in broccoli, and allow to stand for 10 minutes before serving.

Calories Per Serving: 139

Carbohydrates: 31 g

Fat: 1 g

Dietary Fiber: 6 g

Cholesterol: 0 mg

Sodium: 45 mg

Protein: 4 g

❋ *Lentils with Pumpkin* ❋

PREPARATION TIME: *15 minutes*　•　COOKING TIME: *44 minutes*　•
YIELD: *6 servings*

2¼ cups low-sodium nonfat chicken
   broth
2 medium onions, chopped
4 medium carrots, scraped and sliced
5 cloves garlic, minced
2 teaspoons ground cumin
2 teaspoons ground coriander
1 teaspoon curry powder

1 teaspoon ground turmeric
1 cup dried red lentils, rinsed and
   drained
3½ cups low-sodium canned tomatoes, chopped, juice reserved
4 cups cubed pumpkin
½ teaspoon ground black pepper

1. Heat ¼ cup broth in a large saucepan. Add onions, carrots, garlic, cumin, coriander, curry powder, and turmeric, and sauté until onions begin to soften, about 4 minutes.
2. Stir in remaining broth, lentils, and tomatoes with juice. Bring to a boil, reduce heat, cover, and simmer for 10 minutes.
3. Add pumpkin. Return to a boil, reduce heat, cover, and simmer until lentils are tender, about 25 minutes.
4. Stir in black pepper and serve.

Calories Per Serving: 120
Fat: 1 g
Cholesterol: 0 mg
Protein: 5 g

Carbohydrates: 25 g
Dietary Fiber: 6 g
Sodium: 150 mg

❋ *Three-Bean Chili* ❋

PREPARATION TIME: *20 minutes* • COOKING TIME: *28 minutes* •
YIELD: *8 servings*

¼ cup low-sodium vegetable broth
1 medium red bell pepper, cored and
   chopped
1 medium green bell pepper, cored
   and chopped
2 tablespoons minced jalapeño pepper
1 medium onion, chopped
3 cloves garlic, minced
1 tablespoon ground cumin
1 tablespoon chili powder
2 teaspoons paprika

½ cup orange juice
3½ cups low-sodium canned tomatoes, chopped, juice reserved
2 cups low-sodium canned kidney
   beans, rinsed and drained
2 cups low-sodium canned Great
   Northern beans, rinsed and
   drained
2 cups low-sodium canned black
   beans, rinsed and drained
¼ cup chopped fresh parsley

1. Heat broth in a large saucepan. Add bell peppers, jalapeño pepper, onion, and garlic, and sauté until peppers begin to soften, about 6 minutes.
2. Stir in cumin, chili powder, paprika, and orange juice. Add tomatoes with juice, kidney beans, Great Northern beans, and black beans. Bring to a boil, reduce heat, and simmer for 20 minutes.
3. Serve in individual bowls garnished with parsley.

Calories Per Serving: 226

Fat: 2 g

Cholesterol: 0 mg

Protein: 13 g

Carbohydrates: 43 g

Dietary Fiber: 11 g

Sodium: 70 mg

❋ Bean, Couscous, and Vegetable Casserole ❋

PREPARATION TIME: *15 minutes plus 5 minutes standing time* ▪
COOKING TIME: *45 minutes* ▪ YIELD: *8 servings*

Olive oil cooking spray
2 cups cooked or low-sodium canned
   chickpeas, rinsed and drained
4 cups low-sodium canned tomatoes,
   chopped and drained
2 cups low-sodium canned Great
   Northern beans, rinsed and
   drained
4 cloves garlic, minced

1 medium green bell pepper, cored
   and chopped
1 medium onion, thinly sliced
2 cups chopped broccoli
1 cup fresh, drained canned, or
   thawed frozen corn kernels
½ teaspoon ground black pepper
3 cups boiling water
1½ cups uncooked couscous

1. Preheat oven to 375 degrees. Lightly coat a 3-quart casserole with olive oil cooking spray.
2. Combine chickpeas, tomatoes, beans, garlic, bell pepper, onion, broccoli, corn, and black pepper in the prepared casserole and bake for 45 minutes.
3. In a separate bowl, pour boiling water over couscous, cover, and allow to stand for 5 minutes.
4. Serve vegetables over couscous.

Calories Per Serving: 288

Fat: 1 g

Cholesterol: 0 mg

Protein: 14 g

Carbohydrates: 58 g

Dietary Fiber: 14 g

Sodium: 26 mg

❋ *Black Beans and Rice* ❋

PREPARATION TIME: *20 minutes* • COOKING TIME: *22 minutes* •
YIELD: *6 servings*

3¼ cups low-sodium nonfat chicken
  broth
3 medium stalks celery, chopped
1 medium onion, chopped
1 medium green bell pepper, cored
  and chopped

4 scallions, chopped
2 cloves garlic, minced
6 cups low-sodium canned black
  beans, rinsed and drained
½ teaspoon ground black pepper
1½ cups cooked rice

1. Heat broth in a large saucepan. Add celery, onion, bell pepper, three fourths of the chopped scallion, and the garlic, and sauté until onion begins to soften, about 3 minutes.
2. Add beans and black pepper, and simmer until bell pepper is just tender, about 15 minutes.
3. Serve over rice, garnished with remaining chopped scallion.

Calories Per Serving: 436
Fat: 1 g
Cholesterol: 0 mg
Protein: 23 g

Carbohydrates: 84 g
Dietary Fiber: 14 g
Sodium: 123 mg

❋ *Black Beans and Green Chiles* ❋

PREPARATION TIME: *15 minutes* • COOKING TIME: *24 minutes* •
YIELD: *6 servings*

¼ cup low-sodium nonfat chicken
  broth
1 medium onion, chopped
4 cloves garlic, minced
4 teaspoons ground cumin
4 teaspoons dried oregano
½ teaspoon cayenne pepper

½ cup chopped canned mild green
  chiles, drained
6 cups low-sodium canned black
  beans, rinsed and drained
2 cups low-sodium canned tomatoes,
  crushed, juice reserved
¼ teaspoon ground black pepper
¼ cup nonfat plain yogurt

1. Heat broth in a large saucepan. Add onion and garlic, and sauté until onion begins to soften, about 3 minutes. Add cumin, oregano, cayenne pepper, and chiles, and sauté for 1 more minute.

2. Add beans, tomatoes with juice, and black pepper. Bring to a boil, reduce heat, and simmer for 15 minutes.
3. Serve topped with yogurt.

Calories Per Serving: 272
Fat: 2 g
Cholesterol: 0 mg
Protein: 17 g

Carbohydrates: 50 g
Dietary Fiber: 14 g
Sodium: 112 mg

❋ *Baked Black Beans with Jalapeño Pepper* ❋

PREPARATION TIME: *15 minutes* • COOKING TIME: *30 minutes* •
YIELD: *4 servings*

*½ cup low-sodium nonfat chicken
   broth*
1 medium onion, chopped
1 medium carrot, scraped and diced
1 jalapeño pepper, seeded and minced
3 cloves garlic, minced

*4 cups low-sodium canned black
   beans, rinsed and drained*
2 tablespoons ground coriander
½ teaspoon dried marjoram
½ cup grated nonfat cheddar

1. Preheat oven to 350 degrees.
2. Heat ¼ cup broth in a flameproof 2-quart casserole. Add onion, carrot, jalapeño pepper, and garlic, and sauté until carrot begins to soften, about 5 minutes.
3. Add remaining broth, beans, coriander, and marjoram, and stir for 1 minute. Bake for 20 minutes. Sprinkle the top of the casserole with cheddar, then return to the oven until cheese melts, about 2 minutes.

Calories Per Serving: 171
Fat: 1 g
Cholesterol: 3 mg
Protein: 12 g

Carbohydrates: 30 g
Dietary Fiber: 8 g
Sodium: 362 mg

❋ *Oven-Baked Black Bean Tortillas* ❋

PREPARATION TIME: *20 minutes* • COOKING TIME: *12 minutes* •
YIELD: *5 servings*

Olive oil cooking spray
4 cups low-sodium canned black
beans, rinsed and drained
1½ cups low-sodium tomato sauce
1 teaspoon chili powder

½ cup grated nonfat cheddar
½ cup grated nonfat mozzarella
10 6-inch tortillas
½ cup nonfat sour cream

1. Preheat oven to 375 degrees. Lightly coat a 13 × 9-inch nonstick baking dish with olive oil cooking spray.
2. Combine beans, tomato sauce, and chili powder in a blender or food processor and puree very briefly.
3. Combine cheeses in a separate bowl and set aside.
4. Place ⅓ cup bean mixture and 2 teaspoons cheese mixture in the middle of each tortilla. Roll up tortillas, arrange them in the prepared baking dish, and bake until cheese melts and edges of tortillas begin to become crisp, about 12 minutes.
5. Top each tortilla with sour cream and serve.

Calories Per Serving: 387
Fat: 3 g
Cholesterol: 5 mg
Protein: 24 g

Carbohydrates: 71 g
Dietary Fiber: 13 g
Sodium: 566 mg

❊ Black Bean Chili with Cornbread Crust ❊

PREPARATION TIME: 25 minutes plus 10 minutes standing time •
COOKING TIME: 27 minutes • YIELD: 6 servings

¼ cup low-sodium vegetable broth
2 cloves garlic, minced
2 medium onions, chopped
1½ teaspoons ground cumin
2 teaspoons chili powder
1 jalapeño pepper, seeded and minced
2 medium green bell peppers, cored
and chopped
1 medium carrot, scraped and
shredded
1 cup chopped yellow summer squash
3 cups low-sodium canned black
beans, rinsed and drained
2 medium tomatoes, chopped

3 tablespoons low-sodium tomato
juice
¼ cup chopped fresh parsley
1 cup cornmeal
¼ cup all-purpose flour
1½ tablespoons sugar
2 teaspoons low-sodium baking
powder
1 cup nonfat buttermilk
2 egg whites
1 cup fresh or thawed frozen corn
kernels
½ teaspoon dried marjoram
½ teaspoon dried thyme

1. Preheat oven to 425 degrees.
2. Heat broth in a flameproof 3-quart casserole. Add garlic and onions, and sauté until onions begin to soften, about 3 minutes. Stir in cumin, chili powder, jalapeño pepper, bell peppers, carrot, squash, beans, tomatoes, tomato juice, and parsley. Cook and stir for 2 minutes.
3. Combine cornmeal, flour, sugar, and baking powder in a separate large bowl. Stir in buttermilk, egg whites, corn, marjoram, and thyme. Mix just enough to incorporate dry ingredients. Spread batter evenly over the chili. Bake until cornbread is done when fork tested, about 20 minutes.
4. Allow to stand for 10 minutes before serving.

Calories Per Serving: 369	Carbohydrates: 75 g
Fat: 2 g	Dietary Fiber: 11 g
Cholesterol: 1 mg	Sodium: 178 mg
Protein: 17 g	

❈ *Layered Black Bean Casserole* ❈

PREPARATION TIME: *15 minutes* • **COOKING TIME:** *40 minutes* •
YIELD: *6 servings*

Olive oil cooking spray
9 6-inch corn tortillas
1½ cups low-sodium canned black beans, rinsed and drained
1½ cups fresh or thawed frozen corn kernels
1 medium onion, chopped
1 medium green bell pepper, cored and chopped

4 medium tomatoes, chopped
2 cloves garlic, minced
½ teaspoon ground cumin
½ teaspoon chili powder
¼ teaspoon ground black pepper
½ cup grated nonfat cheddar

1. Preheat oven to 350 degrees. Lightly coat a 2-quart casserole with olive oil cooking spray.
2. Arrange a single layer of tortillas on the bottom of the casserole. Top with ½ cup beans and ½ cup corn. Repeat with 2 more layers of tortillas, beans, and corn.
3. In a separate bowl, combine the onion, bell pepper, tomatoes, garlic, cumin, chili powder, and black pepper. Spread this mixture over the beans and corn. Bake for 35 minutes.
4. Top with cheddar and return to the oven until cheese melts, about 5 minutes.

Calories Per Serving: 217
Fat: 2 g
Cholesterol: 2 mg
Protein: 11 g

Carbohydrates: 43 g
Dietary Fiber: 6 g
Sodium: 143 mg

❋ *Spicy Baked Black Beans and Pineapple* ❋

PREPARATION TIME: *15 minutes* ・ COOKING TIME: *40 minutes* ・
YIELD: *4 servings*

Olive oil cooking spray
1 cup low-sodium tomato sauce
1 tablespoon reduced-sodium soy sauce
1 tablespoon molasses
2 teaspoons prepared mustard
2 teaspoons vinegar

3 cloves garlic, minced
½ teaspoon onion powder
2 cups low-sodium canned black beans, rinsed and drained
2 cups juice-packed canned pineapple bits, drained

1. Preheat oven to 375 degrees. Lightly coat a 2-quart casserole with olive oil cooking spray.
2. Combine all ingredients in a large bowl and mix well.
3. Transfer to the prepared casserole and bake, covered, for 40 minutes.

Calories Per Serving: 197
Fat: 1 g
Cholesterol: 0 mg
Protein: 10 g

Carbohydrates: 40 g
Dietary Fiber: 8 g
Sodium: 194 mg

❋ *Black Beans with Sweet Potatoes* ❋

PREPARATION TIME: *15 minutes* ・ COOKING TIME: *22 minutes* ・
YIELD: *8 servings*

½ cup low-sodium nonfat chicken broth

¼ teaspoon cayenne pepper

1 teaspoon ground cumin

1 teaspoon dried thyme

2 medium sweet potatoes, chopped

1 medium leek (white part only), chopped

1 medium red bell pepper, cored and cut into ½-inch slices

1 medium yellow bell pepper, cored and cut into ½-inch slices

1 medium onion, sliced

2 tablespoons lime juice

1 medium tomato, cut into thin wedges

4 cups low-sodium canned black beans, rinsed and drained

4 cups cooked rice

1. Heat ¼ cup broth in a large saucepan. Add cayenne pepper, cumin, and thyme, and sauté for 30 seconds. Add sweet potatoes and continue to sauté until potatoes begin to soften, about 5 minutes.
2. Add remaining broth and leek, and sauté for 4 more minutes. Stir in bell peppers and onion, and continue to sauté for 4 additional minutes. Add lime juice, tomato, and beans, and simmer until potatoes are done and all ingredients are heated through, about 6 minutes.
3. Serve over rice.

Calories Per Serving: 388
Fat: 1 g
Cholesterol: 0 mg
Protein: 13 g

Carbohydrates: 82 g
Dietary Fiber: 12 g
Sodium: 39 mg

❋ Black Beans with Squash and Zucchini ❋

PREPARATION TIME: 20 minutes • COOKING TIME: 28 minutes •
YIELD: 6 servings

¾ cup low-sodium nonfat chicken broth

1 medium onion, chopped

3 cups chopped yellow summer squash

2 medium green bell peppers, cored and chopped

1 cup chopped zucchini

2 medium stalks celery, sliced

2 cups chopped mushrooms

3 medium carrots, scraped and sliced

2 medium tomatoes, chopped

2 cups low-sodium canned black beans, rinsed and drained

½ cup dry white wine

¾ cup low-sodium tomato paste

1½ tablespoons chili powder

1½ teaspoons ground cumin

2 cloves garlic, minced

½ teaspoon ground black pepper

¼ cup shredded nonfat cheddar

1. Heat ¼ cup broth in a large saucepan. Add onion and sauté until onion begins to soften, about 3 minutes.
2. Add squash, bell peppers, zucchini, celery, mushrooms, and carrots, and continue to sauté for 5 more minutes.
3. Stir in remaining broth, tomatoes, beans, wine, tomato paste, chili powder, cumin, garlic, and black pepper. Bring to a boil, reduce heat, cover, and simmer until vegetables are tender, about 15 minutes.
4. Serve topped with cheese.

Calories Per Serving: 191
Fat: 2 g
Cholesterol: 1 mg
Protein: 11 g

Carbohydrates: 35 g
Dietary Fiber: 10 g
Sodium: 125 mg

❀ *Black-eyed Peas with Okra, Corn,* ❀ *and Tomatoes*

PREPARATION TIME: *15 minutes* • COOKING TIME: *12 minutes* •
YIELD: *4 servings*

2 tablespoons low-sodium nonfat
   chicken broth
1 medium onion, chopped
½ cup sliced celery
2 cloves garlic, minced
1 teaspoon dried thyme
½ teaspoon dry mustard
¼ teaspoon ground black pepper
¼ teaspoon paprika

¼ teaspoon cayenne pepper
2 cups low-sodium canned black-eyed
   peas, rinsed and drained
1 cup fresh or thawed frozen corn
   kernels
1¼ cups sliced canned okra, drained
2 medium tomatoes, chopped
2 cups cooked rice

1. Heat broth in a large saucepan. Add onion, celery, and garlic, and sauté until onion begins to soften, about 3 minutes.
2. Stir in thyme, mustard, black pepper, paprika, and cayenne pepper. Add black-eyed peas and corn, and sauté for 4 minutes. Stir in okra and tomatoes, and simmer until heated through, about 3 minutes.
3. Serve over rice.

Calories Per Serving: 398
Fat: 1 g
Cholesterol: 0 mg
Protein: 15 g

Carbohydrates: 85 g
Dietary Fiber: 9 g
Sodium: 237 mg

❋ Black-eyed Peas and Rice ❋

PREPARATION TIME: *15 minutes* • COOKING TIME: *42 minutes* •
YIELD: *6 servings*

2¼ cups low-sodium nonfat chicken
   broth
1 medium onion, chopped
1 medium green bell pepper, cored
   and diced
1 medium red bell pepper, cored and
   diced

1 bay leaf
⅛ teaspoon dried thyme
⅛ teaspoon cayenne pepper
1½ cups low-sodium canned black-
   eyed peas, rinsed and drained
½ cup uncooked white rice

1. Heat ¼ cup broth in a large saucepan. Add onion and bell peppers, and sauté until peppers begin to soften, about 4 minutes.
2. Stir in 1 cup broth, bay leaf, thyme, cayenne pepper, and black-eyed peas. Bring to a boil, reduce heat, cover, and simmer for 15 minutes.
3. Add remaining broth and rice. Bring to a boil, reduce heat, cover, and simmer until rice is just tender, about 15 minutes. Remove bay leaf.

Calories Per Serving: 96
Fat: 1 g
Cholesterol: 0 mg
Protein: 4 g

Carbohydrates: 20 g
Dietary Fiber: 1 g
Sodium: 128 mg

❋ Baked Black-eyed Peas with Tomatoes ❋ and Mushrooms

PREPARATION TIME: *20 minutes* • COOKING TIME: *55 minutes* •
YIELD: *6 servings*

¼ cup low-sodium nonfat chicken
   broth
2 cloves garlic, minced
1 cup chopped onion
1 medium green bell pepper, cored
   and chopped
1 cup sliced mushrooms

2 medium tomatoes, chopped
½ teaspoon ground black pepper
2 cups low-sodium canned tomatoes,
   drained and crushed
1 cup cooked rice
2 cups low-sodium canned black-eyed
   peas, rinsed and drained

1. Preheat oven to 350 degrees.
2. Heat broth in a flameproof 3-quart casserole. Add garlic and onion, and sauté until onion begins to soften, about 3 minutes. Add bell pepper, mushrooms, and fresh tomatoes, and cook, stirring frequently, for 5 minutes.
3. Add black pepper, canned tomatoes, rice, and black-eyed peas. Cover and bake until casserole is heated through, about 45 minutes.

Calories Per Serving: 151
Fat: 1 g
Cholesterol: 0 mg
Protein: 7 g

Carbohydrates: 30 g
Dietary Fiber: 5 g
Sodium: 47 mg

❈ *Cannellini Beans with Cabbage* ❈

PREPARATION TIME: *15 minutes* ▪ COOKING TIME: *15 minutes* ▪
YIELD: *4 servings*

5 cups shredded cabbage
1 cup low-sodium tomato sauce
1 tablespoon lemon juice
1 teaspoon vinegar
1 tablespoon orange juice concentrate
2 tablespoons honey

1 teaspoon Dijon mustard
2 cloves garlic, minced
½ cup seedless raisins
¼ teaspoon ground black pepper
2 cups low-sodium canned cannellini
*   beans, rinsed and drained*

1. Combine cabbage, tomato sauce, lemon juice, vinegar, orange juice concentrate, honey, mustard, garlic, raisins, and black pepper in a large saucepan. Bring to a simmer, cover, and cook for 10 minutes.
2. Add beans and continue to simmer until all ingredients are heated through, about 5 minutes.

Calories Per Serving: 298
Fat: 1 g
Cholesterol: 0 mg
Protein: 13 g

Carbohydrates: 65 g
Dietary Fiber: 12 g
Sodium: 102 mg

❋ *White Beans and Mushrooms in* ❋ *Wine Sauce with Couscous*

PREPARATION TIME: *15 minutes plus 5 minutes standing time* •
COOKING TIME: *20 minutes* • YIELD: *6 servings*

¼ cup low-sodium nonfat chicken broth
6 cups sliced mushrooms
1 medium onion, chopped
2 medium red bell peppers, cored and chopped
1 medium carrot, scraped and sliced
2 cloves garlic, minced
2 cups low-sodium canned tomatoes, chopped, juice reserved

2 cups low-sodium canned Great Northern beans, rinsed and drained
1 tablespoon lemon juice
1 teaspoon paprika
¼ teaspoon dried thyme
½ teaspoon ground black pepper
½ cup dry white wine
1¼ cups boiling water
2¼ cups uncooked couscous

1. Heat broth in a large saucepan. Add mushrooms, onion, bell peppers, carrot, and garlic, and sauté until onion begins to soften, about 5 minutes.
2. Stir in tomatoes with juice, beans, lemon juice, paprika, thyme, black pepper, and wine. Bring to a boil, reduce heat, cover, and simmer for 15 minutes.
3. In a separate bowl, pour boiling water over couscous, cover, and allow to stand for 5 minutes.
4. Divide couscous among individual plates, top with vegetables, and serve.

Calories Per Serving: 394
Fat: 1 g
Cholesterol: 0 mg
Protein: 17 g

Carbohydrates: 79 g
Dietary Fiber: 17 g
Sodium: 38 mg

❋ *Bean-Pineapple Jumble* ❋

PREPARATION TIME: *20 minutes* • COOKING TIME: *35 minutes* •
YIELD: *6 servings*

2 tablespoons low-sodium nonfat chicken broth
2 cups juice-packed canned pineapple chunks, drained

1 medium onion, chopped
4 cloves garlic, minced
1 tablespoon brown sugar
4 medium tomatoes, chopped

2 tablespoons lime juice
1½ teaspoons dried oregano
1 teaspoon grated lime peel
¼ teaspoon cayenne pepper
¼ teaspoon ground black pepper

2 cups low-sodium canned Great
  Northern beans, rinsed and
  drained
2 cups low-sodium canned kidney
  beans, rinsed and drained
2 cups cooked rice

1. Combine broth, pineapple chunks, onion, garlic, and brown sugar in a large saucepan. Cook, stirring frequently, until mixture is dry and onion begins to brown, about 15 minutes.
2. Add tomatoes, lime juice, oregano, lime peel, cayenne pepper, black pepper, and beans. Bring to a simmer and cook, stirring frequently, for 15 minutes.
3 Stir in rice and continue to simmer until rice is heated through, about 5 minutes.

Calories Per Serving: 297
Fat: 1 g
Cholesterol: 0 mg
Protein: 13 g

Carbohydrates: 61 g
Dietary Fiber: 10 g
Sodium: 17 mg

❄ *Cannellini Beans and Green Peas* ❄

PREPARATION TIME: *20 minutes* • COOKING TIME: *30 minutes* •
YIELD: *6 servings*

¼ cup low-sodium nonfat chicken
  broth
½ cup diced celery
⅓ cup chopped onion
2½ cups low-sodium canned tomatoes, chopped and drained
½ teaspoon dried basil

½ teaspoon dried rosemary
½ teaspoon ground black pepper
2 cups fresh, thawed frozen, or
  drained canned green peas
1 cup low-sodium canned cannellini
  beans, rinsed and drained
3 cups cooked rice

1. Heat broth in a large saucepan. Add celery and onion, and sauté until onion begins to soften, about 3 minutes. Stir in tomatoes, basil, rosemary, and black pepper. Cover and simmer, stirring occasionally, for 20 minutes.
2. Add peas and beans, cover, and continue to cook until all ingredients are heated through, about 5 minutes.
3. Serve over rice.

Calories Per Serving: 227 Carbohydrates: 47 g
Fat: 1 g Dietary Fiber: 5 g
Cholesterol: 0 mg Sodium: 39 mg
Protein: 9 g

❋ White Beans and Spinach ❋

PREPARATION TIME: *20 minutes* • COOKING TIME: *27 minutes* •
YIELD: *4 servings*

¼ cup low-sodium vegetable broth   *2 medium tomatoes, chopped*
1 medium onion, chopped   *3 cups low-sodium canned Great*
3 cloves garlic, minced   *   Northern beans, rinsed and*
¼ teaspoon cayenne pepper   *   drained*
1 teaspoon paprika   *¼ teaspoon ground black pepper*
1 teaspoon dried rosemary   *6 cups chopped fresh spinach*
¼ cup chopped fresh parsley

1. Heat broth in a large saucepan. Add onion, garlic, cayenne pepper, paprika, rosemary, and 2 tablespoons parsley. Sauté until onion begins to soften, about 3 minutes.
2. Add tomatoes, beans, and black pepper. Reduce heat and simmer for 15 minutes. Stir in spinach and continue to simmer until spinach is just tender, about 7 minutes. Serve topped with remaining parsley.

Calories Per Serving: 231 Carbohydrates: 40 g
Fat: 1 g Dietary Fiber: 12 g
Cholesterol: 0 mg Sodium: 105 mg
Protein: 15 g

❋ Cannellini Beans with Garlic ❋

PREPARATION TIME: *20 minutes* • COOKING TIME: *39 minutes* •
YIELD: *4 servings*

1 cup low-sodium nonfat chicken   *4 cups low-sodium canned cannellini*
*   broth*   *   beans, rinsed and drained*
1 small onion, chopped   *¼ teaspoon ground black pepper*
3 cloves garlic, minced   *¼ cup chopped fresh parsley*
2 medium stalks celery, chopped

1. Heat ¼ cup broth in a large saucepan. Add onion, garlic, and celery, and sauté until onion begins to soften, about 4 minutes.
2. Add remaining broth, beans, and black pepper. Bring to a boil, reduce heat, cover, and simmer until vegetables are just tender, about 30 minutes.
3. Transfer to individual bowls, garnish with parsley, and serve.

Calories Per Serving: 206
Fat: 1 g
Cholesterol: 0 mg
Protein: 14 g

Carbohydrates: 37 g
Dietary Fiber: 11 g
Sodium: 52 mg

❊ *Stovetop Maple-Mustard Beans* ❊

PREPARATION TIME: *15 minutes* • COOKING TIME: *29 minutes* •
YIELD: *6 servings*

5 cups low-sodium canned Great Northern beans, rinsed and drained
1 cup low-sodium nonfat chicken broth

1 medium onion, chopped
¼ cup maple syrup
2 tablespoons spicy brown mustard
2 tablespoons low-sodium ketchup
1 tablespoon dry mustard

1. Combine all ingredients in a large saucepan. Bring to a boil, reduce heat, cover, and simmer until onion is just tender, about 25 minutes.
2. Drain any excess liquid and serve.

Calories Per Serving: 239
Fat: 1 g
Cholesterol: 0 mg
Protein: 13 g

Carbohydrates: 46 g
Dietary Fiber: 11 g
Sodium: 75 mg

❊ *Great Northern Beans and Eggplant Bake* ❊

PREPARATION TIME: *20 minutes* • COOKING TIME: *53 minutes* •
YIELD: *6 servings*

¼ cup low-sodium nonfat chicken
   broth
2 medium onions, sliced
3 cloves garlic, minced
3 cups diced eggplant
3 cups low-sodium canned tomatoes,
   drained and chopped

¼ teaspoon dried thyme
½ teaspoon ground black pepper
2 cups low-sodium canned Great
   Northern beans, rinsed and
   drained
½ cup bread crumbs
2 tablespoons grated nonfat Parmesan

1. Preheat oven to 350 degrees.
2. Heat broth in a flameproof 3-quart casserole. Add onions and garlic, and sauté until onions begin to soften, about 3 minutes. Add eggplant and continue to sauté for 6 more minutes.
3. Stir in tomatoes, thyme, and ¼ teaspoon black pepper. Bring to a boil, reduce heat, and simmer, stirring frequently, for 10 minutes.
4. Add beans, cover, and bake for 25 minutes. In a separate bowl, combine bread crumbs, Parmesan, and remaining black pepper, and sprinkle over the top of the casserole. Return to the oven for 3 minutes.

Calories Per Serving: 162
Fat: 1 g
Cholesterol: 2 mg
Protein: 9 g

Carbohydrates: 31 g
Dietary Fiber: 6 g
Sodium: 86 mg

❋ Great Northern Beans with Zucchini, ❋ Sweet Potatoes, and Kale

PREPARATION TIME: 20 minutes plus 10 minutes standing time •
COOKING TIME: 32 minutes • YIELD: 6 servings

¼ cup low-sodium nonfat chicken
   broth
1 medium onion, diced
1 medium green bell pepper, cored
   and diced
2 cups diced zucchini
1 cup sliced mushrooms
1 jalapeño pepper, seeded and minced
3 cups water

1½ cups uncooked white rice
2 cups diced sweet potatoes
2 tablespoons chopped fresh parsley
¼ teaspoon dried thyme
½ teaspoon ground allspice
2 cups chopped fresh kale
2 cups low-sodium canned Great
   Northern beans, rinsed and
   drained

1. Heat broth in a large saucepan. Add onion, bell pepper, zucchini, mushrooms, and jalapeño pepper. Sauté until peppers begin to soften, about 5 minutes.

2. Add water, rice, sweet potatoes, parsley, thyme, and allspice. Bring to a boil, reduce heat, cover, and simmer for 15 minutes. Stir in kale and beans, and continue to simmer until kale is wilted and beans are heated through, about 6 minutes.
3. Remove from heat, stir gently, and allow to stand for 10 minutes before serving.

Calories Per Serving: 296
Fat: 1 g
Cholesterol: 0 mg
Protein: 9 g

Carbohydrates: 64 g
Dietary Fiber: 7 g
Sodium: 86 mg

❋ *Orange-Dijon Cannellini Beans* ❋

PREPARATION TIME: *20 minutes* • COOKING TIME: *35 minutes* •
YIELD: *4 servings*

2 cups low-sodium nonfat chicken broth
6 cups low-sodium canned cannellini beans, rinsed and drained
1 medium onion, chopped
½ cup sugarless all-fruit orange marmalade

⅓ cup brown sugar
1 tablespoon Dijon mustard
1 teaspoon dried rosemary
¼ teaspoon ground black pepper

1. Combine all ingredients in a large saucepan.
2. Bring to a simmer, cover, and cook for 30 minutes before serving.

Calories Per Serving: 529
Fat: 2 g
Cholesterol: 0 mg
Protein: 27 g

Carbohydrates: 107 g
Dietary Fiber: 21 g
Sodium: 206 mg

❋ *Navy Beans with Fruit and Vegetables* ❋

PREPARATION TIME: *25 minutes* • COOKING TIME: *40 minutes* •
YIELD: *6 servings*

2 cups low-sodium canned navy
beans, rinsed and drained
2½ cups low-sodium nonfat chicken
broth
2 large potatoes, sliced
2 cups chopped fresh or thawed
frozen green beans (2-inch
lengths)

3 medium apples, peeled, cored, and
sliced
1 medium pear, peeled, cored, and
sliced
2 medium carrots, scraped and sliced
1 tablespoon lemon juice
¼ teaspoon ground black pepper
1 cup fresh, drained canned, or
thawed frozen corn kernels

1. Combine navy beans, broth, potatoes, green beans, apples, pear, carrots, lemon juice, and black pepper in a large pot. Bring to a boil, reduce heat, and simmer until potatoes are tender, about 30 minutes.
2. Add corn and simmer for 5 more minutes before serving.

Calories Per Serving: 287
Fat: 1 g
Cholesterol: 0 mg
Protein: 12 g

Carbohydrates: 62 g
Dietary Fiber: 12 g
Sodium: 97 mg

❋ White Beans and Apples ❋

PREPARATION TIME: 15 minutes • COOKING TIME: 45 minutes •
YIELD: 4 servings

Olive oil cooking spray
4 cups low-sodium canned Great
Northern beans, rinsed and
drained
3 medium apples, peeled, cored, and
diced

1 tablespoon brown sugar
1 teaspoon ground cinnamon
2 tablespoons dry red wine
½ teaspoon ground black pepper
1 cup apple juice

1. Preheat oven to 350 degrees. Lightly coat a 2-quart casserole with olive oil cooking spray.
2. Combine beans, apples, brown sugar, cinnamon, wine, and black pepper in the prepared casserole. Pour apple juice over the mixture, cover, and bake for 45 minutes.

Calories Per Serving: 334
Fat: 1 g
Cholesterol: 0 mg
Protein: 15 g

Carbohydrates: 68 g
Dietary Fiber: 14 g
Sodium: 18 mg

❋ Green Chile and Pinto Bean Casserole ❋

PREPARATION TIME: *20 minutes* • COOKING TIME: *1 hour 16 minutes* •
YIELD: *6 servings*

2 cups low-sodium canned tomatoes, chopped, ¼ cup juice reserved
1 medium onion, chopped
2 cups uncooked white rice
3½ cups water
2 cups low-sodium canned pinto beans, rinsed and drained
2 cups cooked or low-sodium canned chickpeas, rinsed and drained

½ cup canned mild green chiles, chopped and drained
1 teaspoon dried oregano
1 teaspoon dried basil
½ teaspoon ground black pepper
1 cup fresh or thawed frozen green peas
1 cup fresh or thawed frozen corn kernels

1. Preheat oven to 375 degrees.
2. Heat reserved tomato juice in a flameproof 3-quart casserole. Add onion and sauté until it begins to soften, about 3 minutes. Add rice and stir until rice begins to parch, about 2 more minutes.
3. Stir in water, pinto beans, chickpeas, tomatoes, chiles, oregano, basil, and black pepper. Bring to a boil, cover, and bake until rice is just tender, about 50 minutes. Stir in peas and corn, and return to the oven until all ingredients are heated through, about 15 minutes.

Calories Per Serving: 457
Fat: 2 g
Cholesterol: 0 mg
Protein: 17 g

Carbohydrates: 95 g
Dietary Fiber: 11 g
Sodium: 272 mg

❋ Simple Beans and Rice ❋

PREPARATION TIME: *10 minutes* • COOKING TIME: *14 minutes* •
YIELD: *4 servings*

¼ cup low-sodium nonfat chicken broth
1 medium stalk celery, with leaves, chopped
1 cup chopped onion

2 cloves garlic, minced
3 cups low-sodium canned red kidney beans, liquid reserved
½ teaspoon hot pepper sauce
2 cups cooked rice

1. Heat broth in a large saucepan. Add celery, onion, and garlic, and sauté until onion begins to soften, about 5 minutes.
2. Add beans with liquid. Stir in hot pepper sauce, reduce heat, cover, and simmer until beans are heated through, about 7 minutes. Drain any excess liquid.
3. Serve beans over rice on individual plates.

Calories Per Serving: 312
Fat: 1 g
Cholesterol: 0 mg
Protein: 14 g

Carbohydrates: 62 g
Dietary Fiber: 10 g
Sodium: 21 mg

VEGETABLE MAIN DISHES

Asparagus and Orzo Casserole with Rice • Lima Beans and
Zucchini • Lima Beans, Eggplant, and Mushrooms with Couscous
• Chopped Broccoli with Tomatoes and Pasta Shells • Broccoli
with Mushrooms in Tofu Sauce • Broccoli and Parsnips • Carrots
and Leeks with Broccoli • Carrots and Apples • Tropical
Cabbage • Cabbage-Mushroom Casserole • Cabbage and
Carrots with Couscous • Sweet and Tangy Carrots • Spiced
Cauliflower, Potatoes, Carrots, and Green Beans • Curried
Cauliflower with Tomatoes and Green Peas • Curried Cauliflower
and Broccoli • Corn, Shiitake Mushrooms, and Green Beans •
Corn, Lima Beans, and Bell Peppers • Cucumbers and Tomatoes •
Eggplant del Rio • Eggplant and Tomatoes • Eggplant and Red
Peppers • Eggplant, Yellow Pepper, and Mushrooms • Baked
Eggplant, Green Beans, and Zucchini • Lemon-Dilled Eggplant and
Summer Squash • Shiitake-and-Corn-Stuffed Eggplant •
Jalapeño, Eggplant, and Couscous • Summer Vegetable
Ratatouille • Baked Eggplant • Curried Eggplant and Potatoes •
Spiced Eggplant and Potatoes • Island Eggplant • Tomato-
Broccoli Pasta • Mushroom Pilaf • Mushroom-Vegetable Curry •
Spicy Peas and Potatoes in Tomato Sauce • Red Pepper–Rice

Casserole ▪ Shiitake-and-Corn-Stuffed Peppers ▪ Red Bell
Peppers and Pineapple with Tofu ▪ Tofu, Broccoli, and
Mushroom–Stuffed Red Peppers ▪ Corn-Stuffed Green Peppers ▪
Tofu-Stuffed Potatoes ▪ New Potatoes and Green Beans ▪
Potatoes, Apples, and Onions ▪ Curried Sweet Potatoes and Green
Peas ▪ Chili Potatoes with Yogurt ▪ Chopped Potatoes with
Tomatoes and Green Chiles ▪ Curried Potatoes and Zucchini ▪
Spicy Potatoes and Broccoli ▪ Curried Potatoes, Cauliflower, and
Peas with Yogurt ▪ Potatoes, Tomatoes, and Green Beans over
Couscous ▪ Microwaved Sweet Potatoes and Fruit ▪ Sweet
Potatoes, Mushrooms, and Acorn Squash ▪ Spinach and Tomatoes
with Capellini ▪ Fruit-Stuffed Acorn Squash ▪ Stirfried Spinach
and Rice ▪ Quick Couscous-Stuffed Tomatoes ▪ Spinach and
Potatoes ▪ Zucchini with Tomatoes ▪ Zucchini, Corn, and
Mushroom Casserole ▪ Zucchini and Yellow Squash Sauté ▪
Zucchini-Rice Casserole with Green Chiles ▪ Curried Summer
Squash, Broccoli, and Rice ▪ Quick Microwave Ratatouille ▪
Zucchini and Pattypan Casserole ▪ Pattypan Squash and
Tomatoes ▪ Microwaved Spaghetti Squash ▪ Butternut Squash
and Apples in Red Wine ▪ Mixed Curried Vegetables ▪ Mixed
Fruit and Vegetable Curry ▪ Easy Fruit Curry

❋ Asparagus and Orzo Casserole with Rice ❋

PREPARATION TIME: *20 minutes* • COOKING TIME: *40 minutes* •
YIELD: *6 servings*

⅔ *cup uncooked wild rice*
3½ *cups low-sodium nonfat chicken*
   broth
1 *medium onion, chopped*
1 *clove garlic, minced*
1 *teaspoon dried thyme*
1 *teaspoon dried marjoram*

¼ *teaspoon ground black pepper*
½ *cup uncooked orzo*
2 *cups chopped fresh asparagus spears*
   (1-inch lengths)
½ *cup nonfat ricotta*
¼ *cup minced red bell pepper*
¼ *cup grated nonfat Parmesan*

1. Combine rice, broth, onion, garlic, thyme, marjoram, and black pepper in
   a large saucepan. Bring to a boil, reduce heat, cover, and simmer for 20
   minutes.
2. Stir in orzo. Return to a boil, reduce heat, cover, and simmer for 10 minutes. Add asparagus and simmer for 5 more minutes.
3. Drain any excess liquid and stir in ricotta.
4. Serve topped with minced bell pepper and Parmesan.

Calories Per Serving: 233
Fat: 1 g
Cholesterol: 4 mg
Protein: 16 g

Carbohydrates: 44 g
Dietary Fiber: 2 g
Sodium: 222 mg

❋ Lima Beans and Zucchini ❋

PREPARATION TIME: *15 minutes* • COOKING TIME: *17 minutes* •
YIELD: *6 servings*

¼ *cup low-sodium vegetable broth*
1 *medium onion, sliced*
2 *cloves garlic, minced*
2 *cups chopped zucchini*
1 *teaspoon dried thyme*

4 *cups low-sodium canned lima*
   beans, liquid reserved
3 *cups cooked rice*
1 *medium tomato, finely chopped*
3 *tablespoons grated nonfat Parmesan*

1. Heat broth in a large saucepan. Add onion, garlic, zucchini, and thyme.
   Sauté until onion and zucchini begin to soften, about 5 minutes.
2. Add beans with liquid. Bring to a boil, reduce heat, and simmer until
   heated through, about 7 minutes.
3. Serve over rice, topped with chopped tomato and Parmesan.

Calories Per Serving: 265

Carbohydrates: 54 g

Fat: 1 g

Dietary Fiber: 7 g

Cholesterol: 3 mg

Sodium: 72 mg

Protein: 11 g

❋ Lima Beans, Eggplant, and Mushrooms ❋ with Couscous

PREPARATION TIME: *20 minutes* • COOKING TIME: *43 minutes plus 5 minutes standing time* • YIELD: *6 servings*

1¼ cups low-sodium nonfat chicken broth

1 medium onion, chopped

2 medium red bell peppers, cored and chopped

2 cloves garlic, minced

3 cups diced eggplant

1 cup sliced mushrooms

1 cup diced potato

1½ cups thawed frozen lima beans

2 cups low-sodium canned tomatoes, chopped, juice reserved

¼ cup low-sodium tomato sauce

1 teaspoon cider vinegar

1 teaspoon paprika

1 teaspoon dried oregano

½ teaspoon ground black pepper

1¼ cups boiling water

2¼ cups uncooked couscous

1. Heat ¼ cup broth in a large saucepan. Add onion, bell peppers, and garlic, and sauté until onion begins to soften, about 4 minutes. Add eggplant and sauté for 4 more minutes.

2. Add remaining broth, mushrooms, potato, lima beans, tomatoes with juice, tomato sauce, vinegar, paprika, oregano, and black pepper. Bring to a boil, reduce heat, cover, and simmer, stirring frequently, until vegetables are just tender, about 30 minutes.

3. In a separate bowl, pour boiling water over couscous, cover, and allow to stand for 5 minutes.

4. Serve vegetables over couscous.

Calories Per Serving: 394

Carbohydrates: 81 g

Fat: 1 g

Dietary Fiber: 16 g

Cholesterol: 0 mg

Sodium: 100 mg

Protein: 15 g

❋ *Chopped Broccoli with Tomatoes* ❋ *and Pasta Shells*

PREPARATION TIME: *15 minutes* • COOKING TIME: *24 minutes* •
YIELD: *4 servings*

¼ cup low-sodium nonfat chicken
  broth
1 medium onion, chopped
2 cloves garlic, minced
2 tablespoons minced fresh parsley
1 tablespoon minced fresh basil
1 teaspoon sugar
¼ teaspoon cayenne pepper

3 tablespoons low-sodium tomato
  paste
3 cups low-sodium canned tomatoes,
  crushed, juice reserved
4 large pitted ripe olives, sliced
3 cups chopped broccoli
2 cups cooked pasta shells
2 tablespoons grated nonfat Parmesan

1. Heat broth in a large saucepan. Add onion and garlic, and sauté until onion begins to soften, about 3 minutes.
2. Stir in parsley, basil, sugar, cayenne pepper, tomato paste, tomatoes with juice, and olives. Bring to a boil, reduce heat, cover, and simmer for 10 minutes. Stir in broccoli and shells, cover, and simmer until broccoli begins to soften and pasta is heated through, about 5 minutes.
3. Serve topped with Parmesan.

Calories Per Serving: 177
Fat: 2 g
Cholesterol: 3 mg
Protein: 9 g

Carbohydrates: 35 g
Dietary Fiber: 6 g
Sodium: 89 mg

❋ *Broccoli with Mushrooms in Tofu Sauce* ❋

PREPARATION TIME: *20 minutes* • COOKING TIME: *50 minutes* •
YIELD: *4 servings*

1 cup diced potato
1 medium carrot, scraped and sliced
1 medium onion, chopped
1¾ cups low-sodium vegetable broth
½ cup crumbled firm tofu, drained
1 tablespoon lemon juice

2 cloves garlic, minced
2 cups chopped broccoli
1 cup uncooked white rice
1 cup sliced mushrooms
½ teaspoon ground black pepper

1. Preheat oven to 350 degrees.
2. Combine potato, carrot, onion, and 1 cup broth in a flameproof 2-quart casserole. Cover and simmer for 6 minutes.
3. Transfer to a blender or food processor. Add tofu, lemon juice, and garlic, and puree. Return puree to the casserole, and add remaining ingredients. Stir well and bake for 40 minutes.

Calories Per Serving: 310
Fat: 1 g
Cholesterol: 0 mg
Protein: 10 g

Carbohydrates: 66 g
Dietary Fiber: 4 g
Sodium: 57 mg

❋ Broccoli and Parsnips ❋

PREPARATION TIME: *15 minutes* • COOKING TIME: *18 minutes* •
YIELD: *4 servings*

¾ cup low-sodium nonfat chicken
  broth
½ teaspoon ground cumin
4 medium parsnips, peeled and
  chopped
4 cups chopped broccoli

⅛ teaspoon cayenne pepper
¾ teaspoon ground turmeric
1 teaspoon ground coriander
¼ teaspoon ground black pepper
1 teaspoon garam masala

1. Heat ¼ cup broth in a large saucepan. Add cumin, parsnips, broccoli, cayenne pepper, turmeric, coriander, and black pepper. Sauté for 4 minutes.
2. Add remaining broth, cover, and simmer until vegetables are just tender, about 10 minutes.
3. Stir in garam masala and serve.

Calories Per Serving: 131
Fat: 1 g
Cholesterol: 0 mg
Protein: 6 g

Carbohydrates: 28 g
Dietary Fiber: 9 g
Sodium: 89 mg

❋ Carrots and Leeks with Broccoli ❋

PREPARATION TIME: *15 minutes* • COOKING TIME: *51 minutes* •
YIELD: *4 servings*

2 tablespoons low-sodium nonfat
   chicken broth
4 medium leeks (white parts only),
   sliced
1 clove garlic, minced
1 cup uncooked brown rice
3 medium carrots, scraped and sliced

2 cups chopped fresh broccoli
2 cups water
2 tablespoons low-sodium tomato
   paste
¼ cup chopped fresh parsley
1 tablespoon lemon juice
¼ teaspoon ground black pepper

1. Heat broth in a large saucepan. Add leeks and garlic, and sauté until leeks begin to soften, about 4 minutes. Add rice and sauté for another minute.
2. Add remaining ingredients. Bring to a boil, reduce heat, cover, and simmer until the liquid is absorbed, about 40 minutes.

Calories Per Serving: 282
Fat: 2 g
Cholesterol: 0 mg
Protein: 6 g

Carbohydrates: 62 g
Dietary Fiber: 5 g
Sodium: 75 mg

❋ *Carrots and Apples* ❋

PREPARATION TIME: *15 minutes*   ▪   COOKING TIME: *45 minutes*   ▪
YIELD: *6 servings*

Olive oil cooking spray
6 medium apples, peeled, cored, and
   thinly sliced
3 cups scraped and thinly sliced carrots

⅓ cup brown sugar
2 tablespoons all-purpose flour
¾ cup orange juice

1. Preheat oven to 350 degrees. Lightly coat a 3-quart casserole with olive oil cooking spray.
2. Arrange half the apple slices in a layer on the bottom of the prepared casserole and add a layer of half the carrots. In a separate bowl, combine brown sugar and flour, and sprinkle half the mixture over the carrots.
3. Cover with remaining apple slices and a second layer of carrots. Top with the remaining brown sugar–flour mixture. Pour orange juice over all and bake for 45 minutes.

Calories Per Serving: 249
Fat: 1 g
Cholesterol: 0 mg
Protein: 2 g

Carbohydrates: 63 g
Dietary Fiber: 6 g
Sodium: 36 mg

❊ *Tropical Cabbage* ❊

PREPARATION TIME: *20 minutes* • COOKING TIME: *33 minutes* • YIELD: *4 servings*

8 cups shredded cabbage	1 cup water
½ cup seedless raisins	2 tablespoons lime juice
1 cup diced pineapple	½ teaspoon ground black pepper
2 medium onions, diced	

1. Combine all ingredients in a large saucepan. Bring to a boil, reduce heat, and simmer until cabbage is just tender, about 30 minutes.
2. Drain any excess liquid and serve.

Calories Per Serving: 135	Carbohydrates: 33 g
Fat: 1 g	Dietary Fiber: 5 g
Cholesterol: 0 mg	Sodium: 38 mg
Protein: 4 g	

❊ *Cabbage-Mushroom Casserole* ❊

PREPARATION TIME: *20 minutes* • COOKING TIME: *60 minutes* •
YIELD: *4 servings*

Olive oil cooking spray	2 cups sliced mushrooms
2 cups cooked rice	2 cloves garlic, minced
6 cups shredded cabbage	½ teaspoon dried oregano
1 cup low-sodium tomato sauce	½ teaspoon dried basil
1 cup water	½ teaspoon ground black pepper
1 medium onion, minced	¼ cup chopped fresh parsley

1. Preheat oven to 350 degrees. Lightly coat a 3-quart casserole with olive oil cooking spray.
2. Place 1 cup rice in a layer on the bottom of the prepared casserole. Spread half the cabbage over rice.
3. Combine tomato sauce, water, onion, mushrooms, garlic, oregano, basil, and black pepper. Spoon half of this mixture over cabbage.
4. Repeat these layers with remaining rice, cabbage, and tomato sauce mixture. Bake for 60 minutes.
5. Serve topped with parsley.

Calories Per Serving: 238

Carbohydrates: 52 g

Fat: 1 g

Dietary Fiber: 7 g

Cholesterol: 0 mg

Sodium: 78 mg

Protein: 8 g

❊ *Cabbage and Carrots with Couscous* ❊

PREPARATION TIME: *15 minutes plus 5 minutes standing time* •
COOKING TIME: *20 minutes* • YIELD: *4 servings*

½ cup low-sodium tomato juice
1 tablespoon coriander seeds
½ teaspoon cumin seeds
¼ teaspoon cayenne pepper
4 cups chopped cabbage
2 medium carrots, scraped and sliced

1 medium tomato, chopped
¼ teaspoon ground turmeric
½ cup canned mild green chiles,
   chopped and drained
2 cups boiling water
1 cup uncooked couscous

1. Heat ¼ cup tomato juice in a large saucepan. Add coriander, cumin, and cayenne pepper, and sauté for 1 minute. Stir in remaining juice, cabbage, carrots, tomato, turmeric, and chiles. Reduce heat, cover, and simmer until vegetables are just tender, about 12 minutes.
2. In a separate bowl, pour boiling water over couscous, cover, and allow to stand for 5 minutes.
3. Serve vegetables over couscous.

Calories Per Serving: 270

Carbohydrates: 57 g

Fat: 1 g

Dietary Fiber: 13 g

Cholesterol: 0 mg

Sodium: 68 mg

Protein: 10 g

❊ *Sweet and Tangy Carrots* ❊

PREPARATION TIME: *15 minutes* • COOKING TIME: *19 minutes* •
YIELD: *4 servings*

½ cup low-sodium vegetable broth
2 pounds carrots, scraped and grated
1 tablespoon brown sugar

½ cup orange juice
¼ teaspoon ground black pepper

1. Combine broth, carrots, and brown sugar in a saucepan. Bring to a boil, reduce heat, cover, and simmer, stirring occasionally, for 10 minutes.
2. Stir in orange juice and black pepper, and simmer, uncovered, until carrots are tender-crisp, about 5 minutes.

Calories Per Serving: 126	Carbohydrates: 30 g
Fat: 1 g	Dietary Fiber: 6 g
Cholesterol: 0 mg	Sodium: 84 mg
Protein: 3 g	

�֍ Spiced Cauliflower, Potatoes, Carrots, �֍ and Green Beans

PREPARATION TIME: *25 minutes* • COOKING TIME: *32 minutes* •
YIELD: *8 servings*

¼ cup low-sodium nonfat chicken
  broth
2 medium onions, quartered and
  thinly sliced
4 cloves garlic, minced
2 tablespoons minced fresh gingerroot
2 jalapeño peppers, seeded and
  minced
1½ teaspoons ground cumin
¾ teaspoon ground coriander
¾ teaspoon ground cardamom

½ teaspoon ground cinnamon
¼ teaspoon ground cloves
1¼ cups nonfat plain yogurt
5 cups diced boiling potatoes
2 medium carrots, scraped and sliced
4 cups chopped cauliflower
¼ cup chopped fresh or thawed frozen
  green beans (1-inch lengths)
1½ cups water
3 cups cooked rice

1. Heat broth in a large saucepan. Add onions and sauté until they begin to soften, about 4 minutes.
2. Add garlic, gingerroot, and jalapeño peppers, and sauté for 1 more minute. Stir in cumin, coriander, cardamom, cinnamon, cloves, and half the yogurt. Stir for 5 minutes.
3. Add remaining yogurt, potatoes, carrots, cauliflower, green beans, and water. Partially cover and simmer, stirring several times, until vegetables are just tender, about 20 minutes.
4. Serve over rice on individual plates.

Calories Per Serving: 198	Carbohydrates: 43 g
Fat: 0 g	Dietary Fiber: 3 g
Cholesterol: 1 mg	Sodium: 170 mg
Protein: 7 g	

❋ *Curried Cauliflower with Tomatoes* ❋ *and Green Peas*

PREPARATION TIME: *20 minutes* • COOKING TIME: *19 minutes* •
YIELD: *4 servings*

¾ *cup low-sodium vegetable broth*
1 medium onion, chopped
4 cloves garlic, minced
2 teaspoons minced fresh gingerroot
½ *teaspoon dry mustard*
1 teaspoon ground cumin
1 tablespoon curry powder

½ *teaspoon cayenne pepper*
4 cups chopped cauliflower
2 cups low-sodium canned tomatoes, drained and crushed
1 cup fresh or thawed frozen green peas
2 cups cooked rice

1. Heat ¼ cup broth in a large saucepan. Add onion, garlic, and gingerroot, and sauté until onion begins to soften, about 3 minutes. Stir in dry mustard, cumin, curry powder, and cayenne pepper, and sauté for 1 more minute.
2. Add remaining broth, cauliflower, and tomatoes. Cover and simmer for 8 minutes. Add peas and continue to simmer until peas and cauliflower are tender, about 5 more minutes.
3. Serve over rice.

Calories Per Serving: 232
Fat: 1 g
Cholesterol: 0 mg
Protein: 8 g

Carbohydrates: 48 g
Dietary Fiber: 3 g
Sodium: 57 mg

❋ *Curried Cauliflower and Broccoli* ❋

PREPARATION TIME: *20 minutes* • COOKING TIME: *23 minutes* •
YIELD: *4 servings*

¾ *cup low-sodium nonfat chicken broth*
1 medium onion, chopped
2 cloves garlic, minced
3 cups chopped cauliflower
3 cups chopped broccoli

1 cup low-sodium canned tomatoes, chopped, juice reserved
2 teaspoons curry powder
½ *teaspoon ground turmeric*
½ *teaspoon ground black pepper*
2 cups cooked rice

1. Heat ¼ cup broth in a large saucepan. Add onion and garlic, and sauté until onion begins to soften, about 3 minutes.
2. Add remaining broth, cauliflower, broccoli, tomatoes with juice, curry powder, turmeric, and black pepper. Bring to a boil, reduce heat, cover, and simmer until potatoes are tender, about 15 minutes.
3. Divide rice among individual plates, top with curry mixture, and serve.

Calories Per Serving: 190	Carbohydrates: 40 g
Fat: 1 g	Dietary Fiber: 3 g
Cholesterol: 0 mg	Sodium: 105 mg
Protein: 7 g	

❋ Corn, Shiitake Mushrooms, ❋ and Green Beans

PREPARATION TIME: *20 minutes* • COOKING TIME: *26 minutes* •
YIELD: *4 servings*

½ cup low-sodium nonfat chicken
broth
1 cup minced shiitake mushrooms
1 cup chopped onion
2 teaspoons chili powder

2 medium tomatoes, chopped
2 cups fresh, drained canned, or
thawed frozen corn kernels
2 cups chopped fresh or thawed frozen
green beans (2-inch lengths)

1. Heat broth in a large skillet. Add mushrooms, onion, and chili powder, and sauté until onion begins to soften, about 4 minutes.
2. Stir in remaining ingredients. Reduce heat and simmer until beans are just tender, about 20 minutes.

Calories Per Serving: 165	Carbohydrates: 39 g
Fat: 1 g	Dietary Fiber: 6 g
Cholesterol: 0 mg	Sodium: 50 mg
Protein: 7 g	

❋ Corn, Lima Beans, and Bell Peppers ❋

PREPARATION TIME: *15 minutes* • COOKING TIME: *22 minutes* • YIELD: *6 servings*

4 cups fresh or thawed frozen corn
   kernels
3 cups fresh or thawed frozen lima
   beans
1½ cups water

5 scallions, sliced
1 medium green bell pepper, cored
   and diced
1 medium red bell pepper, cored and
   diced

1. Combine corn, lima beans, and water in a large saucepan. Bring to a boil, reduce heat, cover, and simmer for 10 minutes.
2. Stir in scallions and bell peppers, and continue to simmer until beans are done and peppers are tender-crisp, about 8 minutes.
3. Drain any excess liquid and serve.

Calories Per Serving: 202
Fat: 0 g
Cholesterol: 0 mg
Protein: 9 g

Carbohydrates: 44 g
Dietary Fiber: 9 g
Sodium: 22 mg

❈ *Cucumbers and Tomatoes* ❈

PREPARATION TIME: *20 minutes* • COOKING TIME: *41 minutes* • YIELD: *4 servings*

¼ cup low-sodium nonfat chicken
   broth
1 medium onion, chopped
3 medium tomatoes, chopped
½ teaspoon ground black pepper

½ teaspoon sugar
4 medium cucumbers, peeled, halved
   lengthwise, and thickly sliced
1 cup cooked rice

1. Heat broth in a large saucepan. Sauté onion until it begins to soften, about 3 minutes.
2. Add tomatoes, black pepper, sugar, and cucumbers. Bring to a boil, reduce heat, and simmer for 30 minutes. Add rice and heat through, about 3 minutes.

Calories Per Serving: 130
Fat: 1 g
Cholesterol: 0 mg
Protein: 5 g

Carbohydrates: 28 g
Dietary Fiber: 2 g
Sodium: 26 mg

❋ *Eggplant del Rio* ❋

PREPARATION TIME: *15 minutes* • COOKING TIME: *38 minutes* •
YIELD: *8 servings*

8¼ cups low-sodium nonfat chicken
   broth
2 medium onions, chopped
4 cloves garlic, minced
3 cups low-sodium canned tomatoes,
   drained and chopped
1 cup scraped and sliced carrots
1 cup sliced celery

2 cups diced eggplant
2 cups low-sodium canned pinto
   beans, rinsed and drained
2 cups fresh, drained canned, or
   thawed frozen corn kernels
1 teaspoon ground cumin
1 teaspoon chili powder
½ cup grated nonfat cheddar

1. Heat ¼ cup broth in a large pot. Add onions and garlic, and sauté until onions begin to soften, about 4 minutes.
2. Add remaining broth, tomatoes, carrots, and celery. Bring to a boil, reduce heat, and simmer for 10 minutes. Add eggplant and simmer until eggplant is tender, about 10 more minutes.
3. Stir in beans, corn, cumin, and chili powder, and simmer for 5 additional minutes. Transfer 2 cups of the vegetable stew to a food processor or blender and puree. Stir the puree back into the pot.
4. Transfer to individual bowls, sprinkle with cheese, and serve.

Calories Per Serving: 170
Fat: 1 g
Cholesterol: 1 mg
Protein: 15 g

Carbohydrates: 28 g
Dietary Fiber: 1 g
Sodium: 228 mg

❋ *Eggplant and Tomatoes* ❋

PREPARATION TIME: *15 minutes* • COOKING TIME: *21 minutes* •
YIELD: *4 servings*

¼ cup low-sodium nonfat chicken
   broth
4 cups thinly sliced eggplant
4 medium tomatoes, diced

1 medium onion, thinly sliced
3 cloves garlic, minced
¼ teaspoon cayenne pepper

1. Heat broth in a saucepan. Add eggplant and sauté until it begins to soften, about 4 minutes.

2. Add remaining ingredients and simmer until vegetables are just tender, about 15 minutes.

Calories Per Serving: 74
Fat: 1 g
Cholesterol: 0 mg
Protein: 3 g
Carbohydrates: 16 g
Dietary Fiber: 2 g
Sodium: 39 mg

Eggplant and Red Peppers

Preparation Time: *20 minutes* ▪ Cooking Time: *36 minutes* ▪ Yield: *4 servings*

¼ cup low-sodium nonfat chicken broth
3½ cups diced eggplant (1-inch cubes)
3 cloves garlic, minced
1 medium onion, chopped
¾ cup chopped celery
2 medium red bell peppers, cored and chopped
1 cup uncooked white rice
2 cups low-sodium canned tomatoes, chopped, juice reserved
2 bay leaves
½ teaspoon dried thyme
½ teaspoon dried marjoram
¼ teaspoon ground black pepper
¼ cup chopped fresh parsley
½ cup hot water

1. Heat 2 tablespoons broth in a large saucepan. Add eggplant and garlic, and sauté until eggplant begins to soften, about 4 minutes. Remove and set aside.
2. Heat remaining broth in saucepan. Add onion, celery, and bell peppers, and sauté until onion begins to soften, about 4 minutes. Add rice and continue to sauté for 4 more minutes.
3. Stir in tomatoes with juice, bay leaves, thyme, marjoram, black pepper, parsley, and hot water. Cover and simmer for 15 minutes.
4. Add eggplant and continue to simmer until rice is tender, about 5 minutes.
5. Remove bay leaves and serve.

Calories Per Serving: 246
Fat: 1 g
Cholesterol: 0 mg
Protein: 6 g
Carbohydrates: 54 g
Dietary Fiber: 3 g
Sodium: 73 mg

❊ Eggplant, Yellow Pepper, and Mushrooms ❊

PREPARATION TIME: *15 minutes* • COOKING TIME: *11 minutes* •
YIELD: *4 servings*

¼ cup low-sodium nonfat chicken
   broth
1 clove garlic, minced
¼ cup sliced scallion
6 cups diced eggplant (1-inch
   cubes)

1 medium yellow bell pepper, cored
   and chopped
1 cup sliced mushrooms
¼ teaspoon ground black pepper
1½ tablespoons grated nonfat
   Parmesan

1. Heat broth in a large saucepan. Add the garlic, half the scallion, the egg-plant, and the yellow bell pepper, and sauté until the scallion begins to soften, about 4 minutes.
2. Add mushrooms and black pepper, and continue to sauté until eggplant is just tender, about 5 minutes.
3. Stir in Parmesan, transfer to individual plates, sprinkle with remaining scallions, and serve.

Calories Per Serving: 56
Fat: 0 g
Cholesterol: 2 mg
Protein: 3 g

Carbohydrates: 10 g
Dietary Fiber: 1 g
Sodium: 63 mg

❊ Baked Eggplant, Green Beans, and Zucchini ❊

PREPARATION TIME: *25 minutes* • COOKING TIME: *37 minutes* •
YIELD: *6 servings*

¼ cup low-sodium nonfat chicken
   broth
4 cups diced eggplant
1½ cups chopped green beans
   (1-inch lengths)
2 cups low-sodium canned tomatoes,
   chopped and drained

2 cups sliced zucchini
1 clove garlic, minced
¼ teaspoon ground black pepper
2 teaspoons dried oregano
2 tablespoons grated nonfat
   Parmesan

1. Preheat oven to 375 degrees.
2. Heat broth in a flameproof 3-quart casserole. Add eggplant, green beans, tomatoes, zucchini, garlic, black pepper, and oregano, and sauté for 5 min-utes. Cover and bake until vegetables are tender, about 30 minutes.
3. Sprinkle with Parmesan and serve.

Calories Per Serving: 54
Fat: 0 g
Cholesterol: 2 mg
Protein: 3 g

Carbohydrates: 11 g
Dietary Fiber: 2 g
Sodium: 14 mg

❋ Lemon-Dilled Eggplant and ❋ Summer Squash

PREPARATION TIME: *25 minutes* • COOKING TIME: *40 minutes* •
YIELD: *6 servings*

¼ cup low-sodium nonfat chicken
  broth
2 cloves garlic, minced
2 medium onions, thinly sliced
3 medium green bell peppers, cored
  and cut into thin strips
2 cups diced eggplant

4 cups diced yellow summer squash
4 medium tomatoes, chopped and
  drained
¼ teaspoon ground black pepper
½ teaspoon dried oregano
½ teaspoon dried dill
¼ cup lemon juice

1. Heat broth in a large saucepan. Add garlic and onions, and sauté until onions begin to soften, about 3 minutes. Add bell peppers, eggplant, and squash, and sauté for 5 more minutes.
2. Add tomatoes, black pepper, oregano, and dill. Cover and simmer, stirring occasionally, for 15 minutes.
3. Remove cover and continue to simmer until any excess liquid has evaporated, about 15 minutes.
4. Stir in lemon juice and serve at once.

Calories Per Serving: 56
Fat: 1 g
Cholesterol: 0 mg
Protein: 3 g

Carbohydrates: 12 g
Dietary Fiber: 3 g
Sodium: 21 mg

❋ Shiitake-and-Corn-Stuffed Eggplant ❋

PREPARATION TIME: *25 minutes* • COOKING TIME: *52 minutes* •
YIELD: *4 servings*

2 medium eggplants
¼ cup low-sodium nonfat chicken
   broth
1 medium onion, chopped
2 cloves garlic, minced
1 cup chopped green beans (½-inch
   lengths)
¾ cup fresh or thawed frozen corn
   kernels

3 cups low-sodium canned tomatoes,
   chopped, juice reserved
1 cup minced shiitake mushrooms
1 teaspoon dried basil
1 teaspoon dried oregano
1 teaspoon ground cumin
¼ teaspoon ground black pepper
2 tablespoons grated nonfat
   Parmesan

1. Preheat oven to 375 degrees.
2. Halve the eggplants lengthwise. Scoop out the eggplant flesh, leaving a ½-inch shell. Chop the eggplant flesh.
3. Heat broth in a flameproof 3-quart casserole. Add onion and sauté until it begins to soften, about 3 minutes. Add garlic, green beans, corn, and chopped eggplant, and sauté for 2 more minutes. Add tomatoes and mushrooms, and continue to sauté for 3 additional minutes. Remove from the casserole and set aside.
4. Arrange the eggplant shells in the casserole.
5. In a separate bowl, combine reserved tomato juice, basil, oregano, cumin, and black pepper. Fill each eggplant shell with the vegetable mixture, pour the tomato juice mixture over the eggplant, and bake for 40 minutes. Sprinkle each eggplant with Parmesan and return to the oven for 2 minutes.

Calories Per Serving: 17
Fat: 0 g
Cholesterol: 0 mg
Protein: 1 g

Carbohydrates: 4 g
Dietary Fiber: 1 g
Sodium: 4 mg

❋ Jalapeño, Eggplant, and Couscous ❋

PREPARATION TIME: 20 minutes plus 5 minutes standing time   ·
COOKING TIME: 38 minutes   ·   YIELD: 6 servings

¼ cup low-sodium nonfat chicken
   broth
¼ cup chopped onion
1 clove garlic, minced
1 medium green bell pepper, cored
   and chopped

1 medium red bell pepper, cored and
   chopped
1 tablespoon minced fresh gingerroot
1 jalapeño pepper, seeded and minced
4 cups diced eggplant
2 teaspoons ground cumin

1 teaspoon ground coriander
¼ teaspoon ground cinnamon
¼ teaspoon ground black pepper
⅛ teaspoon ground cloves

4 medium tomatoes, chopped
2¼ cups boiling water
1¼ cups uncooked couscous

1. Heat broth in a large saucepan. Add onion, garlic, bell peppers, ginger-root, and jalapeño pepper, and sauté until onion begins to soften, about 5 minutes. Add eggplant, cumin, coriander, cinnamon, black pepper, and cloves, and sauté for 3 more minutes.
2. Stir in tomatoes and bring to a boil. Reduce heat, cover, and simmer until eggplant is tender, about 15 minutes. Remove cover, increase heat, and cook, stirring frequently, until most of the liquid has evaporated, about 10 minutes.
3. In a separate bowl, pour boiling water over couscous, cover, and allow to stand for 5 minutes.
4. Serve eggplant over couscous.

Calories Per Serving: 193
Fat: 1 g
Cholesterol: 0 mg
Protein: 7 g

Carbohydrates: 40 g
Dietary Fiber: 8 g
Sodium: 94 mg

❋ *Summer Vegetable Ratatouille* ❋

PREPARATION TIME: *20 minutes* • COOKING TIME: *31 minutes* •
YIELD: *6 servings*

¼ cup low-sodium nonfat chicken broth
2 medium onions, chopped
2 cloves garlic, minced
5 cups chopped eggplant
1 medium green bell pepper, cored and chopped
1 medium red bell pepper, cored and chopped
2 cups chopped zucchini

2 cups chopped pattypan squash
3 medium tomatoes, chopped
½ cup chopped fresh parsley
1 teaspoon dried basil
½ teaspoon ground black pepper
2 tablespoons low-sodium tomato paste
¼ cup shredded nonfat mozzarella
2 cups cooked rice

1. Heat broth in a large saucepan. Add onions, garlic, eggplant, and bell peppers, and sauté until onions begin to soften, about 4 minutes.
2. Add zucchini, pattypan squash, tomatoes, parsley, and basil. Bring to a boil, reduce heat, cover, and simmer for 15 minutes.

3. Stir in black pepper and simmer for 10 more minutes. Stir in tomato paste.
4. Serve topped with 2 teaspoons cheese per serving over rice.

Calories Per Serving: 173
Fat: 2 g
Cholesterol: 5 mg
Protein: 6 g
Carbohydrates: 34 g
Dietary Fiber: 3 g
Sodium: 55 mg

Baked Eggplant

PREPARATION TIME: *20 minutes* ▪ COOKING TIME: *37 minutes* ▪ YIELD: *4 servings*

2 tablespoons low-sodium nonfat chicken broth
1 medium onion, chopped
1 medium green bell pepper, cored and chopped
3 cloves garlic, minced
3 cups diced eggplant
3 medium tomatoes, chopped
½ cup chopped canned mild green chiles, drained
6 slices whole-wheat toast, crumbled
½ teaspoon ground cumin
½ teaspoon chili powder
½ teaspoon dried oregano
¼ teaspoon ground black pepper
⅓ cup shredded nonfat cheddar
⅓ cup shredded nonfat mozzarella

1. Preheat oven to 375 degrees.
2. Heat broth in a flameproof 2-quart casserole. Add onion, bell pepper, garlic, and eggplant, and sauté until onion begins to soften, about 5 minutes.
3. Remove from heat and stir in tomatoes, chiles, toast crumbs, cumin, chili powder, oregano, and black pepper. Cover and bake until vegetables are just tender, about 20 minutes.
4. Remove from the oven and stir in cheddar and mozzarella. Return to the oven until cheeses melt, about 10 minutes.

Calories Per Serving: 117
Fat: 1 g
Cholesterol: 4 mg
Protein: 10 g
Carbohydrates: 19 g
Dietary Fiber: 3 g
Sodium: 299 mg

❋ *Curried Eggplant and Potatoes* ❋

PREPARATION TIME: *20 minutes* • COOKING TIME: *21 minutes* •
YIELD: *4 servings*

¾ cup low-sodium nonfat chicken
 broth
2 whole peeled cloves garlic
2 teaspoons minced fresh gingerroot
¼ teaspoon chili powder
1 medium onion, chopped
½ teaspoon ground turmeric

2 cups diced potatoes
3 cups chopped eggplant
1 teaspoon curry powder
1 cup fresh or thawed frozen green
 peas
2 cups cooked rice

1. Combine 2 tablespoons broth, the garlic, gingerroot, chili powder, and onion in a blender or food processor and puree.
2. Heat puree in a large saucepan. Add turmeric and stir in potatoes. Cover and simmer for 5 minutes.
3. Add remaining broth and eggplant, cover, and simmer for 8 minutes. Stir in curry powder and peas and continue to simmer until peas and eggplant are cooked through, about 5 more minutes.
4. Serve over rice.

Calories Per Serving: 182
Fat: 1 g
Cholesterol: 0 mg
Protein: 7 g

Carbohydrates: 39 g
Dietary Fiber: 4 g
Sodium: 45 mg

❋ *Spiced Eggplant and Potatoes* ❋

PREPARATION TIME: *20 minutes* • COOKING TIME: *33 minutes* •
YIELD: *4 servings*

1 cup low-sodium nonfat chicken
 broth
1 medium onion, chopped
½ teaspoon ground cumin
½ teaspoon ground coriander
1 teaspoon minced fresh gingerroot
4 cloves garlic, minced
½ teaspoon chili powder
¼ teaspoon ground turmeric
4 cups chopped eggplant

½ teaspoon sugar
½ cup chopped canned mild green
 chiles, drained
2 cups diced potatoes
2 medium tomatoes, chopped
1½ teaspoons dried cilantro
1 tablespoon lemon juice
½ teaspoon ground black pepper
¼ cup nonfat plain yogurt

1. Heat ¼ cup broth in a large saucepan. Add onion, cumin, and coriander, and sauté for 2 minutes. Add gingerroot, half the garlic, chili powder, and turmeric, and sauté for 2 more minutes.
2. Add eggplant, sugar, and chiles, and sauté for 2 additional minutes. Stir in remaining broth. Bring to a boil, reduce heat, cover, and simmer for 10 minutes. Add potatoes and tomatoes, and continue to simmer, stirring occasionally, until potatoes are just tender, about 10 minutes.
3. Stir in cilantro, remaining garlic, lemon juice, and black pepper, and simmer for 2 more minutes. Transfer to individual plates, top each serving with a tablespoon of yogurt, and serve.

Calories Per Serving: 275
Fat: 1 g
Cholesterol: 0 mg
Protein: 7 g

Carbohydrates: 63 g
Dietary Fiber: 3 g
Sodium: 71 mg

❋ *Island Eggplant* ❋

PREPARATION TIME: *15 minutes* • COOKING TIME: *7 minutes* •
YIELD: *5 servings*

¼ cup water
1 tablespoon dry sherry
1 tablespoon reduced-sodium soy
    sauce
1 tablespoon rice vinegar
2 teaspoons sugar
¼ cup low-sodium nonfat chicken
    broth

1 clove garlic, minced
3 scallions, chopped
4 cups diced eggplant (1-inch cubes)
2 cups chopped broccoli
⅓ cup sliced canned water chestnuts,
    drained
2½ cups cooked rice

1. Combine water, sherry, soy sauce, vinegar, and sugar in a small bowl, and set aside.
2. Heat broth in a large saucepan. Add garlic and half the scallions, and sauté for 30 seconds. Add eggplant and broccoli, and continue to sauté for 2 more minutes.
3. Stir in water chestnuts and sherry mixture, and bring to a simmer. Cook, stirring frequently, until liquid begins to thicken, about 2½ minutes.
4. Transfer to a serving bowl, sprinkle with remaining scallions, and serve over rice.

Calories Per Serving: 47

Fat: 0 g

Cholesterol: 0 mg

Protein: 2 g

Carbohydrates: 10 g

Dietary Fiber: 1 g

Sodium: 173 mg

❋ *Tomato-Broccoli Pasta* ❋

PREPARATION TIME: *15 minutes* • COOKING TIME: *18 minutes* •
YIELD: *4 servings*

8 quarts water

8 ounces fresh linguine

4 cups chopped broccoli

3 tablespoons wine vinegar

1 teaspoon olive oil

¼ teaspoon ground black pepper

2 medium tomatoes, chopped

3 scallions, sliced

¼ cup chopped fresh basil

2 tablespoons grated nonfat Parmesan

1. Bring water to a boil in a large saucepan. Add linguine and broccoli, and cook until pasta is just tender, about 3 minutes. Drain well and transfer to a large bowl.
2. Combine vinegar, olive oil, and black pepper in a separate bowl and pour over pasta. Add tomatoes, scallions, and basil, and toss well.
3. Serve topped with Parmesan.

Calories Per Serving: 271

Fat: 3 g

Cholesterol: 0 mg

Protein: 11 g

Carbohydrates: 53 g

Dietary Fiber: 7 g

Sodium: 56 mg

❋ *Mushroom Pilaf* ❋

PREPARATION TIME: *25 minutes plus 1 hour standing time for barley* •
COOKING TIME: *30 minutes* • YIELD: *6 servings*

1 cup boiling water

½ cup pearl barley

3½ cups low-sodium nonfat chicken
  broth

4 cups sliced mushrooms

1½ cups uncooked white rice

2 medium onions, chopped

1 clove garlic, minced

¼ cup chopped fresh parsley

¼ teaspoon ground black pepper

1. Pour boiling water over barley in a small bowl and allow to stand for 1 hour. Drain and set aside.
2. Heat ¼ cup broth in a large saucepan. Add mushrooms and sauté for 3 minutes. Remove and set aside.
3. Heat another ¼ cup broth in the saucepan. Add rice and sauté for 2 minutes. Add onions and garlic, and continue to sauté for 2 more minutes.
4. Add reserved barley and mushrooms to the saucepan. Stir in remaining broth and bring to a boil. Reduce heat, cover, and simmer, stirring occasionally, until grains are just tender, about 15 minutes.
5. Stir in parsley and sprinkle with black pepper.

Calories Per Serving: 217
Fat: 1 g
Cholesterol: 0 mg
Protein: 11 g

Carbohydrates: 42 g
Dietary Fiber: 5 g
Sodium: 121 mg

❋ *Mushroom-Vegetable Curry* ❋

PREPARATION TIME: *25 minutes* • COOKING TIME: *50 minutes* •
YIELD: *4 servings*

2½ cups low-sodium vegetable broth
1 medium onion, sliced
2 cloves garlic, minced
1½ teaspoons ground cumin
1½ teaspoons ground coriander
½ teaspoon ground allspice
½ teaspoon ground turmeric
½ teaspoon ground ginger
¼ teaspoon cayenne pepper
1 medium red bell pepper, cored and chopped
1 medium yellow bell pepper, cored and chopped

2 medium carrots, scraped and chopped
3 cups sliced mushrooms
1 tablespoon low-sodium tomato paste
2 medium potatoes, diced
2 cups chopped cauliflower
2 cups chopped broccoli
1 cup chopped fresh or thawed frozen green beans (1-inch lengths)
3 tablespoons lemon juice
2 cups cooked rice

1. Heat ¼ cup broth in a large saucepan. Add onion and garlic, and sauté until onion begins to soften, about 3 minutes.
2. Add 1¼ cups broth, the cumin, coriander, allspice, turmeric, ginger, cayenne pepper, bell peppers, carrots, and mushrooms. Bring to a boil, reduce heat, and simmer, stirring frequently, until the mixture begins to thicken, about 20 minutes. Stir in tomato paste. Allow to cool slightly.

3. Stir in remaining broth, potatoes, cauliflower, and broccoli. Bring to a boil, reduce heat, cover, and simmer for 12 minutes. Add green beans and continue to simmer until beans are tender, about 5 additional minutes. Stir in lemon juice.
4. Serve over rice.

Calories Per Serving: 312
Fat: 1 g
Cholesterol: 0 mg
Protein: 9 g

Carbohydrates: 69 g
Dietary Fiber: 5 g
Sodium: 78 mg

❀ *Spicy Peas and Potatoes in Tomato Sauce* ❀

PREPARATION TIME: *20 minutes* • COOKING TIME: *39 minutes* •
YIELD: *4 servings*

1 medium tomato, chopped
2 tablespoons nonfat plain yogurt
3 cloves garlic, minced
1 teaspoon minced fresh gingerroot
1 teaspoon ground coriander
½ teaspoon ground cumin
½ teaspoon garam masala
¼ teaspoon ground cinnamon
½ teaspoon ground black pepper

¼ teaspoon ground turmeric
1¾ cups low-sodium tomato juice
1 medium onion, diced
1 tablespoon minced jalapeño pepper
1 cup uncooked white rice
2 cups diced potatoes
¼ cup chopped fresh parsley
¾ cup fresh or thawed frozen green
  peas

1. In a small bowl, combine tomato, yogurt, garlic, gingerroot, coriander, cumin, garam masala, cinnamon, black pepper, and turmeric. Mix well and set aside.
2. Heat ¼ cup tomato juice in a large saucepan. Add onion and jalapeño pepper, and sauté until onion begins to soften, about 4 minutes. Add tomato mixture, cover, and simmer, stirring occasionally, for 10 minutes.
3. Add remaining tomato juice and bring to a boil. Stir in rice and potatoes, reduce heat, cover, and simmer for 15 minutes. Add parsley and peas, and continue to simmer until peas are tender, about 5 more minutes.

Calories Per Serving: 352
Fat: 1 g
Cholesterol: 0 mg
Protein: 9 g

Carbohydrates: 78 g
Dietary Fiber: 5 g
Sodium: 137 mg

❋ Red Pepper–Rice Casserole ❋

PREPARATION TIME: *25 minutes* • COOKING TIME: *51 minutes* •
YIELD: *4 servings*

*½ cup low-sodium nonfat chicken
    broth*
2 medium onions, chopped
*2 medium red bell peppers, cored and
    chopped*
1 cup sliced mushrooms
1 clove garlic, minced
2 cups cooked rice

1 cup nonfat cottage cheese
2 egg whites, lightly beaten
2 teaspoons dried dill
⅓ cup minced fresh parsley
¼ teaspoon ground black pepper
⅓ cup bread crumbs
*2 tablespoons grated nonfat
    Parmesan*

1. Preheat oven to 375 degrees.
2. Combine broth, onions, and bell peppers in a flameproof 2-quart casserole. Bring to a boil, reduce heat, cover, and simmer until vegetables are just tender, about 10 minutes. Add mushrooms and garlic, and simmer, uncovered, until liquid has evaporated, about 10 more minutes. Remove from heat and stir in rice. Mix well.
3. In a separate bowl, combine cottage cheese, egg whites, dill, parsley, and black pepper. Stir into vegetable mixture and bake for 25 minutes. In a separate bowl, combine bread crumbs and Parmesan, sprinkle over casserole, and return to the oven for 3 minutes.

Calories Per Serving: 271
Fat: 1 g
Cholesterol: 5 mg
Protein: 17 g

Carbohydrates: 49 g
Dietary Fiber: 2 g
Sodium: 288 mg

❋ Shiitake-and-Corn-Stuffed Peppers ❋

PREPARATION TIME: *20 minutes* • COOKING TIME: *40 minutes* •
YIELD: *4 servings*

Olive oil cooking spray
1 cup minced shiitake mushrooms
*1 cup fresh or thawed frozen corn
    kernels*

1 medium onion, grated
1 clove garlic, minced
1 tablespoon dried cilantro
2 tablespoons lime juice

1 teaspoon dried oregano
1 teaspoon ground cumin
¼ teaspoon ground cinnamon
¼ teaspoon ground black pepper
2 large red bell peppers, halved
   lengthwise and cored

2 large green bell peppers, halved
   lengthwise and cored
1 cup low-sodium nonfat chicken
   broth

1. Preheat oven to 350 degrees. Lightly coat a 3-quart casserole with olive oil cooking spray.
2. Combine mushrooms, corn, onion, garlic, cilantro, lime juice, oregano, cumin, cinnamon, and black pepper.
3. Fill the bell pepper halves with the mushroom mixture and arrange in the prepared casserole. Pour broth over the peppers, cover, and bake for 40 minutes.

Calories Per Serving: 139
Fat: 0 g
Cholesterol: 0 mg
Protein: 7 g

Carbohydrates: 28 g
Dietary Fiber: 4 g
Sodium: 219 mg

❊ Red Bell Peppers and Pineapple with Tofu ❊

PREPARATION TIME: *20 minutes* ▪ COOKING TIME: *20 minutes* ▪
YIELD: *4 servings*

2½ cups juice-packed canned pineapple chunks, juice reserved
2 tablespoons honey
1 tablespoon vinegar
1 teaspoon dry mustard
¼ teaspoon ground black pepper
¼ cup low-sodium nonfat chicken
   broth
½ pound firm tofu, drained and cut
   into ¾-inch cubes

1 cup sliced onion
1 teaspoon minced fresh gingerroot
2 medium red bell peppers, cored and
   cut into thin strips
2 cloves garlic, minced
½ teaspoon dried thyme
2 cups cooked rice

1. Whisk together the reserved pineapple juice, honey, vinegar, dry mustard, and black pepper in a small bowl. Set aside.
2. Heat 2 tablespoons broth in a large skillet. Add tofu and sauté until brown, about 3 minutes. Remove and set aside.

3. Heat remaining broth in the skillet. Add onion, gingerroot, bell peppers, garlic, and thyme. Sauté until onion begins to soften, about 4 minutes. Add pineapple chunks and sauté for 5 more minutes.
4. Stir in pineapple juice mixture and tofu. Continue to stir gently for about 4 minutes.
5. Divide rice among individual plates, top with pineapple mixture, and serve.

Calories Per Serving: 319
Fat: 2 g
Cholesterol: 0 mg
Protein: 8 g

Carbohydrates: 70 g
Dietary Fiber: 3 g
Sodium: 43 mg

✖ Tofu, Broccoli, and Mushroom—Stuffed ✖ Red Peppers

PREPARATION TIME: 20 minutes • COOKING TIME: 40 minutes •
YIELD: 4 servings

Olive oil cooking spray
1 medium onion, minced
2 medium stalks celery, minced
1 cup finely chopped mushrooms
1 jalapeño pepper, seeded and minced
1 cup cooked rice
1 cup finely chopped broccoli
1 cup crumbled firm tofu, drained

¼ teaspoon ground black pepper
2 cups low-sodium tomato sauce
8 medium red bell peppers, cores
    removed, thin slices removed from
    bottoms so they will stand up
½ cup nonfat plain yogurt
2 tablespoons lemon juice
¼ cup chopped fresh parsley

1. Preheat oven to 350 degrees. Lightly coat a 9″ × 9″ baking pan with olive oil cooking spray.
2. In a large bowl, combine onion, celery, mushrooms, jalapeño pepper, rice, broccoli, tofu, black pepper, and 1 cup tomato sauce. Stuff peppers.
3. Arrange peppers in the prepared pan. Pour remaining tomato sauce over peppers, cover, and bake for 40 minutes.
4. Combine yogurt and lemon juice and spoon over peppers. Top with parsley and serve.

Calories Per Serving: 107
Fat: 2 g
Cholesterol: 1 mg
Protein: 11 g

Carbohydrates: 41 g
Dietary Fiber: 7 g
Sodium: 107 mg

❋ *Corn-Stuffed Green Peppers* ❋

PREPARATION TIME: *20 minutes* • COOKING TIME: *50 minutes* •
YIELD: *4 servings*

Olive oil cooking spray
8 medium green bell peppers, cores
   removed, thin slices removed from
   bottoms so they will stand up
¼ cup low-sodium vegetable broth
4 medium leeks (white parts only),
   chopped
2 scallions, thinly sliced

2 cloves garlic, minced
4 cups fresh, drained canned, or
   thawed frozen corn kernels
½ cup chopped fresh parsley
1 teaspoon dried oregano
½ teaspoon ground black pepper
1 tablespoon paprika
2 cups cooked rice

1. Preheat oven to 350 degrees. Lightly coat a 9″ × 9″ baking pan with olive
   oil cooking spray.
2. Arrange peppers standing up in baking pan.
3. Heat broth in a large skillet. Add leeks, scallions, and garlic, and sauté
   until leeks begin to soften, about 3 minutes. Stir in corn, parsley, oregano,
   and black pepper, and continue to sauté for 5 more minutes.
4. Stuff peppers with the leek-corn mixture, sprinkle each with paprika, and
   bake until peppers are done, about 40 minutes.
5. Serve with rice.

Calories Per Serving: 381
Fat: 1 g
Cholesterol: 0 mg
Protein: 11 g

Carbohydrates: 90 g
Dietary Fiber: 9 g
Sodium: 41 mg

❋ *Tofu-Stuffed Potatoes* ❋

PREPARATION TIME: *25 minutes* • COOKING TIME: *1 hour 10 minutes* •
YIELD: *4 servings*

4 large baking potatoes
¼ cup low-sodium nonfat chicken
   broth
1 cup minced onion
1 cup sliced mushrooms
2 cloves garlic, minced

¼ teaspoon ground black pepper
1 cup diced firm tofu (1-inch cubes),
   drained
3 tablespoons chopped fresh parsley
1 tablespoon Dijon mustard
1 tablespoon paprika

1. Preheat oven to 425 degrees.
2. Bake potatoes for 40 minutes. Remove from the oven and cool sufficiently to handle. Lower oven temperature to 375 degrees.
3. Heat broth in a large skillet. Add onion, mushrooms, and garlic, and sauté until onion begins to soften, about 4 minutes. Sprinkle with black pepper.
4. Halve potatoes lengthwise and scoop out flesh, leaving ¼-inch shells. Combine potato flesh, tofu, parsley, and mustard, and mix well. Stir in onion mixture.
5. Divide stuffing mixture among potato halves, sprinkle with paprika, and return to the oven for 20 minutes.

Calories Per Serving: 267   Carbohydrates: 58 g
Fat: 1 g   Dietary Fiber: 6 g
Cholesterol: 0 mg   Sodium: 103 mg
Protein: 8 g

❊ New Potatoes and Green Beans ❊

PREPARATION TIME: *15 minutes* • COOKING TIME: *15 minutes* •
YIELD: *6 servings*

2 cups water
6 cups chopped fresh or thawed
    frozen green beans (2-inch
    lengths)

1 medium onion, sliced
1 pound small new potatoes, halved
½ teaspoon ground black pepper
½ teaspoon dried thyme

1. Combine water, beans, onion, and potatoes in a large saucepan. Sprinkle with black pepper and thyme, bring to a boil, reduce heat, and simmer until vegetables are just tender, about 15 minutes.
2. Drain and serve.

Calories Per Serving: 164   Carbohydrates: 38 g
Fat: 0 g   Dietary Fiber: 5 g
Cholesterol: 0 mg   Sodium: 16 mg
Protein: 5 g

❊ Potatoes, Apples, and Onions ❊

PREPARATION TIME: *25 minutes* • COOKING TIME: *42 minutes* •
YIELD: *6 servings*

¼ cup low-sodium nonfat chicken
  broth
3 medium onions, thinly sliced
1 clove garlic, minced
4 large potatoes, thinly sliced

4 medium apples, peeled, cored, and
  thinly sliced
¼ teaspoon ground nutmeg
¼ teaspoon ground black pepper
¼ cup skim milk
¼ cup grated nonfat mozzarella

1. Preheat oven to 375 degrees.
2. Heat broth in a large oven-safe pot. Add onions and garlic, and sauté until onions begin to soften, about 3 minutes. Remove mixture and set aside.
3. In the pot, layer potatoes, onion mixture, and apples, with potatoes on bottom and apples on top. Sprinkle each layer with nutmeg and black pepper. Pour the milk over the top, cover, and bake for 35 minutes. Remove the cover, sprinkle the mozzarella on top, and return to the oven until the cheese melts, about 2 minutes.

Calories Per Serving: 156
Fat: 0 g
Cholesterol: 1 mg
Protein: 4 g

Carbohydrates: 35 g
Dietary Fiber: 3 g
Sodium: 51 mg

❊ *Curried Sweet Potatoes and Green Peas* ❊

PREPARATION TIME: *20 minutes* ・ COOKING TIME: *23 minutes* ・
YIELD: *4 servings*

2 tablespoons balsamic vinegar
1¼ cups low-sodium nonfat chicken
  broth
1 medium onion, finely chopped
3 cloves garlic, minced

5 medium sweet potatoes, diced
1 tablespoon curry powder
1 cup fresh or thawed frozen green
  peas
2 cups cooked rice

1. Heat vinegar and ¼ cup broth in a large saucepan. Add onion and garlic, and sauté until onion begins to soften, about 4 minutes.
2. Stir in remaining broth, sweet potatoes, and curry powder. Cover and simmer for 10 minutes. Add peas and simmer until peas are tender, about 5 more minutes.
3. Serve over rice.

Calories Per Serving: 394
Fat: 1 g
Cholesterol: 0 mg
Protein: 8 g

Carbohydrates: 87 g
Dietary Fiber: 8 g
Sodium: 122 mg

❀ Chili Potatoes with Yogurt ❀

PREPARATION TIME: *20 minutes* • COOKING TIME: *22 minutes* •
YIELD: *4 servings*

¼ cup low-sodium nonfat chicken
  broth
1 medium onion, sliced
1 bay leaf
1 teaspoon minced fresh gingerroot
2 cloves garlic, minced
¼ teaspoon ground cumin
4 cups chopped potatoes

2 medium tomatoes, coarsely
  chopped
1 medium green bell pepper, cored
  and chopped
¼ teaspoon ground turmeric
2 teaspoons ground coriander
1 teaspoon chili powder
⅔ cup nonfat plain yogurt

1. Heat broth in a large saucepan. Add onion and bay leaf, and sauté until onion begins to soften, about 3 minutes. Add gingerroot and garlic, and sauté for 1 more minute.
2. Add cumin, potatoes, tomatoes, and bell pepper, and continue to sauté for 4 additional minutes.
3. Stir in turmeric, coriander, chili powder, and yogurt. Cover and simmer until potatoes are tender, about 12 minutes. Remove bay leaf.
4. Transfer to individual plates and serve.

Calories Per Serving: 254
Fat: 1 g
Cholesterol: 1 mg
Protein: 8 g

Carbohydrates: 57 g
Dietary Fiber: 5 g
Sodium: 64 mg

❀ Chopped Potatoes with Tomatoes ❀ and Green Chiles

PREPARATION TIME: *15 minutes* • COOKING TIME: *21 minutes* •
YIELD: *4 servings*

1 cup low-sodium nonfat chicken
  broth
1 medium onion, thinly sliced
2 medium tomatoes, coarsely chopped
¼ teaspoon ground cumin
½ teaspoon ground turmeric

¼ teaspoon ground black pepper
1 teaspoon minced fresh gingerroot
2 tablespoons minced canned mild
  green chiles, drained
4 cups coarsely chopped potatoes
½ teaspoon garam masala

1. Heat ¼ cup broth in a large saucepan. Add onion, tomatoes, cumin, turmeric, black pepper, gingerroot, and chiles. Sauté until onion begins to soften, about 4 minutes.
2. Add potatoes and remaining broth. Cover and simmer until potatoes are just tender, about 12 minutes.
3. Stir in the garam masala, transfer to individual plates, and serve.

Calories Per Serving: 234
Fat: 1 g
Cholesterol: 0 mg
Protein: 7 g

Carbohydrates: 52 g
Dietary Fiber: 4 g
Sodium: 85 mg

❈ *Curried Potatoes and Zucchini* ❈

PREPARATION TIME: *15 minutes* ▪ **COOKING TIME:** *24 minutes* ▪
YIELD: *4 servings*

½ cup apple juice
1 medium onion, chopped
3 cups diced potatoes
1 medium carrot, scraped and sliced
3½ cups chopped zucchini

2 teaspoons curry powder
¼ teaspoon ground black pepper
¼ cup nonfat plain yogurt
2 tablespoons seedless raisins

1. Heat ¼ cup juice in a large saucepan. Add onion and sauté until it begins to soften, about 3 minutes.
2. Add remaining juice, potatoes, carrot, zucchini, curry powder, and black pepper. Cover and simmer until potatoes are just tender, about 17 minutes.
3. Transfer to individual plates, top with yogurt and raisins, and serve.

Calories Per Serving: 251
Fat: 1 g
Cholesterol: 0 mg
Protein: 7 g

Carbohydrates: 58 g
Dietary Fiber: 5 g
Sodium: 39 mg

❋ *Spicy Potatoes and Broccoli* ❋

PREPARATION TIME: *15 minutes* • COOKING TIME: *26 minutes* •
YIELD: *4 servings*

*½ cup low-sodium nonfat chicken
   broth*
½ teaspoon cumin seeds
1 medium onion, chopped
1 teaspoon minced fresh gingerroot
3 cloves garlic, minced
3 cups chopped potatoes

¾ teaspoon ground turmeric
1 teaspoon chili powder
2 medium tomatoes, chopped
3 cups chopped broccoli
1 teaspoon garam masala
2 teaspoons ground coriander
¼ teaspoon ground black pepper

1. Heat ¼ cup broth in a large saucepan. Add cumin seeds and sauté for 1 minute. Add onion, gingerroot, and garlic, and sauté until onion begins to soften, about 4 more minutes.
2. Stir in remaining broth, potatoes, turmeric, chili powder, and tomatoes. Cover and simmer for 5 minutes.
3. Add remaining ingredients. Cover and continue to simmer until broccoli is just tender, about 12 minutes.
4. Transfer to individual plates and serve.

Calories Per Serving: 220
Fat: 1 g
Cholesterol: 0 mg
Protein: 7 g

Carbohydrates: 49 g
Dietary Fiber: 4 g
Sodium: 86 mg

❋ *Curried Potatoes, Cauliflower, and Peas* ❋ *with Yogurt*

PREPARATION TIME: *25 minutes* • COOKING TIME: *36 minutes* •
YIELD: *5 servings*

*2¼ cups low-sodium nonfat chicken
   broth*
*6 medium boiling potatoes, cut into
   1-inch cubes*
2 medium onions, chopped
2 tablespoons minced fresh gingerroot
2 cloves garlic, minced

1 tablespoon curry powder
⅛ teaspoon cayenne pepper
1 cup low-sodium tomato paste
4 cups chopped cauliflower
½ cup nonfat plain yogurt
*1 cup fresh or thawed frozen green
   peas*

1. Heat ¼ cup broth in a large saucepan. Add potatoes and onions, and sauté for 5 minutes. Stir in gingerroot and garlic, and sauté for 1 more minute.
2. Add remaining broth, curry powder, cayenne pepper, tomato paste, cauliflower, and yogurt. Bring to a boil, reduce heat, and simmer until potatoes are just tender, about 20 minutes.
3. Stir in peas and simmer until done, about 5 minutes.

Calories Per Serving: 286	Carbohydrates: 61 g
Fat: 1 g	Dietary Fiber: 7 g
Cholesterol: 0 mg	Sodium: 86 mg
Protein: 10 g	

❋ *Potatoes, Tomatoes, and Green Beans* ❋ *over Couscous*

PREPARATION TIME: *20 minutes plus 5 minutes standing time* •
COOKING TIME: *26 minutes* • YIELD: *4 servings*

1¼ cups low-sodium nonfat chicken broth	1 cup chopped fresh or frozen green beans (1-inch lengths)
2 cloves garlic, minced	1 teaspoon garam masala
1 medium onion, sliced	1 teaspoon chili powder
⅛ teaspoon ground cloves	½ teaspoon ground turmeric
2 bay leaves	½ teaspoon ground coriander
¼ teaspoon ground cinnamon	¼ teaspoon ground black pepper
2 medium tomatoes, coarsely chopped	2 cups boiling water
3 medium potatoes, coarsely chopped	1 cup uncooked couscous

1. Heat ¼ cup broth in a large saucepan. Add garlic and onion, and sauté until onion begins to soften, about 4 minutes. Stir in cloves, bay leaves, and cinnamon, and sauté for 2 more minutes.
2. Add remaining broth, tomatoes, potatoes, green beans, garam masala, chili powder, turmeric, coriander, and black pepper. Bring to a boil, reduce heat, cover, and simmer for 15 minutes.
3. In a separate bowl, pour boiling water over couscous, cover, and allow to stand for 5 minutes.
4. Divide couscous among individual plates, top with the vegetables (remove bay leaves first), and serve.

Calories Per Serving: 357
Fat: 1 g
Cholesterol: 0 mg
Protein: 14 g

Carbohydrates: 74 g
Dietary Fiber: 12 g
Sodium: 102 mg

❋ Microwaved Sweet Potatoes and Fruit ❋

PREPARATION TIME: *15 minutes plus 5 minutes standing time* •
COOKING TIME: *7 minutes* • YIELD: *5 servings*

½ cup coarsely chopped dried prunes
½ cup coarsely chopped dried apricots
½ cup seedless raisins
¼ cup orange juice

½ cup apple juice
¼ teaspoon ground cinnamon
5 cups diced cooked sweet potatoes
   (1-inch cubes)

1. Combine prunes, apricots, raisins, orange juice, apple juice, and cinnamon in a microwave-safe casserole. Cover and microwave on HIGH until fruit is just tender, about 4 minutes.
2. Stir in sweet potatoes, cover, and microwave on HIGH for 3 minutes.
3. Allow casserole to stand for 5 minutes before serving.

Calories Per Serving: 270
Fat: 1 g
Cholesterol: 0 mg
Protein: 4 g

Carbohydrates: 66 g
Dietary Fiber: 5 g
Sodium: 22 mg

❋ Sweet Potatoes, Mushrooms, ❋ and Acorn Squash

PREPARATION TIME: *15 minutes* • COOKING TIME: *1 hour 15 minutes* •
YIELD: *4 servings*

4 cups sliced mushrooms
1 medium onion, thinly sliced
1 cup diced sweet potato
1 cup diced acorn squash
2 cups low-sodium canned tomatoes,
   chopped, juice reserved

3 cloves garlic, minced
¾ cup uncooked wild rice
½ teaspoon ground black pepper
2 cups low-sodium nonfat chicken
   broth

1. Preheat oven to 350 degrees.
2. Combine all ingredients in a 3-quart casserole.
3. Bake for 1 hour 15 minutes.

Calories Per Serving: 250   Carbohydrates: 55 g
Fat: 1 g   Dietary Fiber: 6 g
Cholesterol: 0 mg   Sodium: 52 mg
Protein: 9 g

❈ *Spinach and Tomatoes with Capellini* ❈

PREPARATION TIME: *15 minutes* ▪ COOKING TIME: *10 minutes* ▪
YIELD: *6 servings*

2 quarts water
8 ounces uncooked capellini
2 tablespoons low-sodium nonfat
  chicken broth
2 cloves garlic, minced
3½ cups low-sodium canned tomatoes, chopped, juice reserved

2 cups chopped fresh spinach
1½ teaspoons dried basil
3 tablespoons capers, drained
½ teaspoon ground black pepper
2 tablespoons grated nonfat
  Parmesan

1. Bring water to a rapid boil in a large saucepan. Cook capellini for 5 minutes. Drain well in a colander.
2. Combine capellini, broth, garlic, tomatoes with juice, spinach, basil, capers, and black pepper in the saucepan. Simmer, stirring frequently, for 5 minutes.
3. Transfer to a large platter, top with Parmesan, and serve.

Calories Per Serving: 177   Carbohydrates: 36 g
Fat: 1 g   Dietary Fiber: 3 g
Cholesterol: 0 mg   Sodium: 55 mg
Protein: 7 g

❈ *Fruit-Stuffed Acorn Squash* ❈

PREPARATION TIME: *15 minutes* ▪ COOKING TIME: *1 hour* ▪ YIELD: *4 servings*

2 medium acorn squash, halved
½ cup chopped dried apricots
2 medium apples, peeled, cored, and
    finely chopped
½ cup seedless raisins

3 tablespoons lemon juice
1 tablespoon minced lemon peel
1½ tablespoons honey
¼ teaspoon ground black pepper

1. Preheat oven to 350 degrees.
2. Place squash halves cut side down in a shallow baking dish. Cover them with water and bake for 30 minutes.
3. Combine remaining ingredients and mix well. Turn squash halves upright, place one quarter of the apricot mixture in each half, and return to the oven until squash are cooked through, about 30 more minutes.

Calories Per Serving: 388
Fat: 1 g
Cholesterol: 0 mg
Protein: 6 g

Carbohydrates: 101 g
Dietary Fiber: 11 g
Sodium: 22 mg

❇ Stirfried Spinach and Rice ❇

PREPARATION TIME: 15 minutes   •   COOKING TIME: 13 minutes   •
YIELD: 4 servings

2 tablespoons low-sodium nonfat
    chicken broth
1 medium onion, minced
1 medium carrot, scraped and thinly
    sliced
2 stalks bok choy, chopped
1 medium red bell pepper, cored and
    chopped

1 cup snow peas
1 cup bean sprouts
1 cup shredded fresh spinach
2 cups cooked rice
1 tablespoon reduced-sodium soy
    sauce
½ teaspoon ground black pepper

1. Heat broth in a large skillet. Add onion and carrot, and stirfry until onion begins to soften, about 3 minutes.
2. Add bok choy, bell pepper, snow peas, bean sprouts, and spinach, and cook until spinach is limp, about 4 minutes.
3. Stir in rice, soy sauce, and black pepper. Continue to stir constantly until mixture thickens, about 4 minutes. Transfer to individual plates and serve at once.

Calories Per Serving: 192
Fat: 1 g
Cholesterol: 0 mg
Protein: 9 g

Carbohydrates: 38 g
Dietary Fiber: 6 g
Sodium: 215 mg

❊ *Quick Couscous-Stuffed Tomatoes* ❊

PREPARATION TIME: *20 minutes plus 5 minutes standing time* •
COOKING TIME: *9 minutes* • YIELD: *4 servings*

1 cup boiling water
½ cup uncooked couscous
4 large tomatoes, tops removed and
    flesh and juice scooped out and
    reserved
¼ cup minced onion
3 cups chopped fresh spinach

6 tablespoons grated nonfat
    Parmesan
1 tablespoon bread crumbs
¼ teaspoon dried oregano
¼ teaspoon dried basil
⅛ teaspoon ground nutmeg
¼ teaspoon ground black pepper

1. Preheat broiler.
2. In a bowl, pour boiling water over couscous, cover, and allow to stand for 5 minutes.
3. Combine reserved tomato flesh and juice, onion, and spinach in a large saucepan. Sauté until spinach is limp, about 4 minutes.
4. Mix couscous, 4 tablespoons Parmesan, bread crumbs, oregano, basil, nutmeg, and black pepper. Stir into tomato-onion mixture and mix well.
5. Fill hollowed tomatoes with stuffing mixture, sprinkle remaining Parmesan over the tops, and broil for 3 minutes.

Calories Per Serving: 162
Fat: 1 g
Cholesterol: 10 mg
Protein: 10 g

Carbohydrates: 31 g
Dietary Fiber: 6 g
Sodium: 60 mg

❊ *Spinach and Potatoes* ❊

PREPARATION TIME: *20 minutes* • COOKING TIME: *19 minutes* •
YIELD: *4 servings*

¾ cup low-sodium vegetable broth
2 cups diced potatoes
¼ teaspoon ground turmeric
½ teaspoon chili powder

½ teaspoon ground cumin
6 cups chopped fresh spinach
1 medium tomato, chopped

1. Combine broth, potatoes, turmeric, chili powder, and cumin in a large saucepan. Bring to a boil, reduce heat, and simmer for 10 minutes.
2. Add spinach and tomato, and continue to simmer until spinach is tender, about 5 minutes.
3. Transfer to individual plates and serve.

Calories Per Serving: 134
Fat: 1 g
Cholesterol: 0 mg
Protein: 6 g

Carbohydrates: 28 g
Dietary Fiber: 4 g
Sodium: 111 mg

❋ Zucchini with Tomatoes ❋

PREPARATION TIME: 20 minutes　•　COOKING TIME: 39 minutes　•
YIELD: 6 servings

2¾ cups low-sodium nonfat chicken
　broth
4 cups diced zucchini
2 scallions, minced
4 medium tomatoes, chopped

¼ teaspoon ground black pepper
1 cup uncooked white rice
2 tablespoons grated nonfat
　Parmesan
¼ cup minced fresh parsley

1. Heat ¼ cup broth in a large saucepan. Add zucchini and sauté until soft, about 3 minutes. Remove and set aside.
2. Heat another ¼ cup broth in the saucepan. Add scallions and sauté until soft, about 2 minutes. Add tomatoes and sauté until liquid has evaporated, about 4 minutes.
3. Stir in black pepper, rice, and remaining broth. Bring to a boil, reduce heat, cover, and simmer until rice is just tender, about 20 minutes.
4. Add reserved zucchini, Parmesan, and parsley, and simmer to heat through, about 3 minutes.

Calories Per Serving: 160
Fat: 1 g
Cholesterol: 0 mg
Protein: 6 g

Carbohydrates: 33 g
Dietary Fiber: 2 g
Sodium: 150 mg

❊ Zucchini, Corn, and Mushroom Casserole ❊

PREPARATION TIME: *15 minutes* • COOKING TIME: *24 minutes* •
YIELD: *6 servings*

2 tablespoons low-sodium nonfat
  chicken broth
1 medium onion, chopped
3 scallions, sliced
2 cloves garlic, minced
1 jalapeño pepper, seeded and minced
1 cup sliced zucchini
1 cup fresh, drained canned, or
  thawed frozen corn kernels

2 cups sliced mushrooms
2 cups low-sodium tomato sauce
½ teaspoon dried oregano
½ teaspoon dried thyme
¾ cup cooked rice
½ teaspoon ground black pepper
¼ cup shredded nonfat cheddar

1. Heat broth in a large saucepan. Add onion, scallions, garlic, jalapeño pepper, zucchini, and corn. Sauté until onion begins to soften, about 4 minutes.
2. Stir in mushrooms, tomato sauce, oregano, and thyme, and simmer for 10
   minutes. Add rice and black pepper, and simmer until vegetables are just
   tender and all ingredients are heated through, about 8 more minutes.
3. Serve topped with cheese.

Calories Per Serving: 104
Fat: 0 g
Cholesterol: 1 mg
Protein: 5 g

Carbohydrates: 22 g
Dietary Fiber: 3 g
Sodium: 129 mg

❊ Zucchini and Yellow Squash Sauté ❊

PREPARATION TIME: *15 minutes* • COOKING TIME: *6 minutes* •
YIELD: *4 servings*

¼ cup low-sodium nonfat chicken
  broth
2 cloves garlic, minced
1 medium onion, chopped
2 cups julienned zucchini
2 cups julienned yellow summer
  squash

1 medium red bell pepper, cored and
  julienned
1 medium tomato, chopped
¼ cup chopped fresh parsley
¼ teaspoon dried basil
¼ teaspoon ground black pepper
2 cups cooked rice

1. Heat broth in a large saucepan. Add garlic and onion, and sauté for 2 minutes.
2. Stir in zucchini, squash, and bell pepper, and sauté for 2 more minutes.
3. Add tomato, parsley, basil, and black pepper. Continue to cook until squash is just tender and tomato is heated through, about 2 minutes.
4. Serve over rice.

Calories Per Serving: 163
Fat: 1 g
Cholesterol: 0 mg
Protein: 5 g

Carbohydrates: 36 g
Dietary Fiber: 2 g
Sodium: 29 mg

❈ *Zucchini-Rice Casserole with Green Chiles* ❈

PREPARATION TIME: *15 minutes* ▪ COOKING TIME: *30 minutes* ▪
YIELD: *6 servings*

Olive oil cooking spray
3 cups thinly sliced zucchini
2 cups cooked rice
1 cup nonfat plain yogurt
½ cup canned mild green chiles,
   chopped and drained

1 teaspoon chili powder
2 cloves garlic, minced
¼ teaspoon ground black pepper
½ cup shredded nonfat cheddar

1. Preheat oven to 350 degrees.
2. Lightly coat a 2-quart casserole with olive oil cooking spray. Arrange a layer of half the zucchini on the bottom of the casserole. Spread rice over zucchini.
3. Mix together the yogurt, chiles, chili powder, garlic, and black pepper. Top the rice with the yogurt mixture. Layer on the remaining zucchini and bake for 25 minutes.
4. Top with cheese and return to the oven until cheese melts, about 5 minutes.

Calories Per Serving: 203
Fat: 1 g
Cholesterol: 4 mg
Protein: 12 g

Carbohydrates: 38 g
Dietary Fiber: 2 g
Sodium: 264 mg

❈ *Curried Summer Squash, Broccoli, and Rice* ❈

PREPARATION TIME: *15 minutes* • COOKING TIME: *28 minutes* •
YIELD: *4 servings*

2 cups apple juice
1 medium onion, chopped
3 cloves garlic, minced
1 tablespoon minced fresh gingerroot
1 cup low-sodium tomato juice
3 tablespoons chopped fresh parsley
1 teaspoon ground turmeric

2 teaspoons curry powder
1 teaspoon sugar
1½ cups uncooked white rice
½ cup seedless raisins
3 cups chopped yellow summer
  squash
1 cup chopped broccoli

1. Heat ¼ cup apple juice in a large saucepan. Add onion, garlic, and ginger-root, and sauté until onion begins to soften, about 3 minutes.
2. Add remaining apple juice, tomato juice, parsley, turmeric, curry powder, sugar, and rice. Bring to a boil, reduce heat, cover, and simmer for 15 minutes.
3. Stir in remaining ingredients and simmer until rice is done and vegetables are tender, about 5 more minutes. Drain any excess liquid.
4. Transfer to individual plates and serve.

Calories Per Serving: 430
Fat: 1 g
Cholesterol: 0 mg
Protein: 9 g

Carbohydrates: 99 g
Dietary Fiber: 5 g
Sodium: 30 mg

❈ *Quick Microwave Ratatouille* ❈

PREPARATION TIME: *15 minutes* • COOKING TIME: *10 minutes* •
YIELD: *6 servings*

1 medium onion, chopped
2 cups sliced zucchini
1 medium green bell pepper, cored
  and chopped
2 tablespoons chopped fresh parsley
3 cloves garlic, minced
4 cups diced eggplant

1 teaspoon dried rosemary
1 teaspoon dried basil
½ teaspoon ground black pepper
2 tablespoons low-sodium nonfat
  chicken broth
3 medium tomatoes, chopped

1. Combine onion, zucchini, bell pepper, parsley, garlic, eggplant, rosemary, basil, black pepper, and broth in a microwave-safe 3-quart casserole. Cover and microwave on HIGH for 5 minutes.
2. Stir in tomatoes and microwave until vegetables are tender, about 5 more minutes.

Calories Per Serving: 44
Fat: 0 g
Cholesterol: 0 mg
Protein: 2 g

Carbohydrates: 10 g
Dietary Fiber: 2 g
Sodium: 21 mg

❁ *Zucchini and Pattypan Casserole* ❁

PREPARATION TIME: *15 minutes* • COOKING TIME: *33 minutes* •
YIELD: *6 servings*

Olive oil cooking spray
3 cups cooked rice
2 cups diced zucchini
2 cups diced pattypan squash
1 medium red bell pepper, cored and diced
½ teaspoon dried dill

2 cups nonfat plain yogurt
2 egg whites, lightly beaten
½ teaspoon ground black pepper
¼ cup chopped onion
½ cup nonfat whole-grain bread crumbs
3 tablespoons grated nonfat cheddar

1. Preheat oven to 350 degrees. Lightly coat a 3-quart casserole with olive oil cooking spray.
2. Spread rice on the bottom of the casserole.
3. In a separate bowl, combine zucchini, squash, bell pepper, and dill. Layer over rice.
4. Mix yogurt, egg whites, black pepper, and onion, and spoon over vegetables in the casserole. Top with bread crumbs and bake for 30 minutes. Sprinkle cheese over the top and return to the oven until cheese melts, about 3 more minutes.

Calories Per Serving: 216
Fat: 1 g
Cholesterol: 2 mg
Protein: 10 g

Carbohydrates: 41 g
Dietary Fiber: 3 g
Sodium: 116 mg

❋ *Pattypan Squash and Tomatoes* ❋

PREPARATION TIME: *15 minutes* • COOKING TIME: *18 minutes* •
YIELD: *4 servings*

¼ cup low-sodium nonfat chicken
  broth
1 medium onion, chopped
4 cups thinly sliced pattypan squash

1 clove garlic, minced
2 medium tomatoes, chopped
¼ teaspoon cayenne pepper
1½ cups cooked rice

1. Heat broth in a large skillet. Add onion and sauté until it begins to soften, about 3 minutes.
2. Add squash and sauté for 3 more minutes.
3. Stir in remaining ingredients, cover, and simmer until heated through, about 10 minutes.

Calories Per Serving: 140
Fat: 1 g
Cholesterol: 0 mg
Protein: 5 g

Carbohydrates: 31 g
Dietary Fiber: 3 g
Sodium: 35 mg

❋ *Microwaved Spaghetti Squash* ❋

PREPARATION TIME: *15 minutes* • COOKING TIME: *21 minutes* •
YIELD: *4 servings*

1 spaghetti squash (approximately
  3 pounds)
3 medium tomatoes, chopped
1 cup chopped zucchini

3 scallions, sliced
1 teaspoon dried basil
1 tablespoon balsamic vinegar
¼ teaspoon ground black pepper

1. Pierce the skin of the squash in several places. Microwave, on a paper plate, on HIGH for 8 minutes. Turn the squash and microwave on HIGH until tender, about 8 more minutes. Remove and set aside.
2. Combine tomatoes, zucchini, and scallions in a microwave-safe 3-quart casserole. Cover loosely with wax paper or a paper towel and microwave on HIGH, stirring once, for 5 minutes. Stir in remaining ingredients.
3. Halve the squash and discard the seeds. Scoop out the flesh and strings and transfer to a serving plate. Top with vegetable sauce and serve.

Calories Per Serving: 96

Carbohydrates: 21 g

Fat: 1 g

Dietary Fiber: 6 g

Cholesterol: 0 mg

Sodium: 20 mg

Protein: 5 g

❀ *Butternut Squash and Apples in Red Wine* ❀

PREPARATION TIME: *20 minutes* • COOKING TIME: *31 minutes* •
YIELD: *6 servings*

¼ cup low-sodium nonfat chicken
  broth
¼ cup chopped onion
2 cups chopped apples
3 cups chopped butternut squash

½ cup dry red wine
1½ cups chopped dried apricots
1½ cups chopped pitted prunes
¼ teaspoon ground cinnamon
2 cups cooked rice

1. Heat broth in a large saucepan. Add onion, apples, and squash, and sauté until onion begins to soften, about 4 minutes.
2. Add wine, apricots, prunes, and cinnamon, and simmer for 25 minutes.
3. Serve over rice.

Calories Per Serving: 338

Carbohydrates: 83 g

Fat: 1 g

Dietary Fiber: 9 g

Cholesterol: 0 mg

Sodium: 18 mg

Protein: 5 g

❀ *Mixed Curried Vegetables* ❀

PREPARATION TIME: *15 minutes* • COOKING TIME: *22 minutes* •
YIELD: *4 servings*

2¼ cups low-sodium vegetable broth
1 medium onion, chopped
3 cloves garlic, minced
¼ teaspoon cayenne pepper
½ teaspoon ground cumin
1 tablespoon ground coriander
2 teaspoons ground cardamom
½ teaspoon ground turmeric
½ teaspoon ground cinnamon

1½ teaspoons minced fresh gingerroot
1 cup chopped cauliflower
1 cup chopped broccoli
2 medium carrots, scraped and sliced
2 cups chopped celery
2 cups chopped green beans (1-inch
  lengths)
2 cups cooked rice

1. Heat ¼ cup broth in a large pot. Add onion and sauté until it begins to soften, about 3 minutes.
2. Add garlic, cayenne pepper, cumin, coriander, cardamom, turmeric, cinnamon, and gingerroot. Sauté for 1 more minute.
3. Stir in remaining broth, cauliflower, broccoli, carrots, celery, and green beans. Bring to a boil, reduce heat, cover, and simmer until vegetables are just tender, about 15 minutes.
4. Serve over rice.

Calories Per Serving: 204

Fat: 1 g

Cholesterol: 0 mg

Protein: 6 g

Carbohydrates: 43 g

Dietary Fiber: 4 g

Sodium: 247 mg

❋ *Mixed Fruit and Vegetable Curry* ❋

PREPARATION TIME: *20 minutes* • COOKING TIME: *39 minutes* •
YIELD: *6 servings*

1 teaspoon ground cumin

1 teaspoon ground coriander

1 teaspoon ground cinnamon

1 teaspoon ground turmeric

¼ teaspoon cayenne pepper

½ teaspoon fennel seeds

¼ teaspoon ground cardamom

¼ teaspoon ground cloves

1¾ cups low-sodium nonfat chicken broth

2 medium onions, chopped

2 cloves garlic, minced

1½ teaspoons minced fresh gingerroot

2 cups chopped zucchini

1 cup chopped fresh or thawed frozen green beans (1-inch lengths)

2 medium tart apples, peeled, cored, and chopped

1 medium red bell pepper, cored and chopped

¾ cup dried apricots

½ cup seedless raisins

½ cup sugarless all-fruit apricot jam

2 tablespoons lemon juice

3 cups cooked rice

1. In a bowl, combine cumin, coriander, cinnamon, turmeric, cayenne pepper, fennel seeds, cardamom, and cloves. Mix well and set aside.
2. Heat ¼ cup broth in a large saucepan. Add onions, garlic, and gingerroot, and sauté until onions begin to soften, about 4 minutes. Stir in spice mixture and continue to sauté for 5 more minutes.
3. Add remaining broth, zucchini, green beans, apples, bell pepper, and apricots. Bring to a boil, reduce heat, and simmer until vegetables are just ten-

der, about 20 minutes. Stir in raisins and jam, and heat all ingredients through, about 5 minutes. Stir in lemon juice.
4. Serve over rice.

Calories Per Serving: 264
Fat: 1 g
Cholesterol: 0 mg
Protein: 7 g

Carbohydrates: 61 g
Dietary Fiber: 4 g
Sodium: 58 mg

❊ *Easy Fruit Curry* ❊

PREPARATION TIME: *20 minutes* ▪ COOKING TIME: *45 minutes* ▪
YIELD: *6 servings*

Olive oil cooking spray
3 medium apricots, pitted and halved
3 medium pears, cored and halved
3 medium peaches, pitted and halved
6 slices fresh or canned pineapple

2 medium bananas, sliced
¼ cup orange juice
¼ cup brown sugar
2 tablespoons curry powder

1. Preheat oven to 325 degrees. Lightly coat a 9 × 13-inch baking dish with olive oil cooking spray.
2. Arrange fruit in the prepared baking dish. In a separate bowl, combine orange juice, brown sugar, and curry powder, and pour over fruit.
3. Bake uncovered for 45 minutes.

Calories Per Serving: 259
Fat: 1 g
Cholesterol: 0 mg
Protein: 2 g

Carbohydrates: 67 g
Dietary Fiber: 6 g
Sodium: 19 mg

STEWS

One Potato, Two Potato Chicken Stew • Autumn Harvest
Chicken Stew • Chicken and Green Bean Stew • Chicken-
Linguine Stew • Sherried Chicken Stew • Chicken Stew with
Tomatoes and Zucchini • Chicken–Yellow Squash Stew • Bell
Pepper, Chicken, and Green Pea Stew • Chicken-Vegetable Stew
• Chicken, Potato, and Corn Stew • Chicken–Lima Bean
Stew • Mulligatawny Stew • Turkey Meatball and Vegetable
Stew • Turkey Sangría • Gingered Oyster Stew • Okra-Crab
Gumbo • Vegetable-Scallop Stew • Seafood Stew with White
Wine • Scallop-Spinach Stew • Shrimp Stew with Yellow
Pepper • Jalapeño-Shrimp Gumbo • Spicy Cod and Vegetable
Stew • November Vegetable Fish Stew • Fisherman's Casserole
• Haddock Stew with Rice • Orange Roughy, Scallop, and Shrimp
Stew • Fisherman's Stew with Sun-Dried Tomatoes • Flounder,
Shrimp, Crab, and Clam Stew with Farfalle • Shrimp, Haddock,
and Eggplant Stew • Green Pepper–Tofu Stew • Green Bean,
Turnip, and Eggplant Stew • Tofu Stew with Couscous • Cabbage
Stew • Pumpkin-Corn Stew • African Vegetable Stew •
Shiitake Mushroom and Squash Stew • Broccoli and Cauliflower
Stew • Fruit and Sweet Potato Stew • Winter Squash Stew •

Greek Peasant Stew ▪ Yam and Green Pea Stew with Yellow Bell
Pepper ▪ Vegetarian Okra Gumbo ▪ Sweet Potato–Red
Pepper–Corn Stew ▪ Zucchini-Yam Stew ▪ Spicy Green Bean
and Tomato Stew ▪ Red Lentil Stew ▪ Lentil Stew with Red
Wine and Garlic ▪ Sherried Lentil Stew with Shiitake Mushrooms
▪ Black Bean–Pumpkin Stew ▪ Kidney Bean Stew with Garlic and
Sherry ▪ Eggplant, Red Potato, and Chickpea Stew ▪ Cauliflower,
Spinach, and Chickpea Stew ▪ Kale, Tomato, and Chickpea Stew
▪ Zucchini and Chickpea Stew ▪ Eggplant, Navy Bean, and
Mushroom Stew ▪ Great Northern Bean and Red Pepper Stew
with Rosemary ▪ Navy Bean and Clam Stew with White Wine ▪
Great Northern Bean and Pumpkin Stew ▪ Zucchini–Great
Northern Bean Stew with Moroccan Spices ▪ Lobster, Clam,
and Shrimp Stew

❋ *One Potato, Two Potato Chicken Stew* ❋

PREPARATION TIME: *15 minutes* • COOKING TIME: *35 minutes* •
YIELD: *7 servings*

2¼ cups low-sodium nonfat chicken
 broth
2 skinless boneless chicken breast tenderloins, about 4 ounces each,
 chopped
2 medium onions, sliced
4 scallions, sliced
2 cloves garlic, minced
1 jalapeño pepper, seeded and minced

4 medium stalks celery, sliced
2 medium tomatoes, chopped
1 cup diced potato
1 cup diced sweet potato
½ teaspoon dried oregano
2 bay leaves
½ teaspoon ground black pepper
¼ cup chopped fresh parsley

1. Heat ¼ cup broth in a large saucepan. Add chicken and sauté until no
   longer pink, about 8 minutes.
2. Add onions, scallions, garlic, jalapeño pepper, and celery, and sauté until
   onion begins to soften, about 4 more minutes.
3. Stir in remaining broth, tomatoes, potato, sweet potato, oregano, bay
   leaves, and black pepper. Bring to a boil, reduce heat, cover, and simmer
   until chicken is cooked through and vegetables are just tender, about 18
   minutes.
4. Remove bay leaves and serve topped with parsley.

Calories Per Serving: 145
Fat: 1 g
Cholesterol: 30 mg
Protein: 12 g

Carbohydrates: 23 g
Dietary Fiber: 3 g
Sodium: 159 mg

❋ *Autumn Harvest Chicken Stew* ❋

PREPARATION TIME: *25 minutes* • COOKING TIME: *46 minutes* •
YIELD: *8 servings*

¼ cup dry white wine

4 skinless boneless chicken breast tenderloins, about 4 ounces each,
chopped

5¼ cups low-sodium nonfat chicken
broth

2 medium onions, chopped

4 cloves garlic, minced

2 medium leeks (white parts only),
chopped

4 medium potatoes, peeled and
chopped

4 medium carrots, scraped and sliced

1 medium turnip, peeled and chopped

1 medium sweet potato, peeled and
chopped

2 teaspoons dried oregano

2 teaspoons dried thyme

1 cup chopped broccoli

1 cup chopped cauliflower

¼ teaspoon ground black pepper

3 cups cooked rice

1. Heat wine in a large pot. Add chicken and sauté until chicken is no longer
   pink, about 8 minutes. Remove and set aside.
2. Heat ¼ cup broth in the pot. Add onions and garlic, and sauté until onions
   begin to soften, about 4 minutes.
3. Add remaining broth, leeks, potatoes, carrots, turnip, sweet potato,
   oregano, and thyme. Bring to a boil, reduce heat, cover, and simmer for 15
   minutes.
4. Add broccoli and cauliflower, and simmer until chicken is cooked through
   and vegetables are just tender, about 10 more minutes. Stir in black pepper.
5. Serve over rice.

Calories Per Serving: 332
Fat: 1 g
Cholesterol: 26 mg
Protein: 21 g

Carbohydrates: 60 g
Dietary Fiber: 1 g
Sodium: 172 mg

✳ Chicken and Green Bean Stew ✳

PREPARATION TIME: 15 minutes ▪ COOKING TIME: 36 minutes ▪
YIELD: 4 servings

6 tablespoons low-sodium nonfat
chicken broth

3 skinless boneless chicken breast tenderloins, about 4 ounces each,
chopped

1 medium onion, chopped

3 medium stalks celery, chopped

6 medium carrots, scraped and sliced

1 cup sliced mushrooms

2 cups low-sodium canned tomatoes,
chopped, juice reserved

⅓ cup dry white wine

2 cloves garlic, minced

¾ teaspoon dried rosemary

¼ teaspoon ground black pepper
2 cups diced potatoes

1 cup chopped fresh or thawed frozen
green beans (2-inch lengths)

1. Heat 4 tablespoons broth in a large saucepan. Add chicken and sauté until no longer pink, about 8 minutes. Remove and set aside.
2. Heat remaining broth in the saucepan. Add onion, celery, carrots, and mushrooms. Sauté until onion begins to soften, about 4 minutes.
3. Stir in tomatoes with juice, white wine, garlic, rosemary, black pepper, potatoes, and green beans. Return chicken to the saucepan, cover, and simmer, stirring frequently, until chicken is cooked through and vegetables are tender, about 20 minutes.

Calories Per Serving: 247
Fat: 1 g
Cholesterol: 35 mg
Protein: 19 g

Carbohydrates: 41 g
Dietary Fiber: 6 g
Sodium: 99 mg

❈ *Chicken Linguine Stew* ❈

PREPARATION TIME: *20 minutes* • COOKING TIME: *38 minutes* •
YIELD: *5 servings*

3¾ cups low-sodium nonfat chicken
broth
2 skinless boneless chicken breast
tenderloins, about 4 ounces each
1 medium onion, chopped
2 cloves garlic, minced
2 medium green bell peppers, cored
and chopped
2 cups low-sodium canned tomatoes,
chopped, juice reserved

1 cup diced potato
½ cup chopped fresh parsley
½ teaspoon dried basil
½ teaspoon dried oregano
1 bay leaf
½ teaspoon ground black pepper
2 ounces uncooked linguine, broken
into small pieces

1. Heat ¼ cup broth in a large saucepan. Add chicken and sauté until no longer pink, about 8 minutes. Remove and set aside.
2. Heat 2 tablespoons broth in the saucepan. Add onion and garlic, and sauté until onion begins to soften, about 3 minutes. Add bell peppers and sauté for 5 more minutes. Add more broth if necessary.
3. Stir in remaining broth, tomatoes with juice, potato, ¼ cup parsley, the basil, oregano, bay leaf, and black pepper. Return chicken to the saucepan. Bring to a boil and stir in pasta. Reduce heat and simmer until pasta is tender and chicken is cooked through, about 15 minutes.
4. Remove bay leaf. Serve sprinkled with remaining parsley.

Calories Per Serving: 138
Fat: 1 g
Cholesterol: 28 mg
Protein: 14 g

Carbohydrates: 16 g
Dietary Fiber: 1 g
Sodium: 252 mg

❋ *Sherried Chicken Stew* ❋

PREPARATION TIME: *20 minutes* • COOKING TIME: *32 minutes* •
YIELD: *6 servings*

3 cups low-sodium nonfat chicken
   broth
4 skinless boneless chicken breast tenderloins, about 4 ounces each,
   chopped
1½ cups uncooked white rice
3 scallions, sliced
2 cloves garlic, minced

2 medium carrots, scraped and grated
¾ cup minced dried apricots
¼ cup seedless raisins
¼ teaspoon ground allspice
1 tablespoon curry powder
1 cup orange juice
½ cup dry sherry
½ teaspoon ground black pepper

1. Heat ¼ cup broth in a large saucepan. Add chicken and sauté until no longer pink, about 8 minutes.
2. Stir in remaining ingredients. Bring to a boil, reduce heat, cover, and simmer until chicken is cooked through and rice is tender, about 20 minutes.

Calories Per Serving: 341
Fat: 1 g
Cholesterol: 47 mg
Protein: 23 g

Carbohydrates: 54 g
Dietary Fiber: 2 g
Sodium: 186 mg

❋ *Chicken Stew with Tomatoes and Zucchini* ❋

PREPARATION TIME: *20 minutes plus 1 hour marinating time* •
COOKING TIME: *54 minutes* • YIELD: *6 servings*

1 teaspoon dried oregano
6 skinless boneless chicken breast tenderloins, about 4 ounces each,
   chopped

7¼ cups low-sodium nonfat chicken
   broth
1 medium onion, diced
2 cloves garlic, minced

1 jalapeño pepper, seeded and minced
4 medium tomatoes, chopped
1½ cups uncooked white rice
2 cups diced zucchini

¼ teaspoon ground black pepper
½ cup green peas
3 tablespoons grated nonfat
　Parmesan

1. Sprinkle oregano on chicken. Place chicken in a covered bowl and refrigerate for 1 hour.
2. Heat ¼ cup broth in a large pot. Add chicken and sauté until no longer pink, about 8 minutes.
3. Add onion, garlic, and jalapeño pepper, and sauté until onion begins to soften, about 3 minutes. Stir in tomatoes, reduce heat, cover, and simmer until chicken is cooked through, about 20 minutes. Add broth if necessary. Remove chicken and set aside.
4. Add remaining broth, rice, zucchini, and black pepper to the pot. Bring to a boil, reduce heat, cover, and simmer until rice is just tender, about 15 minutes. Return chicken to the pot, add green peas and Parmesan, and simmer for about 4 minutes. Drain any excess liquid before serving.

Calories Per Serving: 412
Fat: 2 g
Cholesterol: 73 mg
Protein: 44 g

Carbohydrates: 54 g
Dietary Fiber: 4 g
Sodium: 375 mg

❋ Chicken–Yellow Squash Stew ❋

PREPARATION TIME: 25 minutes　•　COOKING TIME: 51 minutes　•　YIELD: 6 servings

6¼ cups low-sodium nonfat chicken
　broth
4 skinless boneless chicken breast tenderloins, about 4 ounces each, cut into 1-inch cubes
2 medium onions, quartered
2 medium red potatoes, cubed

1 clove garlic, minced
1 bay leaf
½ teaspoon dried oregano
3 cups diced yellow summer squash
3 medium tomatoes, quartered
2 tablespoons minced fresh parsley
½ teaspoon ground black pepper

1. Heat ¼ cup broth in a large saucepan. Add chicken and sauté until no longer pink, about 8 minutes.
2. Add remaining broth. Bring to a boil, reduce heat, and simmer for 15 minutes.
3. Add onions, potatoes, garlic, bay leaf, oregano, squash, and tomatoes, and simmer until vegetables are tender and chicken is cooked through, about 20 minutes. Remove bay leaf.
4. Stir in parsley and black pepper, transfer to individual bowls, and serve.

Calories Per Serving: 246
Fat: 1 g
Cholesterol: 47 mg
Protein: 31 g

Carbohydrates: 28 g
Dietary Fiber: 6 g
Sodium: 226 mg

❋ Bell Pepper, Chicken, and Green Pea Stew ❋

PREPARATION TIME: *20 minutes* • COOKING TIME: *35 minutes* •
YIELD: *4 servings*

½ cup low-sodium nonfat chicken
broth
3 skinless boneless chicken breast tenderloins, about 4 ounces each,
chopped
1 medium onion, chopped
3 cloves garlic, minced
2 medium green bell peppers, cored
and cut into thin strips
4 medium tomatoes, chopped

1 cup low-sodium tomato sauce
1½ teaspoons dried oregano
½ teaspoon dried basil
1 tablespoon honey
¼ teaspoon ground black pepper
¾ cup fresh or thawed frozen green
peas
1 tablespoon balsamic vinegar
3 cups cooked rice

1. Heat ¼ cup broth in a large saucepan. Add chicken, onion, garlic, and bell
   peppers, and sauté until chicken is no longer pink, about 8 minutes.
2. Stir in remaining broth, tomatoes, tomato sauce, oregano, basil, honey,
   and black pepper. Cover and simmer, stirring occasionally, for 20 minutes.
3. Add peas and balsamic vinegar, and simmer for 5 more minutes.
4. Serve over rice.

Calories Per Serving: 387
Fat: 2 g
Cholesterol: 53 mg
Protein: 29 g

Carbohydrates: 64 g
Dietary Fiber: 4 g
Sodium: 97 mg

❋ Chicken-Vegetable Stew ❋

PREPARATION TIME: *15 minutes* • COOKING TIME: *38 minutes* •
YIELD: *4 servings*

1¼ cups low-sodium nonfat chicken broth
2 skinless boneless chicken breast tenderloins, about 4 ounces each, chopped
1½ cups diced potatoes
3 medium carrots, scraped and sliced
1 medium onion, sliced
5 medium stalks celery, sliced
½ cup chopped fresh parsley
½ teaspoon dried basil
½ teaspoon dried oregano
1 teaspoon paprika
¼ teaspoon ground white pepper
2 cloves garlic, peeled and chopped

1. In a large saucepan, bring ¾ cup broth and the chopped chicken to a boil, reduce heat, cover, and simmer for 10 minutes.
2. Add remaining ingredients. Return to a boil. Reduce heat, cover, and simmer until chicken is cooked through and vegetables are tender, about 25 minutes.
3. Transfer to individual bowls and serve.

Calories Per Serving: 218
Fat: 1 g
Cholesterol: 53 mg
Protein: 23 g
Carbohydrates: 28 g
Dietary Fiber: 4 g
Sodium: 200 mg

Chicken, Potato, and Corn Stew

Preparation Time: *20 minutes* ▪ Cooking Time: *44 minutes* ▪ Yield: *6 servings*

2¼ cups low-sodium nonfat chicken broth
4 skinless boneless chicken breast tenderloins, about 4 ounces each, chopped
2 scallions, sliced
6 tablespoons chopped fresh parsley
¼ teaspoon ground cumin
¼ teaspoon ground black pepper
3 medium carrots, scraped and sliced
3 medium white potatoes, cubed
2 cups fresh or thawed frozen corn kernels
½ cup skim milk

1. Heat ¼ cup broth in a large saucepan. Add chicken and sauté until chicken is no longer pink, about 8 minutes. Add scallions and 4 tablespoons parsley, and sauté for 1 more minute.
2. Stir in remaining broth, cumin, and black pepper. Bring to a boil. Reduce heat, cover, and simmer for 10 minutes.
3. Add carrots and potatoes, cover, and simmer for 10 more minutes.

4. Stir in corn and milk, and simmer uncovered until carrots and potatoes are just tender, about 10 minutes.
5. Transfer to individual bowls, garnish with remaining parsley, and serve.

Calories Per Serving: 423
Fat: 2 g
Cholesterol: 47 mg
Protein: 27 g

Carbohydrates: 78 g
Dietary Fiber: 13 g
Sodium: 296 mg

❋ Chicken—Lima Bean Stew ❋

PREPARATION TIME: *20 minutes* • COOKING TIME: *34 minutes* •
YIELD: *8 servings*

¼ cup low-sodium nonfat chicken
 broth
6 skinless boneless chicken breast tenderloins, about 4 ounces each,
 chopped
4 cups low-sodium canned tomatoes,
 juice reserved
1 cup fresh or thawed frozen corn
 kernels

3 cups fresh or thawed frozen lima
 beans
1 medium potato, peeled and cubed
1 medium onion, chopped
¼ teaspoon ground black pepper
⅛ teaspoon cayenne pepper
2 tablespoons all-purpose flour

1. Heat broth in a large pot. Add chicken and sauté until no longer pink, about 8 minutes.
2. Stir in tomatoes with juice, corn, lima beans, potato, onion, black pepper, and cayenne pepper. Bring to a boil, reduce heat, cover, and simmer until chicken is cooked through, about 20 minutes. Stir in flour and bring to a boil, stirring constantly, for 1 minute.

Calories Per Serving: 199
Fat: 2 g
Cholesterol: 53 mg
Protein: 24 g

Carbohydrates: 24 g
Dietary Fiber: 6 g
Sodium: 68 mg

❋ Mulligatawny Stew ❋

PREPARATION TIME: *15 minutes* • COOKING TIME: *23 minutes* •
YIELD: *8 servings*

¼ cup low-sodium nonfat chicken
  broth
2 skinless boneless chicken breast tenderloins, about 4 ounces each,
  chopped
1 teaspoon curry powder
4 cups water
1 teaspoon lemon juice
¼ teaspoon ground cloves
⅛ teaspoon ground mace

1 medium onion, chopped
1 medium carrot, scraped and sliced
1 medium apple, peeled, cored, and
  chopped
1 medium green bell pepper, cored
  and chopped
2 cups low-sodium canned tomatoes,
  drained and chopped
½ teaspoon ground black pepper
¼ cup chopped fresh parsley

1. Heat broth in a large Dutch oven. Add chicken and curry powder, and sauté until chicken is no longer pink, about 8 minutes.
2. Add water, lemon juice, cloves, mace, onion, carrot, apple, bell pepper, tomatoes, and black pepper. Bring to a boil, reduce heat, and simmer until carrots are just tender, about 15 minutes.
3. Serve topped with parsley.

Calories Per Serving: 84
Fat: 1 g
Cholesterol: 10 mg
Protein: 10 g

Carbohydrates: 10 g
Dietary Fiber: 2 g
Sodium: 35 mg

❆ *Turkey Meatball and Vegetable Stew* ❆

PREPARATION TIME: 43 minutes • COOKING TIME: 1 hour 20 minutes •
YIELD: 8 *servings*

¾ pound ground turkey breast
½ cup rolled oats
2 egg whites
4 scallions, minced
1 medium green bell pepper, cored
  and minced
1 teaspoon ground black pepper
3 cloves garlic, minced
¼ cup skim milk
3¼ cups low-sodium nonfat chicken
  broth

1 medium onion, chopped
2 tablespoons all-purpose flour
1 cup dry white wine
2 medium sweet potatoes, diced
2 cups chopped fresh or frozen green
  beans (1-inch lengths)
3 medium stalks celery, sliced
3 medium turnips, diced
¼ cup chopped fresh parsley
1 teaspoon dried thyme

1. Combine ground turkey, oats, egg whites, scallions, bell pepper, ½ teaspoon black pepper, garlic, and skim milk. Mix well and form into 1-inch meatballs.

2. Place meatballs on a steamer rack in a large soup pot over 1 cup chicken broth. Steam for 10 minutes or until no longer pink.
3. Remove meatballs and discard any remaining steaming liquid.
4. Heat ¼ cup broth in the pot. Add onion and sauté until it begins to soften, about 3 minutes. Whisk together remaining broth, flour, and wine. Pour into the pot.
5. Add all remaining ingredients. Bring to a boil, reduce heat, and simmer until vegetables are tender, about 30 minutes.

Calories Per Serving: 180
Fat: 1 g
Cholesterol: 26 mg
Protein: 17 g

Carbohydrates: 22 g
Dietary Fiber: 4 g
Sodium: 123 mg

❋ Turkey Sangría ❋

PREPARATION TIME: *20 minutes* • COOKING TIME: *32 minutes* •
YIELD: *8 servings*

1 medium onion, finely chopped
1 medium tart apple, peeled, cored, and finely chopped
1 tablespoon brown sugar
3 tablespoons lemon juice
1 tablespoon minced lemon peel
½ cup sangría

1½ cups low-sodium nonfat chicken broth
8 skinless boneless turkey breast tenderloins, about 4 ounces each
2 teaspoons cornstarch
3 tablespoons hot water
1 cup sliced juice-packed canned peaches, juice reserved

1. Preheat oven to 350 degrees.
2. Combine onion, apple, brown sugar, lemon juice, and lemon peel in a flameproof 3-quart casserole. Stir over medium heat until liquid has evaporated, about 4 minutes.
3. Stir in sangría and broth. Add turkey, cover, and bake for 25 minutes.
4. In a separate bowl, combine cornstarch and water, and mix well. Stir into turkey casserole, add peaches with juice, and simmer on top of the stove until mixture begins to thicken, about 3 minutes.
5. Transfer turkey to individual plates, top with peach mixture, and serve.

Calories Per Serving: 173
Fat: 1 g
Cholesterol: 70 mg
Protein: 27 g

Carbohydrates: 10 g
Dietary Fiber: 1 g
Sodium: 111 mg

❋ *Gingered Oyster Stew* ❋

PREPARATION TIME: *15 minutes* • COOKING TIME: *5 minutes* •
YIELD: *4 servings*

6 tablespoons low-sodium vegetable
   broth
1 tablespoon reduced-sodium soy
   sauce
1 teaspoon grated fresh gingerroot
1½ cups shucked oysters, liquid reserved

2 cups chopped bok choy
2 cups chopped mushrooms
½ cup bean sprouts
1½ cups snow peas
4 scallions, sliced

1. Combine broth, soy sauce, and gingerroot in a large saucepan. Bring to a boil, add oysters with liquid, bok choy, mushrooms, bean sprouts, and snow peas. Return to boil, reduce heat, cover, and simmer until bok choy is just beginning to soften, about 2 minutes.
2. Serve topped with scallions.

Calories Per Serving: 200
Fat: 2 g
Cholesterol: 22 mg
Protein: 12 g

Carbohydrates: 35 g
Dietary Fiber: 6 g
Sodium: 347 mg

❋ *Okra-Crab Gumbo* ❋

PREPARATION TIME: *25 minutes* • COOKING TIME: *1 hour 5 minutes* •
YIELD: *8 servings*

4¼ cups low-sodium nonfat chicken
   broth
1 cup chopped onion
2 medium carrots, scraped and sliced
2 medium stalks celery, sliced
2 bay leaves
2 teaspoons dried thyme
¼ cup chopped fresh parsley
1 tablespoon paprika

1 medium green bell pepper, cored
   and chopped
1 cup diced potato
3 cups sliced okra
2 cups low-sodium canned tomatoes,
   drained and chopped
½ teaspoon cayenne pepper
½ teaspoon ground black pepper
1½ pounds crabmeat

1. Heat ¼ cup broth in a large saucepan. Add onion, carrots, and celery, and sauté until onion begins to soften, about 4 minutes. Stir in remaining

broth, bay leaves, thyme, parsley, paprika, bell pepper, potato, okra, tomatoes, and cayenne pepper. Mix well, bring to a boil, reduce heat, and simmer for 45 minutes. Remove bay leaves.
2. Stir in black pepper and crabmeat, and simmer for 10 more minutes.

Calories Per Serving: 209
Fat: 2 g
Cholesterol: 76 mg
Protein: 25 g

Carbohydrates: 24 g
Dietary Fiber: 3 g
Sodium: 405 mg

❊ *Vegetable-Scallop Stew* ❊

PREPARATION TIME: *20 minutes* • COOKING TIME: *33 minutes* •
YIELD: *4 servings*

¼ cup low-sodium nonfat chicken
  broth
1 medium onion, chopped
1 clove garlic, minced
¼ teaspoon ground cumin
¼ teaspoon cayenne pepper
3½ cups low-sodium canned tomatoes, crushed, juice reserved
3 cups water

½ teaspoon dried oregano
2 cups chopped cauliflower
1 cup chopped green beans (1-inch
  lengths)
1 medium carrot, scraped and sliced
2 cups fresh scallops
½ teaspoon ground black pepper
¼ cup chopped fresh parsley

1. Heat broth in a large saucepan. Add onion and garlic, and sauté until onion begins to soften, about 4 minutes.
2. Add cumin, cayenne pepper, tomatoes with juice, water, and oregano. Simmer for 10 minutes.
3. Add cauliflower, green beans, and carrot, and continue to simmer for 15 more minutes.
4. Stir in scallops and black pepper, and simmer until scallops are opaque, about 2 minutes.
5. Serve topped with parsley.

Calories Per Serving: 144
Fat: 1 g
Cholesterol: 22 mg
Protein: 15 g

Carbohydrates: 20 g
Dietary Fiber: 3 g
Sodium: 182 mg

❈ *Seafood Stew with White Wine* ❈

PREPARATION TIME: *20 minutes* • COOKING TIME: *19 minutes* •
YIELD: *6 servings*

2 cups dry white wine
3 cups bottled clam juice
½ cup minced onion
2 tablespoons minced fresh parsley
1 pound fresh medium shrimp,
   peeled, deveined, and halved

½ cup crabmeat
½ pound fresh scallops, halved
½ teaspoon ground black pepper

1. Bring wine, clam juice, onion, and parsley to a boil. Reduce heat, cover, and simmer for 5 minutes.
2. Add shrimp, crabmeat, and scallops. Cover and simmer for 10 more minutes.
3. Stir in black pepper, transfer to individual bowls, and serve.

Calories Per Serving: 191
Fat: 2 g
Cholesterol: 140 mg
Protein: 25 g

Carbohydrates: 4 g
Dietary Fiber: 0 g
Sodium: 787 mg

❈ *Scallop-Spinach Stew* ❈

PREPARATION TIME: *20 minutes* • COOKING TIME: *24 minutes* •
YIELD: *4 servings*

2 teaspoons sesame oil
1 medium onion, thinly sliced
3 cloves garlic, minced
1 medium green bell pepper, cored
   and diced
2 teaspoons minced fresh gingerroot
1 tablespoon reduced-sodium soy
   sauce

2 cups low-sodium nonfat chicken
   broth
2 medium carrots, scraped and sliced
2 cups chopped fresh spinach
3 scallions, sliced
½ cup sliced shiitake mushrooms
1 cup canned bamboo shoots, drained
2 cups fresh scallops

1. Heat oil in a large skillet. Add onion, garlic, and bell pepper, and sauté for 2 minutes.
2. Add gingerroot, soy sauce, broth, and carrots. Simmer for 10 minutes.

3. Stir in spinach, scallions, mushrooms, and bamboo shoots, and simmer for 5 more minutes.
4. Add scallops and cook until scallops are opaque, about 5 minutes.

Calories Per Serving: 196   Carbohydrates: 19 g
Fat: 3 g   Dietary Fiber: 4 g
Cholesterol: 29 mg   Sodium: 476 mg
Protein: 17 g

❋ *Shrimp Stew with Yellow Pepper* ❋

PREPARATION TIME: *20 minutes* • COOKING TIME: *27 minutes* •
YIELD: *6 servings*

*¼ cup low-sodium nonfat chicken
  broth*
1 medium onion, diced
*1 medium yellow bell pepper, cored
  and diced*
3 cups boiling water
2 cups diced potatoes
*2 cups low-sodium canned tomatoes,
  chopped, juice reserved*

1 bay leaf
½ teaspoon ground black pepper
⅛ teaspoon hot pepper sauce
*1½ pounds fresh medium shrimp,
  peeled and deveined*
¼ cup chopped fresh parsley

1. Heat broth in a large saucepan. Add onion and bell pepper, and sauté until onion begins to soften, about 4 minutes.
2. Stir in boiling water, potatoes, tomatoes with juice, bay leaf, black pepper, and hot pepper sauce. Bring to a boil, reduce heat, cover, and simmer until potatoes are just tender, about 15 minutes.
3. Add shrimp and parsley, cover, and simmer until shrimp turn pink, about 4 minutes. Remove bay leaf.
4. Transfer to individual bowls and serve at once.

Calories Per Serving: 185   Carbohydrates: 25 g
Fat: 2 g   Dietary Fiber: 2 g
Cholesterol: 115 mg   Sodium: 132 mg
Protein: 18 g

❋ *Jalapeño-Shrimp Gumbo* ❋

PREPARATION TIME: *25 minutes* • COOKING TIME: *42 minutes* •
YIELD: *8 servings*

4¼ cups low-sodium nonfat chicken
 broth
2 medium onions, diced
1 medium green bell pepper, cored
 and diced
1 medium red bell pepper, cored and
 diced
4 cloves garlic, minced
1 jalapeño pepper, seeded and minced
3 medium stalks celery, sliced
3 cups low-sodium canned tomatoes,
 drained and crushed
1 cup low-sodium tomato paste
1 cup low-sodium ketchup

¼ teaspoon ground white pepper
¼ teaspoon ground black pepper
½ teaspoon granulated sugar
½ teaspoon brown sugar
1 tablespoon molasses
½ teaspoon hot pepper sauce
1 tablespoon Worcestershire sauce
1 teaspoon dried thyme
2 bay leaves
3 tablespoons lemon juice
1 pound fresh medium shrimp, peeled
 and deveined
6 cups cooked white rice
2 scallions, minced

1. Heat ¼ cup broth in a large pot. Add onions, bell peppers, and garlic, and
   sauté until onions begin to soften, about 4 minutes.
2. Add jalapeño pepper, celery, tomatoes, tomato paste, ketchup, white pepper, black pepper, granulated sugar, brown sugar, molasses, hot pepper
   sauce, Worcestershire sauce, thyme, bay leaves, and lemon juice. Bring to
   a boil, reduce heat, and simmer for 30 minutes.
3. Stir in shrimp and simmer until shrimp turn pink, about 2 minutes. Remove bay leaves.
4. Serve over rice, garnished with minced scallions.

Calories Per Serving: 332
Fat: 2 g
Cholesterol: 86 mg
Protein: 18 g

Carbohydrates: 59 g
Dietary Fiber: 3 g
Sodium: 355 mg

❋ *Spicy Cod and Vegetable Stew* ❋

PREPARATION TIME: *25 minutes* • COOKING TIME: *39 minutes* •
YIELD: *6 servings*

1½ cups low-sodium nonfat chicken
   broth
2 medium onions, chopped
4 cloves garlic, minced
2 medium carrots, scraped and sliced
2 medium stalks celery, sliced
4 medium tomatoes, chopped
2 tablespoons paprika
4 bay leaves

½ teaspoon ground cumin
½ teaspoon ground coriander
¼ teaspoon ground ginger
¼ teaspoon ground cloves
1 pound fresh cod fillet, cut into
   1-inch cubes
¼ teaspoon cayenne pepper
¼ teaspoon ground black pepper

1. Heat ¼ cup broth in a large saucepan. Add onions, garlic, carrots, and celery, and sauté until onions begin to soften, about 4 minutes.
2. Add remaining broth, tomatoes, paprika, bay leaves, cumin, coriander,
   ginger, and cloves. Bring to a boil, reduce heat, and simmer for 15 minutes.
3. Add cod and cayenne pepper, and simmer until fish flakes easily, about 15
   minutes.
4. Remove bay leaves, stir in black pepper, transfer to individual bowls, and
   serve.

Calories Per Serving: 114
Fat: 1 g
Cholesterol: 33 mg
Protein: 15 g

Carbohydrates: 10 g
Dietary Fiber: 2 g
Sodium: 142 mg

❋ November Vegetable Fish Stew ❋

PREPARATION TIME: 20 minutes • COOKING TIME: 28 minutes •
YIELD: 6 servings

¼ cup low-sodium nonfat chicken
   broth
3 medium onions, sliced
2 medium carrots, scraped and diced
3 cups diced potatoes
1 cup dry white wine
3 medium tomatoes, chopped

½ teaspoon ground black pepper
½ teaspoon dried oregano
½ teaspoon dried basil
6 fresh cod fillets, about 4 ounces
   each
3 tablespoons lemon juice
¼ cup chopped fresh parsley

1. Heat broth in a large saucepan. Add onions and sauté until they begin to
   soften, about 3 minutes. Add carrots and potatoes, and sauté for 3 more
   minutes.

2. Stir in wine, tomatoes, black pepper, oregano, and basil. Top with fish fillets, cover, and simmer until fish flakes easily, about 20 minutes. Drain any excess liquid. Stir in lemon juice.
3. Serve fish fillets over vegetables on individual plates, garnished with parsley.

Calories Per Serving: 237	Carbohydrates: 27 g
Fat: 1 g	Dietary Fiber: 3 g
Cholesterol: 49 mg	Sodium: 95 mg
Protein: 23 g	

❊ *Fisherman's Casserole* ❊

PREPARATION TIME: *25 minutes* ▪ COOKING TIME: *22 minutes* ▪
YIELD: *6 servings*

¾ cup low-sodium nonfat chicken broth
2 medium onions, chopped
2 cloves garlic, minced
2 medium stalks celery, sliced
2 cups sliced mushrooms
1 medium green bell pepper, cored and diced
½ teaspoon ground black pepper
1 teaspoon dried oregano
¼ teaspoon ground turmeric

2 cups low-sodium canned tomatoes, chopped, juice reserved
2 medium potatoes, diced
2 cups low-sodium canned cannellini beans, rinsed and drained
½ pound fresh cod fillet, cut into 2-inch cubes
¼ cup sliced green olives
1 medium red bell pepper, cored and cut into thin strips

1. Heat ¼ cup broth in a large saucepan. Add onions, garlic, celery, mushrooms, and diced bell pepper, and sauté until onions begin to soften, about 4 minutes. Stir in black pepper, oregano, and turmeric, and sauté for 1 more minute.
2. Add remaining broth, tomatoes with juice, potatoes, beans, and cod. Bring to a boil, reduce heat, cover, and simmer until fish flakes easily, about 15 minutes.
3. Serve topped with olives and red pepper strips.

Calories Per Serving: 196	Carbohydrates: 32 g
Fat: 2 g	Dietary Fiber: 7 g
Cholesterol: 16 mg	Sodium: 210 mg
Protein: 15 g	

❋ *Haddock Stew with Rice* ❋

PREPARATION TIME: *15 minutes* · COOKING TIME: *24 minutes* ·
YIELD: *4 servings*

¼ cup low-sodium nonfat chicken
    broth
1 medium onion, chopped
1 clove garlic, minced
1 medium carrot, scraped and sliced
1 medium red bell pepper, cored and
    diced
4 medium stalks celery, sliced
2 cups low-sodium canned tomatoes,
    crushed, juice reserved

1 cup bottled clam juice
½ teaspoon ground black pepper
¼ teaspoon dried oregano
¼ teaspoon dried thyme
⅛ teaspoon hot pepper sauce
¾ pound fresh haddock fillet, cut into
    1-inch cubes
2 cups cooked rice

1. Heat broth in a large saucepan. Add onion, garlic, carrot, bell pepper, and celery, and sauté until onion begins to soften, about 4 minutes.
2. Add tomatoes with juice, clam juice, black pepper, oregano, thyme, hot pepper sauce, and haddock. Bring to a boil, reduce heat, cover, and simmer until fish flakes easily, about 15 minutes.
3. Serve over rice.

Calories Per Serving: 245
Fat: 1 g
Cholesterol: 37 mg
Protein: 20 g

Carbohydrates: 39 g
Dietary Fiber: 3 g
Sodium: 398 mg

❋ *Orange Roughy, Scallop, and Shrimp Stew* ❋

PREPARATION TIME: *20 minutes* · COOKING TIME: *47 minutes* ·
YIELD: *8 servings*

3¼ cups low-sodium nonfat chicken
    broth
1 cup chopped onion
4 cloves garlic, minced
6 medium tomatoes, chopped
3 medium stalks celery, sliced
2 cups diced potatoes
¼ cup chopped fresh parsley

1 tablespoon dried dill
1 bay leaf
½ cup dry white wine
½ pound fresh orange roughy fillet,
    cut into 1-inch cubes
1½ cups fresh scallops
½ pound fresh medium shrimp, peeled
    and deveined

1. Heat ¼ cup broth in a large saucepan. Add onion and garlic, and sauté until onion begins to soften, about 4 minutes.
2. Add remaining broth, tomatoes, celery, potatoes, parsley, dill, bay leaf, and wine. Bring to a boil, reduce heat, and simmer for 30 minutes.
3. Stir in orange roughy and scallops, and simmer for 4 minutes. Add shrimp and simmer until fish flakes easily and shrimp have turned pink, about 3 more minutes. Remove bay leaf before serving.

Calories Per Serving: 174
Fat: 1 g
Cholesterol: 65 mg
Protein: 18 g

Carbohydrates: 19 g
Dietary Fiber: 2 g
Sodium: 248 mg

❊ *Fisherman's Stew with Sun-Dried Tomatoes* ❊

PREPARATION TIME: *20 minutes plus 20 minutes soaking time* •
COOKING TIME: *1 hour 14 minutes* • YIELD: *4 servings*

3 sun-dried tomatoes
2 cups boiling water
6 tablespoons low-sodium vegetable
  broth
1 medium onion, diced
1 shallot, diced
4 cloves garlic, minced
1 jalapeño pepper, seeded and minced
⅛ teaspoon cayenne pepper
5 medium tomatoes, chopped
1 teaspoon dried basil

¼ cup chopped fresh parsley
1 bay leaf
1½ cups low-sodium canned tomatoes, drained and chopped
1½ cups dry white wine
¼ teaspoon ground black pepper
12 clams, in their shells
¼ pound fresh medium shrimp, peeled
  and deveined
½ pound fresh haddock fillet, cut into
  1-inch cubes

1. Soak sun-dried tomatoes in boiling water for 20 minutes. Drain, mince and set aside.
2. Heat broth in a large saucepan. Add onion, shallot, garlic, jalapeño pepper, and cayenne pepper. Sauté until onion begins to soften, about 3 minutes.
3. Add sun-dried tomatoes, fresh tomatoes, basil, parsley, and bay leaf. Sauté for 3 more minutes. Stir in canned tomatoes, bring to a simmer, cover, and cook for 45 minutes. Stir in wine and black pepper, and simmer for 15 additional minutes.

4. Add remaining ingredients and simmer until shrimp have turned pink and haddock flakes easily, about 4 minutes. Remove bay leaf. Discard any unopened clams.
5. Transfer to individual serving bowls and serve at once.

Calories Per Serving: 261
Fat: 1 g
Cholesterol: 35 mg
Protein: 16 g

Carbohydrates: 33 g
Dietary Fiber: 5 g
Sodium: 494 mg

❋ *Flounder, Shrimp, Crab, and Clam Stew* ❋ *with Farfalle*

PREPARATION TIME: *25 minutes* • COOKING TIME: *56 minutes* •
YIELD: *8 servings*

2¼ cups low-sodium nonfat chicken
  broth
1 cup chopped onion
2 cloves garlic, minced
1 medium red bell pepper, cored and
  chopped
6 cups low-sodium canned tomatoes,
  drained and crushed
2 cups diced potatoes
2 medium stalks celery, sliced
1 teaspoon dried basil

1 teaspoon dried oregano
1 teaspoon ground black pepper
1½ cups uncooked farfalle pasta
¾ pound fresh flounder fillet, cut into
  1-inch cubes
½ pound fresh medium shrimp, peeled
  and deveined
1½ cups crabmeat
1 cup canned clams, drained
½ cup chopped fresh parsley

1. Heat ¼ cup broth in a large saucepan. Add onion, garlic, and bell pepper, and sauté until onion begins to soften, about 4 minutes.
2. Add remaining broth, tomatoes, potatoes, celery, basil, oregano, and black pepper. Bring to a boil, reduce heat, cover, and simmer for 30 minutes.
3. Stir in farfalle and simmer for 8 more minutes. Add flounder and simmer for 4 additional minutes. Stir in shrimp, crabmeat, and clams. Simmer until shrimp turn pink, about 4 minutes.
4. Transfer to individual bowls, garnish with parsley, and serve.

Calories Per Serving: 294
Fat: 2 g
Cholesterol: 87 mg
Protein: 27 g

Carbohydrates: 39 g
Dietary Fiber: 3 g
Sodium: 304 mg

❀ *Shrimp, Haddock, and Eggplant Stew* ❀

PREPARATION TIME: *20 minutes*   •   COOKING TIME: *41 minutes*   •   YIELD: *4 servings*

¾ *pound fresh haddock or cod fillet,*
   cut into 1-inch cubes
1 *tablespoon poultry seasoning*
¼ *cup low-sodium nonfat chicken*
   broth
4 *cups diced eggplant (½-inch cubes)*
1 *medium onion, chopped*

1 *medium green bell pepper, cored*
   and chopped
2 *medium tomatoes, quartered*
¼ *teaspoon cayenne pepper*
1 *cup water*
½ *teaspoon ground black pepper*
¼ *pound fresh medium shrimp, peeled*
   und deveined

1. Preheat oven to 350 degrees.
2. Sprinkle haddock with poultry seasoning and set aside.
3. Heat broth in a flameproof 3-quart casserole. Add eggplant, onion, bell pepper, and tomatoes, and sauté until onion begins to soften, about 4 minutes.
4. Add cayenne pepper, water, and black pepper. Reduce heat, cover, and simmer for 5 minutes.
5. Arrange haddock and shrimp on top of vegetables, cover, and bake for 30 minutes.

Calories Per Serving: 133
Fat: 1 g
Cholesterol: 67 mg
Protein: 18 g

Carbohydrates: 67 g
Dietary Fiber: 2 g
Sodium: 95 mg

❀ *Green Pepper–Tofu Stew* ❀

PREPARATION TIME: *20 minutes*   •   COOKING TIME: *28 minutes*   •
YIELD: *4 servings*

2 *tablespoons low-sodium nonfat*
   chicken broth
1 *medium onion, chopped*
2 *medium green bell peppers, cored*
   and chopped
3 *cloves garlic, minced*
2 *cups low-sodium tomato sauce*

1 *tablespoon red wine vinegar*
1 *teaspoon ground cumin*
1 *bay leaf*
4 *green olives, chopped*
½ *teaspoon ground black pepper*
½ *pound firm tofu, drained and cut*
   into ½-inch cubes

1. Heat broth in a large saucepan. Add onion, bell peppers, and garlic, and sauté until onion begins to soften, about 3 minutes. Remove from heat.
2. Stir in tomato sauce, vinegar, cumin, bay leaf, olives, and black pepper. Gently mix in tofu. Return the saucepan to the heat and bring to a boil. Reduce heat, cover, and simmer, stirring frequently, for 20 minutes. Remove bay leaf.

Calories Per Serving: 143
Fat: 2 g
Cholesterol: 0 mg
Protein: 8 g

Carbohydrates: 25 g
Dietary Fiber: 4 g
Sodium: 163 mg

❊ *Green Bean, Turnip, and Eggplant Stew* ❊

PREPARATION TIME: *25 minutes* • COOKING TIME: *33 minutes* •
YIELD: *6 servings*

2¼ cups low-sodium nonfat chicken
  broth
1 medium onion, minced
2 cloves garlic, minced
3 cups chopped green beans (1-inch
  lengths)
3 medium carrots, scraped and sliced

3 cups diced turnip
3 cups diced eggplant
½ teaspoon ground black pepper
1 teaspoon dried basil
1 teaspoon dried oregano
3 scallions, minced

1. Heat ¼ cup broth in a large saucepan. Add onion and garlic, and sauté until onion begins to soften, about 3 minutes.
2. Stir in remaining broth, beans, carrots, turnips, eggplant, black pepper, basil, and oregano, and bring to a boil. Reduce heat, cover, and simmer until vegetables are just tender, about 25 minutes.
3. Serve topped with scallions.

Calories Per Serving: 54
Fat: 0 g
Cholesterol: 0 mg
Protein: 3 g

Carbohydrates: 11 g
Dietary Fiber: 3 g
Sodium: 153 mg

❊ *Tofu Stew with Couscous* ❊

PREPARATION TIME: *20 minutes plus 5 minutes standing time* •
COOKING TIME: *30 minutes* • YIELD: *4 servings*

½ cup low-sodium nonfat chicken
   broth
1 medium onion, chopped
2 cloves garlic, minced
2 medium tomatoes, chopped
¾ cup low-sodium tomato paste
¼ cup dry white wine
2 tablespoons lemon juice

1 teaspoon sugar
½ teaspoon ground cinnamon
½ teaspoon ground cloves
½ teaspoon ground black pepper
½ pound firm tofu, drained and cut
   into 1-inch cubes
2 cups boiling water
1 cup uncooked couscous

1. Heat ¼ cup broth in a large saucepan. Add onion and garlic, and sauté until onion begins to soften, about 3 minutes.
2. Stir in remaining broth, tomatoes, tomato paste, wine, lemon juice, sugar, cinnamon, cloves, and black pepper. Add tofu. Reduce heat, cover, and simmer, gently stirring occasionally, for 25 minutes.
3. In a separate bowl, pour boiling water over couscous, cover, and allow to stand for 5 minutes.
4. Serve couscous topped with tofu stew on individual plates.

Calories Per Serving: 300
Fat: 2 g
Cholesterol: 0 mg
Protein: 15 g

Carbohydrates: 56 g
Dietary Fiber: 2 g
Sodium: 112 mg

❋ Cabbage Stew ❋

PREPARATION TIME: 20 minutes • COOKING TIME: 29 minutes •
YIELD: 6 servings

4¼ cups low-sodium nonfat chicken
   broth
2 medium onions, chopped
2 cloves garlic, minced
1 medium boiling potato, chopped

8 cups shredded cabbage
1 cup low-sodium tomato sauce
½ teaspoon caraway seeds
½ teaspoon dill seeds
½ teaspoon ground black pepper

1. Heat ¼ cup broth in a large saucepan. Add onions and garlic, and sauté until onions begin to soften, about 3 minutes.
2. Add remaining broth, potato, cabbage, tomato sauce, caraway seeds, and dill seeds. Bring to a boil, reduce heat, cover, and simmer until potato and cabbage are just tender, about 20 minutes.
3. Stir in black pepper.

Calories Per Serving: 106   Carbohydrates: 20 g
Fat: 1 g   Dietary Fiber: 6 g
Cholesterol: 0 mg   Sodium: 266 mg
Protein: 4 g

❊ *Pumpkin-Corn Stew* ❊

PREPARATION TIME: *25 minutes* ▪ COOKING TIME: *30 minutes* ▪
YIELD: *4 servings*

2¼ cups low-sodium nonfat chicken   2 cups diced pumpkin
   broth   2 cups fresh or thawed frozen corn
1 medium onion, diced   kernels
1 jalapeño pepper, seeded and minced 1 tablespoon low-sodium tomato
2 cups diced turnips   paste
1 medium carrot, scraped and sliced   ¼ teaspoon ground black pepper

1. Heat broth in a large saucepan. Add onion and jalapeño pepper, and sauté
   until onion begins to soften, about 3 minutes.
2. Add remaining broth, turnips, carrot, and pumpkin. Bring to a boil, reduce heat, and simmer for 15 minutes. Stir in corn, tomato paste, and
   black pepper, and simmer for 5 additional minutes.

Calories Per Serving: 264   Carbohydrates: 57 g
Fat: 1 g   Dietary Fiber: 6 g
Cholesterol: 0 mg   Sodium: 246 mg
Protein: 11 g

❊ *African Vegetable Stew* ❊

PREPARATION TIME: *20 minutes* ▪ COOKING TIME: *27 minutes* ▪
YIELD: *6 servings*

¼ cup low-sodium nonfat chicken
  broth
1 medium onion, chopped
2 cups chopped cabbage
4 cloves garlic, minced
2 cups canned sweet potatoes,
  drained
2 cups low-sodium canned tomatoes,
  juice reserved

1½ cups low-sodium tomato juice
¾ cup apple juice
2 teaspoons grated fresh gingerroot
½ teaspoon cayenne pepper
2 cups thawed frozen or fresh green
  beans, cut into 1-inch lengths
2 tablespoons reduced-fat peanut
  butter

1. Heat broth in a large saucepan. Add onion and sauté until it begins to
   soften, about 3 minutes. Add cabbage and garlic, and sauté for 3 more
   minutes.
2. Stir in sweet potatoes, tomatoes with juice, tomato juice, apple juice, gingerroot, and cayenne pepper. Bring to a boil, reduce heat, cover, and simmer until heated through, about 5 minutes.
3. Add green beans and simmer for 10 more minutes. Add peanut butter and
   mix thoroughly before serving.

Calories Per Serving: 178
Fat: 2 g
Cholesterol: 0 mg
Protein: 5 g

Carbohydrates: 38 g
Dietary Fiber: 4 g
Sodium: 141 mg

❃ *Shiitake Mushroom and Squash Stew* ❃

PREPARATION TIME: *20 minutes* • COOKING TIME: *33 minutes* •
YIELD: *6 servings*

4¼ cups low-sodium nonfat chicken
  broth
1 cup minced shiitake mushrooms
1 medium onion, chopped
1 medium green bell pepper, cored
  and chopped

2 teaspoons chili powder
¼ teaspoon ground black pepper
4 cups fresh or frozen corn kernels
2 cups chopped zucchini
2 cups chopped yellow summer
  squash

1. Heat ¼ cup broth in a large saucepan. Add mushrooms and sauté for 4
   minutes. Add onion, bell pepper, and chili powder, and sauté until onion
   begins to soften, about 3 minutes.
2. Add black pepper, corn, zucchini, squash, and remaining broth. Bring to a
   boil, reduce heat, and simmer until vegetables are tender, about 20 minutes.

Calories Per Serving: 78

Carbohydrates: 13 g

Fat: 0 g

Dietary Fiber: 3 g

Cholesterol: 0 mg

Sodium: 142 mg

Protein: 8 g

❋ *Broccoli and Cauliflower Stew* ❋

PREPARATION TIME: *20 minutes* • COOKING TIME: *26 minutes* •
YIELD: *8 servings*

2¼ cups low-sodium nonfat chicken
 broth
1 medium onion, chopped
2 cloves garlic, minced
2 teaspoons minced fresh gingerroot
¼ teaspoon cayenne pepper
6 cups chopped broccoli
2 cups chopped cauliflower
1 cup water-packed canned artichoke
 hearts, drained and diced

1 medium red bell pepper, cored and
 chopped
1 cup sliced mushrooms
¼ cup chopped fresh basil
1 tablespoon reduced-sodium soy
 sauce
1 teaspoon ground white pepper
½ cup dry white wine
¼ teaspoon ground black pepper

1. Heat ¼ cup broth in a large saucepan. Add onion, garlic, gingerroot, and
   cayenne pepper, and sauté until onion begins to soften, about 4 minutes.
2. Stir in all remaining ingredients. Simmer until vegetables are just tender,
   about 20 minutes.
3. Transfer to individual bowls and serve.

Calories Per Serving: 86

Carbohydrates: 14 g

Fat: 1 g

Dietary Fiber: 4 g

Cholesterol: 0 mg

Sodium: 197 mg

Protein: 4 g

❋ *Fruit and Sweet Potato Stew* ❋

PREPARATION TIME: *20 minutes* • COOKING TIME: *30 minutes* •
YIELD: *8 servings*

1¾ cups low-sodium nonfat chicken
  broth
2 medium onions, chopped
2 tablespoons sugar
2 tablespoons all-purpose flour
½ cup dry white wine
4 medium sweet potatoes, diced

2½ cups juice-packed canned pineapple chunks, juice reserved
½ teaspoon dried thyme
1 teaspoon ground black pepper
3 cups chopped apples
3 cups chopped pears

1. Heat ¼ cup broth in a large saucepan. Add onions and sauté until they begin to soften, about 3 minutes.
2. In a separate bowl, whisk together remaining broth, sugar, flour, and wine. Stir into the saucepan. Add sweet potatoes, pineapple chunks with juice, thyme, and black pepper. Bring to a boil, reduce heat, cover, and simmer until sweet potatoes are just tender, about 15 minutes.
3. Add apples and pears, and simmer until fruit is tender, about 10 more minutes.

Calories Per Serving: 252
Fat: 1 g
Cholesterol: 0 mg
Protein: 2 g

Carbohydrates: 58 g
Dietary Fiber: 7 g
Sodium: 77 mg

❋ *Winter Squash Stew* ❋

PREPARATION TIME: *25 minutes* • COOKING TIME: *57 minutes* •
YIELD: *8 servings*

2¾ cups low-sodium nonfat chicken
  broth
1 medium onion, sliced
2 medium leeks (white parts only),
  sliced
2 cloves garlic, minced
1 tablespoon brown sugar
1 tablespoon minced fresh gingerroot
2 tablespoons all-purpose flour
1 medium green bell pepper, cored
  and chopped

1 medium red bell pepper, cored and
  chopped
3 cups chopped butternut squash
3 cups chopped Hubbard squash
½ cup dry red wine
½ cup orange juice
¼ cup chopped fresh parsley
2 tablespoons lemon juice
½ teaspoon ground black pepper

1. Preheat oven to 375 degrees.
2. Heat 1 cup broth in a flameproof 3-quart casserole. Add onion, leeks, garlic, brown sugar, gingerroot, and flour, and cook, stirring, until mixture begins to thicken, about 5 minutes.

3. Add remaining broth, bell peppers, butternut squash, Hubbard squash, wine, orange juice, parsley, and lemon juice. Mix well, cover, and bake until vegetables begin to soften, about 25 minutes. Remove the cover and continue to bake until vegetables are done, about 25 more minutes.
4. Stir in black pepper.

Calories Per Serving: 138
Fat: 0 g
Cholesterol: 0 mg
Protein: 3 g

Carbohydrates: 31 g
Dietary Fiber: 4 g
Sodium: 117 mg

❋ Greek Peasant Stew ❋

PREPARATION TIME: 20 minutes • COOKING TIME: 30 minutes •
YIELD: 6 servings

¼ cup low-sodium nonfat chicken broth
2 cups chopped green beans (2-inch lengths)
1 medium onion, chopped
2 medium carrots, scraped and sliced
3 medium stalks celery, sliced

4 cups low-sodium canned tomatoes, chopped, juice reserved
3 medium potatoes, chopped
¼ cup chopped fresh parsley
1 teaspoon dried dill
2 teaspoons dried oregano
½ teaspoon ground black pepper
3 cups sliced zucchini

1. Combine broth, beans, onion, carrots, celery, tomatoes with juice, potatoes, parsley, dill, oregano, and black pepper in a large saucepan. Bring to a boil, reduce heat, cover, and simmer, stirring frequently, for 20 minutes.
2. Add zucchini, cover, and simmer until vegetables are just tender, about 10 minutes.

Calories Per Serving: 122
Fat: 1 g
Cholesterol: 0 mg
Protein: 4 g

Carbohydrates: 27 g
Dietary Fiber: 4 g
Sodium: 54 mg

❋ Yam and Green Pea Stew with ❋ Yellow Bell Pepper

PREPARATION TIME: 20 minutes • COOKING TIME: 36 minutes •
YIELD: 8 servings

1¼ cups low-sodium nonfat chicken
 broth
1 medium onion, sliced
3 cloves garlic, minced
6 medium yams, diced
3 medium stalks celery, sliced
2 medium carrots, scraped and sliced
2 medium tomatoes, chopped

¼ cup chopped fresh parsley
1 teaspoon dried thyme
1 cup apple juice
1 cup orange juice
1 medium yellow bell pepper, cored
 and chopped
1 cup fresh or frozen green peas
½ teaspoon ground black pepper

1. Heat ¼ cup broth in a large saucepan. Add onion and garlic, and sauté until onion begins to soften, about 3 minutes.
2. Add remaining broth, yams, celery, carrots, tomatoes, parsley, thyme, apple juice, and orange juice. Bring to a boil, reduce heat, and simmer for 15 minutes. Stir in bell pepper and peas and simmer for 10 more minutes.
3. Stir in black pepper and simmer for about 2 minutes.

Calories Per Serving: 169
Fat: 0 g
Cholesterol: 0 mg
Protein: 4 g

Carbohydrates: 39 g
Dietary Fiber: 5 g
Sodium: 80 mg

❊ *Vegetarian Okra Gumbo* ❊

PREPARATION TIME: *20 minutes* • COOKING TIME: *1 hour 14 minutes* •
YIELD. *8 servings*

8¼ cups low-sodium vegetable broth
3 cloves garlic, minced
2 cups minced onion
1½ cups chopped celery
2 medium red bell peppers, cored and
 chopped
2 cups low-sodium canned tomatoes,
 crushed, juice reserved

¼ teaspoon dried thyme
4 bay leaves
¼ teaspoon ground black pepper
⅛ teaspoon hot pepper sauce
2 cups sliced okra
1 cup uncooked white rice

1. Heat ¼ cup broth in a large pot. Stir in garlic and onion, and sauté until onion begins to soften, about 3 minutes.
2. Add celery, bell peppers, and tomatoes with juice. Bring to a boil, reduce heat, and simmer for 10 minutes.
3. Stir in remaining broth, thyme, bay leaves, black pepper, hot pepper sauce, and okra. Simmer for 30 minutes.

4. Add rice and bring to a boil. Reduce heat, cover, and simmer until rice is tender, about 20 minutes. Remove bay leaf before serving.

Calories Per Serving: 173
Fat: 1 g
Cholesterol: 0 mg
Protein: 5 g

Carbohydrates: 38 g
Dietary Fiber: 3 g
Sodium: 62 mg

❊ Sweet Potato–Red Pepper–Corn Stew ❊

PREPARATION TIME: 25 minutes • COOKING TIME: 39 minutes •
YIELD: 8 servings

8 cups low-sodium vegetable broth
1 medium onion, chopped
5 cloves garlic, minced
3 scallions, sliced
1 medium stalk celery, sliced
3 medium red bell peppers, cored and
  chopped
4 medium sweet potatoes, chopped

1 teaspoon dried thyme
1 teaspoon dried basil
1 bay leaf
¼ teaspoon ground black pepper
5 cups fresh or thawed frozen corn
  kernels
¼ cup minced fresh parsley

1. Heat ¼ cup broth in a large saucepan. Add onion, garlic, scallions, celery, and bell peppers, and sauté until onion begins to soften, about 4 minutes.
2. Stir in remaining broth, sweet potatoes, thyme, basil, bay leaf, and black pepper. Bring to a boil, reduce heat, cover, and simmer until potatoes are just tender, about 20 minutes. Add corn and continue to simmer until corn is done, about 5 minutes. Remove bay leaf.
3. Serve topped with parsley.

Calories Per Serving: 207
Fat: 0 g
Cholesterol: 0 mg
Protein: 7 g

Carbohydrates: 48 g
Dietary Fiber: 5 g
Sodium: 272 mg

❊ Zucchini-Yam Stew ❊

PREPARATION TIME: 20 minutes • COOKING TIME: 37 minutes •
YIELD: 4 servings

6¼ cups low-sodium vegetable broth
1 medium onion, diced
1 medium green bell pepper, cored
 and diced
1 cup diced zucchini
2 cloves garlic, minced

2 cups diced yams
1 tablespoon dried parsley
1 teaspoon dried thyme
½ teaspoon ground black pepper
½ teaspoon ground allspice

1. Heat ¼ cup broth in a large saucepan. Add onion, bell pepper, zucchini, and garlic, and sauté until pepper begins to soften, about 5 minutes.
2. Add all remaining ingredients. Bring to a boil, reduce heat, and simmer, stirring occasionally, until yams are tender, about 25 minutes.

Calories Per Serving: 233
Fat: 1 g
Cholesterol: 0 mg
Protein: 11 g

Carbohydrates: 46 g
Dietary Fiber: 6 g
Sodium: 205 mg

❊ *Spicy Green Bean and Tomato Stew* ❊

PREPARATION TIME: *15 minutes* • COOKING TIME: *24 minutes* •
YIELD: *6 servings*

¼ cup low-sodium nonfat chicken
 broth
2 medium onions, chopped
½ jalapeño pepper, seeded and minced
8 cups chopped fresh or thawed
 frozen green beans (1-inch
 lengths)

½ cup water
2 teaspoons dried dill
½ teaspoon ground black pepper
3 cups low-sodium canned tomatoes,
 chopped, juice reserved
3 tablespoons grated nonfat
 Parmesan

1. Heat broth in a large pot. Add onions and jalapeño pepper, and sauté until onions begin to soften, about 3 minutes.
2. Add green beans, water, dill, and black pepper. Bring to a boil, reduce heat, and simmer for 10 minutes.
3. Stir in tomatoes with juice and simmer until beans are tender, about 8 more minutes.
4. Serve topped with Parmesan.

Calories Per Serving: 100
Fat: 1 g
Cholesterol: 3 mg
Protein: 6 g

Carbohydrates: 22 g
Dietary Fiber: 4 g
Sodium: 69 mg

❊ *Red Lentil Stew* ❊

PREPARATION TIME: *15 minutes* ∙ COOKING TIME: *1 hour 10 minutes* ∙
YIELD: *6 servings*

¼ cup low-sodium nonfat chicken
   broth
1 medium onion, chopped
2 cloves garlic, minced
6 cups water
4 cups dried red lentils, rinsed and
   drained

½ teaspoon dried oregano
1 bay leaf
6 medium carrots, scraped and sliced
4 medium stalks celery, sliced
3 medium tomatoes, chopped
½ teaspoon ground black pepper
½ cup chopped fresh parsley

1. Heat broth in a large saucepan. Add onion and garlic, and sauté until
   onion begins to soften, about 3 minutes.
2. Stir in water, lentils, oregano, and bay leaf. Bring to a boil, reduce heat,
   cover, and simmer for 40 minutes.
3. Add carrots, celery, tomatoes, and black pepper. Cover and simmer until
   vegetables are tender, about 20 minutes. Remove bay leaf.
4. Transfer stew to individual plates, garnish with parsley, and serve.

Calories Per Serving: 121
Fat: 1 g
Cholesterol: 0 mg
Protein: 7 g

Carbohydrates: 26 g
Dietary Fiber: 7 g
Sodium: 97 mg

❊ *Lentil Stew with Red Wine and Garlic* ❊

PREPARATION TIME: *25 minutes* ∙ COOKING TIME: *51 minutes* ∙
YIELD: *6 servings*

3 cups water
3½ cups low-sodium canned tomatoes, chopped, juice reserved
¼ cup low-sodium tomato paste
½ cup dry red wine
¾ teaspoon dried basil
¾ teaspoon dried thyme
½ teaspoon cayenne pepper

2 cups dried lentils, rinsed and
   drained
1 medium onion, chopped
4 medium carrots, scraped and sliced
4 medium stalks celery, chopped
3 cloves garlic, minced
¼ teaspoon ground black pepper
¼ cup chopped fresh parsley

1. Combine all ingredients except parsley in a large saucepan. Bring to a boil, reduce heat, cover, and simmer until vegetables and lentils are just tender, about 45 minutes.
2. Serve topped with parsley.

Calories Per Serving: 125
Fat: 1 g
Cholesterol: 0 mg
Protein: 6 g

Carbohydrates: 27 g
Dietary Fiber: 7 g
Sodium: 108 mg

❈ *Sherried Lentil Stew with Shiitake* ❈ *Mushrooms*

PREPARATION TIME: *25 minutes plus 30 minutes soaking time* ▪
COOKING TIME: *31 minutes* ▪ YIELD: *6 servings*

2¼ cups low-sodium nonfat chicken broth
½ cup minced shiitake mushrooms
1 medium onion, diced
3 cloves garlic, minced
1 small carrot, scraped and diced
1 medium stalk celery, diced
3 bay leaves
½ teaspoon cayenne pepper
6 medium tomatoes, diced

1½ cups low-sodium tomato juice
1 teaspoon dried basil
½ teaspoon dried thyme
½ teaspoon dried tarragon
½ teaspoon sugar
½ teaspoon ground black pepper
1 cup dried lentils, soaked in water for 30 minutes and drained
2 tablespoons dry sherry

1. Heat ¼ cup broth in a large saucepan. Add mushrooms, onion, garlic, carrot, and celery, and sauté until onion begins to soften, about 3 minutes.
2. Add remaining broth, bay leaves, cayenne pepper, tomatoes, tomato juice, basil, thyme, tarragon, sugar, and black pepper. Bring to a boil and add lentils. Reduce heat and simmer until lentils are just tender, about 25 minutes. Stir in sherry. Remove bay leaves before serving.

Calories Per Serving: 83
Fat: 1 g
Cholesterol: 0 mg
Protein: 6 g

Carbohydrates: 16 g
Dietary Fiber: 4 g
Sodium: 92 mg

❋ Black Bean–Pumpkin Stew ❋

PREPARATION TIME: *20 minutes* • COOKING TIME: *35 minutes* •
YIELD: *6 servings*

1½ cups low-sodium nonfat chicken
 broth
1 medium onion, chopped
1 medium yellow bell pepper, cored
 and chopped
4 cloves garlic, minced
1 tablespoon reduced-sodium soy
 sauce
4 cups chopped pumpkin

2 cups low-sodium canned tomatoes,
 chopped, juice reserved
1½ teaspoons dried oregano
1½ teaspoons chili powder
½ teaspoon ground cumin
½ teaspoon ground black pepper
2 cups low-sodium canned black
 beans, rinsed and drained
1½ cups fresh or thawed frozen corn
 kernels

1. Heat ¼ cup broth in a large saucepan. Add onion, bell pepper, and garlic, and sauté until onion begins to soften, about 4 minutes.
2. Stir in remaining broth, soy sauce, pumpkin, tomatoes with juice, oregano, chili powder, cumin, and black pepper. Bring to a boil, reduce heat, cover, and simmer until pumpkin is just tender, about 20 minutes.
3. Add beans and corn and simmer until corn is tender and beans are heated through, about 6 more minutes.

Calories Per Serving: 169
Fat: 1 g
Cholesterol: 0 mg
Protein: 9 g

Carbohydrates: 34 g
Dietary Fiber: 8 g
Sodium: 185 mg

❋ Kidney Bean Stew with Garlic and Sherry ❋

PREPARATION TIME: *20 minutes* • COOKING TIME: *55 minutes* •
YIELD: *6 servings*

¼ cup low-sodium nonfat chicken
 broth
3 medium onions, chopped
4 medium green bell peppers, cored
 and chopped

1 cup low-sodium tomato sauce
3 medium tomatoes, chopped
½ cup water
¼ cup dry sherry
2 tablespoons red wine vinegar

3 cups diced potatoes
2 cups low-sodium canned kidney
   beans, rinsed and drained
8 cloves garlic, minced

12 green olives, sliced
1 bay leaf
1 teaspoon sugar
½ teaspoon ground black pepper

1. Heat broth in a large saucepan. Add onions and bell peppers, and sauté until onions begin to soften, about 5 minutes.
2. Stir in remaining ingredients. Bring to a boil, reduce heat, cover, and simmer, stirring occasionally, for 45 minutes. Remove bay leaf.
3. Transfer stew to individual bowls and serve.

Calories Per Serving: 285
Fat: 2 g
Cholesterol: 0 mg
Protein: 10 g

Carbohydrates: 59 g
Dietary Fiber: 9 g
Sodium: 201 mg

❋ *Eggplant, Red Potato, and Chickpea Stew* ❋

PREPARATION TIME: *25 minutes* • COOKING TIME: *31 minutes* •
YIELD: *6 servings*

1½ teaspoons grated fresh gingerroot
4 medium tomatoes, chopped
1 cup cooked or low-sodium canned
   chickpeas, rinsed and drained
5 cups water
½ teaspoon ground turmeric

¼ cup chopped fresh parsley
6 cups diced eggplant
3 cups chopped red potatoes
1½ teaspoons ground coriander
1½ tablespoons lime juice
¼ teaspoon ground black pepper

1. Place gingerroot, tomatoes, chickpeas, water, turmeric, 2 tablespoons parsley, the eggplant, potatoes, and coriander in a large saucepan. Bring to a boil, reduce heat, cover, and simmer until potatoes are tender and eggplant is cooked through, about 25 minutes. Remove from heat and drain any excess liquid.
2. Stir in lime juice and black pepper. Serve sprinkled with remaining parsley.

Calories Per Serving: 184
Fat: 1 g
Cholesterol: 0 mg
Protein: 6 g

Carbohydrates: 40 g
Dietary Fiber: 4 g
Sodium: 150 mg

❋ Cauliflower, Spinach, and Chickpea Stew ❋

PREPARATION TIME: *20 minutes* · COOKING TIME: *20 minutes* ·
YIELD: *6 servings*

¼ cup low-sodium nonfat chicken
  broth
1 cup chopped onion
1 medium green bell pepper, cored
  and chopped
1 medium red bell pepper, cored and
  chopped
3 cloves garlic, minced
1 teaspoon minced fresh gingerroot

1 tablespoon curry powder
2 cups low-sodium canned tomatoes,
  chopped, juice reserved
2 cups cooked or low-sodium canned
  chickpeas, rinsed and drained
¾ cup low-sodium tomato juice
3 cups chopped fresh spinach
2 cups chopped cauliflower
¼ teaspoon cayenne pepper

1. Heat broth in a large saucepan. Add onion, bell peppers, garlic, and gingerroot, and sauté for 2 minutes. Add curry powder and sauté for 3 more
   minutes.
2. Add tomatoes with juice, chickpeas, tomato juice, spinach, and cauliflower, and bring to a boil. Reduce heat, cover, and simmer until cauliflower is tender, about 10 minutes.
3. Stir in cayenne pepper.

Calories Per Serving: 144
Fat: 1 g
Cholesterol: 0 mg
Protein: 8 g

Carbohydrates: 29 g
Dietary Fiber: 7 g
Sodium: 320 mg

❋ Kale, Tomato, and Chickpea Stew ❋

PREPARATION TIME: *15 minutes* · COOKING TIME: *20 minutes* ·
YIELD: *4 servings*

¼ cup low-sodium vegetable broth
1 medium onion, sliced
2 cloves garlic, minced
3 medium potatoes, cut into 1-inch
  cubes
2 cups low-sodium canned tomatoes,
  chopped, juice reserved

2 cups cooked or low-sodium canned
  chickpeas, liquid reserved
4 cups chopped fresh kale
1 tablespoon dried basil
2 tablespoons grated nonfat
  Parmesan

1. Heat broth in a large saucepan. Add onion, garlic, and potatoes, and sauté until onion begins to soften, about 3 minutes.
2. Add tomatoes with juice, chickpeas with liquid, kale, and basil. Bring to a boil, reduce heat, cover, and simmer until kale is tender, about 12 minutes.
3. Serve on individual plates, sprinkled with Parmesan.

Calories Per Serving: 190
Fat: 1 g
Cholesterol: 2 mg
Protein: 9 g

Carbohydrates: 39 g
Dietary Fiber: 6 g
Sodium: 305 mg

❈ *Zucchini and Chickpea Stew* ❈

PREPARATION TIME: *20 minutes* • COOKING TIME: *12 minutes* •
YIELD: *4 servings*

¼ cup low-sodium nonfat chicken
  broth
1 medium onion, chopped
1 clove garlic, peeled and minced
4 cups chopped zucchini
4 cups low-sodium canned tomatoes,
  chopped, juice reserved

2 cups cooked or low-sodium canned
  chickpeas, rinsed and drained
¼ teaspoon ground black pepper
¼ cup chopped fresh parsley

1. Heat broth in a large saucepan. Add onion and garlic, and sauté until onion begins to soften, about 3 minutes.
2. Stir in zucchini, tomatoes with juice, chickpeas, and black pepper. Simmer until zucchini is cooked through, about 7 minutes.
3. Serve in individual bowls garnished with parsley.

Calories Per Serving: 177
Fat: 1 g
Cholesterol: 0 mg
Protein: 9 g

Carbohydrates: 35 g
Dietary Fiber: 7 g
Sodium: 420 mg

❈ *Eggplant, Navy Bean, and Mushroom Stew* ❈

PREPARATION TIME: *20 minutes* • COOKING TIME: *30 minutes* •
YIELD: *6 servings*

½ cup low-sodium nonfat chicken
  broth
3 cups diced eggplant
2 medium leeks (white parts only),
  sliced
2 medium green bell peppers, cored
  and chopped
3 cloves garlic, minced
3 cups sliced mushrooms

2 cups low-sodium tomato sauce
¼ cup dry sherry
2 cups low-sodium canned navy
  beans, rinsed and drained
1 teaspoon vinegar
1 teaspoon dried oregano
¼ teaspoon dried thyme
1 bay leaf
½ teaspoon ground black pepper

1. Heat ¼ cup broth in a large saucepan. Add eggplant, leeks, bell peppers, and garlic, and simmer, stirring frequently, for 10 minutes. Add mushrooms and simmer for 5 more minutes.
2. Stir in all remaining ingredients. Bring to a boil, reduce heat, cover, and simmer for 15 minutes. Remove bay leaf.

Calories Per Serving: 166
Fat: 1 g
Cholesterol: 0 mg
Protein: 8 g

Carbohydrates: 33 g
Dietary Fiber: 7 g
Sodium: 43 mg

❈ Great Northern Bean and Red Pepper Stew ❈ with Rosemary

PREPARATION TIME: 15 minutes ▪ COOKING TIME: 23 minutes ▪
YIELD: 4 servings

2¼ cups low-sodium vegetable broth
1 medium onion, chopped
2 cloves garlic, minced
2 cups low-sodium canned Great
  Northern beans, rinsed and drained

½ teaspoon dried rosemary
½ teaspoon ground black pepper
1 cup canned roasted red bell peppers,
  drained and cut into thin strips
1 tablespoon balsamic vinegar

1. Heat ¼ cup broth in a large saucepan. Add onion and garlic, and sauté until onion begins to soften, about 3 minutes.
2. Add remaining broth, beans, rosemary, and black pepper. Bring to a boil, reduce heat, and simmer, stirring occasionally, for 10 minutes.
3. Stir in roasted peppers and balsamic vinegar, and heat through, about 5 minutes.
4. Transfer to individual bowls and serve.

Calories Per Serving: 159
Fat: 1 g
Cholesterol: 0 mg
Protein: 9 g

Carbohydrates: 31 g
Dietary Fiber: 8 g
Sodium: 30 mg

❊ Navy Bean and Clam Stew ❊ with White Wine

PREPARATION TIME: *20 minutes* ▪ COOKING TIME: *18 minutes* ▪
YIELD: *4 servings*

1 cup dry white wine
1 medium onion, minced
2 cloves garlic, minced
2 cups low-sodium canned tomatoes,
    drained and chopped
4 cups low-sodium canned navy
    beans, rinsed and drained

2 bay leaves
1 teaspoon ground black pepper
1 cup canned clams, drained
2 tablespoons minced fresh parsley

1. Combine wine, onion, garlic, tomatoes, beans, bay leaves, and black pepper in a large saucepan. Bring to a boil, reduce heat, cover, and simmer for
   15 minutes.
2. Add clams and simmer until clams are heated through, about 3 minutes.
   Remove bay leaves.
3. Transfer stew to individual bowls, garnish with parsley, and serve.

Calories Per Serving: 249
Fat: 2 g
Cholesterol: 27 mg
Protein: 19 g

Carbohydrates: 31 g
Dietary Fiber: 8 g
Sodium: 69 mg

❊ Great Northern Bean and Pumpkin Stew ❊

PREPARATION TIME: *25 minutes* ▪ COOKING TIME: *41 minutes* ▪
YIELD: *8 servings*

1 ¼ cups low-sodium nonfat chicken
  broth
1 medium onion, sliced
2 medium leeks (white parts only),
  sliced
2 medium carrots, scraped and
  chopped
2 tablespoons brown sugar
2 cups diced pumpkin
2 medium green bell peppers, cored
  and chopped

2 cups low-sodium canned Great
  Northern beans, rinsed and
  drained
2 medium turnips, chopped
1 ½ teaspoons dried thyme
1 tablespoon curry powder
1 cup chopped fresh parsley
1 cup orange juice
½ cup dry red wine
½ teaspoon ground black pepper

1. Heat ¼ cup broth in a large saucepan. Add onion, leeks, and carrots, and
   sauté until onion begins to soften, about 4 minutes. Add brown sugar and
   stir for 2 more minutes.
2. Add remaining broth, pumpkin, bell peppers, beans, turnips, thyme, curry
   powder, ½ cup parsley, the orange juice, and wine. Bring to a boil, reduce
   heat, and simmer until vegetables are tender, about 30 minutes. Stir in
   black pepper.
3. Serve topped with remaining parsley.

Calories Per Serving: 139
Fat: 1 g
Cholesterol: 0 mg
Protein: 5 g

Carbohydrates: 28 g
Dietary Fiber: 6 g
Sodium: 65 mg

❇ Zucchini—Great Northern Bean Stew ❇ with Moroccan Spices

PREPARATION TIME: 20 minutes • COOKING TIME: 44 minutes •
YIELD: 6 servings

1 cup low-sodium nonfat chicken
  broth
2 medium onions, chopped
3 cloves garlic, minced
1 medium carrot, scraped and sliced
2 medium green bell peppers, cored
  and chopped

1 teaspoon ground cumin
½ teaspoon ground allspice
½ teaspoon ground ginger
½ teaspoon ground turmeric
¼ teaspoon cayenne pepper
½ teaspoon ground cinnamon
4 cups diced zucchini

3 medium tomatoes, chopped
½ cup seedless raisins

2 cups low-sodium canned Great
Northern beans, rinsed and
drained

1. Heat ¼ cup broth in a large saucepan. Add onions and garlic, and sauté until onions begin to soften, about 4 minutes.
2. Add carrot, bell peppers, cumin, allspice, ginger, turmeric, cayenne pepper, and cinnamon, and sauté for 5 more minutes.
3. Stir in all remaining ingredients. Bring to a boil, reduce heat, cover, and simmer until vegetables are just tender, about 30 minutes.

Calories Per Serving: 178
Fat: 1 g
Cholesterol: 0 mg
Protein: 8 g

Carbohydrates: 38 g
Dietary Fiber: 7 g
Sodium: 28 mg

❋ Lobster, Clam, and Shrimp Stew ❋

PREPARATION TIME: 25 minutes • COOKING TIME: 61 minutes •
YIELD: 6 servings

1 cup dry red wine
1 medium green bell pepper, cored
and chopped
1 medium red bell pepper, cored and
chopped
2 medium stalks celery, sliced
1 medium carrot, scraped and sliced
3 medium leeks (white parts only),
sliced
4 cloves garlic, minced
3 medium tomatoes, chopped
¼ cup chopped fresh parsley
1 bay leaf
½ teaspoon dried oregano
½ teaspoon dried basil

¼ teaspoon dried saffron threads,
crushed
1 teaspoon sugar
5 cups low-sodium nonfat chicken
broth
2 cups sliced yellow summer squash
2 cups sliced zucchini
2 cups diced potatoes
½ pound fresh medium shrimp, peeled
and deveined
2 fresh lobster tails, each cut into 3
pieces
12 fresh clams, in their shells
½ teaspoon ground black pepper

1. Combine wine, bell peppers, celery, carrot, leeks, garlic, tomatoes, parsley, bay leaf, oregano, basil, saffron, sugar, and broth in a large pot. Bring to a boil, reduce heat, cover, and simmer for 30 minutes.

2. Add squash, zucchini, and potatoes, and simmer until potatoes are tender, about 12 more minutes. Add shrimp and lobster, and simmer for 2 additional minutes. Add clams, cover, and simmer until clams open, about 10 more minutes. Discard any unopened clams. Remove bay leaf.
3. Stir in black pepper, transfer to individual bowls, and serve.

Calories Per Serving: 281
Fat: 3 g
Cholesterol: 111 mg
Protein: 27 g

Carbohydrates: 31 g
Dietary Fiber: 4 g
Sodium: 527 mg

SEAFOOD SOUPS

Oyster-Spinach Soup • Oyster Soup with Celery and Green Bell
Pepper • Oyster-Celery Soup with Artichokes • Mussel Soup •
Carrot-Clam Soup • Clam-Mushroom Soup • Clam-Corn
Chowder • Manhattan Clam Chowder • Spiced Potato Puree
with Clams • Clam-Succotash Soup • Turnip-Potato-Clam
Chowder • Scallop Soup with White Wine and Green Peas •
Tangy Scallop Chowder with Asparagus • Curried Tomato and
Crab Soup • Maryland Crab Soup • Sherried Crab Soup •
Crab-Cauliflower Chowder • Asparagus-Shrimp Soup • Shrimp
and Artichoke Soup • Shrimp Soup with Corn • Shrimp Soup
with Red Peppers and Chiles • Spicy Shrimp and Vegetable
Soup • Shrimp-Potato Chowder • Haddock-Orzo Soup •
Orange Roughy Soup with Shiitake Mushrooms and Spinach •
Flounder-Vegetable Soup • Codfish Chowder • Orange Roughy
Soup with Mushrooms and Red Wine • Smoked Salmon–Spinach
Soup • Salmon Chowder • Haddock–Lima Bean Soup •
Catfish Soup • Marinated Codfish Soup with Tomatoes •
Curried Cod Soup • Sherried Flounder Soup with Mushrooms •
Leftover Wild Rice–Salmon–Mushroom Soup • Simple Haddock

Chowder • Cod-Cauliflower Chowder • Shrimp and Flounder Soup with Spinach, Lemon, and Thyme • Orange Roughy and Shrimp Soup with Vegetables • Seafood Soup with Cabbage and New Potatoes • Scallop-Shrimp Minestrone • Bouillabaisse with White Wine and Saffron • Cioppino

❋ Oyster-Spinach Soup ❋

PREPARATION TIME: *15 minutes* • COOKING TIME: *30 minutes* •
YIELD: *4 servings*

¼ cup chopped onion
3 cups low-sodium vegetable broth
¾ cup chopped fresh spinach
1 cup shucked oysters, liquid reserved

1 cup skim milk
½ teaspoon ground black pepper
1 tablespoon sliced almonds

1. Combine onion and broth in a large saucepan. Bring to a boil. Reduce heat, cover, and simmer for 20 minutes
2. Add spinach and oysters with liquid, and simmer for 5 minutes. Stir in milk and black pepper, and heat through. Sprinkle with almonds and serve.

Calories Per Serving: 118
Fat: 3 g
Cholesterol: 35 mg
Protein: 8 g

Carbohydrates: 15 g
Dietary Fiber: 1 g
Sodium: 139 mg

❋ Oyster Soup with Celery and ❋ Green Bell Pepper

PREPARATION TIME: *20 minutes* • COOKING TIME: *20 minutes* •
YIELD: *4 servings*

¼ cup low-sodium nonfat chicken
    broth
1 medium onion, chopped
2 medium stalks celery, chopped
1 medium green bell pepper, cored
    and chopped
2 cups shucked oysters, liquid reserved

¼ cup chopped fresh parsley
2 scallions (green parts only),
    chopped
¼ cup chopped celery leaves
4 cups skim milk
⅛ teaspoon cayenne pepper
⅛ teaspoon hot pepper sauce

1. Heat broth in a large saucepan. Add onion, celery, and bell pepper, and sauté until onion begins to soften, about 3 minutes. Add oysters with liquid and simmer for 10 minutes.
2. Add parsley, scallions, celery leaves, and milk, and heat through, about 5 minutes.
3. Stir in cayenne pepper and hot pepper sauce.

Calories Per Serving: 133   Carbohydrates: 15 g
Fat: 2 g   Dietary Fiber: 1 g
Cholesterol: 46 mg   Sodium: 287 mg
Protein: 12 g

❋ Oyster-Celery Soup with Artichokes ❋

PREPARATION TIME: 20 minutes · COOKING TIME: 55 minutes ·
YIELD: 8 servings

6½ cups low-sodium nonfat chicken
  broth
8 scallions, sliced
3 medium stalks celery, sliced
4 cloves garlic, minced
3 cups water-packed canned artichoke hearts, drained and chopped
3 tablespoons all-purpose flour

¼ teaspoon cayenne pepper
1 tablespoon Worcestershire sauce
¼ teaspoon dried thyme
3 cups shucked oysters, liquid reserved
⅓ cup dry sherry
2 cups skim milk

1. Heat ¼ cup broth in a large saucepan. Add scallions, celery, and garlic, and sauté until scallions begin to soften, about 4 minutes. Add artichokes.
2. Sprinkle flour into the saucepan. Gradually add remaining broth, stirring constantly. Add cayenne pepper, Worcestershire sauce, and thyme. Bring to a boil, reduce heat, cover, and simmer for 30 minutes.
3. Add oysters with liquid and sherry, and simmer for 10 more minutes. Stir in milk and heat, about 3 additional minutes.

Calories Per Serving: 153   Carbohydrates: 18 g
Fat: 3 g   Dietary Fiber: 4 g
Cholesterol: 50 mg   Sodium: 551 mg
Protein: 12 g

❋ Mussel Soup ❋

PREPARATION TIME: 25 minutes · COOKING TIME: 45 minutes ·
YIELD: 5 servings

3 dozen mussels, in their shells
1 cup dry white wine

2 tablespoons low-sodium nonfat
  chicken broth

2 teaspoons jalapeño pepper, seeded
    and minced
1 cup chopped leek
3 cloves garlic, minced
¼ teaspoon dried saffron threads,
    crushed
¼ cup dry sherry

1 medium tomato, chopped
1 medium carrot, scraped and diced
2 medium potatoes, diced
½ cup skim milk
¼ teaspoon ground white pepper
½ cup minced fresh parsley

1. Place mussels and wine in a large saucepan with a lid. Heat wine, cover the saucepan, and steam mussels for 5 minutes. Discard any mussels that do not open during the steaming.
2. Shuck mussels and strain steaming liquid. Add water to make 5 cups of liquid total. Set mussels and liquid aside.
3. Heat broth in the saucepan. Add jalapeño pepper, leek, and garlic, and sauté for 2 minutes. Add saffron and sherry, and cook until liquid has evaporated, about 5 minutes. Add tomato and carrot.
4. Stir in reserved mussel cooking liquid and potatoes, bring mixture to a boil, reduce heat, and simmer until potatoes are tender, about 20 minutes. Remove from heat and allow to cool slightly.
5. Set aside 1½ dozen of the most attractive mussels. Add remaining mussels to soup mixture and puree in a blender or food processor.
6. Return puree to the saucepan, add milk and white pepper, and heat gently.
7. Serve topped with parsley.

Calories Per Serving: 142
Fat: 1 g
Cholesterol: 11 mg
Protein: 7 g

Carbohydrates: 21 g
Dietary Fiber: 2 g
Sodium: 190 mg

✳ Carrot-Clam Soup ✳

PREPARATION TIME: 20 minutes • COOKING TIME: 35 minutes •
YIELD: 4 servings

2¼ cups low-sodium nonfat chicken
    broth
¼ onion, chopped
1 medium tomato, chopped
4 medium carrots, scraped and
    chopped
1 cup diced potato

2 tablespoons all-purpose flour
¼ teaspoon cayenne pepper
2 cups canned clams, liquid reserved
½ cup skim milk
¼ teaspoon ground black pepper
¼ cup chopped fresh parsley

1. Heat ¼ cup broth in a large saucepan. Add onion and sauté until it begins to soften, about 3 minutes. Add tomato, carrots, potato, flour, and cayenne pepper, and stir for 4 more minutes.
2. Stir in remaining broth and reserved clam liquid. Bring to a boil, reduce heat, and simmer for 20 minutes.
3. Puree mixture in a food processor or blender. Return puree to the saucepan and stir in milk and black pepper. Add clams and simmer until all ingredients are heated through, about 3 minutes.
4. Serve topped with parsley.

Calories Per Serving: 148
Fat: 1 g
Cholesterol: 5 mg
Protein: 9 g

Carbohydrates: 28 g
Dietary Fiber: 4 g
Sodium: 148 mg

✳ Clam-Mushroom Soup ✳

PREPARATION TIME: *20 minutes* · COOKING TIME: *32 minutes* ·
YIELD: *6 servings*

6¼ cups low-sodium nonfat chicken broth
1 medium onion, chopped
1 medium stalk celery, sliced
1 medium carrot, scraped and thinly sliced
6 cups sliced mushrooms

2 medium tomatoes, chopped
½ teaspoon dried thyme
2 cups diced potatoes
1 cup canned clams, liquid reserved
¼ teaspoon ground black pepper
¼ cup chopped fresh parsley

1. Heat ¼ cup broth in a large saucepan. Add onion, celery, carrot, and mushrooms, and sauté until onion begins to soften, about 4 minutes.
2. Add remaining broth, tomatoes, thyme, and potatoes, and bring to a boil. Reduce heat, cover, and simmer until potatoes are just tender, about 15 minutes. Add clams with liquid and simmer for 5 more minutes.
3. Stir in black pepper. Serve topped with parsley.

Calories Per Serving: 126
Fat: 1 g
Cholesterol: 0 mg
Protein: 4 g

Carbohydrates: 26 g
Dietary Fiber: 3 g
Sodium: 256 mg

❋ *Clam-Corn Chowder* ❋

PREPARATION TIME: *20 minutes* • COOKING TIME: *27 minutes* •
YIELD: *4 servings*

2¼ cups low-sodium nonfat chicken
  broth
1 medium onion, chopped
1 medium stalk celery, sliced
1 10-ounce can minced clams, liquid
  reserved
1 bay leaf

¼ teaspoon dried thyme
½ teaspoon ground black pepper
2 cups diced potatoes
2 cups fresh or thawed frozen corn
  kernels
1 cup skim milk

1. Heat ¼ cup broth in a large saucepan. Add onion and celery, and sauté until onion begins to soften, about 4 minutes. Stir in remaining broth.
2. Add reserved clam liquid, bay leaf, thyme, black pepper, and potatoes. Bring to a boil, reduce heat, cover, and simmer, stirring occasionally, for 10 minutes. Add corn and simmer for 5 more minutes. Remove bay leaf.
3. Stir in clams and milk, and simmer until heated through, about 3 minutes.

Calories Per Serving: 331
Fat: 3 g
Cholesterol: 1 mg
Protein: 10 g

Carbohydrates: 72 g
Dietary Fiber: 4 g
Sodium: 381 mg

❋ *Manhattan Clam Chowder* ❋

PREPARATION TIME: *20 minutes* • COOKING TIME: *26 minutes* •
YIELD: *4 servings*

1¼ cups low-sodium nonfat chicken
  broth
1 medium onion, chopped
2 cloves garlic, minced
2 medium stalks celery, thinly sliced
1 cup canned clams, liquid reserved
1 medium green bell pepper, cored
  and diced
1 cup diced potato

2 cups low-sodium canned tomatoes,
  chopped, juice reserved
2 cups low-sodium tomato juice
⅛ teaspoon cayenne pepper
1 bay leaf
½ teaspoon dried thyme
½ teaspoon sugar
¼ teaspoon ground black pepper

1. Heat ¼ cup broth in a large saucepan. Add onion, garlic, and celery, and sauté until onion begins to soften, about 4 minutes.
2. Add remaining broth, reserved clam liquid, bell pepper, and potato. Bring to a boil, reduce heat, cover, and simmer, stirring occasionally, until potato is just tender, about 12 minutes.
3. Stir in remaining ingredients. Return to a boil, reduce heat, cover, and simmer for 5 more minutes. Remove bay leaf.

Calories Per Serving: 124   Carbohydrates: 27 g
Fat: 2 g   Dietary Fiber: 4 g
Cholesterol: 0 mg   Sodium: 317 mg
Protein: 5 g

❀ *Spiced Potato Puree with Clams* ❀

PREPARATION TIME: *20 minutes* ▪ COOKING TIME: *32 minutes* ▪
YIELD: *6 servings*

1 cup bottled clam juice
5 cups low-sodium nonfat chicken
  broth
2 cups diced potato
1 medium onion, finely chopped
1 scallion, minced
½ teaspoon dried thyme

¼ teaspoon ground black pepper
⅛ teaspoon hot pepper sauce
1 tablespoon low-sodium tomato
  paste
2 cups canned clams, drained
1 tablespoon lime juice

1. Combine clam juice and broth in a large saucepan. Add potato, onion, and scallion. Bring to a boil and reduce heat. Stir in thyme and black pepper, and simmer until potatoes are tender, about 20 minutes.
2. Puree potato mixture in a blender or food processor.
3. Return potato puree to the saucepan. Stir in hot pepper sauce, tomato paste, and clams, and cook gently until all ingredients are heated through, about 5 minutes.
4. Stir in lime juice, transfer to individual bowls, and serve.

Calories Per Serving: 184   Carbohydrates: 22 g
Fat: 1 g   Dietary Fiber: 2 g
Cholesterol: 36 mg   Sodium: 395 mg
Protein: 21 g

❀ *Clam-Succotash Soup* ❀

PREPARATION TIME: *20 minutes* • COOKING TIME: *23 minutes* •
YIELD: *6 servings*

1¼ cups low-sodium nonfat chicken
  broth
1 medium onion, finely chopped
2 cloves garlic, minced
2 medium stalks celery, with leaves,
  chopped
1½ cups canned clams, liquid reserved
1 medium red bell pepper, cored and
  diced
1½ cups thawed frozen lima beans

4 cups low-sodium canned tomatoes,
  chopped, juice reserved
1½ cups fresh or thawed frozen corn
  kernels
⅛ teaspoon cayenne pepper
1 bay leaf
½ teaspoon dried thyme
½ teaspoon dried basil
½ teaspoon sugar
¼ teaspoon ground black pepper

1. Heat ¼ cup broth in a large pot. Add onion, garlic, and celery, and sauté until onion begins to soften, about 3 minutes.
2. Add remaining broth, reserved clam liquid, bell pepper, and lima beans, and bring to a boil. Reduce heat, cover, and simmer, stirring occasionally, until beans are just tender, about 10 minutes.
3. Add remaining ingredients. Return to a boil, reduce heat, cover, and simmer for 5 minutes.
4. Remove bay leaf, transfer to individual bowls, and serve.

Calories Per Serving: 210
Fat: 1 g
Cholesterol: 35 mg
Protein: 16 g

Carbohydrates: 35 g
Dietary Fiber: 4 g
Sodium: 119 mg

❀ *Turnip-Potato-Clam Chowder* ❀

PREPARATION TIME: *20 minutes* • COOKING TIME: *47 minutes* •
YIELD: *6 servings*

2 medium turnips, diced
2 medium potatoes, diced
1 medium carrot, scraped and diced
1 small onion, diced
1 medium stalk celery, diced
2 cups water
4 cups skim milk
2 cups fresh, drained canned, or
    thawed frozen corn kernels

1 cup chopped canned clams, liquid
    reserved
⅛ teaspoon ground cumin
⅛ teaspoon dried sage
⅛ teaspoon dried rosemary
¼ teaspoon ground black pepper

1. Combine turnips, potatoes, carrot, onion, celery, and water. Bring to a boil, reduce heat, cover, and simmer until turnips are tender, about 25 minutes.
2. Stir in milk, corn, clams with liquid, cumin, sage, and rosemary. Cover and simmer gently for 15 minutes. Stir in black pepper.

Calories Per Serving: 199
Fat: 1 g
Cholesterol: 5 mg
Protein: 4 g

Carbohydrates: 41 g
Dietary Fiber: 3 g
Sodium: 201 mg

❋ Scallop Soup with White Wine ❋ and Green Peas

PREPARATION TIME: 20 minutes • COOKING TIME: 35 minutes •
YIELD: 4 servings

4¼ cups low-sodium nonfat chicken
    broth
1 medium onion, chopped
2 cloves garlic, minced
1 cup dry white wine
2 medium stalks celery, sliced
1 medium carrot, scraped and thinly
    sliced

½ cup chopped fresh parsley
1 teaspoon dried thyme
1½ cups fresh or frozen green peas
1 teaspoon dried saffron threads,
    crushed
2 scallions, chopped
1 pound fresh scallops, halved
½ teaspoon ground black pepper

1. Heat ¼ cup broth in a large saucepan. Add onion and garlic, and sauté until onion begins to soften, about 4 minutes. Add remaining broth, wine, celery, carrot, ¼ cup parsley, thyme, peas, and saffron. Bring to a boil, reduce heat, and simmer for 20 minutes.

2. Add scallions and scallops, and simmer for 3 minutes. Stir in black pepper and evaporated milk, and heat through, about 2 minutes.
3. Transfer to individual bowls, garnish with remaining parsley, and serve.

Calories Per Serving: 271
Fat: 1 g
Cholesterol: 39 mg
Protein: 26 g

Carbohydrates: 22 g
Dietary Fiber: 3 g
Sodium: 562 mg

❈ *Tangy Scallop Chowder with Asparagus* ❈

PREPARATION TIME: *20 minutes* • COOKING TIME: *33 minutes* •
YIELD: *10 servings*

5¼ cups low-sodium nonfat chicken broth
3 medium leeks (white part only), sliced
5 cloves garlic, minced
2 cups skim milk
½ cup dry white wine
⅓ cup chopped fresh parsley
1 teaspoon dried tarragon

2 bay leaves
5 cups chopped potato
3 medium stalks celery, sliced
¼ teaspoon hot pepper sauce
1 tablespoon lime juice
4 cups chopped fresh asparagus spears (1-inch lengths)
½ teaspoon ground black pepper
1 pound fresh scallops, halved

1. Heat ¼ cup broth in a large saucepan. Add leeks and garlic, and sauté for 2 minutes.
2. Stir in remaining broth, milk, wine, parsley, tarragon, bay leaves, potato, and celery. Bring to a boil, reduce heat, cover, and simmer until potato is just tender, about 12 minutes.
3. Stir in hot pepper sauce, lime juice, and asparagus, and simmer until asparagus is tender, about 8 minutes. Remove bay leaves. Add black pepper and scallops, and simmer until scallops are opaque, about 3 minutes.

Calories Per Serving: 181
Fat: 1 g
Cholesterol: 16 mg
Protein: 13 g

Carbohydrates: 27 g
Dietary Fiber: 2 g
Sodium: 276 mg

❈ Curried Tomato and Crab Soup ❈

PREPARATION TIME: *20 minutes plus 3 hours chilling time* •
COOKING TIME: *26 minutes* • YIELD: *4 servings*

¾ cup low-sodium nonfat chicken
   broth
2 scallions, sliced
1 tablespoon curry powder
⅛ teaspoon cayenne pepper
¼ teaspoon ground coriander
3 tablespoons all-purpose flour

5 medium tomatoes, chopped
½ cup skim milk
½ teaspoon ground black pepper
1½ cups fresh cooked or shredded
   canned crabmeat
¼ cup chopped fresh parsley

1. Heat ¼ cup broth in a large saucepan. Add scallions and sauté for 3 minutes.
2. Add curry powder, cayenne pepper, coriander, and flour, and stir for 3 more minutes.
3. Add remaining broth and tomatoes, and bring to a boil. Reduce heat and simmer for 15 minutes.
4. Refrigerate soup, covered, for 3 hours. Before serving, stir in milk, black pepper, and crabmeat. Serve topped with parsley.

Calories Per Serving: 128
Fat: 2 g
Cholesterol: 51 mg
Protein: 14 g

Carbohydrates: 15 g
Dietary Fiber: 3 g
Sodium: 229 mg

❈ Maryland Crab Soup ❈

PREPARATION TIME: *25 minutes* • COOKING TIME: *42 minutes* •
YIELD: *8 servings*

6¾ cups low-sodium nonfat chicken
   broth
2 medium onions, finely chopped
2 medium carrots, scraped and thinly
   sliced
2 medium stalks celery, finely
   chopped
½ cup chopped fresh parsley
2 cups water
2 bay leaves

½ teaspoon dry mustard
1 tablespoon Old Bay seasoning (if
   not available, substitute ¼ teaspoon cayenne pepper)
3 cups diced potatoes
3 cups low-sodium canned tomatoes,
   chopped, juice reserved
1 cup fresh or frozen corn kernels
3 cups fresh cooked or shredded
   canned crabmeat

1. Heat ¼ cup broth in a large saucepan. Add onions, carrots, celery, and parsley, and sauté until onions begin to soften, about 4 minutes. Add remaining broth, water, bay leaves, dry mustard, and Old Bay seasoning. Bring to a boil, reduce heat, cover, and simmer for 10 minutes.
2. Add potatoes and simmer for 10 more minutes. Add tomatoes with juice and corn, cover, and simmer for 10 additional minutes.
3. Stir in crabmeat and simmer until crab is heated through. Remove bay leaves, and serve at once.

Calories Per Serving: 273
Fat: 2 g
Cholesterol: 68 mg
Protein: 19 g

Carbohydrates: 42 g
Dietary Fiber: 4 g
Sodium: 608 mg

❋ *Sherried Crab Soup* ❋

PREPARATION TIME: *15 minutes* • COOKING TIME: *44 minutes* •
YIELD: *6 servings*

6¼ cups low-sodium nonfat chicken broth
2 medium leeks (white parts only), chopped
1 medium onion, chopped
4 medium stalks celery, sliced
3½ cups low-sodium canned tomatoes, drained and chopped
1 cup diced potato

2 teaspoons dried basil
1 teaspoon dried thyme
1½ cups fresh or thawed frozen green peas
½ teaspoon ground black pepper
1½ cups fresh cooked or shredded canned crabmeat
⅓ cup dry sherry

1. Heat ¼ cup broth in a large saucepan. Add leeks, onion, and celery, and sauté until onion begins to soften, about 4 minutes.
2. Add remaining broth, tomatoes, potato, basil, and thyme. Bring to a boil, reduce heat, and simmer for 20 minutes.
3. Stir in peas and black pepper, and simmer until peas are tender, about 10 minutes. Add crabmeat and sherry, and heat through, about 3 more minutes.

Calories Per Serving: 193
Fat: 1 g
Cholesterol: 30 mg
Protein: 19 g

Carbohydrates: 27 g
Dietary Fiber: 4 g
Sodium: 321 mg

❀ Crab-Cauliflower Chowder ❀

PREPARATION TIME: 20 minutes ▪ COOKING TIME: 29 minutes ▪
YIELD: 6 servings

2¼ cups low-sodium nonfat chicken
    broth
1 medium onion, chopped
1 medium stalk celery, sliced
2 cloves garlic, minced
1 cup skim milk
2½ cups diced potatoes
2 cups chopped cauliflower

1 medium carrot, scraped and thinly
    sliced
1½ teaspoons dried basil
¼ teaspoon dried thyme
¼ teaspoon dry mustard
3 cups fresh cooked or shredded
    canned crabmeat
½ teaspoon ground black pepper

1. Heat ¼ cup broth in a large saucepan. Add onion, celery, and garlic, and sauté until onion begins to soften, about 4 minutes.
2. Add remaining broth, milk, potatoes, cauliflower, carrot, basil, thyme, and dry mustard. Bring to a boil, reduce heat, cover, and simmer, stirring occasionally, until potatoes are just tender, about 15 minutes.
3. Add crabmeat and simmer until heated through, about 4 minutes. Stir in black pepper.

Calories Per Serving: 229
Fat: 1 g
Cholesterol: 66 mg
Protein: 21 g

Carbohydrates: 32 g
Dietary Fiber: 2 g
Sodium: 293 mg

❀ Asparagus-Shrimp Soup ❀

PREPARATION TIME: 15 minutes ▪ COOKING TIME: 21 minutes ▪
YIELD: 4 servings

5¼ cups low-sodium nonfat chicken
    broth
¾ pound fresh medium shrimp, peeled
    and deveined
6 cups chopped fresh asparagus spears
    (2-inch lengths)

½ cup dry white wine
¼ cup chopped onion
1 teaspoon dried tarragon
½ cup skim milk
½ teaspoon ground black pepper

1. Heat ¼ cup broth in a large saucepan. Add shrimp and sauté until shrimp turn pink, about 3 minutes. Remove and set aside.

2. Heat another ¼ cup broth in the saucepan. Add asparagus, cover, and simmer until just tender, about 5 minutes. Remove and set aside.
3. Combine wine, onion, and tarragon in the saucepan. Cook and stir until liquid is reduced by half, about 6 minutes.
4. Puree milk and 2 cups asparagus in a food processor or blender. Bring puree and remaining broth to a simmer in the saucepan. Return shrimp and remaining asparagus to the saucepan, and simmer until heated through, about 3 minutes.
5. Stir in black pepper.

Calories Per Serving: 166	Carbohydrates: 4 g
Fat: 2 g	Dietary Fiber: 0 g
Cholesterol: 130 mg	Sodium: 367 mg
Protein: 28 g	

❊ *Shrimp and Artichoke Soup* ❊

PREPARATION TIME: *20 minutes plus 1 hour marinating time* •
COOKING TIME: *38 minutes* • YIELD: *8 servings*

¼ cup lime juice
¼ cup orange juice
1 dried chile pepper
1 pound fresh medium shrimp, peeled, deveined, and halved
3¼ cups low-sodium nonfat chicken broth
6 scallions, sliced
1 medium red bell pepper, cored and chopped
2 cloves garlic, minced

3 cups diced potatoes
1 cup diced zucchini
1 cup water-packed canned artichoke hearts, drained and chopped
1 bay leaf
½ teaspoon dried thyme
3 cups water
1 cup skim milk
½ teaspoon ground black pepper
¼ cup chopped fresh parsley

1. In a large bowl, combine lime juice, orange juice, and chile pepper. Add the shrimp and marinate, tossing occasionally, for 1 hour at room temperature.
2. Heat ¼ cup broth in a large saucepan. Add scallions, bell pepper, and garlic, and sauté until scallions begin to soften, about 5 minutes. Add remaining broth, potatoes, zucchini, artichokes, bay leaf, thyme, and water. Bring to a boil, reduce heat, and simmer for 20 minutes.
3. Drain shrimp and add to the saucepan. Simmer for 5 more minutes. Stir in milk and black pepper, and simmer to heat through, about 2 more minutes. Remove bay leaf.
4. Transfer soup to individual bowls, garnish with parsley, and serve.

Calories Per Serving: 178

Carbohydrates: 27 g

Fat: 1 g

Dietary Fiber: 3 g

Cholesterol: 87 mg

Sodium: 128 mg

Protein: 16 g

❈ *Shrimp Soup with Corn* ❈

PREPARATION TIME: *20 minutes* • COOKING TIME: *27 minutes* •
YIELD: *6 servings*

6¼ cups low-sodium nonfat chicken
  broth
¾ pound fresh medium shrimp, peeled
  and deveined
6 scallions, chopped
2 cloves garlic, minced
1 jalapeño pepper, seeded and minced

½ teaspoon dried oregano
2 medium tomatoes, chopped
4 cups fresh or thawed frozen corn
  kernels
1 cup skim milk
½ teaspoon ground black pepper
¼ cup chopped fresh parsley

1. Heat ¼ cup broth in a large saucepan. Add shrimp and sauté until shrimp turn pink, about 2 minutes. Remove and set aside.
2. Heat another ¼ cup broth in the saucepan. Add scallions, garlic, and jalapeño pepper, and sauté until scallions begin to soften, about 3 minutes. Add oregano and tomatoes, and stir for 2 more minutes.
3. Add remaining broth, corn, and milk to the saucepan. Bring to a boil, reduce heat, and simmer for 10 minutes.
4. Return shrimp to soup, stir in black pepper, and heat for about 2 minutes.
5. Serve topped with parsley.

Calories Per Serving: 149

Carbohydrates: 21 g

Fat: 1 g

Dietary Fiber: 2 g

Cholesterol: 65 mg

Sodium: 365 mg

Protein: 13 g

❈ *Shrimp Soup with Red Peppers and Chiles* ❈

PREPARATION TIME: *20 minutes* • COOKING TIME: *1 hour* • YIELD: *8 servings*

¼ cup low-sodium nonfat chicken
   broth
2 medium onions, chopped
2 medium red bell peppers, cored and
   chopped
3 cloves garlic, minced
4 medium stalks celery, chopped
1¼ cups low-sodium canned tomatoes
   with chiles, drained and chopped

2 cups low-sodium canned tomatoes,
   drained and chopped
6 cups fresh or thawed frozen corn
   kernels
12 cups water
½ teaspoon ground black pepper
¼ teaspoon cayenne pepper
1 pound fresh medium shrimp, peeled
   and deveined
½ cup minced scallion

1. Heat broth in a large saucepan. Add onions, bell peppers, garlic, and celery. Sauté until onions begin to soften, about 3 minutes. Add tomatoes with chiles and canned tomatoes, and simmer for 10 minutes.
2. Stir in corn, water, black pepper, and cayenne pepper. Bring to a boil, reduce heat, and simmer for 25 minutes.
3. Add shrimp and simmer for 10 more minutes.
4. Serve topped with scallion.

Calories Per Serving: 196
Fat: 1 g
Cholesterol: 86 mg
Protein: 17 g

Carbohydrates: 34 g
Dietary Fiber: 4 g
Sodium: 258 mg

❈ Spicy Shrimp and Vegetable Soup ❈

PREPARATION TIME: 25 minutes • COOKING TIME: 18 minutes •
YIELD: 6 servings

3¼ cups low-sodium nonfat chicken
   broth
1 medium onion, chopped
2 cloves garlic, minced
1½ cups fresh or thawed frozen corn
   kernels
1 cup chopped cauliflower
1 cup diced potato
1 cup diced zucchini
1 medium carrot, scraped and sliced
1 medium green bell pepper, cored
   and diced
1 medium red bell pepper, cored and
   diced

⅓ cup dry sherry
¾ teaspoon dried basil
½ teaspoon dried thyme
¼ teaspoon chili powder
¼ teaspoon dry mustard
⅛ teaspoon cayenne pepper
¼ teaspoon ground black pepper
½ pound fresh medium shrimp,
   peeled, deveined, and halved
1 cup low-sodium tomato sauce
½ cup skim milk

1. Heat ¼ cup broth in a large saucepan. Add onion and garlic, and sauté until onion begins to soften, about 4 minutes.
2. Add remaining broth, corn, cauliflower, potato, zucchini, carrot, bell peppers, sherry, basil, thyme, chili powder, dry mustard, cayenne pepper, and black pepper. Bring to a boil, reduce heat, cover, and simmer for 5 minutes. Add shrimp and simmer until shrimp turn pink, about 3 more minutes.
3. Stir in tomato sauce and milk, and simmer to heat through, about 3 minutes.

Calories Per Serving: 176
Fat: 1 g
Cholesterol: 63 mg
Protein: 11 g

Carbohydrates: 29 g
Dietary Fiber: 3 g
Sodium: 261 mg

❈ *Shrimp-Potato Chowder* ❈

PREPARATION TIME: *20 minutes* • COOKING TIME: *45 minutes* •
YIELD: *6 servings*

1¾ cups low-sodium nonfat chicken broth
2 medium onions, finely chopped
1 medium carrot, scraped and thinly sliced
2 medium stalks celery, sliced
1 medium red bell pepper, cored and diced
½ cup chopped fresh parsley
2 cloves garlic, minced
2 cups diced potatoes
3½ cups low-sodium canned tomatoes, drained and chopped

¾ cup dry white wine
1 teaspoon sugar
1 bay leaf
2 teaspoons paprika
2 teaspoons chili powder
¼ teaspoon celery seed
½ teaspoon ground black pepper
¼ teaspoon dried thyme
¼ teaspoon cayenne pepper
1½ pounds fresh medium shrimp, peeled and deveined

1. Heat ¼ cup broth in a large saucepan. Add onions, carrot, celery, bell pepper, ¼ cup parsley, and garlic, and sauté until onions begin to soften, about 4 minutes.
2. Stir in remaining broth and potatoes, and bring to a boil. Reduce heat, cover, and simmer, stirring occasionally, until potatoes begin to soften, about 12 minutes. Add tomatoes, wine, sugar, bay leaf, paprika, chili pow-

der, celery seed, black pepper, thyme, and cayenne pepper. Cover and simmer until mixture thickens, about 20 minutes.

3. Add shrimp and continue to simmer until shrimp turn pink, about 3 minutes. Remove bay leaf.
4. Sprinkle with remaining parsley and serve.

Calories Per Serving: 230
Fat: 2 g
Cholesterol: 90 mg
Protein: 25 g

Carbohydrates: 27 g
Dietary Fiber: 3 g
Sodium: 217 mg

❋ *Haddock-Orzo Soup* ❋

PREPARATION TIME: *20 minutes* • COOKING TIME: *1 hour 7 minutes* •
YIELD: *6 servings*

4¼ cups low-sodium nonfat chicken
    broth
1 medium onion, thinly sliced
2 cloves garlic, minced
1 medium red bell pepper, cored and
    cut into thin strips
1 teaspoon dried oregano
½ teaspoon cayenne pepper

3½ cups low-sodium canned tomatoes, drained and chopped
½ cup dry white wine
1 cup uncooked orzo
1½ pounds fresh haddock fillet, cut
    into 1-inch cubes
½ teaspoon ground black pepper

1. Heat ¼ cup broth in a large saucepan. Add onion, garlic, and bell pepper, and sauté until onion begins to soften, about 4 minutes.
2. Add oregano, cayenne pepper, and tomatoes. Bring to a boil, reduce heat, and simmer for 10 minutes. Add wine and puree in a blender or food processor.
3. Return puree to the saucepan, add remaining broth, and bring to a boil. Stir in orzo, reduce heat, and simmer for 20 minutes. Add haddock and simmer until fish flakes easily, about 5 minutes. Stir in black pepper.

Calories Per Serving: 226
Fat: 1 g
Cholesterol: 49 mg
Protein: 24 g

Carbohydrates: 22 g
Dietary Fiber: 2 g
Sodium: 291 mg

❋ Orange Roughy Soup with Shiitake ❋ Mushrooms and Spinach

PREPARATION TIME: *20 minutes* • COOKING TIME: *24 minutes* •
YIELD: *6 servings*

1 teaspoon sesame oil
6¼ cups low-sodium nonfat chicken broth
3 scallions, chopped
2 cloves garlic, minced
2 tablespoons minced fresh gingerroot
½ cup thinly sliced shiitake mushrooms

1 tablespoon rice vinegar
1 tablespoon reduced-sodium soy sauce
1½ pounds fresh orange roughy fillet, cut into 1-inch cubes
8 cups chopped fresh spinach
½ teaspoon ground black pepper

1. Heat sesame oil and ¼ cup broth in a large saucepan. Add scallions, garlic, and gingerroot, and sauté until scallions begin to soften, about 3 minutes. Add mushrooms and sauté for 3 more minutes.
2. Add remaining broth, vinegar, and soy sauce, and bring to a boil. Reduce heat and simmer for 5 minutes.
3. Add orange roughy and spinach, and simmer until fish flakes easily, about 5 minutes.
4. Stir in black pepper, transfer to individual bowls, and serve.

Calories Per Serving: 173
Fat: 2 g
Cholesterol: 65 mg
Protein: 32 g

Carbohydrates: 7 g
Dietary Fiber: 3 g
Sodium: 403 mg

❋ Flounder-Vegetable Soup ❋

PREPARATION TIME: *15 minutes* • COOKING TIME: *35 minutes* •
YIELD: *6 servings*

2¼ cups low-sodium nonfat chicken broth
1 medium onion, chopped
2 medium stalks celery, sliced
4 cups low-sodium tomato juice

1 medium carrot, scraped and sliced
1½ cups chopped fresh or frozen green beans (1-inch lengths)
1½ cups fresh or frozen corn kernels
1 cup diced potato

1 bay leaf
½ teaspoon dried thyme
¼ teaspoon dry mustard
⅛ teaspoon cayenne pepper

¼ teaspoon ground black pepper
¾ pound fresh flounder fillet, cut into
 1-inch cubes

1. Heat ¼ cup broth in a large saucepan. Add onion and celery, and sauté until onion begins to soften, about 4 minutes.
2. Add remaining broth, tomato juice, carrot, green beans, corn, potato, bay leaf, thyme, dry mustard, cayenne pepper, and black pepper. Bring to a boil, reduce heat, cover, and simmer until vegetables are tender, about 20 minutes.
3. Add flounder and simmer until fish flakes easily, about 5 more minutes. Remove bay leaf.
4. Transfer soup to individual bowls and serve.

Calories Per Serving: 151
Fat: 1 g
Cholesterol: 25 mg
Protein: 14 g

Carbohydrates: 25 g
Dietary Fiber: 4 g
Sodium: 77 mg

❋ *Codfish Chowder* ❋

PREPARATION TIME: *20 minutes* • COOKING TIME: *34 minutes* •
YIELD: *6 servings*

2¼ cups low-sodium nonfat chicken
 broth
1 medium onion, chopped
2 cloves garlic, minced
1 medium stalk celery, sliced
2½ cups diced potato
1 cup frozen lima beans
1 medium carrot, scraped and sliced
1½ teaspoons dried basil

¼ teaspoon dried thyme
¼ teaspoon dry mustard
¼ teaspoon ground black pepper
1 pound fresh cod fillet, cut into
 1-inch cubes
1 cup fresh or thawed frozen corn
 kernels
2 cups skim milk
¼ cup chopped fresh parsley

1. Heat ¼ cup broth in a large saucepan. Add onion, garlic, and celery, and sauté until onion begins to soften, about 4 minutes.
2. Stir in remaining broth, potato, lima beans, carrot, basil, thyme, dry mustard, and black pepper. Bring to a boil, reduce heat, cover, and simmer until potatoes are just tender, about 12 minutes.
3. Add cod and corn, and simmer until fish flakes easily, about 6 minutes.

4. Stir in milk and heat through.
5. Serve topped with parsley.

Calories Per Serving: 211   Carbohydrates: 41 g
Fat: 1 g   Dietary Fiber: 4 g
Cholesterol: 8 mg   Sodium: 184 mg
Protein: 10 g

❊ Orange Roughy Soup with Mushrooms ❊ and Red Wine

PREPARATION TIME: *25 minutes* ▪ COOKING TIME: *51 minutes* ▪
YIELD: *10 servings*

5¼ cups low-sodium nonfat chicken
   broth
1 medium onion, chopped
6 cloves garlic, minced
½ teaspoon cayenne pepper
2 medium stalks celery, sliced
1 cup sliced mushrooms
3 tablespoons lemon juice

3½ cups low-sodium canned tomatoes, drained and crushed
½ cup dry red wine
1 teaspoon dried basil
¼ cup chopped fresh parsley
1 teaspoon ground black pepper
2 pounds fresh orange roughy fillet,
   cut into 1-inch cubes

1. Heat ¼ cup broth in a large saucepan. Add onion, garlic, cayenne pepper, celery, and mushrooms, and sauté until onion begins to soften, about 4 minutes. Sprinkle lemon juice on vegetables.
2. Add remaining broth, tomatoes, wine, basil, 2 tablespoons parsley, and black pepper. Bring to a boil, reduce heat, and simmer for 30 minutes.
3. Add orange roughy, cover, and simmer until fish flakes easily, about 10 minutes.
4. Transfer to individual bowls, garnish with remaining parsley, and serve.

Calories Per Serving: 146   Carbohydrates: 8 g
Fat: 1 g   Dietary Fiber: 1 g
Cholesterol: 49 mg   Sodium: 266 mg
Protein: 22 g

❊ *Smoked Salmon–Spinach Soup* ❊

PREPARATION TIME: *15 minutes* • COOKING TIME: *32 minutes* •
YIELD: *6 servings*

6 cups low-sodium nonfat chicken
　broth
6 scallions, sliced
3 small potatoes, chopped

¼ teaspoon ground black pepper
4 cups chopped fresh spinach
4 ounces smoked salmon, cut into
　½-inch cubes

1. Combine broth, scallions, and potatoes in a saucepan. Bring to a boil, reduce heat, cover, and simmer until potatoes are just tender, about 15 minutes.
2. Stir in black pepper and spinach, and simmer for 5 more minutes. Add
salmon and heat through, about 5 minutes.
3. Transfer to individual bowls and serve.

Calories Per Serving: 129
Fat: 2 g
Cholesterol: 11 mg
Protein: 13 g

Carbohydrates: 14 g
Dietary Fiber: 2 g
Sodium: 213 mg

❊ *Salmon Chowder* ❊

PREPARATION TIME: *20 minutes* • COOKING TIME: *41 minutes* •
YIELD: *6 servings*

2 tablespoons low-sodium vegetable
　broth
4 medium potatoes, diced
5 scallions, sliced
¼ teaspoon dried dill
6 cups skim milk
2 cups fresh or thawed frozen corn
　kernels

1 cup chopped fresh or thawed frozen
　green beans (1-inch lengths)
1 medium green bell pepper, cored
　and chopped
¼ pound fresh salmon fillet, cut into
　½-inch cubes
½ teaspoon ground black pepper
2 tablespoons minced fresh parsley

1. Heat broth in a saucepan. Add potatoes, scallions, and dill, and sauté for
3 minutes.
2. Stir in milk, corn, green beans, and bell pepper, and simmer until vegetables are just tender, about 25 minutes.

3. Add salmon, sprinkle with black pepper, and simmer until fish flakes easily, about 7 minutes.
4. Transfer to individual bowls, garnish with parsley, and serve.

Calories Per Serving: 258	Carbohydrates: 45 g
Fat: 3 g	Dietary Fiber: 3 g
Cholesterol: 15 mg	Sodium: 147 mg
Protein: 16 g	

❊ Haddock–Lima Bean Soup ❊

PREPARATION TIME: *20 minutes* • COOKING TIME: *32 minutes* •
YIELD: *6 servings*

5 cups low-sodium nonfat chicken
  broth
1 cup chopped onion
2 tablespoons cornmeal
½ pound fresh haddock fillet, cut into
  1-inch cubes

2 cups fresh or thawed frozen lima
  beans
4 shiitake mushrooms, thinly sliced
2 tablespoons chopped fresh parsley
1 teaspoon dried dill
¼ teaspoon ground black pepper

1. Combine broth, onion, and cornmeal in a large saucepan. Bring to a boil, reduce heat, and simmer for 10 minutes.
2. Add haddock, lima beans, and mushrooms, and simmer until fish flakes easily, about 15 minutes. Stir in parsley, dill, and black pepper, and simmer for 1 more minute.

Calories Per Serving: 157	Carbohydrates: 20 g
Fat: 1 g	Dietary Fiber: 5 g
Cholesterol: 22 mg	Sodium: 179 mg
Protein: 18 g	

❊ Catfish Soup ❊

PREPARATION TIME: *15 minutes* • COOKING TIME: *24 minutes* •
YIELD: *6 servings*

¾ cup low-sodium nonfat chicken
  broth

2 cups chopped onion
3 medium stalks celery, chopped

4 cloves garlic, minced
1 medium green bell pepper, cored
   and chopped
¾ pound fresh catfish fillet, cut into
   1-inch cubes

¼ teaspoon ground black pepper
¼ teaspoon cayenne pepper
2 cups low-sodium canned tomatoes,
   drained and chopped
2 cups water

1. Heat ¼ cup broth in a large pot. Add onion, celery, garlic, and bell pepper. Sauté until onion begins to soften, about 4 minutes.
2. Sprinkle catfish with black pepper and cayenne pepper, and add to the onion mixture. Stir in all remaining ingredients. Bring to a boil, reduce heat, cover, and simmer until fish flakes easily, about 15 minutes.

Calories Per Serving: 104
Fat: 2 g
Cholesterol: 33 mg
Protein: 12 g

Carbohydrates: 10 g
Dietary Fiber: 2 g
Sodium: 78 mg

❊ Marinated Codfish Soup with Tomatoes ❊

PREPARATION TIME: 15 minutes plus 1 hour marinating time   •
COOKING TIME: 20 minutes   •   YIELD: 6 servings

½ cup lime juice
1 teaspoon cayenne pepper
3 cloves garlic, minced
2 cups water
6 fresh cod fillets, about 4 ounces
   each
¼ cup low-sodium nonfat chicken
   broth

1 medium onion, finely chopped
4 scallions, finely chopped
4 medium tomatoes, chopped
¼ teaspoon ground black pepper
1 bay leaf
⅓ teaspoon dried thyme
2 teaspoons olive oil
3 cups cooked rice

1. Combine 6 tablespoons lime juice, the cayenne pepper, two thirds of the garlic, and water. Pour over fish and marinate for 1 hour in the refrigerator.
2. Heat broth in a large pot. Add onion and scallions, and sauté until onion begins to soften, about 3 minutes. Add tomatoes, black pepper, bay leaf, and thyme, and simmer, stirring occasionally, for 5 minutes.
3. Add cod, marinade, and enough water to just cover, and simmer covered until fish flakes easily, about 10 minutes. Remove bay leaf.
4. Divide rice among individual soup bowls. Transfer soup to bowls and serve topped with remaining lime juice and garlic, and olive oil.

Calories Per Serving: 261
Fat: 3 g
Cholesterol: 49 mg
Protein: 24 g

Carbohydrates: 35 g
Dietary Fiber: 1 g
Sodium: 85 mg

❋ *Curried Cod Soup* ❋

PREPARATION TIME: *15 minutes*   •   COOKING TIME: *20 minutes*   •
YIELD: *6 servings*

1¾ cups low-sodium nonfat chicken
   broth
1 cup chopped onion
¾ cup low-sodium tomato paste
1 teaspoon minced fresh gingerroot
1 teaspoon curry powder

¼ teaspoon cayenne pepper
2 tablespoons reduced-fat peanut
   butter
1½ pounds fresh cod fillet, cut into
   2-inch cubes

1. Heat ¼ cup broth in a large pot. Add onion and sauté until it begins to soften, about 3 minutes.
2. Stir in remaining broth, tomato paste, gingerroot, curry powder, cayenne pepper, and peanut butter. Simmer for 5 minutes.
3. Add cod and simmer, covered, until fish flakes easily, about 10 minutes.

Calories Per Serving: 155
Fat: 2 g
Cholesterol: 49 mg
Protein: 24 g

Carbohydrates: 11 g
Dietary Fiber: 2 g
Sodium: 161 mg

❋ *Sherried Flounder Soup with Mushrooms* ❋

PREPARATION TIME: *20 minutes*   •   COOKING TIME: *32 minutes*   •
YIELD: *6 servings*

1 cup water
2 medium potatoes, diced
¼ cup low-sodium nonfat chicken
   broth
2 medium onions, diced
1 cup sliced mushrooms

3 medium red bell peppers, cored and
   chopped
¾ pound fresh flounder fillet, cut into
   1-inch cubes
¼ teaspoon ground black pepper

2 teaspoons reduced-sodium soy
   sauce

¼ cup chopped fresh parsley
½ cup dry sherry

1. Bring water to a boil in a large pot. Add potatoes and boil until they are just tender, about 10 minutes. Remove and set aside. Drain remaining liquid.
2. Heat broth in the pot. Add onions, mushrooms, and bell peppers, and sauté until onions begin to soften, about 4 minutes.
3. Add flounder, black pepper, and soy sauce, and simmer until fish flakes easily, about 10 minutes.
4. Add 2 tablespoons parsley and the sherry, and heat through, about 3 minutes.
5. Serve topped with remaining parsley.

Calories Per Serving: 235
Fat: 1 g
Cholesterol: 28 mg
Protein: 19 g

Carbohydrates: 36 g
Dietary Fiber: 2 g
Sodium: 308 mg

❊ Leftover Wild Rice–Salmon– ❊ Mushroom Soup

PREPARATION TIME: 20 minutes • COOKING TIME: 19 minutes •
YIELD: 6 servings

2½ cups low-sodium nonfat chicken
   broth
1 medium onion, sliced
1 medium stalk celery, thinly sliced
2 cups sliced mushrooms

½ teaspoon dry mustard
¼ teaspoon dried rosemary
1 cup cooked wild rice
1 cup skim milk
¼ pound cooked salmon fillet

1. Heat ¼ cup broth in a large pot. Add onion, celery, and mushrooms, and sauté until onion begins to soften, about 4 minutes.
2. Add dry mustard, rosemary, remaining broth, and wild rice. Bring to a boil, reduce heat, cover, and simmer for 10 minutes.
3. Add milk and salmon, and heat through, about 3 minutes.

Calories Per Serving: 113
Fat: 2 g
Cholesterol: 14 mg
Protein: 11 g

Carbohydrates: 13 g
Dietary Fiber: 1 g
Sodium: 97 mg

❀ *Simple Haddock Chowder* ❀

PREPARATION TIME: *15 minutes* ▪ COOKING TIME: *35 minutes* ▪
YIELD: *4 servings*

3 tablespoons low-sodium nonfat
   chicken broth
1 medium onion, chopped
1 clove garlic, minced
1½ cups water
1 bay leaf

¼ cup chopped fresh parsley
½ teaspoon dried thyme
¼ teaspoon ground black pepper
½ cup skim milk
¾ pound fresh haddock fillet, cut into
   2-inch cubes

1. Heat broth in a large pot. Add onion and garlic, and sauté until onion begins to soften, about 3 minutes.
2. Add water, bay leaf, parsley, thyme, black pepper, and milk. Simmer for 20 minutes. Add haddock and simmer until fish flakes easily, about 10 minutes. Remove bay leaf.

Calories Per Serving: 100
Fat: 1 g
Cholesterol: 50 mg
Protein: 18 g

Carbohydrates: 5 g
Dietary Fiber: 1 g
Sodium: 96 mg

❀ *Cod-Cauliflower Chowder* ❀

PREPARATION TIME: *20 minutes* ▪ COOKING TIME: *27 minutes* ▪
YIELD: *6 servings*

2¼ cups low-sodium nonfat chicken
   broth
1 medium onion, chopped
2 cloves garlic, minced
1 cup bottled clam juice
1 medium carrot, scraped and diced
2 medium potatoes, diced
1½ cups chopped cauliflower
¼ cup dry sherry

1 bay leaf
1½ teaspoons dried basil
1½ teaspoons dried thyme
¼ teaspoon dry mustard
¼ teaspoon ground white pepper
1½ cups low-sodium tomato sauce
1 pound fresh cod fillet, cut into
   1-inch cubes

1. Heat ¼ cup broth in a large pot. Add onion and garlic, and sauté until onion begins to soften, about 3 minutes.

2. Stir in remaining broth, clam juice, carrot, potatoes, cauliflower, sherry, bay leaf, basil, thyme, dry mustard, and white pepper. Bring to a boil.
3. Reduce heat, cover, and simmer, stirring occasionally, until vegetables are just tender, about 12 minutes. Remove bay leaf.
4. Puree 2 cups of vegetable mixture in a blender or food processor and return to the pot. Stir in tomato sauce and mix well. Add cod and simmer until fish flakes easily, about 7 minutes.

Calories Per Serving: 222	Carbohydrates: 31 g
Fat: 1 g	Dietary Fiber: 2 g
Cholesterol: 35 mg	Sodium: 389 mg
Protein: 21 g	

❈ *Shrimp and Flounder Soup with Spinach,* ❈
Lemon, and Thyme

PREPARATION TIME: *20 minutes* • COOKING TIME: *38 minutes* •
YIELD: *8 servings*

2 tablespoons low-sodium nonfat chicken broth	*1 bay leaf*
1 medium leek (white part only), chopped	*1 pound fresh flounder fillet, cut into 2-inch cubes*
4 scallions, chopped	*½ pound fresh medium shrimp, peeled and deveined*
8 cups water	*2 cups chopped fresh spinach*
¼ cup chopped fresh parsley	*1 tablespoon lemon juice*
1 teaspoon dried thyme	*¼ teaspoon ground black pepper*

1. Heat broth in a large saucepan. Add leek and scallions, and sauté until leek begins to soften, about 3 minutes. Add water, parsley, thyme, and bay leaf. Bring to a boil, reduce heat, cover, and simmer for 15 minutes.
2. Remove bay leaf. Return to a boil and add flounder. Reduce heat and simmer for 5 minutes. Add shrimp and simmer until fish flakes easily and shrimp have turned pink, about 4 minutes.
3. Stir in remaining ingredients, heat through, and serve.

Calories Per Serving: 141	Carbohydrates: 9 g
Fat: 2 g	Dietary Fiber: 1 g
Cholesterol: 90 mg	Sodium: 138 mg
Protein: 23 g	

❋ Orange Roughy and Shrimp Soup ❋ with Vegetables

PREPARATION TIME: *20 minutes* • COOKING TIME: *30 minutes* •
YIELD: *8 servings*

1 pound fresh orange roughy fillet,
   cut into 1-inch cubes
2 cups water
¼ cup low-sodium nonfat chicken
   broth
1 medium onion, chopped
2 medium tomatoes, chopped

1 medium green bell pepper, cored
   and chopped
¼ teaspoon dried thyme
¼ teaspoon cayenne pepper
10 cups shredded fresh spinach
½ pound fresh medium shrimp, peeled
   and deveined

1. Combine orange roughy and water in a large pot. Bring to a boil, reduce heat, and simmer for 10 minutes.
2. Add broth, onion, tomatoes, bell pepper, thyme, and cayenne pepper. Simmer for 5 more minutes.
3. Stir in spinach and shrimp, and simmer until spinach is just tender and shrimp have turned pink, about 10 minutes.

Calories Per Serving: 107
Fat: 1 g
Cholesterol: 67 mg
Protein: 19 g

Carbohydrates: 6 g
Dietary Fiber: 3 g
Sodium: 138 mg

❋ Seafood Soup with Cabbage ❋ and New Potatoes

PREPARATION TIME: *20 minutes* • COOKING TIME: *45 minutes* •
YIELD: *8 servings*

7¼ cups low-sodium nonfat chicken
   broth
3 cups chopped onion
1 cup chopped cabbage
2 medium carrots, scraped and thinly
   sliced
2 cups diced new potatoes

1 teaspoon dried thyme
1 teaspoon dried dill
⅛ teaspoon ground cardamom
1 pound fresh cod fillet, cut into
   1-inch cubes
¼ teaspoon ground black pepper
1 cup canned clams, drained

½ *pound fresh medium shrimp, peeled*   ½ *cup minced scallions*
  and deveined

1. Combine ½ cup broth, onion, cabbage, carrots, potatoes, thyme, dill, and cardamom in a large pot. Cover and simmer until cabbage begins to soften, about 10 minutes.
2. Add remaining broth. Bring to a boil, reduce heat, cover, and simmer until potatoes are tender, about 20 minutes.
3. Add cod and simmer until fish is almost cooked through, about 7 minutes. Stir in black pepper, clams, and shrimp, and simmer until shrimp turn pink, about 2 minutes.
4. Serve topped with scallions.

Calories Per Serving: 199   Carbohydrates: 22 g
Fat: 1 g   Dietary Fiber: 2 g
Cholesterol: 68 mg   Sodium: 311 mg
Protein: 25 g

❁ *Scallop-Shrimp Minestrone* ❁

PREPARATION TIME: *25 minutes*   •   COOKING TIME: *30 minutes*   •
YIELD: *8 servings*

6¼ *cups low-sodium nonfat chicken*   ½ *teaspoon dried oregano*
  broth   ½ *teaspoon dried thyme*
1 *medium onion, chopped*   2 *medium tomatoes, chopped*
1 *medium carrot, scraped and sliced*   ½ *cup dry white wine*
2 *medium stalks celery, sliced*   1 *cup uncooked small pasta shells*
1 *medium red bell pepper, cored and*   1 *pound fresh medium shrimp, peeled*
  cut into thin strips   *and deveined*
2 *cups shredded cabbage*   2 *cups fresh scallops, quartered*
1 *cup sliced zucchini*   ½ *teaspoon ground black pepper*

1. Heat ¼ cup broth in a large saucepan. Add onion, carrot, celery, bell pepper, cabbage, and zucchini. Sauté until vegetables begin to soften, about 4 minutes. Stir in oregano and thyme, and sauté for 1 more minute.
2. Add tomatoes and wine, and stir for 3 minutes. Stir in remaining broth and bring to a boil. Add pasta shells, reduce heat, and simmer, stirring occasionally, for 10 minutes. Add shrimp and scallops, and continue to simmer until pasta shells are just tender, about 4 minutes.
3. Stir in black pepper, transfer to individual bowls, and serve.

Calories Per Serving: 210
Fat: 2 g
Cholesterol: 76 mg
Protein: 28 g

Carbohydrates: 17 g
Dietary Fiber: 2 g
Sodium: 269 mg

❊ Bouillabaisse with White Wine and Saffron ❊

PREPARATION TIME: 25 minutes • COOKING TIME: 55 minutes •
YIELD: 10 servings

4¼ cups low-sodium nonfat chicken
  broth
1 medium onion, chopped
3 medium leeks (white parts only),
  sliced
3 cloves garlic, minced
6 medium tomatoes, chopped
1 medium red bell pepper, cored and
  finely chopped
1 bay leaf
2 cups low-sodium tomato juice
2 cups dry white wine
1 teaspoon dried basil

¼ cup chopped fresh parsley
1 teaspoon dried thyme
½ teaspoon dried saffron threads,
  crushed
½ teaspoon ground black pepper
10 clams, in their shells
1 pound fresh cod fillet, cut into
  1-inch cubes
1 pound fresh medium shrimp, peeled
  and deveined
½ cup fresh cooked or shredded
  canned crabmeat

1. Heat ¼ cup broth in a large saucepan. Add onion, leeks, and garlic, and
   sauté until onion begins to soften, about 3 minutes. Add tomatoes and
   bell pepper, and cook, stirring, for 2 more minutes.
2. Add remaining broth, bay leaf, tomato juice, wine, basil, parsley, thyme,
   and saffron. Bring to a boil, reduce heat, and simmer for 30 minutes. Stir
   in black pepper.
3. Add clams and simmer for 8 minutes. Add cod, shrimp, and crabmeat, and
   simmer until clams are open, fish flakes easily, and shrimp have turned
   pink, about 5 more minutes. Discard any unopened clams. Remove bay
   leaf.
4. Transfer to individual bowls and serve.

Calories Per Serving: 213
Fat: 2 g
Cholesterol: 134 mg
Protein: 31 g

Carbohydrates: 15 g
Dietary Fiber: 3 g
Sodium: 367 mg

❊ *Cioppino* ❊

PREPARATION TIME: *25 minutes* • COOKING TIME: *1 hour 5 minutes* •
YIELD: *8 servings*

3¼ cups low-sodium nonfat chicken
　broth
3 cups chopped onion
3 cloves garlic, minced
1 medium green bell pepper, cored
　and chopped
1 medium red bell pepper, cored and
　chopped
2 medium stalks celery, sliced
3 tablespoons lemon juice
6 cups low-sodium canned tomatoes,
　drained and crushed
¾ cup low-sodium tomato paste

3 cups bottled clam juice
1½ teaspoons dried basil
¼ cup chopped fresh parsley
1½ teaspoons dried oregano
½ teaspoon dried thyme
½ teaspoon cayenne pepper
1¼ pounds fresh haddock fillet, cut
　into 1-inch cubes
2 cups canned clams, liquid reserved
¾ pound fresh medium shrimp, peeled
　and deveined
½ pound fresh scallops
½ teaspoon ground black pepper

1. Heat ¼ cup broth in a large saucepan. Add onion, garlic, bell peppers, and celery, and sauté until onion begins to soften, about 4 minutes.
2. Stir in remaining broth, lemon juice, tomatoes, tomato paste, clam juice, basil, parsley, oregano, thyme, and cayenne pepper. Bring to a boil, reduce heat, and simmer for 45 minutes.
3. Add haddock and simmer for 5 minutes. Add clams with liquid, shrimp, and scallops, and continue to simmer until fish flakes easily, shrimp have turned pink, and scallops are opaque, about 5 minutes. Stir in black pepper.
4. Transfer to individual bowls and serve.

Calories Per Serving: 200
Fat: 1 g
Cholesterol: 28 mg
Protein: 17 g

Carbohydrates: 25 g
Dietary Fiber: 4 g
Sodium: 465 mg

CHICKEN SOUPS

Butternut Squash–Spinach–Chicken Soup • Chicken-Asparagus
Soup • Chicken–Bell Pepper Soup • Chicken-Corn Soup •
Chicken-Succotash Soup • Curried Chicken-Vegetable Soup •
Chicken, Lima Bean, and Sweet Potato Soup

❀ Butternut Squash–Spinach–Chicken Soup ❀

PREPARATION TIME: *20 minutes* • COOKING TIME: *37 minutes* •
YIELD: *6 servings*

6¼ cups low-sodium vegetable broth
4 skinless boneless chicken breast tenderloins, about 4 ounces each, chopped
2 medium onions, chopped
⅛ teaspoon ground nutmeg

¼ teaspoon ground cumin
1 jalapeño pepper, seeded and minced
1½ cups diced butternut squash
4 cups chopped fresh spinach
1 cup cooked or low-sodium canned chickpeas, rinsed and drained

1. Heat ¼ cup broth in a large pot. Add chicken, onions, nutmeg, and cumin, and sauté until onions begin to soften, about 4 minutes. Stir in jalapeño pepper.
2. Add remaining broth and squash. Bring to a boil, reduce heat, and simmer until chicken is cooked through, about 20 minutes.
3. Stir in the spinach and chickpeas, and simmer for 5 more minutes.

Calories Per Serving: 195
Fat: 1 g
Cholesterol: 47 mg
Protein: 23 g

Carbohydrates: 25 g
Dietary Fiber: 5 g
Sodium: 47 mg

❀ Chicken-Asparagus Soup ❀

PREPARATION TIME: *20 minutes* • COOKING TIME: *38 minutes* •
YIELD: *6 servings*

6¼ cups low-sodium nonfat chicken broth
6 skinless boneless chicken breast tenderloins, about 4 ounces each, chopped
3 tablespoons all-purpose flour
½ cup dry white wine

6 scallions, sliced
3 medium carrots, scraped and sliced
4 cups chopped fresh asparagus spears (2-inch lengths)
1 cup skim milk
½ teaspoon ground black pepper
¼ cup chopped fresh parsley

1. Heat ¼ cup broth in a large saucepan. Add chicken and sauté until no longer pink, about 8 minutes. Remove and set aside.

2. Add 2 tablespoons broth and the flour to the saucepan. Stir for 2 minutes. Add wine and stir until mixture thickens, about 3 minutes.
3. Stir in remaining broth, scallions, and carrots. Return chicken to the saucepan. Bring to a boil, reduce heat, and simmer for 8 minutes. Add asparagus and simmer for 5 more minutes. Stir in milk and black pepper, and heat through, about 4 minutes.
4. Serve topped with parsley.

Calories Per Serving: 219
Fat: 2 g
Cholesterol: 71 mg
Protein: 31 g

Carbohydrates: 11 g
Dietary Fiber: 2 g
Sodium: 394 mg

❊ *Chicken—Bell Pepper Soup* ❊

PREPARATION TIME: *15 minutes* • COOKING TIME: *44 minutes* •
YIELD: *8 servings*

7 cups low-sodium vegetable broth
4 skinless boneless chicken breast tenderloins, about 4 ounces each, cut into ½-inch cubes
1 medium onion, chopped
3 cloves garlic, minced
1 bay leaf
1 tablespoon paprika

3 tablespoons red wine vinegar
2 medium red bell peppers, cored and chopped
2 medium green bell peppers, cored and chopped
8 small new potatoes, halved
¼ teaspoon ground black pepper

1. Heat ¼ cup broth in a large pot. Add chicken, onion, and garlic, and sauté until onion begins to soften, about 3 minutes. Stir in bay leaf, paprika, and vinegar, and simmer for 2 minutes.
2. Add remaining broth and bring to a boil. Reduce heat, cover, and simmer for 15 minutes. Add bell peppers and potatoes, cover, and simmer for 12 more minutes. Stir in black pepper. Remove bay leaf before serving.

Calories Per Serving: 169
Fat: 1 g
Cholesterol: 35 mg
Protein: 16 g

Carbohydrates: 25 g
Dietary Fiber: 2 g
Sodium: 60 mg

❋ *Chicken-Corn Soup* ❋

PREPARATION TIME: *15 minutes* ▪ COOKING TIME: *44 minutes* ▪
YIELD: *6 servings*

3 skinless boneless chicken breast tenderloins, about 4 ounces each,
   chopped
8 cups low-sodium nonfat chicken
   broth
1 medium stalk celery, sliced
1 medium onion, chopped

12 ounces uncooked egg-free noodles
4 cups fresh or thawed frozen corn
   kernels
½ teaspoon ground black pepper
¼ teaspoon dried saffron threads
¼ cup chopped fresh parsley
4 hard-boiled egg whites, chopped

1. Place chicken, broth, celery, and onion in a large saucepan. Bring to a
   boil, reduce heat, and simmer until chicken is cooked through, about 20
   minutes. Remove and set aside.
2. Return broth to a boil, add noodles, and simmer until tender, about 10
   minutes. Return chicken to the saucepan. Add corn, black pepper, saffron,
   and parsley, and simmer until corn is tender, about 5 minutes.
3. Transfer to individual bowls, garnish with chopped egg whites, and serve.

Calories Per Serving: 454
Fat: 2 g
Cholesterol: 35 mg
Protein: 28 g

Carbohydrates: 77 g
Dietary Fiber: 3 g
Sodium: 464 mg

❋ *Chicken-Succotash Soup* ❋

PREPARATION TIME: *20 minutes* ▪ COOKING TIME: *46 minutes* ▪
YIELD: *6 servings*

6¼ cups low-sodium nonfat chicken
   broth
4 skinless boneless chicken breast tenderloins, about 4 ounces each, cut
   into thin strips
1 medium onion, chopped
1 cup fresh or thawed frozen green
   peas

1 cup thawed frozen lima beans
2 cups fresh or thawed frozen corn
   kernels
3 cups diced potatoes
½ teaspoon dried thyme
½ teaspoon ground white pepper
1 cup skim milk
¼ cup chopped fresh parsley

1. Heat ¼ cup broth in a large saucepan. Add chicken and sauté until no longer pink, about 8 minutes. Remove and set aside.
2. Add onion and sauté until it begins to soften, about 3 minutes. Add additional broth if necessary. Stir in remaining broth, peas, lima beans, corn, and potatoes. Bring to a boil, reduce heat, add thyme and white pepper, and simmer for 20 minutes.
3. Return chicken to the saucepan. Add milk and simmer until heated through, about 7 minutes.
4. Serve garnished with parsley.

Calories Per Serving: 333	Carbohydrates: 51 g
Fat: 1 g	Dietary Fiber: 6 g
Cholesterol: 47 mg	Sodium: 369 mg
Protein: 27 g	

❋ Curried Chicken-Vegetable Soup ❋

PREPARATION TIME: *25 minutes plus 5 minutes standing time* •
COOKING TIME: *29 minutes* • YIELD: *8 servings*

8½ cups low-sodium nonfat chicken
    broth
4 skinless boneless chicken breast ten-
    derloins, about 4 ounces each, cut
    into thin strips
2 medium onions, chopped
3 cloves garlic, minced
1 medium green bell pepper, cored
    and diced
2 teaspoons curry powder
1 teaspoon ground cumin

½ teaspoon ground turmeric
2 medium tomatoes, chopped
2 medium carrots, scraped and sliced
2 cups chopped acorn squash
1 medium turnip, diced
2 cups sliced zucchini
½ teaspoon ground cinnamon
2¼ cups boiling water
1½ cups uncooked couscous
¼ cup chopped fresh parsley

1. Heat ¼ cup broth in a large saucepan. Add chicken and sauté until no longer pink, about 8 minutes. Remove and set aside.
2. Heat another 2 tablespoons broth in the saucepan. Add onions, garlic, and bell pepper, and sauté until onions begin to soften, about 4 minutes. Stir in curry powder, cumin, and turmeric, and sauté for 1 more minute.
3. Return chicken to the saucepan. Add remaining broth, tomatoes, carrots, squash, turnip, zucchini, and cinnamon, and bring to a boil. Reduce heat and simmer until chicken is cooked through and vegetables are just tender, about 15 minutes.

4. In a separate bowl, pour boiling water over couscous, cover, and allow to stand for 5 minutes.
5. Stir couscous into soup. Serve topped with parsley.

Calories Per Serving: 286
Fat: 1 g
Cholesterol: 35 mg
Protein: 20 g

Carbohydrates: 44 g
Dietary Fiber: 9 g
Sodium: 415 mg

❀ *Chicken, Lima Bean, and* ❀ *Sweet Potato Soup*

PREPARATION TIME: *15 minutes* • COOKING TIME: *42 minutes* •
YIELD: *4 servings*

4¼ cups low-sodium nonfat chicken broth
3 skinless boneless chicken breast tenderloins, about 4 ounces each, chopped
1 medium onion, chopped
3 medium stalks celery, sliced
1 medium green bell pepper, cored and chopped

2 cloves garlic, minced
2 cups water
2 sweet potatoes, diced
1½ cups thawed frozen lima beans
½ teaspoon ground black pepper
2 scallions, minced

1. Heat ¼ cup broth in a large saucepan. Add chicken and sauté until no longer pink, about 8 minutes. Add onion, celery, bell pepper, and garlic, and sauté for 2 more minutes.
2. Stir in remaining broth, water, and sweet potatoes. Bring to a boil, reduce heat, and simmer for 20 minutes. Add lima beans and simmer for 5 more minutes. Stir in black pepper.
3. Serve topped with scallions.

Calories Per Serving: 244
Fat: 1 g
Cholesterol: 53 mg
Protein: 26 g

Carbohydrates: 31 g
Dietary Fiber: 6 g
Sodium: 267 mg

BEAN SOUPS

Curried Tomato-Lentil Soup • Lentil-Leek Soup • Chickpea
Puree • Rotelle-Vegetable Soup • Split Pea Soup with Barley •
Black-eyed Pea Soup • Northern Bean and Black-eyed Pea Soup •
Lazy Day Yellow Pea and White Bean Soup • White Bean and
Spinach Soup • Quick Northern Bean Soup with Cabbage •
White Bean, Corn, and Acorn Squash Soup • White Bean Soup
with Turnips • Squash and Navy Bean Pistou • Great Northern
Bean Minestrone • Kidney Bean and Potato Soup • Pinto Bean
and Corn Chowder • Pinto Bean and Vegetable Soup • Pureed
Black Bean Soup with Rice • Black Bean Soup with Shrimp •
Black Bean and Bell Pepper Soup • Sherried Black Bean Soup •
Pinto Bean Soup

✳ Curried Tomato-Lentil Soup ✳

PREPARATION TIME: *20 minutes* • COOKING TIME: *56 minutes* •
YIELD: *7 servings*

5¼ tablespoons low-sodium nonfat
   chicken broth
2 cups chopped onion
2 cloves garlic, minced
2 cups water
1 medium stalk celery, sliced
1 medium carrot, scraped and thinly
   sliced

1 cup dried lentils, rinsed and drained
2 teaspoons curry powder
½ teaspoon chili powder
¼ teaspoon ground black pepper
1½ cups fresh or thawed frozen
   chopped spinach
2 cups low-sodium canned tomatoes,
   chopped, juice reserved

1. Heat ¼ cup broth in a large pot. Add onion and garlic, and sauté until onion begins to soften, about 3 minutes.
2. Add remaining broth, water, celery, carrot, lentils, curry powder, chili powder, and black pepper. Bring to a boil, reduce heat, cover, and simmer until lentils are just tender, about 35 minutes.
3. Add spinach and tomatoes with juice. Simmer for 10 more minutes.

Calories Per Serving: 77
Fat: 0 g
Cholesterol: 0 mg
Protein: 8 g

Carbohydrates: 12 g
Dietary Fiber: 3 g
Sodium: 161 mg

✳ Lentil-Leek Soup ✳

PREPARATION TIME: *20 minutes* • COOKING TIME: *48 minutes* •
YIELD: *6 servings*

¼ cup low-sodium nonfat chicken
   broth
1 medium onion, chopped
2 medium leeks (white parts only),
   chopped
1 clove garlic, minced
3 medium stalks celery, diced
1 medium carrot, scraped and diced

¼ teaspoon dried thyme
¼ teaspoon ground cumin
6 cups water
¼ teaspoon ground black pepper
1 cup dried lentils, rinsed and drained
2 medium tomatoes, chopped
2 tablespoons chopped scallion

1. Heat broth in a large saucepan. Add onion, leeks, garlic, celery, and carrot, and sauté until onion begins to soften, about 5 minutes. Stir in the thyme and cumin, and sauté for 1 more minute.
2. Add water, black pepper, and lentils. Bring to a boil, reduce heat, cover, and simmer until lentils are tender, about 35 minutes.
3. Transfer to individual bowls, top with tomatoes and scallion, and serve.

Calories Per Serving: 226 Carbohydrates: 46 g
Fat: 2 g Dietary Fiber: 4 g
Cholesterol: 0 mg Sodium: 80 mg
Protein: 10 g

❈ *Chickpea Puree* ❈

PREPARATION TIME: *20 minutes* • COOKING TIME: *19 minutes* •
YIELD: *4 servings*

3 tablespoons low-sodium nonfat chicken broth
4 cloves garlic, minced
3 cups cooked or low-sodium canned chickpeas, liquid reserved
3 tablespoons lemon juice

1 teaspoon dried oregano
¼ teaspoon cayenne pepper
1 cup water
3 tablespoons mango chutney
1 tablespoon toasted sesame seeds

1. Heat broth in a large saucepan. Add garlic and sauté for 2 minutes. Add chickpeas with liquid, lemon juice, oregano, and cayenne pepper. Simmer for 10 minutes.
2. Puree mixture in a blender or food processor, and return to the saucepan. Stir in water and simmer to heat through, about 5 minutes. (Add more water if thinner consistency is desired.)
3. Serve in soup bowls topped with chutney and sesame seeds.

Calories Per Serving: 218 Carbohydrates: 42 g
Fat: 2 g Dietary Fiber: 8 g
Cholesterol: 0 mg Sodium: 584 mg
Protein: 10 g

❊ *Rotelle-Vegetable Soup* ❊

PREPARATION TIME: *15 minutes* • COOKING TIME: *20 minutes* •
YIELD: *8 servings*

3 tablespoons low-sodium nonfat
   chicken broth
3 cloves garlic, minced
1 medium green bell pepper, cored
   and diced
1 medium zucchini, diced
1 medium carrot, scraped and diced
2 cups cooked or low-sodium canned
   chickpeas, liquid reserved

2 cups low-sodium canned tomatoes,
   drained and chopped
1 cup low-sodium canned tomato
   sauce
1 teaspoon dried thyme
4 cups low-sodium vegetable broth
3 cups water
1 cup uncooked rotelle
¼ teaspoon ground black pepper
2 tablespoons grated nonfat Parmesan

1. Heat chicken broth in a large pot. Add garlic, bell pepper, zucchini, and carrot, and sauté for 4 minutes.
2. Add chickpeas with liquid, tomatoes, tomato sauce, thyme, vegetable broth, and water. Bring to a boil, add rotelle, and simmer until pasta is just tender, about 8 minutes. Stir in black pepper.
3. Serve topped with Parmesan.

Calories Per Serving: 152
Fat: 1 g
Cholesterol: 1 mg
Protein: 10 g

Carbohydrates: 28 g
Dietary Fiber: 5 g
Sodium: 199 mg

❊ *Split Pea Soup with Barley* ❊

PREPARATION TIME: *20 minutes* • COOKING TIME: *46 minutes* •
YIELD: *8 servings*

¼ cup low-sodium nonfat chicken
   broth
1 medium onion, chopped
2 medium carrots, scraped and
   chopped
1½ cups dried split peas, rinsed and
   drained
½ cup pearl barley

8 cups water
2 tablespoons grated lemon peel
1 tablespoon reduced-sodium soy
   sauce
2 teaspoons dried thyme
½ teaspoon ground black pepper
3 tablespoons lemon juice

1. Heat broth in a large saucepan. Add onion and carrots, and sauté until onion begins to soften, about 3 minutes.
2. Add split peas, barley, water, lemon peel, soy sauce, thyme, and black pepper. Bring to a boil, reduce heat, and simmer until peas and barley are tender, about 35 minutes. Stir in lemon juice.

Calories Per Serving: 190   Carbohydrates: 37 g
Fat: 1 g   Dietary Fiber: 4 g
Cholesterol: 0 mg   Sodium: 194 mg
Protein: 11 g

❋ *Black-eyed Pea Soup* ❋

PREPARATION TIME: *15 minutes* • COOKING TIME: *26 minutes* •
YIELD: *4 servings*

3 tablespoons low-sodium nonfat chicken broth
1 medium onion, chopped
4 cloves garlic, minced
6 cups water
2 cups low-sodium canned black-eyed peas, rinsed and drained

1 medium red bell pepper, cored and chopped
2 teaspoons dried basil
1 teaspoon dried thyme
½ teaspoon ground black pepper
¼ teaspoon cayenne pepper

1. Heat broth in a large saucepan. Add onion and garlic, and sauté until onion begins to soften, about 3 minutes.
2. Add remaining ingredients and bring to a boil. Reduce heat and simmer for 15 minutes.

Calories Per Serving: 260   Carbohydrates: 49 g
Fat: 1 g   Dietary Fiber: 14 g
Cholesterol: 0 mg   Sodium: 52 mg
Protein: 16 g

❋ *Northern Bean and Black-eyed Pea Soup* ❋

PREPARATION TIME: *20 minutes* • COOKING TIME: *1 hour 7 minutes* •
YIELD: *7 servings*

7¼ cups low-sodium vegetable broth
1 medium onion, chopped
2 cloves garlic, minced
¼ cup pearl barley
¼ cup dried lentils, rinsed and drained
2 cups low-sodium canned tomatoes,
    drained and chopped
1 medium carrot, scraped and sliced
1 medium stalk celery, with leaves,
    sliced
1 tablespoon brown sugar
2 bay leaves

½ teaspoon chili powder
½ teaspoon dry mustard
¼ teaspoon dried thyme
⅛ teaspoon ground cloves
¼ teaspoon ground black pepper
1 cup low-sodium canned Great
    Northern beans, rinsed and
    drained
2 cups low-sodium canned black-eyed
    peas, rinsed and drained
Lemon slices

1. Heat ¼ cup broth in a large saucepan. Add onion and garlic, and sauté
   until onion begins to soften, about 3 minutes.
2. Add remaining broth, barley, lentils, tomatoes, carrot, celery, brown sugar,
   bay leaves, chili powder, dry mustard, thyme, cloves, and black pepper.
   Bring to a boil, reduce heat, cover, and simmer, stirring occasionally, for
   45 minutes.
3. Add Great Northern beans and black-eyed peas, and simmer until all ingredients are heated through, about 10 minutes. Remove bay leaves.
4. Transfer to individual bowls, garnish with lemon slices, and serve.

Calories Per Serving: 162
Fat: 1 g
Cholesterol: 0 mg
Protein: 5 g

Carbohydrates: 36 g
Dietary Fiber: 6 g
Sodium: 98 mg

❋ Lazy Day Yellow Pea and White Bean Soup ❋

PREPARATION TIME: 20 minutes ▪ COOKING TIME: 3 hours 14 minutes ▪
YIELD: 8 servings

6¼ cups low-sodium vegetable broth
1½ cups chopped onion
4 cloves garlic, minced
2 medium stalks celery, sliced
2 cups low-sodium canned tomatoes,
    chopped, juice reserved
2 cups dried navy beans, rinsed and
    drained

1½ cups dried yellow split peas, rinsed
    and drained
1 medium red bell pepper, cored and
    chopped
½ cup minced fresh parsley
1 teaspoon dried tarragon
1 teaspoon dried oregano
½ teaspoon ground black pepper

1. Heat ¼ cup broth in a large saucepan. Add onion, garlic, and celery, and sauté until onion begins to soften, about 4 minutes.
2. Add all remaining ingredients and boil for 2 minutes. Reduce heat, cover, and simmer, stirring occasionally, until beans and peas are tender, about 3 hours. Thin soup with additional broth if necessary.

Calories Per Serving: 361
Fat: 1 g
Cholesterol: 0 mg
Protein: 23 g

Carbohydrates: 67 g
Dietary Fiber: 6 g
Sodium: 61 mg

❈ *White Bean and Spinach Soup* ❈

PREPARATION TIME: *15 minutes* • COOKING TIME: *18 minutes* •
YIELD: *6 servings*

2 cups low-sodium nonfat chicken broth
1 medium onion, chopped
4 cloves garlic, minced
2 medium stalks celery, sliced
3 medium carrots, scraped and sliced
3½ cups low-sodium canned tomatoes, chopped, juice reserved
½ cup uncooked small pasta shells

2 tablespoons chopped fresh parsley
2 teaspoons dried basil
2 cups low-sodium canned Great Northern beans, rinsed and drained
6 cups chopped fresh spinach
½ teaspoon ground black pepper
2 tablespoons grated nonfat Parmesan

1. Heat ¼ cup broth in a large saucepan. Add onion, garlic, celery, and carrots, and sauté until onion begins to soften, about 5 minutes.
2. Stir in remaining broth, tomatoes with juice, pasta shells, parsley, basil, beans, spinach, and black pepper. Bring to a boil, reduce heat, cover, and simmer until pasta is just tender, about 8 minutes.
3. Transfer to individual bowls, sprinkle with Parmesan, and serve.

Calories Per Serving: 187
Fat: 1 g
Cholesterol: 0 mg
Protein: 10 g

Carbohydrates: 36 g
Dietary Fiber: 10 g
Sodium: 208 mg

❋ Quick Northern Bean Soup with Cabbage ❋

PREPARATION TIME: *20 minutes* • COOKING TIME: *14 minutes* •
YIELD: *6 servings*

¼ cup low-sodium nonfat chicken
   broth
1 cup shredded cabbage
1 medium green bell pepper, cored
   and chopped
3 cloves garlic, minced
1½ teaspoons dried basil
1 teaspoon dried thyme

½ teaspoon ground black pepper
4 cups water
2 cups low-sodium canned Great
   Northern beans, rinsed and
   drained
¼ cup low-sodium tomato paste
6 ripe olives

1. Heat broth in a large saucepan. Add cabbage, bell pepper, garlic, basil, thyme, and black pepper. Sauté until cabbage begins to soften, about 6 minutes.
2. Add water, beans, and tomato paste, and simmer until all ingredients are heated through, about 6 minutes.
3. Transfer soup to individual bowls, top each serving with an olive, and serve at once.

Calories Per Serving: 101
Fat: 1 g
Cholesterol: 0 mg
Protein: 6 g

Carbohydrates: 19 g
Dietary Fiber: 5 g
Sodium: 78 mg

❋ White Bean, Corn, and Acorn Squash Soup ❋

PREPARATION TIME: *15 minutes* • COOKING TIME: *38 minutes* •
YIELD: *4 servings*

2¼ cups low-sodium nonfat chicken
   broth
1 medium onion, chopped
2 cloves garlic, minced
2 cups cubed acorn squash
3 medium tomatoes, chopped
1 teaspoon dried oregano

1 teaspoon dried thyme
1 teaspoon dried basil
2 cups low-sodium canned Great
   Northern beans, rinsed and
   drained
2 cups fresh, drained canned, or
   thawed frozen corn kernels

1. Heat ¼ cup broth in a large saucepan. Add onion and garlic, and sauté until onion begins to soften, about 3 minutes. Add squash and sauté for 5 more minutes.
2. Stir in remaining broth, tomatoes, oregano, thyme, basil, and beans. Cover and simmer, stirring occasionally, for 15 minutes.
3. Add corn and simmer until squash is just tender, about 10 minutes.

Calories Per Serving: 283   Carbohydrates: 64 g
Fat: 1 g   Dietary Fiber: 12 g
Cholesterol: 0 mg   Sodium: 188 mg
Protein: 14 g

❋ *White Bean Soup with Turnips* ❋

PREPARATION TIME: *20 minutes* • COOKING TIME: *28 minutes* •
YIELD: *4 servings*

2 cups diced turnips   *2 tablespoons minced onion*
1 cup water   *2 tablespoons minced fresh parsley*
2 cups low-sodium canned Great   *2 cups skim milk*
* Northern beans, liquid reserved*   *¼ teaspoon ground black pepper*

1. Combine turnips and water in a large saucepan. Bring to a boil, reduce heat, cover, and simmer until turnips are just tender, about 15 minutes. Drain and discard liquid.
2. In a blender or food processor, puree turnips and 1 cup beans with bean liquid until smooth.
3. Return pureed turnips and beans to the saucepan and add remaining beans, onion, parsley, milk, and black pepper. Simmer covered until all ingredients are heated through, about 10 minutes.
4. Transfer to individual bowls and serve.

Calories Per Serving: 100   Carbohydrates: 22 g
Fat: 0 g   Dietary Fiber: 8 g
Cholesterol: 1 mg   Sodium: 79 mg
Protein: 9 g

❋ Squash and Navy Bean Pistou ❋

PREPARATION TIME: *15 minutes* • COOKING TIME: *34 minutes* •
YIELD: *8 servings*

8 cups water
5 cups sliced yellow summer squash
 (½-inch rounds)
4 cups chopped fresh or thawed frozen
 green beans (1-inch lengths)
2 cups low-sodium canned navy
 beans, rinsed and drained

1 cup uncooked small pasta shells
3 cloves garlic, minced
½ teaspoon dried basil
2 cups low-sodium canned tomatoes,
 drained, chopped
1 tablespoon olive oil

1. Bring water to a boil in a large pot. Add squash, green beans, and navy beans, and simmer for 8 minutes. Add pasta, return to a boil, and simmer for 12 more minutes.
2. Stir in garlic, basil, tomatoes, and olive oil, and simmer for 5 minutes.
3. Transfer to individual bowls and serve at once.

Calories Per Serving: 163
Fat: 2 g
Cholesterol: 0 mg
Protein: 8 g

Carbohydrates: 30 g
Dietary Fiber: 5 g
Sodium: 26 mg

❋ Great Northern Bean Minestrone ❋

PREPARATION TIME: *20 minutes* • COOKING TIME: *1 hour 9 minutes* •
YIELD: *8 servings*

3 tablespoons low-sodium nonfat
 chicken broth
1 cup sliced onion
2 cloves garlic, minced
8 cups water
1 cup shredded cabbage
3 medium tomatoes, chopped
2 cups sliced zucchini
2 medium carrots, scraped and sliced

2 cups low-sodium canned tomatoes,
 chopped, juice reserved
2 teaspoons dried basil
1 teaspoon dried marjoram
½ teaspoon ground black pepper
1 cup low-sodium canned Great
 Northern beans, rinsed and
 drained
1 cup cooked elbow macaroni

1. Heat broth in a large pot. Add onion and garlic, and sauté until onion just begins to soften, about 3 minutes.

2. Add water, cabbage, fresh tomatoes, zucchini, carrots, and canned tomatoes with juice. Stir in basil and marjoram. Bring to a boil, reduce heat, and simmer for 45 minutes.
3. Add black pepper, beans, and macaroni, and simmer for 12 more minutes.
4. Transfer to individual bowls and serve at once.

Calories Per Serving: 90	Carbohydrates: 18 g
Fat: 1 g	Dietary Fiber: 4 g
Cholesterol: 0 mg	Sodium: 36 mg
Protein: 4 g	

❊ *Kidney Bean and Potato Soup* ❊

PREPARATION TIME: *20 minutes* • COOKING TIME: *31 minutes* •
YIELD: *8 servings*

4¼ cups low-sodium vegetable broth
1 medium onion, chopped
2 cloves garlic, minced
1½ cups skim milk
5 cups diced potatoes

¼ teaspoon ground black pepper
1 teaspoon chili powder
4 cups low-sodium canned kidney
    beans, rinsed and drained
⅓ cup shredded nonfat cheddar

1. Heat ¼ cup broth in a large saucepan. Add onion and garlic, and sauté until onion begins to soften, about 3 minutes.
2. Add remaining broth, milk, potatoes, and black pepper. Bring to a boil, reduce heat, cover, and simmer until potatoes are just tender, about 10 minutes.
3. Add chili powder and beans. Simmer until all ingredients are heated through, about 10 minutes.
4. Transfer to individual bowls, stir 2 teaspoons cheese into each bowl, and serve.

Calories Per Serving: 320	Carbohydrates: 65 g
Fat: 1 g	Dietary Fiber: 8 g
Cholesterol: 2 mg	Sodium: 103 mg
Protein: 15 g	

❈ *Pinto Bean and Corn Chowder* ❈

PREPARATION TIME: 20 minutes · COOKING TIME: 18 minutes ·
YIELD: 5 servings

2 tablespoons low-sodium nonfat
  chicken broth
1 medium onion, chopped
1 medium red bell pepper, cored and
  chopped
3 medium carrots, scraped and sliced
2 tablespoons all-purpose flour

3 cups skim milk
2 cups fresh or thawed frozen corn
  kernels
2 cups low-sodium canned pinto
  beans, rinsed and drained
1 tablespoon wine vinegar
½ teaspoon ground black pepper

1. Heat broth in a large saucepan. Add onion, bell pepper, and carrots, and
   sauté until onion begins to soften, about 4 minutes. Add flour and stir for
   1 more minute.
2. Add milk, corn, beans, vinegar, and black pepper. Bring to a boil, reduce
   heat, cover, and simmer until corn is tender and all ingredients are heated
   through, about 7 minutes.

Calories Per Serving: 240
Fat: 1 g
Cholesterol: 2 mg
Protein: 14 g

Carbohydrates: 47 g
Dietary Fiber: 8 g
Sodium: 103 mg

❈ *Pinto Bean and Vegetable Soup* ❈

PREPARATION TIME: 20 minutes · COOKING TIME: 30 minutes ·
YIELD: 8 servings

1¼ cups low-sodium nonfat chicken
  broth
1 medium onion, diced
1 medium red bell pepper, cored and
  diced
1 cup diced zucchini
1 medium carrot, scraped and diced
2 cloves garlic, minced
1 jalapeño pepper, seeded and minced
2 cups low-sodium canned pinto
  beans, liquid reserved

1 medium potato, diced
3½ cups low-sodium canned tomatoes, drained and chopped
2 tablespoons sugar
1 tablespoon chili powder
1 tablespoon dried oregano
1 teaspoon ground cumin
1 teaspoon hot pepper sauce
2 teaspoons dried thyme
¼ teaspoon ground black pepper
¼ cup diced red onion

1. Heat ¼ cup broth in a large pot. Add onion, bell pepper, zucchini, carrot, garlic, and jalapeño pepper. Sauté until bell pepper begins to soften, about 5 minutes.
2. Stir in remaining broth, beans with liquid, potato, tomatoes, sugar, chili powder, oregano, cumin, hot pepper sauce, thyme, and black pepper. Bring to a boil, reduce heat, and simmer until potato is just tender, about 20 minutes.
3. Transfer to individual bowls, top with diced red onion, and serve.

Calories Per Serving: 150
Fat: 1 g
Cholesterol: 0 mg
Protein: 7 g

Carbohydrates: 31 g
Dietary Fiber: 6 g
Sodium: 103 mg

❊ *Pureed Black Bean Soup with Rice* ❊

PREPARATION TIME: *20 minutes* • COOKING TIME: *14 minutes* •
YIELD: *8 servings*

3 cups low-sodium canned black beans, rinsed and drained
2 tablespoons minced lemon peel
3¼ cups low-sodium vegetable broth
1 medium onion, chopped
4 cloves garlic, minced
1 cup chopped celery
1 medium green bell pepper, cored and diced

1 cup water
2 medium tomatoes, chopped
1 teaspoon dried thyme
1½ teaspoons ground cumin
½ teaspoon ground black pepper
3 tablespoons lemon juice
2 cups cooked rice

1. In a blender or food processor, puree beans, lemon peel, and 3 cups vegetable broth.
2. Heat remaining broth in a large saucepan. Add onion, garlic, celery, and bell pepper, and sauté until onion begins to soften, about 4 minutes. Add water, tomatoes, thyme, cumin, black pepper, and lemon juice.
3. Stir in bean puree and simmer until soup is heated through, about 8 minutes.
4. Serve over rice in soup bowls.

Calories Per Serving: 193
Fat: 1 g
Cholesterol: 0 mg
Protein: 8 g

Carbohydrates: 40 g
Dietary Fiber: 7 g
Sodium: 47 mg

❋ Black Bean Soup with Shrimp ❋

PREPARATION TIME: *20 minutes* • COOKING TIME: *52 minutes* •
YIELD: *6 servings*

¼ cup low-sodium nonfat chicken
  broth
1 medium onion, chopped
2 medium carrots, scraped and grated
2 medium stalks celery, sliced
3 cloves garlic, minced
½ teaspoon dried thyme
½ teaspoon dried oregano
½ teaspoon dried basil

2 medium tomatoes, diced
4 cups low-sodium canned black
  beans, rinsed and drained
½ teaspoon ground black pepper
½ pound fresh medium shrimp,
  cooked, peeled, and deveined
¼ cup dry sherry
¼ cup chopped fresh parsley

1. Heat broth in a large saucepan. Add onion, carrots, celery, garlic, thyme, oregano, and basil, and sauté until onion begins to soften, about 4 minutes.
2. Stir in tomatoes. Bring to a boil, reduce heat, cover, and simmer for 15 minutes. Add beans and simmer for 25 more minutes.
3. Stir in black pepper, shrimp, and sherry, and simmer until all ingredients are heated through, about 3 minutes.
4. Serve topped with parsley.

Calories Per Serving: 231
Fat: 2 g
Cholesterol: 57 mg
Protein: 19 g

Carbohydrates: 35 g
Dietary Fiber: 10 g
Sodium: 136 mg

❋ Black Bean and Bell Pepper Soup ❋

PREPARATION TIME: *20 minutes* • COOKING TIME: *27 minutes* •
YIELD: *10 servings*

2¼ cups low-sodium nonfat chicken
  broth
1 medium onion, minced
1 medium carrot, scraped and grated
2 medium stalks celery, finely
  chopped
1 medium green bell pepper, cored
  and chopped

1 medium red bell pepper, cored and
  chopped
1 jalapeño pepper, seeded and minced
3 cups low-sodium tomato puree
2 cups low-sodium canned black
  beans, rinsed and drained
1 cup skim milk

2 cups diced potatoes
1 teaspoon ground cumin
1 teaspoon dried oregano

1 teaspoon dried basil
½ teaspoon ground black pepper
1 cup evaporated skim milk

1. Heat ¼ cup broth in a large saucepan. Add onion, carrot, and celery, and sauté until onion begins to soften, about 3 minutes.
2. Add remaining broth, bell peppers, jalapeño pepper, tomato puree, beans, skim milk, potatoes, cumin, oregano, and basil. Bring to a boil, reduce heat, and simmer until potatoes are just tender, about 15 minutes.
3. Stir in black pepper and evaporated milk, and simmer for 3 more minutes.
4. Transfer to individual bowls and serve.

Calories Per Serving: 165
Fat: 1 g
Cholesterol: 1 mg
Protein: 8 g

Carbohydrates: 33 g
Dietary Fiber: 5 g
Sodium: 169 mg

❋ *Sherried Black Bean Soup* ❋

PREPARATION TIME: *25 minutes* ▪ COOKING TIME: *34 minutes* ▪
YIELD: *6 servings*

4 cups low-sodium canned black
  beans, rinsed and drained
2 cups water
1 medium onion, chopped
4 scallions, sliced
4 medium tomatoes, chopped
2 medium green bell peppers, cored
  and chopped

2 cloves garlic, minced
2 bay leaves
½ teaspoon ground black pepper
¼ teaspoon dried basil
1 tablespoon dry sherry
¼ cup minced onion

1. In a large saucepan, combine beans, water, onion, scallions, tomatoes, bell peppers, garlic, bay leaves, black pepper, and basil. Bring to a boil, reduce heat, cover, and simmer until vegetables are just tender, about 30 minutes.
2. Stir in sherry and remove bay leaves. Transfer to individual bowls, garnish with minced onion, and serve.

Calories Per Serving: 202
Fat: 1 g
Cholesterol: 0 mg
Protein: 12 g

Carbohydrates: 39 g
Dietary Fiber: 11 g
Sodium: 17 mg

❊ *Pinto Bean Soup* ❊

PREPARATION TIME: *20 minutes* ▪ COOKING TIME: *35 minutes* ▪
YIELD: *6 servings*

¼ cup low-sodium nonfat chicken
  broth
½ cup chopped onion
1 medium stalk celery, chopped
1 medium carrot, scraped and
  chopped
1 medium green bell pepper, cored
  and chopped
1 clove garlic, minced

2 cups low-sodium canned pinto
  beans, rinsed and drained
2 cups water
2 cups low-sodium canned tomatoes,
  chopped, juice reserved
½ teaspoon dried basil
½ teaspoon dried oregano
1 bay leaf
¼ teaspoon ground black pepper
2 tablespoons grated nonfat Parmesan

1. Heat broth in a large saucepan. Add onion, celery, carrot, bell pepper, and
   garlic, and sauté until onion begins to soften, about 4 minutes.
2. Add beans, water, tomatoes with juice, basil, oregano, bay leaf, and black
   pepper. Bring to a boil, reduce heat, and simmer until vegetables are just
   tender, about 25 minutes. Remove bay leaf.
3. Serve in bowls topped with Parmesan.

Calories Per Serving: 106
Fat: 1 g
Cholesterol: 2 mg
Protein: 7 g

Carbohydrates: 20 g
Dietary Fiber: 5 g
Sodium: 31 mg

VEGETABLE SOUPS

Asparagus, Leek, and Mushroom Soup • Hot Borscht • Broccoli
and Chinese Cabbage Soup • Broccoflower Soup • Broccoli
Soup • Brussels Sprout Soup • Cabbage-Mushroom Soup •
Cabbage-Potato Soup • Spicy Cabbage-Apple Soup • Cabbage,
Carrot, and Turnip Soup • Ginger-Dill-Carrot Soup • Carrot-
Potato Soup • Cream of Carrot Soup • Spicy Carrot Soup •
Carrot-Garlic Soup • Cream of Cauliflower Soup • Cauliflower-
Spinach Soup • Celery-Potato Soup • Collard Greens Soup •
Corn and Green Pepper Chowder • Gingered Corn Soup • Corn
and Shiitake Mushroom Soup • Corn and Potato Soup • Corn
and Red Pepper Soup • Jalapeño-Corn Chowder • Corn and
Cabbage Soup • Corn and Zucchini Soup • Cranberry Borscht •
Eggplant Soup • Green Bean Soup • Gingered Green Bean
and Zucchini Chowder • Spicy Green Bean–Yellow Squash–
Tomato Soup • Easy Green Bean and Red Pepper Soup with
Leftover Pasta • Kale Soup • Mushroom Soup • Mushroom,
Corn, and Potato Chowder • Mushroom and Quinoa Soup •
Onion Soup with Red Wine • Parsnip Soup • Split Pea Soup •
Green Pea Soup • Green Pea and Zucchini Soup • Santa Fe
Potato-Corn Chowder • Two-Potato Soup with Pumpkin and Okra

• Potato-Onion Soup • Jalapeño-Potato Soup with Green Chiles • Southwestern Pumpkin Soup • Potato-Carrot Soup • Pumpkin-Apple Soup • Pumpkin Soup • Potato-Vegetable Chowder • Simple Potato Puree • Summer Squash Soup • Butternut Squash Soup • Acorn Squash Soup • Tomato-Rice Soup • Tomato-Onion-Potato Soup • Cream of Tomato-Corn Soup • Cream of Tomato Soup with Rice • Tomato-Hominy Soup • Turnip and Shiitake Mushroom Soup • Sherried Pear and Turnip Soup • Zucchini Soup • Gingered Zucchini-Tomato Soup • Zucchini, Potato, and Snow Pea Soup • Yellow Squash Soup • Yuca Soup • Cream of Tomato and Yellow Squash Soup • Spring Watercress Soup • Garden Vegetable Soup • Hearty Vegetable Soup • Rotini-Vegetable Soup • Creamy Vegetable Soup • Quick Vegetable Soup

❀ *Asparagus, Leek, and Mushroom Soup* ❀

PREPARATION TIME: *20 minutes* • COOKING TIME: *51 minutes* •
YIELD: *10 servings*

8½ cups low-sodium nonfat chicken
   broth
4 medium leeks (white parts only),
   sliced
5 cups chopped fresh asparagus spears
   (½-inch lengths)
1 medium red bell pepper, cored and
   chopped
1 medium green bell pepper, cored
   and chopped

1 cup shredded potato
½ cup dry white wine
1 teaspoon dried basil
1 teaspoon ground black pepper
3 cups sliced mushrooms
1 medium carrot, scraped and
   shredded
1½ cups uncooked small pasta shells

1. Heat ¼ cup broth in a large saucepan. Add leeks and sauté until leeks begin to soften, about 3 minutes.
2. Add 8 cups broth, 3 cups asparagus, the bell peppers, potato, wine, basil, and black pepper. Bring to a boil, reduce heat, and simmer for 20 minutes. Transfer to a blender or food processor and puree.
3. Heat remaining broth in the saucepan. Add mushrooms and sauté for 2 minutes. Return puree to the saucepan. Add remaining asparagus, carrot, and pasta shells, and simmer until pasta and asparagus are done, about 15 minutes.
4. Transfer to individual bowls and serve.

Calories Per Serving: 154
Fat: 1 g
Cholesterol: 0 mg
Protein: 5 g

Carbohydrates: 28 g
Dietary Fiber: 2 g
Sodium: 257 mg

❀ *Hot Borscht* ❀

PREPARATION TIME: *20 minutes* • COOKING TIME: *57 minutes* •
YIELD: *8 servings*

2¼ cups low-sodium vegetable broth
2 cups finely chopped onion
1 clove garlic, minced
2 medium stalks celery, thinly sliced
4 cups water
2 medium carrots, scraped and grated
1 medium turnip, grated

2½ cups grated beets
2 cups shredded cabbage
1½ cups grated potatoes
2 tablespoons cider vinegar
3 bay leaves
½ teaspoon dried thyme
½ teaspoon ground black pepper

1. Heat ¼ cup broth in a large pot. Add onion, garlic, and celery, and sauté until onion begins to soften, about 4 minutes.
2. Add water, remaining broth, carrots, turnip, beets, cabbage, potatoes, vinegar, bay leaves, thyme, and black pepper. Bring to a boil, reduce heat, cover, and simmer until soup thickens, about 40 minutes.
3. Remove bay leaves. Puree soup in a blender or food processor. Return puree to the pot and heat to serving temperature, about 5 minutes. Serve at once.

Calories Per Serving: 114
Fat: 1 g
Cholesterol: 0 mg
Protein: 4 g

Carbohydrates: 25 g
Dietary Fiber: 4 g
Sodium: 174 mg

❊ Broccoli and Chinese Cabbage Soup ❊

PREPARATION TIME: 15 minutes • COOKING TIME: 13 minutes •
YIELD: 6 servings

6 cups low-sodium vegetable broth
2 tablespoons grated fresh gingerroot
1 jalapeño pepper, seeded and
  chopped
4 cups chopped broccoli
4 cups shredded Chinese cabbage

1 cup sliced mushrooms
3 tablespoons minced fresh parsley
2 scallions, sliced
2 tablespoons reduced-sodium soy
  sauce
1 medium lemon, cut into wedges

1. Heat broth in a large pot. Add gingerroot and jalapeño pepper, and bring to a boil. Add broccoli, cabbage, and mushrooms, and return to a boil. Reduce heat, cover, and simmer until broccoli is just tender, about 5 minutes.
2. Stir in parsley, scallions, soy sauce, and lemon wedges, and simmer for 1 more minute. Remove lemon wedges before serving.

Calories Per Serving: 72
Fat: 0 g
Cholesterol: 0 mg
Protein: 3 g

Carbohydrates: 16 g
Dietary Fiber: 3 g
Sodium: 293 mg

❋ *Broccoflower Soup* ❋

PREPARATION TIME: *20 minutes* • COOKING TIME: *25 minutes* •
YIELD: *4 servings*

¼ cup low-sodium nonfat chicken
  broth
1 medium onion, chopped
1 medium leek (white part only),
  chopped
3 cloves garlic, minced
1 teaspoon grated fresh gingerroot
1 teaspoon seeded and minced
  jalapeño pepper

¼ teaspoon ground nutmeg
8 cups chopped broccoflower (or 4
  cups chopped broccoli and 4 cups
  chopped cauliflower)
6 cups water
¼ cup chopped scallion

1. Heat broth in a large saucepan. Add onion, leek, garlic, gingerroot, and jalapeño pepper, and sauté until onion begins to soften, about 3 minutes. Add nutmeg and broccoflower and sauté for 2 more minutes.
2. Add water, bring to a boil, reduce heat, and simmer until broccoflower is just tender, about 10 minutes.
3. Puree soup in a blender or food processor.
4. Return soup to the saucepan and simmer to heat through, about 4 minutes.
5. Serve topped with scallion.

Calories Per Serving: 55
Fat: 1 g
Cholesterol: 0 mg
Protein: 4 g

Carbohydrates: 11 g
Dietary Fiber: 5 g
Sodium: 102 mg

❋ *Broccoli Soup* ❋

PREPARATION TIME: *15 minutes* • COOKING TIME: *23 minutes* •
YIELD: *4 servings*

3 cups low-sodium nonfat chicken
    broth
½ cup minced onion
1 clove garlic, minced

1 medium stalk celery, diced
4 cups chopped broccoli
2 cups skim milk
¼ teaspoon ground black pepper

1. Heat ¼ cup broth in a large saucepan. Add onion, garlic, and celery, and sauté for 3 minutes.
2. Add remaining broth and broccoli. Bring to a boil, reduce heat, and simmer until broccoli is just tender, about 10 minutes.
3. Puree soup in a blender or food processor.
4. Return puree to the saucepan, stir in milk and black pepper, and simmer to heat through, about 4 minutes.

Calories Per Serving: 91
Fat: 1 g
Cholesterol: 2 mg
Protein: 12 g

Carbohydrates: 11 g
Dietary Fiber: 3 g
Sodium: 218 mg

❈ Brussels Sprout Soup ❈

PREPARATION TIME: 20 minutes ▪ COOKING TIME: 26 minutes ▪
YIELD: 5 servings

3¾ cups low-sodium nonfat chicken
    broth
6 scallions, chopped
2 medium stalks celery, chopped
3½ tablespoons all-purpose flour

¼ teaspoon ground white pepper
⅛ teaspoon dried tarragon
¼ teaspoon dried thyme
2½ cups halved brussels sprouts
⅔ cup skim milk

1. Heat ¼ cup broth in a large saucepan. Add scallions and celery, and sauté until celery begins to soften, about 4 minutes. Add flour and stir for 2 more minutes.
2. Gradually add remaining broth, stirring until smooth. Add white pepper, tarragon, thyme, and brussels sprouts. Bring to a boil, reduce heat, and simmer until brussels sprouts are just tender, about 10 minutes.
3. Puree soup in a blender or food processor.
4. Return soup to the saucepan, stir in milk, and simmer to heat through, about 4 minutes.
5. Divide soup among individual bowls and serve.

Calories Per Serving: 73
Fat: 0 g
Cholesterol: 0 mg
Protein: 8 g

Carbohydrates: 11 g
Dietary Fiber: 3 g
Sodium: 145 mg

✳ *Cabbage-Mushroom Soup* ✳

PREPARATION TIME: *20 minutes* • COOKING TIME: *57 minutes* •
YIELD: *6 servings*

7¼ cups low-sodium vegetable broth
2 medium onions, diced
2 cups sliced mushrooms
2 cloves garlic, minced
4 cups shredded cabbage

2 small potatoes, diced
½ teaspoon dried thyme
½ teaspoon cayenne pepper
¼ teaspoon ground black pepper

1. Heat ¼ cup broth in a large saucepan. Add onions, mushrooms, and garlic, and sauté until onions begin to soften, about 3 minutes.
2. Add all remaining ingredients. Bring to a boil, reduce heat, and simmer for 45 minutes.

Calories Per Serving: 95
Fat: 0 g
Cholesterol: 2 mg
Protein: 4 g

Carbohydrates: 20 g
Dietary Fiber: 3 g
Sodium: 58 mg

✳ *Cabbage-Potato Soup* ✳

PREPARATION TIME: *15 minutes* • COOKING TIME: *33 minutes* •
YIELD: *6 servings*

6¼ cups low-sodium nonfat chicken
   broth
1 medium onion, sliced
2 cups shredded cabbage
1 tablespoon brown sugar

1 tablespoon caraway seeds
4 medium potatoes, chopped
½ teaspoon ground black pepper
½ cup nonfat plain yogurt
¼ cup chopped fresh dill

1. Heat ¼ cup broth in a large saucepan. Add onion and sauté until it begins to soften, about 3 minutes.

2. Add cabbage and sauté for 5 more minutes. Stir in brown sugar and caraway seeds, and cook for 2 additional minutes.
3. Stir in remaining broth and potatoes, and bring to a boil. Reduce heat and simmer until potatoes are tender, about 15 minutes. Stir in black pepper.
4. Serve topped with yogurt and dill.

Calories Per Serving: 178
Fat: 0 g
Cholesterol: 0 mg
Protein: 4 g

Carbohydrates: 36 g
Dietary Fiber: 3 g
Sodium: 329 mg

❋ Spicy Cabbage-Apple Soup ❋

PREPARATION TIME: *20 minutes* • COOKING TIME: *53 minutes* •
YIELD: *8 servings*

¼ cup low-sodium nonfat chicken
  broth
1 medium onion, sliced
1 clove garlic, minced
3 medium tart apples, peeled, cored,
  and diced
1 tablespoon brown sugar

½ teaspoon ground allspice
¼ cup dry sherry
9 cups water
6 cups shredded cabbage
¼ teaspoon ground black pepper
3 tablespoons chopped scallion

1. Heat broth in a large saucepan. Add onion and garlic, and sauté until onion begins to soften, about 3 minutes. Add apples, brown sugar, allspice, and sherry, and sauté until apples begin to soften, about 4 minutes.
2. Add water and cabbage. Bring to a boil, reduce heat, and simmer until cabbage is tender, about 35 minutes. Stir in black pepper.
3. Serve topped with scallion.

Calories Per Serving: 105
Fat: 1 g
Cholesterol: 0 mg
Protein: 1 g

Carbohydrates: 21 g
Dietary Fiber: 3 g
Sodium: 42 mg

❋ Cabbage, Carrot, and Turnip Soup ❋

PREPARATION TIME: *20 minutes* • COOKING TIME: *1 hour 3 minutes* •
YIELD: *8 servings*

2¼ cups low-sodium nonfat chicken
   broth
2 cups minced onion
2 cloves garlic, minced
1 medium stalk celery, thinly sliced
2 medium carrots, scraped and
   shredded
1 small turnip, diced
6 cups water

2 tablespoons cider vinegar
1½ teaspoons sugar
½ teaspoon dry mustard
½ teaspoon dried marjoram
¼ teaspoon dried thyme
¼ teaspoon ground black pepper
2 cups shredded cabbage
1 cup grated potato

1. Heat ¼ cup broth in a large saucepan. Add onion, garlic, and celery, and sauté until onion begins to soften, about 3 minutes.
2. Add remaining broth, carrots, turnip, water, vinegar, sugar, dry mustard, marjoram, thyme, and black pepper. Bring to a boil, reduce heat, and simmer for 25 minutes.
3. Add cabbage and potato. Return to a boil, reduce heat, and simmer for another 25 minutes.

Calories Per Serving: 174
Fat: 0 g
Cholesterol: 0 mg
Protein: 2 g

Carbohydrates: 15 g
Dietary Fiber: 2 g
Sodium: 174 mg

✳ *Ginger-Dill-Carrot Soup* ✳

PREPARATION TIME: *20 minutes* • COOKING TIME: *36 minutes* •
YIELD: *6 servings*

6¼ cups low-sodium vegetable broth
3 medium leeks (white parts only),
   chopped
2 cloves garlic, minced
1 teaspoon minced fresh gingerroot
4 medium carrots, scraped and
   chopped

1 medium potato, quartered and
   sliced
2 teaspoons dry white wine
¼ teaspoon ground white pepper
1 tablespoon dried dill
¼ cup chopped fresh dill

1. Heat ¼ cup broth in a large saucepan. Add leeks, garlic, and gingerroot, and sauté until leeks begin to soften, about 3 minutes.
2. Add remaining broth, carrots, and potato, and bring to a boil. Reduce heat, cover, and simmer until carrots are just tender, about 20 minutes. Stir in wine, white pepper, and dried dill.
3. Puree soup in a blender or food processor.

4. Return soup to the saucepan and gently heat through, about 5 minutes. Serve topped with fresh dill.

Calories Per Serving: 135
Fat: 0 g
Cholesterol: 0 mg
Protein: 3 g

Carbohydrates: 30 g
Dietary Fiber: 4 g
Sodium: 68 mg

❋ *Carrot-Potato Soup* ❋

PREPARATION TIME: *20 minutes* • COOKING TIME: *50 minutes* •
YIELD: *5 servings*

5¼ cups low-sodium vegetable broth
1 cup chopped onion
6 medium carrots, scraped and sliced
2 cups diced potatoes

½ teaspoon ground black pepper
½ teaspoon dried sage
3 scallions, minced

1. Heat ¼ cup broth in a large saucepan. Add onion and sauté until it begins to soften, about 3 minutes. Add carrots and potatoes, and sauté for 5 more minutes.
2. Add remaining broth, black pepper, and sage. Bring to a boil, reduce heat, and simmer until carrots are just tender, about 30 minutes. Remove from heat and allow to cool.
3. Puree soup in a blender or food processor.
4. Return soup to the saucepan and heat through, about 5 minutes. Transfer to individual bowls, garnish with scallion, and serve.

Calories Per Serving: 142
Fat: 0 g
Cholesterol: 0 mg
Protein: 3 g

Carbohydrates: 33 g
Dietary Fiber: 4 g
Sodium: 70 mg

❋ *Cream of Carrot Soup* ❋

PREPARATION TIME: *20 minutes* • COOKING TIME: *34 minutes* •
YIELD: *4 servings*

4¼ cups low-sodium nonfat chicken
   broth
1 medium potato, chopped
2 medium carrots, scraped and sliced
1 medium onion, chopped
1 bay leaf
1 teaspoon dried basil

1 teaspoon sugar
½ teaspoon ground nutmeg
⅓ cup uncooked white rice
1 cup skim milk
⅛ teaspoon ground black pepper
¼ cup minced fresh parsley

1. Heat ¼ cup broth in a large saucepan. Add potato, carrots, and onion, and sauté until onion begins to soften, about 4 minutes.
2. Stir in remaining broth, bay leaf, basil, sugar, nutmeg, and rice. Bring to a boil, reduce heat, cover, and simmer until rice is just tender, about 20 minutes.
3 Stir in milk and black pepper, and heat through, about 5 minutes. Remove bay leaf.
4. Serve topped with parsley.

Calories Per Serving: 204
Fat: 1 g
Cholesterol: 1 mg
Protein: 13 g

Carbohydrates: 37 g
Dietary Fiber: 3 g
Sodium: 231 mg

❊ *Spicy Carrot Soup* ❊

PREPARATION TIME: *20 minutes* • COOKING TIME: *42 minutes* •
YIELD: *6 servings*

6¼ cups low-sodium nonfat chicken
   broth
1 medium onion, minced
1 tablespoon brown sugar
½ teaspoon ground coriander
1 tablespoon curry powder

⅛ teaspoon ground nutmeg
6 medium carrots, scraped and diced
2 medium potatoes, diced
¼ teaspoon ground black pepper
½ cup skim milk

1. Heat ¼ cup broth in a large saucepan. Add onion and sauté until it begins to soften, about 3 minutes. Stir in brown sugar, coriander, curry powder, and nutmeg, and sauté for 1 more minute.
2. Add remaining broth, carrots, and potatoes, and bring to a boil. Reduce heat and simmer until carrots are tender, about 25 minutes.
3. Puree soup in a blender or food processor and return to the saucepan. Stir in black pepper and milk, and simmer until soup is heated through, about 5 minutes.

Calories Per Serving: 106
Fat: 1 g
Cholesterol: 3 mg
Protein: 10 g

Carbohydrates: 15 g
Dietary Fiber: 3 g
Sodium: 207 mg

❊ Carrot-Garlic Soup ❊

PREPARATION TIME: 20 minutes • COOKING TIME: 30 minutes •
YIELD: 4 servings

1 medium onion, chopped
4 cups low-sodium vegetable broth
16 cloves garlic, whole, unpeeled,
    and tied in a cheesecloth bag
1 medium carrot, scraped and diced

2 medium potatoes, diced
2 teaspoons minced fresh gingerroot
1 tablespoon orange juice concentrate
1 tablespoon honey
¼ teaspoon ground black pepper

1. Combine onion, broth, garlic bag, carrot, and potatoes in a large saucepan. Bring to a boil, reduce heat, cover, and simmer until carrot begins to soften, about 20 minutes. Remove garlic bag.
2. Puree soup in a blender or food processor and return to the saucepan. Stir in gingerroot, orange juice concentrate, honey, and black pepper, and simmer to heat through, about 5 minutes.

Calories Per Serving: 172
Fat: 0 g
Cholesterol: 0 mg
Protein: 4 g

Carbohydrates: 40 g
Dietary Fiber: 4 g
Sodium: 52 mg

❊ Cream of Cauliflower Soup ❊

PREPARATION TIME: 15 minutes • COOKING TIME: 20 minutes •
YIELD: 4 servings

3½ cups chopped cauliflower
¼ cup minced onion
3¼ cups low-sodium nonfat chicken
    broth
1 cup skim milk

1 tablespoon minced fresh parsley
¼ teaspoon ground black pepper
¼ teaspoon paprika
⅛ teaspoon ground nutmeg

1. Combine cauliflower, onion, and broth in a large saucepan. Bring to a boil, reduce heat, cover, and simmer until cauliflower softens, about 10 minutes. Remove from heat and allow to cool slightly.
2. Puree soup in a blender or food processor and return to the saucepan. Stir in milk, parsley, black pepper, paprika, and nutmeg. Simmer until heated through, about 5 minutes.

Calories Per Serving: 74
Fat: 0 g
Cholesterol: 1 mg
Protein: 10 g

Carbohydrates: 9 g
Dietary Fiber: 0 g
Sodium: 197 mg

❋ *Cauliflower-Spinach Soup* ❋

PREPARATION TIME: *15 minutes* • COOKING TIME: *27 minutes* •
YIELD: *6 servings*

6 cups chopped cauliflower
3 medium leeks (white parts only),
   sliced
2 cloves garlic, minced
5 cups low-sodium nonfat chicken
   broth

½ teaspoon ground cumin
½ teaspoon ground nutmeg
¼ teaspoon cayenne pepper
6 cups chopped fresh spinach
½ teaspoon ground black pepper

1. Combine cauliflower, leeks, garlic, and broth in a large saucepan. Bring to a boil, reduce heat, cover, and simmer until vegetables are just tender, about 15 minutes.
2. Stir in cumin, nutmeg, cayenne pepper, and spinach, and simmer until spinach is tender, about 5 minutes.
3. Stir in black pepper, transfer to individual bowls, and serve.

Calories Per Serving: 97
Fat: 1 g
Cholesterol: 0 mg
Protein: 5 g

Carbohydrates: 17 g
Dietary Fiber: 3 g
Sodium: 329 mg

❋ *Celery-Potato Soup* ❋

PREPARATION TIME: *15 minutes* • COOKING TIME: *32 minutes* •
YIELD: *6 servings*

6¼ cups low-sodium vegetable broth
1 medium onion, chopped
6 medium stalks celery, chopped, leaves reserved for garnish
1 clove garlic, minced
1 medium potato, diced
¼ teaspoon ground nutmeg
⅛ teaspoon dried thyme
¼ teaspoon ground black pepper

1. Heat ¼ cup broth in a large saucepan. Add onion, celery, and garlic, and sauté until onion begins to soften, about 4 minutes.
2. Stir in remaining broth, potato, nutmeg, thyme, and black pepper. Bring to a boil, reduce heat, and simmer until celery and potato are tender, about 15 minutes.
3. Puree soup in a blender or food processor and return to the saucepan. Simmer to heat through, about 5 minutes.
4. Garnish with celery leaves and serve at once.

Calories Per Serving: 102
Fat: 0 g
Cholesterol: 0 mg
Protein: 2 g
Carbohydrates: 23 g
Dietary Fiber: 3 g
Sodium: 74 mg

Collard Greens Soup

Preparation Time: *15 minutes* ▪ Cooking Time: *38 minutes* ▪ Yield: *6 servings*

3¼ cups low-sodium nonfat chicken broth
1 medium onion, minced
1 clove garlic, minced
3 cups water
1 medium stalk celery, sliced
1 medium carrot, scraped and sliced
½ cup uncooked white rice
¼ teaspoon ground black pepper
¼ teaspoon dry mustard
¼ teaspoon dried thyme
½ teaspoon dried basil
¼ teaspoon dried oregano
½ teaspoon dried marjoram
4 cups chopped fresh collard greens
1 cup fresh or thawed frozen corn kernels

1. Heat ¼ cup broth in a large pot. Add onion and garlic, and sauté until onion begins to soften, about 3 minutes.
2. Add remaining broth, water, celery, carrot, rice, black pepper, dry mustard, thyme, basil, oregano, and marjoram. Bring to a boil, reduce heat, cover, and simmer until rice is just tender, about 15 minutes.
3. Stir in collard greens and corn. Return to a boil, reduce heat, cover, and simmer until collards are just tender, about 10 more minutes.

Calories Per Serving: 208
Fat: 1 g
Cholesterol: 0 mg
Protein: 7 g

Carbohydrates: 45 g
Dietary Fiber: 3 g
Sodium: 206 mg

✳ *Corn and Green Pepper Chowder* ✳

PREPARATION TIME: *20 minutes* • COOKING TIME: *44 minutes* •
YIELD: *6 servings*

3¼ cups low-sodium nonfat chicken
  broth
½ cup chopped scallions
2 medium carrots, scraped and
  chopped
2 medium green bell peppers, cored
  and chopped
2 cups diced potatoes

2 cups skim milk
1 bay leaf
1 teaspoon dried thyme
½ teaspoon ground black pepper
4 cups fresh or thawed frozen corn
  kernels
¼ cup chopped fresh parsley

1. Heat ¼ cup broth in a large saucepan. Add scallions and carrots, and sauté for 4 minutes.
2. Add bell peppers and sauté for 4 more minutes.
3. Stir in remaining broth, potatoes, milk, bay leaf, thyme, and black pepper. Bring to a boil, reduce heat, cover, and simmer until potatoes are just tender, about 20 minutes.
4. Add corn and simmer for 10 more minutes. Remove bay leaf.
5. Serve topped with parsley.

Calories Per Serving: 251
Fat: 1 g
Cholesterol: 1 mg
Protein: 9 g

Carbohydrates: 55 g
Dietary Fiber: 5 g
Sodium: 228 mg

✳ *Gingered Corn Soup* ✳

PREPARATION TIME: *25 minutes* • COOKING TIME: *35 minutes* •
YIELD: *4 servings*

2 tablespoons low-sodium nonfat
  chicken broth
1 tablespoon grated fresh gingerroot
1 medium green bell pepper, cored
  and chopped
1 medium baking potato, diced

5½ cups water
5 cups fresh, drained canned, or
  thawed frozen corn kernels
1 tablespoon lime juice
¼ cup ground black pepper
¼ cup chopped fresh parsley

1. Heat broth in a large saucepan. Add gingerroot, bell pepper, potato, and ½ cup water. Cover and simmer for 10 minutes.
2. Add remaining water and bring to a boil. Add corn, reduce heat, and simmer until potato is just tender, about 15 minutes.
3. Puree soup in a blender or food processor and return to the saucepan. Gently reheat.
4. Stir in lime juice and black pepper. Serve topped with parsley.

Calories Per Serving: 396
Fat: 0 g
Cholesterol: 0 mg
Protein: 8 g

Carbohydrates: 98 g
Dietary Fiber: 7 g
Sodium: 45 mg

❋ Corn and Shiitake Mushroom Soup ❋

PREPARATION TIME: 15 minutes • COOKING TIME: 25 minutes •
YIELD: 4 servings

6¼ cups low-sodium nonfat chicken
  broth
5 scallions, sliced
1 cup minced shiitake mushrooms

4 cups fresh, drained canned, or
  frozen corn kernels
1 teaspoon chili powder
¼ teaspoon ground black pepper
1 tablespoon dried cilantro

1. Heat ¼ cup broth in a large saucepan. Add scallions and sauté for 2 minutes.
2. Stir in remaining broth, mushrooms, corn, chili powder, and black pepper. Bring to a boil, reduce heat, and simmer until corn is tender, about 15 minutes. Stir in cilantro.
3. Transfer to individual bowls and serve.

Calories Per Serving: 225
Fat: 0 g
Cholesterol: 0 mg
Protein: 17 g

Carbohydrates: 45 g
Dietary Fiber: 5 g
Sodium: 284 mg

❋ *Corn and Potato Soup* ❋

PREPARATION TIME: *20 minutes* · COOKING TIME: *26 minutes* ·
YIELD: *4 servings*

2 teaspoons dry sherry
1¼ cups low-sodium vegetable broth
1½ cups chopped onion
1 medium carrot, scraped and sliced
2 medium stalks celery, chopped
1 bay leaf

2 medium potatoes, cubed
1 cup skim milk
1 cup fresh, drained canned, or
    thawed frozen corn kernels
⅛ teaspoon cayenne pepper
¼ cup nonfat plain yogurt

1. Heat sherry and ¼ cup broth in a large saucepan. Add onion and sauté
   until it begins to soften, about 3 minutes.
2. Add carrot, celery, bay leaf, potatoes, and remaining broth. Bring to a boil,
   reduce heat, and simmer until potatoes are tender, about 15 minutes. Add
   milk and corn, and simmer until corn is tender, about 3 minutes. Remove
   bay leaf.
3. Puree 1 cup of soup in a blender or food processor. Stir puree and cayenne
   pepper into remaining soup in the saucepan.
4. Serve topped with yogurt.

Calories Per Serving: 222
Fat: 1 g
Cholesterol: 1 mg
Protein: 8 g

Carbohydrates: 49 g
Dietary Fiber: 5 g
Sodium: 87 mg

❋ *Corn and Red Pepper Soup* ❋

PREPARATION TIME: *20 minutes* · COOKING TIME: *20 minutes* ·
YIELD: *6 servings*

2 cups skim milk
4 cups fresh, drained canned, or
    thawed frozen corn kernels
2¾ cups low-sodium nonfat chicken
    broth
2 medium red bell peppers, cored and
    chopped

6 scallions, sliced
1 tablespoon ground cumin
2 cups diced potatoes
½ teaspoon ground black pepper
¼ cup chopped fresh parsley

1. Puree milk and 2 cups corn kernels in a blender or food processor and set aside.
2. Heat ¼ cup broth in a large saucepan. Add bell peppers and scallions, and sauté until peppers begin to soften, about 4 minutes. Stir in remaining broth, cumin, potatoes, remaining corn kernels, and corn puree. Bring to a boil, reduce heat, and simmer until potatoes are tender, about 10 minutes. Add black pepper.
3. Serve topped with parsley.

Calories Per Serving: 338
Fat: 1 g
Cholesterol: 3 mg
Protein: 19 g

Carbohydrates: 69 g
Dietary Fiber: 6 g
Sodium: 250 mg

❁ *Jalapeño-Corn Chowder* ❁

PREPARATION TIME: *15 minutes* · COOKING TIME: *29 minutes* ·
YIELD: *4 servings*

3¼ cups low-sodium vegetable broth
1 medium onion, minced
½ jalapeño pepper, seeded and minced
½ cup minced red bell pepper
½ cup all-purpose flour
¼ cup dry white wine

2 cups skim milk
½ teaspoon dried marjoram
3 cups fresh or thawed frozen corn
   kernels
¼ cup chopped fresh parsley

1. Heat ¼ cup broth in a large saucepan. Add onion, jalapeño pepper, and bell pepper, and sauté until onion begins to soften, about 4 minutes. Add flour and stir for 3 more minutes.
2. Stir in remaining broth, wine, milk, and marjoram. Bring to a boil, reduce heat, and simmer for 10 minutes. Add corn and simmer until tender, about 4 minutes.
3. Serve topped with parsley.

Calories Per Serving: 261
Fat: 1 g
Cholesterol: 2 mg
Protein: 11 g

Carbohydrates: 54 g
Dietary Fiber: 5 g
Sodium: 153 mg

✳ Corn and Cabbage Soup ✳

PREPARATION TIME: *20 minutes plus 1 hour standing time* •
COOKING TIME: *43 minutes* • YIELD: *6 servings*

4¾ cups low-sodium vegetable broth
1 medium onion, chopped
2 tablespoons all-purpose flour
4 cups shredded cabbage
1 medium potato, diced
3 cups fresh or thawed frozen corn
   kernels

2 medium tomatoes, chopped
¾ teaspoon dried basil
¾ teaspoon dried thyme
½ cup skim milk
¼ teaspoon ground black pepper
¼ cup chopped fresh parsley

1. Heat ¼ cup broth in a large pot. Add onion and sauté until it begins to soften, about 3 minutes. Stir in flour.
2. Add remaining broth, cabbage, potato, corn, and tomatoes. Bring to a boil and reduce heat. Stir in basil and thyme, cover, and simmer until vegetables are tender, about 25 minutes.
3. Stir in milk and black pepper, and simmer for 10 more minutes.
4. Serve topped with parsley.

Calories Per Serving: 178
Fat: 0 g
Cholesterol: 0 mg
Protein: 6 g

Carbohydrates: 41 g
Dietary Fiber: 4 g
Sodium: 58 mg

✳ Corn and Zucchini Soup ✳

PREPARATION TIME: *20 minutes* • COOKING TIME: *39 minutes* •
YIELD: *6 servings*

2¼ cups low-sodium nonfat chicken
   broth
1 teaspoon sugar
2 cups fresh or thawed frozen corn
   kernels
1 medium onion, minced
1 medium green bell pepper, cored
   and finely diced

1 medium red bell pepper, cored and
   finely diced
3 medium tomatoes, chopped
2 tablespoons all-purpose flour
2½ cups skim milk
1 cup diced zucchini
¼ teaspoon ground black pepper
¼ cup chopped fresh parsley

1. Heat ¼ cup broth in a large saucepan. Add sugar and corn, and sauté until corn begins to soften, about 4 minutes. Remove corn and set aside.
2. Heat another ¼ cup broth in the saucepan. Add onion and bell peppers, and sauté until onion begins to soften, about 3 minutes. Add tomatoes and sauté for 3 more minutes. Stir in flour and blend well.
3. Return corn to the saucepan. Add remaining broth, milk, and zucchini. Bring to a boil, reduce heat, and simmer for 20 minutes. Stir in black pepper.
4. Serve topped with parsley.

Calories Per Serving: 132
Fat: 1 g
Cholesterol: 2 mg
Protein: 9 g

Carbohydrates: 25 g
Dietary Fiber: 3 g
Sodium: 124 mg

❋ *Cranberry Borscht* ❋

PREPARATION TIME: *15 minutes* • COOKING TIME: *25 minutes* •
YIELD: *4 servings*

6 medium carrots, scraped and
   chopped
3 cups fresh or thawed frozen cranberries
4 cups low-sodium nonfat chicken
   broth

3 tablespoons sugar
2 tablespoons lemon juice
½ cup nonfat sour cream
2 tablespoons chopped fresh dill

1. In a large saucepan, combine carrots, cranberries, broth, and sugar, and simmer until carrots are tender, about 20 minutes.
2. Puree mixture in a blender or food processor and return to the saucepan. Whisk in lemon juice and sour cream. Simmer to heat through, about 5 minutes.
3. Serve topped with dill.

Calories Per Serving: 160
Fat: 0 g
Cholesterol: 1 mg
Protein: 3 g

Carbohydrates: 34 g
Dietary Fiber: 6 g
Sodium: 349 mg

❋ *Eggplant Soup* ❋

PREPARATION TIME: *20 minutes* • COOKING TIME: *34 minutes* •
YIELD: *6 servings*

6¼ cups low-sodium vegetable broth
1 medium onion, chopped
2 cloves garlic, minced
1 medium carrot, scraped and diced
2 tablespoons dry sherry

⅛ teaspoon dried saffron threads,
   crushed
3 medium tomatoes, chopped
4 cups chopped eggplant
¼ teaspoon ground black pepper
¼ cup chopped fresh parsley

1. Heat ¼ cup broth in a large saucepan. Add onion, garlic, and carrot, and sauté until onion begins to soften, about 3 minutes. In a separate bowl, mix sherry and saffron. Stir into the onion mixture, and sauté for 3 more minutes.
2. Add remaining broth, tomatoes, and eggplant. Bring to a boil, reduce heat, and simmer until vegetables are soft, about 15 minutes. Remove from heat.
3. Remove and reserve 1 cup of vegetables. Puree the rest of the soup in a blender or food processor.
4. Return puree to the saucepan, stir in black pepper, and simmer to heat through, about 5 minutes.
5. Stir in reserved vegetables and serve garnished with parsley.

Calories Per Serving: 100
Fat: 0 g
Cholesterol: 0 mg
Protein: 3 g

Carbohydrates: 21 g
Dietary Fiber: 3 g
Sodium: 55 mg

❋ *Green Bean Soup* ❋

PREPARATION TIME: *15 minutes* • COOKING TIME: *24 minutes* •
YIELD: *6 servings*

3¼ cups low-sodium vegetable broth
½ medium onion, chopped
1 medium stalk celery, chopped
1 medium tomato, chopped
2 medium carrots, scraped and sliced
1 clove garlic, minced
¼ teaspoon cayenne pepper
¼ teaspoon ground cardamom

¼ teaspoon ground cumin
1 teaspoon ground coriander
1 teaspoon ground ginger
½ teaspoon ground turmeric
3 cups chopped green beans (1-inch
   lengths)
¼ cup chopped fresh parsley

1. Heat ¼ cup broth in a large pot. Add onion, celery, tomato, carrots, and garlic, and sauté until onion begins to soften, about 4 minutes. Stir in cayenne pepper, cardamom, cumin, coriander, ginger, and turmeric.
2. Add remaining broth and bring to a boil. Add green beans, reduce heat, and simmer until beans are just tender, about 20 minutes.
3. Serve topped with parsley.

Calories Per Serving: 47
Fat: 0 g
Cholesterol: 0 mg
Protein: 2 g

Carbohydrates: 11 g
Dietary Fiber: 2 g
Sodium: 27 mg

❈ Gingered Green Bean and ❈ Zucchini Chowder

PREPARATION TIME: 20 minutes • COOKING TIME: 55 minutes •
YIELD: 8 servings

6¼ cups low-sodium nonfat chicken broth
1 medium onion, sliced
6 scallions, sliced
3 cloves garlic, minced
1 tablespoon minced fresh gingerroot
¼ teaspoon cayenne pepper
½ cup dry sherry
2 cups diced potatoes
2 medium carrots, scraped and sliced

2 medium stalks celery, sliced
2 medium tomatoes, diced
1½ cups chopped green beans (1-inch lengths)
½ cup chopped fresh parsley
2 cups skim milk
½ teaspoon ground black pepper
1½ cups chopped zucchini
½ cup evaporated skim milk

1. Heat ¼ cup broth in a large saucepan. Add onion, scallions, garlic, gingerroot, cayenne pepper, and sherry, and sauté until onion begins to soften, about 4 minutes.
2. Add remaining broth, potatoes, carrots, celery, tomatoes, green beans, ¼ cup parsley, skim milk, and black pepper. Bring to a boil, reduce heat, and simmer for 30 minutes.
3. Add zucchini and simmer until vegetables are just tender, about 10 more minutes. Stir in evaporated milk and simmer for 1 additional minute.
4. Serve topped with remaining parsley.

Calories Per Serving: 106
Fat: 0 g
Cholesterol: 1 mg
Protein: 5 g

Carbohydrates: 18 g
Dietary Fiber: 2 g
Sodium: 242 mg

❋ Spicy Green Bean–Yellow Squash– ❋ Tomato Soup

PREPARATION TIME: *15 minutes* • COOKING TIME: *23 minutes* •
YIELD: *6 servings*

¾ cup low-sodium nonfat chicken
 broth
1 medium onion, chopped
1 jalapeño pepper, seeded and minced
1 teaspoon ground cumin
1 teaspoon dried marjoram
1 teaspoon ground coriander

2 cups chopped fresh or thawed
 frozen green beans (1-inch
 lengths)
1 cup sliced yellow summer squash
3½ cups low-sodium canned tomatoes, chopped, juice reserved

1. Heat ¼ cup broth in a large saucepan. Add onion and jalapeño pepper, and sauté until onion begins to soften, about 3 minutes.
2. Stir in remaining broth, cumin, marjoram, coriander, and green beans. Bring to a boil, reduce heat, and simmer for 5 minutes. Add squash and tomatoes with juice, and simmer until squash is just tender, about 10 minutes.

Calories Per Serving: 56
Fat: 1 g
Cholesterol: 0 mg
Protein: 3 g

Carbohydrates: 12 g
Dietary Fiber: 2 g
Sodium: 109 mg

❋ Easy Green Bean and Red Pepper Soup ❋ with Leftover Pasta

PREPARATION TIME: *15 minutes* • COOKING TIME: *40 minutes* •
YIELD: *6 servings*

4¼ cups low-sodium nonfat chicken
  broth
1 medium onion, minced
2 cups chopped fresh or thawed frozen
  green beans (1-inch lengths)
1 cup diced fresh or thawed frozen
  yellow wax beans

¼ teaspoon ground black pepper
2 cups water
1 cup cooked small pasta shells
½ cup canned roasted red peppers
2 tablespoons minced fresh basil
2 tablespoons grated nonfat
  Parmesan

1. Heat ¼ cup broth in a large pot. Add onion, green and yellow beans, and black pepper. Cover and simmer, stirring frequently, for about 12 minutes.
2. Add remaining broth and water, and bring to a boil. Reduce heat and simmer for 15 minutes. Stir in cooked pasta shells and roasted peppers and heat through, about 5 minutes.
3. Transfer to individual bowls, garnish with minced basil, top with Parmesan, and serve.

Calories Per Serving: 76
Fat: 0 g
Cholesterol: 0 mg
Protein: 2 g

Carbohydrates: 13 g
Dietary Fiber: 3 g
Sodium: 227 mg

❈ Kale Soup ❈

PREPARATION TIME: *20 minutes* • COOKING TIME: *33 minutes* •
YIELD: *6 servings*

6¼ cups low-sodium vegetable broth
5 scallions, chopped
1 clove garlic, minced
8 cups chopped fresh kale
3 cups cubed potatoes

2 teaspoons lemon juice
¼ teaspoon ground black pepper
⅛ teaspoon cayenne pepper
1½ cups skim milk

1. Heat ¼ cup broth in a large pot. Add scallions and garlic, and sauté for 3 minutes. Add kale and sauté for 2 more minutes.
2. Stir in remaining broth, potatoes, lemon juice, and black pepper. Bring to a boil, reduce heat, and simmer, stirring occasionally, until potatoes and kale are tender, about 15 minutes.
3. Puree soup in a blender or food processor.
4. Return puree to the saucepan, stir in cayenne pepper and milk, and simmer for about 5 minutes to heat through.

Calories Per Serving: 77
Fat: 0 g
Cholesterol: 1 mg
Protein: 5 g

Carbohydrates: 15 g
Dietary Fiber: 3 g
Sodium: 88 mg

❊ *Mushroom Soup* ❊

PREPARATION TIME: *15 minutes* • COOKING TIME: *15 minutes* •
YIELD: *4 servings*

2¼ cups low-sodium nonfat chicken
　broth
6 cups sliced mushrooms
2 cups skim milk

1 scallion, sliced
1 tablespoon dried parsley
1 tablespoon dry sherry
¼ teaspoon ground black pepper

1. Heat ¼ cup broth in a large saucepan. Add mushrooms and sauté for 3
   minutes. Remove mushrooms, mince, and set aside.
2. Puree remaining broth, milk, scallion, parsley, and sherry in a blender or
   food processor.
3. Transfer puree to the saucepan, add minced mushrooms, and simmer for
   about 10 minutes to heat through. Stir in black pepper and serve.

Calories Per Serving: 90
Fat: 1 g
Cholesterol: 2 mg
Protein: 10 g

Carbohydrates: 11 g
Dietary Fiber: 1 g
Sodium: 164 mg

❊ *Mushroom, Corn, and Potato Chowder* ❊

PREPARATION TIME: *20 minutes* • COOKING TIME: *22 minutes* •
YIELD: *4 servings*

1¼ cups low-sodium vegetable broth
4 cups sliced mushrooms
¼ cup chopped onion
2 cloves garlic, minced
2 cups diced potatoes
1 medium carrot, scraped and
　chopped

1½ cups fresh or thawed frozen corn
　kernels
1 cup skim milk
¼ teaspoon ground black pepper

1. Heat ¼ cup broth in a large saucepan. Add mushrooms, onion, and garlic, and sauté until mushrooms are tender, about 4 minutes.
2. Stir in remaining broth, potatoes, and carrot. Bring to a boil, reduce heat, cover, and simmer until potatoes are just tender, about 10 minutes.
3. Add corn, milk, and black pepper, and simmer until heated through, about 5 minutes.

Calories Per Serving: 213	Carbohydrates: 47 g
Fat: 0 g	Dietary Fiber: 4 g
Cholesterol: 1 mg	Sodium: 56 mg
Protein: 7 g	

❊ *Mushroom and Quinoa Soup* ❊

PREPARATION TIME: *20 minutes* ▪ COOKING TIME: *55 minutes* ▪
YIELD: *8 servings*

7¼ cups low-sodium vegetable broth
1 cup chopped onion
2 cloves garlic, minced
1 medium carrot, scraped and sliced
½ cup pearl barley
2 cups low-sodium canned tomatoes,
* drained and chopped*

2 bay leaves
1 teaspoon honey
¼ teaspoon ground black pepper
1 teaspoon dried basil
1 cup sliced mushrooms
½ cup quinoa

1. Heat ¼ cup broth in a large pot. Add onion and garlic, and sauté until onion begins to soften, about 3 minutes.
2. Add all remaining ingredients and bring to a boil. Reduce heat, cover, and simmer, stirring occasionally, until all ingredients are tender, about 50 minutes.
3. Remove bay leaves and serve.

Calories Per Serving: 123	Carbohydrates: 26 g
Fat: 1 g	Dietary Fiber: 3 g
Cholesterol: 0 mg	Sodium: 47 mg
Protein: 4 g	

❈ *Onion Soup with Red Wine* ❈

PREPARATION TIME: *25 minutes* • COOKING TIME: *1 hour 8 minutes* •
YIELD: *6 servings*

4 cups low-sodium vegetable broth
3 cups water
1 ½ cups dry red wine
8 cups coarsely chopped red onion
1 medium carrot, scraped and
   shredded
1 clove garlic, minced
2 bay leaves

½ teaspoon dried thyme
¼ teaspoon dry mustard
¼ teaspoon ground black pepper
⅛ teaspoon cayenne pepper
6 ½-inch-thick slices French bread,
   toasted
6 teaspoons grated nonfat Parmesan

1. Combine broth, water, wine, onion, carrot, garlic, bay leaves, thyme, dry mustard, black pepper, and cayenne pepper in a large pot. Bring to a boil, reduce heat, cover, and simmer, stirring occasionally, for 1 hour. Remove bay leaves.
2. Serve in individual bowls topped with a slice of French bread and a teaspoon of Parmesan.

Calories Per Serving: 156
Fat: 0 g
Cholesterol: 0 mg
Protein: 4 g

Carbohydrates: 30 g
Dietary Fiber: 3 g
Sodium: 144 mg

❈ *Parsnip Soup* ❈

PREPARATION TIME: *15 minutes* • COOKING TIME: *29 minutes* •
YIELD: *6 servings*

6¼ cups low-sodium vegetable broth
3 medium stalks celery, chopped
1 medium onion, chopped
1 clove garlic, minced
1 bay leaf

¼ teaspoon ground nutmeg
¼ teaspoon dried thyme
4 cups diced parsnips
¼ teaspoon ground white pepper

1. Heat ¼ cup broth in a large saucepan. Add celery, onion, and garlic, and sauté until onion begins to soften, about 4 minutes.
2. Add remaining broth, bay leaf, nutmeg, thyme, and parsnips. Bring to a boil, reduce heat, and simmer until parsnips are just tender, about 12 minutes. Remove bay leaf.

3. Puree soup in a blender or food processor and return it to the saucepan. Stir in white pepper and simmer to heat through, about 5 minutes.

Calories Per Serving: 146 Carbohydrates: 34 g
Fat: 0 g Dietary Fiber: 7 g
Cholesterol: 0 mg Sodium: 66 mg
Protein: 3 g

❈ Split Pea Soup ❈

PREPARATION TIME: *15 minutes* • COOKING TIME: *1 hour 3 minutes* •
YIELD: *4 servings*

2 tablespoons low-sodium vegetable
  broth
¼ cup chopped onion
4 cups water
1 cup dried green split peas, rinsed
  and drained

1 medium carrot, scraped and diced
¼ teaspoon ground black pepper
½ teaspoon dried marjoram
¼ teaspoon dried thyme
2 tablespoons chopped fresh parsley

1. Heat broth in a large saucepan. Add onion and sauté until it begins to soften, about 3 minutes.
2. Add water, split peas, carrot, black pepper, marjoram, and thyme, and bring to a boil. Reduce heat, cover, and simmer, stirring occasionally, until peas are tender, about 50 minutes.
3. Puree soup in a blender or food processor and return it to the saucepan. Simmer to heat through, about 5 minutes, and serve topped with parsley.

Calories Per Serving: 183 Carbohydrates: 33 g
Fat: 1 g Dietary Fiber: 3 g
Cholesterol: 0 mg Sodium: 29 mg
Protein: 13 g

❈ Green Pea Soup ❈

PREPARATION TIME: *20 minutes* • COOKING TIME: *25 minutes* •
YIELD: *6 servings*

6¼ cups low-sodium nonfat chicken
  broth
2 medium onions, chopped
1 medium leek (white part only),
  chopped
2 tablespoons minced fresh gingerroot
1 clove garlic, minced

2 medium stalks celery, chopped
⅛ teaspoon ground cloves
1 teaspoon dried tarragon
6 cups fresh or thawed frozen green
  peas
¼ teaspoon ground white pepper

1. Heat ¼ cup broth in a large saucepan. Add onions, leek, gingerroot, garlic, and celery, and sauté until onion begins to soften, about 4 minutes.
2. Add remaining broth, cloves, tarragon, and peas. Bring to a boil, reduce heat, and simmer until peas are tender, about 8 minutes.
3. Puree soup in a blender or food processor and return it to the saucepan. Stir in white pepper and simmer to heat through, about 5 minutes.

Calories Per Serving: 202

Carbohydrates: 40 g

Fat: 1 g

Dietary Fiber: 8 g

Cholesterol: 0 mg

Sodium: 61 mg

Protein: 10 g

❋ *Green Pea and Zucchini Soup* ❋

PREPARATION TIME: *25 minutes* • COOKING TIME: *38 minutes* •
YIELD: *5 servings*

6¼ cups low-sodium nonfat chicken
  broth
1 jalapeño pepper, seeded and
  chopped
2 cups diced zucchini

2½ cups fresh or thawed frozen green
  peas
1 medium baking potato, chopped
½ teaspoon curry powder
¼ teaspoon ground black pepper

1. Heat ¼ cup broth in a large saucepan. Add jalapeño pepper, zucchini, peas, and potato, and sauté for 5 minutes.
2. Stir in remaining broth and curry powder. Bring to a boil, reduce heat, cover, and simmer until vegetables are just tender, about 20 minutes.
3. Puree soup in a blender or food processor and return it to the saucepan. Stir in black pepper and gently reheat before serving.

Calories Per Serving: 149

Carbohydrates: 23 g

Fat: 0 g

Dietary Fiber: 4 g

Cholesterol: 0 mg

Sodium: 300 mg

Protein: 14 g

❋ Santa Fe Potato-Corn Chowder ❋

PREPARATION TIME: 20 minutes • COOKING TIME: 28 minutes •
YIELD: 5 servings

3¼ cups low-sodium nonfat chicken
  broth
5 scallions, chopped
3 cups diced potatoes
1 bay leaf
½ teaspoon dry mustard
¼ teaspoon dried marjoram
¼ teaspoon ground black pepper

1½ cups fresh or thawed frozen corn
  kernels
2½ cups skim milk
½ cup chopped canned mild green
  chiles, drained
¼ cup grated nonfat cheddar
2 tablespoons chopped fresh parsley

1. Heat ¼ cup broth in a large saucepan. Add scallions and sauté until they begin to soften, about 3 minutes.
2. Add remaining broth and stir until well blended. Add potatoes, bay leaf, dry mustard, marjoram, and black pepper. Stir well and simmer for 10 minutes. Add corn and simmer until corn and potatoes are tender, about 5 more minutes.
3. Add milk and chiles, and simmer for about 3 minutes. Remove bay leaf.
4. Serve topped with cheese and parsley.

Calories Per Serving: 284
Fat: 1 g
Cholesterol: 4 mg
Protein: 13 g

Carbohydrates: 55 g
Dietary Fiber: 4 g
Sodium: 343 mg

❋ Two-Potato Soup with Pumpkin and Okra ❋

PREPARATION TIME: 25 minutes • COOKING TIME: 25 minutes •
YIELD: 8 servings

1 turnip, chopped
3 cups chopped potatoes
3 cups chopped sweet potatoes
2 medium carrots, scraped and
  chopped
1½ cups chopped pumpkin

1 medium onion, chopped
6 fresh or frozen okra, sliced
½ teaspoon dried thyme
½ teaspoon ground black pepper
3 cups skim milk

Combine all ingredients in a large saucepan. Bring to a boil, reduce heat, cover, and simmer until turnip and potatoes are just tender, about 25 minutes.

Calories Per Serving: 230
Fat: 1 g
Cholesterol: 2 mg
Protein: 8 g

Carbohydrates: 51 g
Dietary Fiber: 6 g
Sodium: 78 mg

✖ *Potato-Onion Soup* ✖

PREPARATION TIME: *15 minutes* • COOKING TIME: *11 minutes* •
YIELD: *6 servings*

3 medium potatoes, chopped
2 medium onions, chopped
4 cups water

4 cups skim milk
¼ teaspoon white pepper
¼ cup minced fresh parsley

1. Combine potatoes, onions, water, milk, and white pepper in a saucepan. Bring to a boil, reduce heat, and simmer until potatoes are tender, about 30 minutes.
2. Puree soup in a blender or food processor and return it to the saucepan. Simmer to heat through.
3. Transfer to individual bowls, sprinkle with parsley, and serve.

Calories Per Serving: 216
Fat: 1 g
Cholesterol: 4 mg
Protein: 11 g

Carbohydrates: 42 g
Dietary Fiber: 3 g
Sodium: 143 mg

✖ *Jalapeño-Potato Soup with Green Chiles* ✖

PREPARATION TIME: *25 minutes* • COOKING TIME: *42 minutes* •
YIELD: *4 servings*

5¼ cups low-sodium nonfat chicken
 broth
1 medium onion, finely chopped
1 clove garlic, minced
½ teaspoon ground cumin
½ teaspoon ground black pepper
⅛ teaspoon dried oregano

3 medium potatoes, diced
1 4-ounce can chopped green chiles,
 drained
1 jalapeño pepper, seeded and minced
¼ tablespoon dried cilantro
¼ cup shredded nonfat cheddar

1. Heat ¼ cup broth in a large saucepan. Add onion and garlic, and sauté until onion begins to soften, about 3 minutes. Add cumin and black pepper, and sauté for 2 more minutes.
2. Add remaining broth, oregano, potatoes, chiles, and jalapeño pepper. Bring to a boil, reduce heat, cover, and simmer until potatoes are just tender, about 30 minutes. Stir in cilantro.
3. Serve topped with cheddar.

Calories Per Serving: 302
Fat: 0 g
Cholesterol: 3 mg
Protein: 20 g
Carbohydrates: 56 g
Dietary Fiber: 5 g
Sodium: 312 mg

Southwestern Pumpkin Soup

PREPARATION TIME: *20 minutes* ▪ COOKING TIME: *32 minutes* ▪ YIELD: *4 servings*

3¼ cups low-sodium nonfat chicken broth
2 medium tomatoes, chopped
1 medium green bell pepper, cored and chopped
1 medium onion, chopped
½ teaspoon sugar
½ teaspoon ground nutmeg
2 cups cubed pumpkin
½ cup skim milk
2 tablespoons chopped fresh cilantro

1. Heat ¼ cup broth in a large saucepan. Add tomatoes, bell pepper, onion, sugar, and nutmeg, and sauté until onion begins to soften, about 3 minutes.
2. Stir in remaining broth and pumpkin. Bring to a boil, reduce heat, cover, and simmer for 20 minutes.
3. Add milk and simmer to heat through, about 3 minutes.
4. Serve topped with cilantro.

Calories Per Serving: 83
Fat: 0 g
Cholesterol: 0 mg
Protein: 6 g
Carbohydrates: 15 g
Dietary Fiber: 3 g
Sodium: 103 mg

❊ *Potato-Carrot Soup* ❊

PREPARATION TIME: *20 minutes* • COOKING TIME: *17 minutes* •
YIELD: *6 servings*

3 cups diced potatoes
2 cups water
1 medium onion, chopped
2 medium carrots, scraped and
  chopped

¼ teaspoon ground black pepper
½ teaspoon dried dill
1½ cups skim milk
3 tablespoons all-purpose flour
¼ cup chopped fresh parsley

1. Combine potatoes, water, onion, carrots, black pepper, and dill in a large
   saucepan. Bring to a boil, reduce heat, cover, and simmer until potatoes
   are tender, about 12 minutes.
2. In a separate bowl, mix milk and flour, and stir until smooth. Stir into the
   saucepan and bring to a boil for 1 minute.
3. Serve topped with parsley.

Calories Per Serving: 168
Fat: 0 g
Cholesterol: 2 mg
Protein: 5 g

Carbohydrates: 36 g
Dietary Fiber: 3 g
Sodium: 49 mg

❊ *Pumpkin-Apple Soup* ❊

PREPARATION TIME: *25 minutes* • COOKING TIME: *39 minutes* •
YIELD: *8 servings*

5¼ cups low-sodium vegetable broth
6 cups cubed pumpkin
1 medium baking potato, cubed
1 medium carrot, scraped and
  chopped
1 medium tart apple, peeled, cored,
  and sliced

¾ cup cranberries
½ tablespoon ground coriander
1 tablespoon grated fresh gingerroot
1½ cups apple juice
¼ teaspoon ground black pepper
¼ teaspoon ground nutmeg

1. Heat ¼ cup broth in a large saucepan. Add pumpkin, potato, carrot, apple,
   cranberries, coriander, and gingerroot. Sauté for 6 minutes.
2. Add remaining broth and apple juice. Bring to a boil, reduce heat, and
   simmer until vegetables are just tender, about 20 minutes.

3. Stir in black pepper and nutmeg. Puree in a blender or food processor.
4. Return soup to the saucepan and gently reheat.

Calories Per Serving: 394   Carbohydrates: 88 g
Fat: 1 g   Dietary Fiber: 8 g
Cholesterol: 0 mg   Sodium: 248 mg
Protein: 12 g

❈ *Pumpkin Soup* ❈

PREPARATION TIME: *15 minutes* • COOKING TIME: *16 minutes* •
YIELD: *8 servings*

2 tablespoons all-purpose flour   7¼ cups low-sodium nonfat chicken
¼ teaspoon ground ginger   broth
⅛ teaspoon ground turmeric   3 scallions, sliced
2 cups skim milk   2 cups canned pumpkin puree
                                         ¼ cup chopped fresh parsley

1. In a bowl, combine flour, ginger, turmeric, and ½ cup milk.
2. Heat ¼ cup broth in a large saucepan. Add scallions and sauté for 3 min-
    utes. Stir in pumpkin, then flour mixture.
3. Gradually add remaining milk and stir constantly until mixture thickens,
    about 8 minutes. Stir in remaining broth and heat gently.
4. Serve topped with parsley.

Calories Per Serving: 92   Carbohydrates: 19 g
Fat: 0 g   Dietary Fiber: 3 g
Cholesterol: 1 mg   Sodium: 68 mg
Protein: 4 g

❈ *Potato-Vegetable Chowder* ❈

PREPARATION TIME: *20 minutes* • COOKING TIME: *55 minutes* •
YIELD: *10 servings*

8 cups low-sodium nonfat chicken   2 cups skim milk
   broth   4 cups diced potatoes

3 medium carrots, scraped and sliced
3 medium stalks celery, sliced
1 cup thawed frozen lima beans
1 cup uncooked small elbow macaroni
2 cups chopped fresh spinach

1 cup fresh or thawed frozen green peas
¼ cup chopped fresh parsley
1 teaspoon dried marjoram
1 teaspoon ground black pepper
1 cup evaporated skim milk
3 scallions, minced

1. Combine broth, skim milk, potatoes, carrots, and celery in a large saucepan. Bring to a boil, reduce heat, and simmer for 20 minutes.
2. Add lima beans, macaroni, spinach, peas, parsley, marjoram, and black pepper. Return to a boil, reduce heat, and simmer for 20 more minutes.
3. Remove from heat and stir in evaporated milk. Simmer until heated through, about 3 minutes. Serve topped with scallions.

Calories Per Serving: 214
Fat: 1 g
Cholesterol: 2 mg
Protein: 14 g

Carbohydrates: 39 g
Dietary Fiber: 4 g
Sodium: 233 mg

❋ *Simple Potato Puree* ❋

PREPARATION TIME: *15 minutes* ▪ COOKING TIME: *21 minutes* ▪
YIELD: *4 servings*

4¼ cups low-sodium nonfat chicken broth
½ cup minced onion
2 tablespoons minced fresh parsley

4 medium potatoes, boiled and mashed
¼ teaspoon ground black pepper
1 tablespoon dried dill

1. Heat ¼ cup broth in a saucepan. Add onion and sauté for 3 minutes. Add parsley and sauté for 1 more minute.
2. In a separate bowl, combine remaining broth and potatoes. Add to onions, stir in black pepper, and bring to a boil. Reduce heat and simmer for 10 minutes.
3. Transfer to a blender or food processor and puree.
4. Serve sprinkled with dill.

Calories Per Serving: 185
Fat: 0 g
Cholesterol: 0 mg
Protein: 4 g

Carbohydrates: 42 g
Dietary Fiber: 3 g
Sodium: 33 mg

❋ *Summer Squash Soup* ❋

PREPARATION TIME: *10 minutes* • COOKING TIME: *20 minutes* •
YIELD: *4 servings*

4 cups low-sodium vegetable broth
1 medium onion, sliced
5 cups chopped yellow summer
  squash

¼ teaspoon ground black pepper
¼ cup nonfat plain yogurt

1. Heat ¼ cup broth in a large saucepan. Add onion and sauté until it begins to soften, about 3 minutes.
2. Add remaining broth and squash, and bring to a boil. Reduce heat and simmer until squash is just tender, about 10 minutes.
3. Stir in black pepper and yogurt, and serve.

Calories Per Serving: 74
Fat: 0 g
Cholesterol: 0 mg
Protein: 3 g

Carbohydrates: 16 g
Dietary Fiber: 2 g
Sodium: 49 mg

❋ *Butternut Squash Soup* ❋

PREPARATION TIME: *20 minutes* • COOKING TIME: *36 minutes* •
YIELD: *4 servings*

3¼ cups low-sodium nonfat chicken
  broth
1 medium onion, chopped
2 cloves garlic, minced
1 tablespoon curry powder
1 teaspoon ground cumin

⅛ teaspoon cayenne pepper
3 cups chopped butternut squash
3 medium tart apples, peeled, cored,
  and chopped
2 tablespoons chopped fresh parsley

1. Heat ¼ cup broth in a large pot. Add onion and garlic, and sauté until onion begins to soften, about 3 minutes. Add curry powder, cumin, and cayenne pepper, and sauté for 1 more minute.
2. Add remaining broth, squash, and apples, and bring to a boil. Reduce heat, cover, and simmer until squash and apples are just tender, about 25 minutes.
3. Serve topped with parsley.

Calories Per Serving: 211
Fat: 1 g
Cholesterol: 0 mg
Protein: 11 g
Carbohydrates: 44 g
Dietary Fiber: 7 g
Sodium: 227 mg

Acorn Squash Soup

PREPARATION TIME: *15 minutes* ▪ COOKING TIME: *41 minutes* ▪ YIELD: *8 servings*

5¼ cups low-sodium nonfat chicken broth
2 medium onions, thinly sliced
4 cups diced acorn squash
1 large potato, diced
1 teaspoon dried marjoram
3 cups water
4 cups chopped fresh spinach
¼ teaspoon ground black pepper

1. Heat ¼ cup broth in a large pot. Add onions and sauté until they begin to soften, about 3 minutes.
2. Add squash, potato, marjoram, water, and remaining broth. Bring to a boil, reduce heat, and simmer until squash and potato are just tender, about 20 minutes. Stir in spinach and simmer for 5 more minutes.
3. Remove from heat. Puree half the soup in a blender or food processor and return it to the pot. Stir in black pepper. Simmer to heat through, about 5 minutes.

Calories Per Serving: 110
Fat: 1 g
Cholesterol: 0 mg
Protein: 6 g
Carbohydrates: 21 g
Dietary Fiber: 5 g
Sodium: 156 mg

Tomato-Rice Soup

PREPARATION TIME: *20 minutes* ▪ COOKING TIME: *55 minutes* ▪ YIELD: *6 servings*

4¼ cups low-sodium nonfat chicken broth
2 medium onions, thinly sliced
½ teaspoon dried thyme
¼ teaspoon dried marjoram
1 teaspoon dried parsley
1 clove garlic, minced
4 medium tomatoes, chopped
¾ cup cooked rice
½ cup nonfat plain yogurt

1. Heat ¼ cup broth in a large saucepan. Add onions and sauté until they begin to soften, about 3 minutes.
2. Add thyme, marjoram, parsley, garlic, tomatoes, and remaining broth. Bring to a boil, reduce heat, and simmer for 40 minutes.
3. Puree soup in a blender or food processor and return it to the saucepan. Add rice and yogurt, and heat through, about 5 minutes.

Calories Per Serving: 90　　　　　Carbohydrates: 14 g
Fat: 0 g　　　　　　　　　　　　　Dietary Fiber: 2 g
Cholesterol: 0 mg　　　　　　　　Sodium: 143 mg
Protein: 8 g

❋ *Tomato-Onion-Potato Soup* ❋

PREPARATION TIME: *20 minutes* • COOKING TIME: *34 minutes* •
YIELD: *6 servings*

2¾ cups low-sodium vegetable broth　⅛ teaspoon ground cloves
2 medium onions, sliced　　　　　　¼ teaspoon ground black pepper
3 medium potatoes, cubed　　　　　¼ cup nonfat plain yogurt
3½ cups low-sodium canned tomatoes　2 teaspoons dried basil
2 teaspoons sugar

1. Heat ¼ cup broth in a large saucepan. Add onions and sauté until they begin to soften, about 3 minutes.
2. Add remaining broth and potatoes, and bring to a boil. Reduce heat, cover, and simmer until potatoes are tender, about 15 minutes.
3. Puree soup in a blender or food processor and return it to the saucepan.
4. Puree tomatoes, sugar, cloves, and black pepper in the blender or food processor. Stir tomato mixture into the saucepan and simmer to heat through, about 10 minutes.
5. Serve topped with yogurt and basil.

Calories Per Serving: 124　　　　　Carbohydrates: 28 g
Fat: 0 g　　　　　　　　　　　　　Dietary Fiber: 3 g
Cholesterol: 0 mg　　　　　　　　Sodium: 40 mg
Protein: 4 g

❇ *Cream of Tomato-Corn Soup* ❇

PREPARATION TIME: *15 minutes* • COOKING TIME: *16 minutes* •
YIELD: *4 servings*

3 tablespoons low-sodium nonfat
   chicken broth
1 medium onion, chopped
2 tablespoons all-purpose flour
2 cups low-sodium tomato juice

3 cups fresh, drained canned, or
   thawed frozen corn kernels
2 cups skim milk
¼ teaspoon ground black pepper
¼ cup chopped fresh parsley

1. Heat broth in a large saucepan. Add onion and sauté until it begins to soften, about 3 minutes. Stir in flour until mixture thickens, about 3 minutes.
2. Puree onion mixture, tomato juice, and corn in a blender or food processor and return mixture to the saucepan.
3. Add milk and black pepper. Simmer to heat all ingredients through, about 10 minutes.
4. Serve topped with parsley.

Calories Per Serving: 175
Fat: 0 g
Cholesterol: 2 mg
Protein: 9 g

Carbohydrates: 38 g
Dietary Fiber: 4 g
Sodium: 92 mg

❇ *Cream of Tomato Soup with Rice* ❇

PREPARATION TIME: *20 minutes* • COOKING TIME: *16 minutes* •
YIELD: *4 servings*

¼ cup low-sodium nonfat chicken
   broth
½ cup chopped onion
½ cup chopped green bell pepper
1 medium stalk celery, chopped
¼ cup chopped carrot
1 clove garlic, minced
⅔ cup nonfat cottage cheese

2 cups low-sodium canned tomatoes,
   chopped, juice reserved
½ cup water
¼ teaspoon dried thyme
½ teaspoon dried oregano
½ teaspoon dried basil
¼ teaspoon ground black pepper
1 cup cooked rice

1. Heat broth in a large saucepan. Add onion, bell pepper, celery, carrot, and garlic. Sauté until onion begins to soften, about 4 minutes.

2. Combine cottage cheese, tomatoes with juice, water, thyme, oregano, basil, and black pepper in a blender or food processor and blend until smooth.
3. Stir cottage cheese mixture into vegetables, add rice, and simmer, stirring occasionally, until all ingredients are heated through, about 10 minutes.

Calories Per Serving: 110
Fat: 0 g
Cholesterol: 2 mg
Protein: 7 g

Carbohydrates: 20 g
Dietary Fiber: 1 g
Sodium: 124 mg

❋ *Tomato-Hominy Soup* ❋

PREPARATION TIME: *20 minutes* • COOKING TIME: *24 minutes* •
YIELD: *4 servings*

3¼ cups low-sodium vegetable broth
3 cloves garlic, minced
1 cup chopped onion
2 teaspoons chili powder
½ teaspoon dried oregano
½ teaspoon honey
2 tablespoons lime juice

1 jalapeño pepper, seeded and minced
½ cup canned mild green chiles, diced and drained
1 cup canned hominy, drained
2 medium tomatoes, chopped
¼ cup chopped fresh parsley
2 tablespoons chopped black olives

1. Heat ¼ cup broth in a large saucepan. Add garlic and onion, and sauté until onion begins to soften, about 3 minutes.
2. Add remaining broth, chili powder, oregano, honey, lime juice, jalapeño pepper, chiles, hominy, and tomatoes. Bring to a boil, reduce heat, cover, and simmer for 15 minutes.
3. Serve topped with parsley and olives.

Calories Per Serving: 119
Fat: 1 g
Cholesterol: 0 mg
Protein: 3 g

Carbohydrates: 25 g
Dietary Fiber: 3 g
Sodium: 388 mg

❋ *Turnip and Shiitake Mushroom Soup* ❋

PREPARATION TIME: *20 minutes* • COOKING TIME: *27 minutes* •
YIELD: *6 servings*

1 cup minced shiitake mushrooms
6 cups low-sodium nonfat chicken
  broth
2 cups diced turnips

1 cup fresh or thawed frozen corn
  kernels
¼ teaspoon ground black pepper

1. Combine mushrooms, broth, turnips, and corn in a large saucepan. Bring
   to a boil, reduce heat, cover, and simmer until turnips are just tender,
   about 20 minutes.
2. Transfer to individual bowls, sprinkle with black pepper, and serve.

Calories Per Serving: 89
Fat: 0 g
Cholesterol: 0 mg
Protein: 9 g

Carbohydrates: 15 g
Dietary Fiber: 3 g
Sodium: 199 mg

❋ *Sherried Pear and Turnip Soup* ❋

PREPARATION TIME: *20 minutes* • COOKING TIME: *31 minutes* •
YIELD: *8 servings*

¼ cup low-sodium vegetable broth
1 medium onion, chopped
3 cups diced turnips
2 tablespoons dry sherry
1 medium carrot, scraped and chopped
1 jalapeño pepper, seeded and minced

¼ teaspoon dried tarragon
½ teaspoon ground cloves
6 medium Bosc pears, peeled, cored,
  and chopped
8 cups water
1 tablespoon lemon juice

1. Heat broth in a large saucepan. Add onion and turnips, and sauté until
   onion begins to soften, about 3 minutes. Add sherry and cook for 1 more
   minute.
2. Add carrot, jalapeño pepper, tarragon, cloves, pears, and water. Bring to a
   boil, reduce heat, and simmer until vegetables are soft, about 12 minutes.
3. Puree soup in a blender or food processor and return it to the saucepan.
   Stir in lemon juice and simmer to heat through, about 5 minutes.

Calories Per Serving: 81
Fat: 1 g
Cholesterol: 0 mg
Protein: 1 g

Carbohydrates: 20 g
Dietary Fiber: 4 g
Sodium: 67 mg

❊ *Zucchini Soup* ❊

PREPARATION TIME: *15 minutes* • COOKING TIME: *18 minutes* •
YIELD: *4 servings*

2¼ cups low-sodium nonfat chicken
    broth
1 small onion, chopped
1 tablespoon seeded and minced
    jalapeño pepper
¼ teaspoon ground black pepper

2 cups chopped zucchini
1 cup fresh, drained canned, or
    thawed frozen corn kernels
1 cup skim milk
¼ cup shredded nonfat cheddar
¼ cup chopped fresh parsley

1. Heat ¼ cup broth in a large saucepan. Add onion and sauté until it begins to soften, about 3 minutes.
2. Add remaining broth, jalapeño pepper, black pepper, zucchini, and corn. Bring to a boil, reduce heat, cover, and simmer for 5 minutes. Stir in milk and simmer to heat through, about 5 minutes.
3. Serve topped with cheese and parsley.

Calories Per Serving: 99
Fat: 0
Cholesterol: 2 mg
Protein: 11 g

Carbohydrates: 15 g
Dietary Fiber: 2 g
Sodium: 215 mg

❊ *Gingered Zucchini-Tomato Soup* ❊

PREPARATION TIME: *20 minutes* • COOKING TIME: *25 minutes* •
YIELD: *4 servings*

2¾ cups low-sodium nonfat chicken
    broth
1 teaspoon grated fresh gingerroot
1 medium stalk celery, diced
6 medium tomatoes, chopped
1½ cups diced zucchini

1 medium red bell pepper, cored and
    diced
2½ cups low-sodium tomato juice
¼ teaspoon cayenne pepper
¼ cup chopped fresh parsley

1. Heat ¼ cup broth in a large saucepan. Add gingerroot, celery, tomatoes, zucchini, and bell pepper. Simmer for 10 minutes.
2. Add remaining broth and tomato juice, and simmer for 10 more minutes. Stir in cayenne pepper. Serve topped with parsley.

Calories Per Serving: 82	Carbohydrates: 18 g
Fat: 1 g	Dietary Fiber: 5 g
Cholesterol: 0 mg	Sodium: 60 mg
Protein: 4 g	

❋ *Zucchini, Potato, and Snow Pea Soup* ❋

PREPARATION TIME. *20 minutes* • COOKING TIME: *35 minutes* •
YIELD: *4 servings*

6¼ cups low-sodium vegetable broth
4 cups cubed new potatoes
¼ teaspoon dried saffron threads, crushed
1 tablespoon dried cilantro

½ teaspoon dry mustard
¼ teaspoon ground black pepper
4 cups chopped zucchini
3 cups snow peas

1. Combine broth, potatoes, saffron, cilantro, dry mustard, and black pepper in a large saucepan. Bring to a boil, reduce heat, cover, and simmer for 10 minutes.
2. Add zucchini, cover, and simmer for 15 more minutes. Add snow peas and simmer for 3 additional minutes.

Calories Per Serving: 331	Carbohydrates: 62 g
Fat: 1 g	Dietary Fiber: 8 g
Cholesterol: 0 mg	Sodium: 279 mg
Protein: 20 g	

❋ *Yellow Squash Soup* ❋

PREPARATION TIME: *10 minutes* • COOKING TIME: *20 minutes* •
YIELD: *4 servings*

4¼ cups low-sodium nonfat chicken broth
1 medium onion, chopped
2 cloves garlic, minced

3 cups sliced yellow summer squash
¼ cup nonfat plain yogurt
1½ teaspoons dried dill

1. Heat ¼ cup broth in a large saucepan. Add onion, garlic, and squash, and sauté until onion begins to soften, about 3 minutes.
2. Add remaining broth, bring to a boil, reduce heat, cover, and simmer for 10 minutes.
3. Serve topped with yogurt and dill.

Calories Per Serving: 87
Fat: 0 g
Cholesterol: 0 mg
Protein: 4 g

Carbohydrates: 19 g
Dietary Fiber: 3 g
Sodium: 52 mg

✳ *Yuca Soup* ✳

PREPARATION TIME: *20 minutes* • COOKING TIME: *38 minutes* •
YIELD: *8 servings*

¼ cup low-sodium nonfat chicken
  broth
2 medium onions, chopped
4 cloves garlic, minced
1 teaspoon minced fresh gingerroot
¼ teaspoon dried thyme
¼ teaspoon ground cumin
3 medium stalks celery, thinly sliced
1 medium carrot, scraped and diced

8 cups water
2½ cups diced yuca (also known as
  cassava) (¾-inch cubes)
1 cup chopped green beans (1-inch
  lengths)
2 medium yellow bell peppers, cored
  and diced
½ teaspoon ground white pepper
1 cup canned hominy, drained

1. Heat broth in a large pot. Add onions, garlic, and gingerroot, and sauté until onions begin to soften, about 3 minutes.
2. Stir in thyme, cumin, celery, and carrot, and sauté for 3 more minutes. Remove mixture and set aside.
3. Add water to the pot and bring to a boil. Stir in yuca and boil for 5 minutes. Stir reserved onion mixture into the pot, cover, and simmer until yuca and carrots are just soft, about 10 minutes.
4. Add remaining ingredients and simmer for 5 more minutes.

Calories Per Serving: 54
Fat: 0 g
Cholesterol: 1 mg
Protein: 2 g

Carbohydrates: 12 g
Dietary Fiber: 2 g
Sodium: 102 mg

�֎ *Cream of Tomato and Yellow Squash Soup* �֎

PREPARATION TIME: *20 minutes* • COOKING TIME: *40 minutes* •
YIELD: *6 servings*

4¼ cups low-sodium nonfat chicken
  broth
1 medium onion, minced
1 clove garlic, crushed
4 cups sliced yellow summer squash
4 medium tomatoes, chopped

1 medium red bell pepper, cored and
  chopped
1 teaspoon dried oregano
¼ teaspoon ground black pepper
½ cup nonfat plain yogurt
2 tablespoons minced fresh basil

1. Heat ¼ cup broth in a large saucepan. Add onion, garlic, and squash, and
   sauté until onion begins to soften, about 3 minutes.
2. Add tomatoes, bell pepper, oregano, and remaining broth. Bring to a boil,
   reduce heat, and simmer until vegetables are tender, about 25 minutes.
   Remove from heat and allow to cool.
3. Puree soup in a blender or food processor and return it to the saucepan.
   Stir in black pepper and yogurt, and simmer to heat through, about 5 minutes.
4. Serve in individual bowls topped with basil.

Calories Per Serving: 73
Fat: 0 g
Cholesterol: 0 mg
Protein: 8 g

Carbohydrates: 11 g
Dietary Fiber: 2 g
Sodium: 145 mg

�֎ *Spring Watercress Soup* �֎

PREPARATION TIME: *20 minutes* • COOKING TIME: *33 minutes* •
YIELD: *6 servings*

6¼ cups low-sodium nonfat chicken
  broth
3 scallions, sliced
2 cloves garlic, minced
1 cup diced turnips
1 cup diced potato
2 medium carrots, scraped and sliced
½ teaspoon dried thyme

½ cup chopped fresh parsley
2 cups chopped fresh asparagus spears
  (1-inch lengths)
1 cup fresh or thawed frozen green
  peas
2 cups watercress leaves
2 tablespoons vinegar
½ teaspoon ground black pepper

1. Heat ¼ cup broth in a large saucepan. Add scallions, garlic, turnips, potato, and carrots. Sauté until scallions begin to soften, about 5 minutes.
2. Stir in remaining broth, thyme, and parsley, and bring to a boil. Reduce heat and simmer for 15 minutes. Stir in asparagus and peas, and simmer for 5 more minutes.
3. Add watercress and puree half the soup in a blender or food processor. Return puree to the saucepan. Stir in vinegar and black pepper, simmer to heat through, and serve.

Calories Per Serving: 110   Carbohydrates: 19 g
Fat: 0 g   Dietary Fiber: 3 g
Cholesterol: 0 mg   Sodium: 330 mg
Protein: 4 g

❀ *Garden Vegetable Soup* ❀

PREPARATION TIME: *15 minutes* • COOKING TIME: *35 minutes* •
YIELD: *6 servings*

5¼ cups low-sodium nonfat chicken broth
2 medium carrots, scraped and sliced
2 medium onions, thinly sliced
4 medium tomatoes, quartered
2 medium red bell peppers, cored and diced

1 medium zucchini, diced
¼ teaspoon ground black pepper
⅛ teaspoon cayenne pepper
½ cup nonfat plain yogurt
3 tablespoons minced fresh parsley

1. Heat ¼ cup broth in a large saucepan. Add carrots and onions, cover, and cook until carrots begin to soften, about 6 minutes.
2. Add remaining broth, tomatoes, and bell peppers, and simmer for 10 minutes. Add zucchini and simmer for 10 more minutes.
3. Stir in black pepper, cayenne pepper, and yogurt, and simmer to heat through, about 3 minutes.
4. Serve topped with parsley.

Calories Per Serving: 84   Carbohydrates: 12 g
Fat: 0 g   Dietary Fiber: 3 g
Cholesterol: 0 mg   Sodium: 180 mg
Protein: 9 g

❋ *Hearty Vegetable Soup* ❋

PREPARATION TIME: *20 minutes* • COOKING TIME: *51 minutes* •
YIELD: *6 servings*

5¼ cups low-sodium nonfat chicken
   broth
2 medium onions, thinly sliced
2 medium red potatoes, diced
2 medium carrots, scraped and diced
2 medium stalks celery, diced
2 cups diced zucchini

6 medium tomatoes, diced
¼ teaspoon ground black pepper
¼ cup uncooked small elbow macaroni
4 cups julienned fresh spinach
2 teaspoons dried basil

1. Heat ¼ cup broth in a large pot. Add onions and sauté until they begin to soften, about 3 minutes.
2. Add potatoes, carrots, celery, zucchini, tomatoes, and 4 cups broth. Bring to a boil and stir in black pepper. Reduce heat and simmer until vegetables are just tender, about 30 minutes.
3. Stir macaroni into soup and simmer until macaroni is just tender, about 8 minutes. Add spinach and basil, and simmer for 3 more minutes. Stir in remaining broth to thin as necessary.

Calories Per Serving: 128
Fat: 1 g
Cholesterol: 2 mg
Protein: 7 g

Carbohydrates: 26 g
Dietary Fiber: 4 g
Sodium: 281 mg

❋ *Rotini-Vegetable Soup* ❋

PREPARATION TIME: *20 minutes* • COOKING TIME: *39 minutes* •
YIELD: *6 servings*

¼ cup low-sodium nonfat chicken
   broth
1 medium onion, chopped
1 medium carrot, scraped and
   chopped
2 medium stalks celery, chopped
2 cloves garlic, minced
1½ cups diced potatoes

2 cups low-sodium canned tomatoes,
   chopped, juice reserved
2 cups water
1 bay leaf
1 teaspoon dried thyme
½ teaspoon dried basil
¼ teaspoon ground black pepper
1½ cups cooked rotini
¼ cup chopped fresh parsley

1. Heat broth in a large saucepan. Add onion, carrot, celery, and garlic. Sauté until onion begins to soften, about 3 minutes.
2. Add potatoes, tomatoes with juice, water, bay leaf, thyme, basil, and black pepper. Bring to a boil, reduce heat, cover, and simmer until vegetables are just tender, about 25 minutes.
3. Add rotini and simmer to heat through, about 5 minutes. Remove bay leaf.
4. Serve topped with parsley.

Calories Per Serving: 119
Fat: 1 g
Cholesterol: 0 mg
Protein: 4 g

Carbohydrates: 26 g
Dietary Fiber: 3 g
Sodium: 41 mg

❋ *Creamy Vegetable Soup* ❋

PREPARATION TIME: *15 minutes* • COOKING TIME: *20 minutes* •
YIELD: *6 servings*

2 cups water
1 cup chopped green beans (1-inch lengths)
¾ cup green peas
2 cups chopped cauliflower
2 medium carrots, scraped and sliced

1 medium potato, cut into 1-inch cubes
2 cups chopped fresh spinach
2 cups skim milk
¼ teaspoon ground black pepper
¼ cup chopped fresh parsley

1. Combine water, green beans, peas, cauliflower, carrots, and potato in a large pot. Bring to a boil, reduce heat, cover, and simmer until vegetables just begin to become tender, about 10 minutes.
2. Add spinach and simmer for 1 more minute.
3. Return soup to a boil, reduce heat, and stir in milk and black pepper. Simmer until all ingredients are heated through, about 3 minutes.
4. Serve topped with parsley.

Calories Per Serving: 124
Fat: 1 g
Cholesterol: 1 mg
Protein: 8 g

Carbohydrates: 24 g
Dietary Fiber: 3 g
Sodium: 109 mg

❋ *Quick Vegetable Soup* ❋

PREPARATION TIME: *10 minutes* • COOKING TIME: *22 minutes* •
YIELD: *6 servings*

2 tablespoons low-sodium nonfat
 chicken broth
½ cup chopped onion
2 cloves garlic, minced
1 cup chopped cabbage

4 cups thawed frozen mixed vegetables
4 cups low-sodium tomato juice
1 cup water
¼ teaspoon ground black pepper

1. Heat broth in a large pot. Add onion and garlic, and sauté until onion begins to soften, about 3 minutes.
2. Stir in cabbage and sauté for 2 more minutes. Add remaining ingredients.
   Bring to a boil, reduce heat, and simmer until vegetables are just tender,
   about 10 minutes.

Calories Per Serving: 178
Fat: 2 g
Cholesterol: 0 mg
Protein: 7 g

Carbohydrates: 31 g
Dietary Fiber: 6 g
Sodium: 164 mg

COLD SOUPS

Cold Beet Soup ▪ Chilled Green Pea Soup ▪ Chilled Pumpkin
Soup ▪ Simple Gazpacho ▪ Creamy Cucumber-Tomato Soup ▪
Tomato-Spinach Soup ▪ Chunky Jalapeño–Yellow Bell Pepper
Gazpacho ▪ Sherried Red Pepper Gazpacho ▪ Pineapple-Papaya
Soup ▪ Roasted Red Pepper–Jalapeño Soup ▪ Zucchini-
Buttermilk Soup ▪ Cold Cream of Cauliflower Soup ▪
Chilled Shrimp and Horseradish Soup ▪ Spiced Mango Soup ▪
Melon Soup ▪ Blueberry Soup

❀ *Cold Beet Soup* ❀

PREPARATION TIME: *15 minutes plus 2 hours chilling time* ▪
COOKING TIME: *30 minutes* ▪ YIELD: *4 servings*

4 cups thinly sliced beets
1 medium potato, thinly sliced
2 bay leaves
4 cups water

3 tablespoons lemon juice
¼ cup sugar
1 cup nonfat plain yogurt
1 tablespoon dried dill

1. Combine beets, potato, bay leaves, and water in a large saucepan. Bring to a boil, reduce heat, cover, and simmer until beets soften, about 25 minutes.
2. Remove from heat. Discard bay leaves. Stir in lemon juice and sugar.
3. Puree soup in a blender or food processor and chill for 2 hours.
4. Divide soup among individual bowls, top with yogurt, sprinkle with dill, and serve.

Calories Per Serving: 121
Fat: 0 g
Cholesterol: 1 mg
Protein: 4 g

Carbohydrates: 27 g
Dietary Fiber: 4 g
Sodium: 116 mg

❀ *Chilled Green Pea Soup* ❀

PREPARATION TIME: *20 minutes plus 2 hours chilling time* ▪
COOKING TIME: *18 minutes* ▪ YIELD: *6 servings*

1 cup fresh or thawed frozen green
  peas
1 medium onion, sliced
2 medium carrots, scraped and sliced
1 medium potato, sliced
1 clove garlic, minced

1½ teaspoons curry powder
¼ teaspoon ground black pepper
2 cups low-sodium nonfat chicken
  broth
⅔ cup nonfat buttermilk

1. Combine peas, onion, carrots, potato, garlic, curry powder, black pepper, and 1 cup broth in a large saucepan. Bring to a boil, reduce heat, cover, and simmer until carrots are just tender, about 15 minutes.
2. Puree soup in a blender or food processor and return it to the saucepan. Whisk in remaining broth and buttermilk.
3. Chill for 2 hours before serving.

Calories Per Serving: 99   Carbohydrates: 19 g
Fat: 0 g   Dietary Fiber: 3 g
Cholesterol: 0 mg   Sodium: 83 mg
Protein: 6 g

❀ *Chilled Pumpkin Soup* ❀

PREPARATION TIME: *20 minutes plus 2 hours chilling time* ·
COOKING TIME: *35 minutes* · YIELD: *6 servings*

4½ cups low-sodium nonfat chicken   ¼ teaspoon ground nutmeg
   broth   ¼ cup chopped fresh parsley
1 medium onion, sliced   2 cups skim milk
2 cups pumpkin puree   ¼ teaspoon ground black pepper
1 bay leaf   ½ cup nonfat plain yogurt
½ teaspoon ground ginger   ¼ cup minced scallions
½ teaspoon curry powder

1. Heat ¼ cup broth in a large saucepan. Add onion and sauté for 3 minutes.
2. Stir in pumpkin, remaining broth, bay leaf, ginger, curry powder, nutmeg, and parsley. Bring to a boil, reduce heat, and simmer for 15 minutes.
3. Remove bay leaf. Puree soup in a blender or food processor and return it to the saucepan. Stir in milk and black pepper, and simmer to heat through, about 10 minutes.
4. Chill for two hours, and serve topped with yogurt and scallions.

Calories Per Serving: 103   Carbohydrates: 15 g
Fat: 1 g   Dietary Fiber: 3 g
Cholesterol: 2 mg   Sodium: 190 mg
Protein: 11 g

❀ *Simple Gazpacho* ❀

PREPARATION TIME: *20 minutes plus 3 hours chilling time* · YIELD: *8 servings*

5 medium tomatoes, finely diced
½ cup finely diced cucumber
1 medium green bell pepper, cored
   and minced
2 scallions, minced

½ cup chopped fresh parsley
¼ cup lime juice
4 teaspoons sugar
⅛ teaspoon cayenne pepper
2 cups low-sodium tomato juice

1. Combine tomatoes, cucumber, bell pepper, scallions, and parsley in a large bowl.
2. Combine lime juice, sugar, cayenne pepper, and tomato juice, and mix well into vegetables. Cover and chill for 3 hours.

Calories Per Serving: 42
Fat: 0 g
Cholesterol: 0 mg
Protein: 1 g

Carbohydrates: 10 g
Dietary Fiber: 2 g
Sodium: 15 mg

❋ Creamy Cucumber-Tomato Soup ❋

PREPARATION TIME: *10 minutes plus 2 hours chilling time*   •   YIELD: *8 servings*

1 medium cucumber, peeled and
   thinly sliced
3 medium tomatoes, chopped
3 cups nonfat plain yogurt

1 cup skim milk
1 tablespoon dried dill
2 cloves garlic, minced

Combine cucumber slices and tomatoes. Stir in yogurt, milk, dill, and garlic. Cover and chill for 2 hours.

Calories Per Serving: 97
Fat: 0 g
Cholesterol: 3 mg
Protein: 9 g

Carbohydrates: 16 g
Dietary Fiber: 1 g
Sodium: 109 mg

❋ Tomato-Spinach Soup ❋

PREPARATION TIME: *20 minutes plus 2 hours chilling time*   •
COOKING TIME: *23 minutes*   •   YIELD: *4 servings*

2 tablespoons low-sodium vegetable
   broth
2 cloves garlic, minced
4 medium tomatoes, diced
1 tablespoon low-sodium tomato
   paste
¼ cup dry red wine
½ teaspoon dried oregano

2 teaspoons minced scallions
1 teaspoon sugar
¼ teaspoon ground black pepper
1 cup thawed frozen chopped spinach
1 teaspoon dried basil
⅛ teaspoon ground nutmeg
½ cup nonfat plain yogurt
½ cup skim milk

1. Heat broth in a large saucepan. Add garlic and sauté for 1 minute. Mix in tomatoes, tomato paste, and wine, and simmer, stirring occasionally, until tomatoes cook down, about 20 minutes.
2. Puree soup in a blender or food processor and return it to the saucepan. Stir in oregano, scallions, sugar, and black pepper. Transfer to a covered glass bowl and chill for 2 hours.
3. Puree spinach, basil, nutmeg, yogurt, and milk in the blender or food processor. Transfer to a separate glass bowl and chill for 2 hours.
4. Blend tomato mixture and spinach soup, and serve.

Calories Per Serving: 79
Fat: 1 g
Cholesterol: 1 mg
Protein: 7 g

Carbohydrates: 13 g
Dietary Fiber: 3 g
Sodium: 107 mg

✳ *Chunky Jalapeño–Yellow* ✳ *Bell Pepper Gazpacho*

PREPARATION TIME: *20 minutes* • YIELD: *4 servings*

2 medium onions, minced
1 medium cucumber, peeled and
   minced
2 medium yellow bell peppers, cored
   and minced
6 small tomatoes, finely chopped

2 cloves garlic, minced
1 jalapeño pepper, seeded and
   chopped
2 cups low-sodium tomato juice
2 teaspoons olive oil
¼ teaspoon ground black pepper

1. In a large bowl, combine onions, cucumber, bell peppers, and half the tomatoes.
2. Puree all remaining ingredients in a blender or food processor.
3. Stir puree into vegetables and mix well before serving.

Calories Per Serving: 119
Fat: 3 g
Cholesterol: 0 mg
Protein: 4 g

Carbohydrates: 23 g
Dietary Fiber: 5 g
Sodium: 136 mg

❈ *Sherried Red Pepper Gazpacho* ❈

PREPARATION TIME: *15 minutes plus 2 hours chilling time* ∙ YIELD: *6 servings*

8 medium tomatoes, chopped
2 medium red bell peppers, cored and
    chopped
½ cucumber, peeled and chopped

2 cloves garlic, chopped
⅓ cup dry sherry
½ teaspoon ground black pepper
2 tablespoons minced red onion

1. Combine tomatoes, bell peppers, cucumber, garlic, sherry, and black pepper in a blender or food processor and pulse briefly to reach the desired consistency. Transfer to a bowl, cover, and chill for 2 hours.
2. Divide soup among individual bowls, top with minced red onion, and serve.

Calories Per Serving: 86
Fat: 1 g
Cholesterol: 0 mg
Protein: 3 g

Carbohydrates: 19 g
Dietary Fiber: 3 g
Sodium: 73 mg

❈ *Pineapple-Papaya Soup* ❈

PREPARATION TIME: *15 minutes plus 3 hours chilling time* ∙ YIELD: *6 servings*

2 cups pineapple juice
2 cups low-sodium tomato juice
1 medium papaya, peeled, seeded,
    and chopped
¾ cup fresh or juice-packed canned
    pineapple chunks, drained
1 medium green bell pepper, cored
    and chopped

1 medium red bell pepper, cored and
    chopped
½ jalapeño pepper, seeded and minced
3 tablespoons lime juice
1 tablespoon dried cilantro
¼ teaspoon ground black pepper

1. Puree all ingredients in a blender or food processor to the desired consistency.
2. Transfer to a large bowl, cover, and chill for 3 hours.

Calories Per Serving: 83
Fat: 0 g
Cholesterol: 0 mg
Protein: 1 g

Carbohydrates: 21 g
Dietary Fiber: 2 g
Sodium: 45 mg

❋ *Roasted Red Pepper–Jalapeño Soup* ❋

PREPARATION TIME: *10 minutes plus 2 hours chilling time* • YIELD: *4 servings*

*2 medium tomatoes, cored and
    chopped*
*1 7-ounce jar roasted red peppers,
    drained and chopped*
2 cloves garlic, minced

1 jalapeño pepper, seeded and minced
¼ cup minced onion
2 teaspoons olive oil
1 cup water
2 tablespoons chopped fresh parsley

1. Combine tomatoes, roasted peppers, garlic, jalapeño pepper, onion, olive oil, and water. Cover and chill for 2 hours.
2. Serve topped with parsley.

Calories Per Serving: 62
Fat: 2 g
Cholesterol: 0 mg
Protein: 1 g

Carbohydrates: 11 g
Dietary Fiber: 1 g
Sodium: 206 mg

❋ *Zucchini-Buttermilk Soup* ❋

PREPARATION TIME: *15 minutes plus 2 hours chilling time* • YIELD: *4 servings*

3 cups nonfat buttermilk
1 cup finely chopped zucchini
1 jalapeño pepper, seeded and minced
3 medium tomatoes, diced
½ cup diced cucumber

*1 medium red bell pepper, cored and
    diced*
¼ teaspoon ground black pepper
¼ teaspoon paprika
2 tablespoons minced fresh parsley

1. Combine buttermilk, zucchini, jalapeño pepper, tomatoes, cucumber, bell pepper, and black pepper in a large bowl. Cover and chill for 2 hours.
2. Serve topped with paprika and parsley.

Calories Per Serving: 117	Carbohydrates: 20 g
Fat: 1 g	Dietary Fiber: 2 g
Cholesterol: 3 mg	Sodium: 209 mg
Protein: 9 g	

❋ Cold Cream of Cauliflower Soup ❋

PREPARATION TIME: *20 minutes plus 3 hours chilling time*　•
COOKING TIME: *30 minutes*　•　YIELD: *6 servings*

*3¼ cups low-sodium nonfat chicken
　broth*
*4 medium leeks (white parts only),
　chopped*
1 medium onion, chopped

6 cups chopped cauliflower
¼ teaspoon ground black pepper
1 cup skim milk
1½ cups evaporated skim milk
¼ cup chopped fresh parsley

1. Heat ¼ cup broth in a large saucepan. Add leeks and onion, and sauté until onion begins to soften, about 3 minutes.
2. Add remaining broth, cauliflower, and black pepper. Bring to a boil, reduce heat, cover, and simmer until cauliflower is tender, about 15 minutes.
3. Puree soup in a blender or food processor and return it to the saucepan. Stir in skim milk and evaporated milk, and bring to a simmer. Remove from heat, cool, cover, and chill for 3 hours.
4. Serve topped with parsley.

Calories Per Serving: 162	Carbohydrates: 27 g
Fat: 1 g	Dietary Fiber: 2 g
Cholesterol: 3 mg	Sodium: 234 mg
Protein: 13 g	

❋ Chilled Shrimp and Horseradish Soup ❋

PREPARATION TIME: *20 minutes plus 3 hours chilling time*　•　YIELD: *4 servings*

2 cups low-sodium tomato juice
1 teaspoon olive oil
1 teaspoon prepared horseradish
½ teaspoon chili powder
¼ teaspoon dried thyme
¼ teaspoon cayenne pepper
2 medium tomatoes, finely chopped

*1 medium cucumber, peeled and
　finely chopped*
*1 medium green bell pepper, cored
　and minced*
2 scallions, finely chopped
2 cloves garlic, minced
1 cup chopped cooked shrimp
2 tablespoons minced fresh parsley

1. Combine tomato juice and olive oil in a large bowl. Stir in horseradish, chili powder, thyme, and cayenne pepper.
2. Add tomatoes, cucumber, bell pepper, scallions, and garlic, and mix well. Stir in shrimp, cover, and chill for 3 hours.
3. Serve topped with parsley.

Calories Per Serving: 94	Carbohydrates: 12 g
Fat: 2 g	Dietary Fiber: 3 g
Cholesterol: 63 mg	Sodium: 109 mg
Protein: 9 g	

❋ *Spiced Mango Soup* ❋

PREPARATION TIME: *15 minutes plus 2 hours chilling time* • YIELD: *4 servings*

2 medium mangoes, peeled, cored, and cut into chunks
½ cup nonfat plain yogurt
1 small jalapeño pepper, seeded and minced

3 tablespoons lime juice
2 tablespoons honey
¾ cup chilled sugar-free ginger ale
¼ cup apple juice

1. Puree mangoes, yogurt, jalapeño pepper, lime juice, and honey in a blender or food processor.
2. Transfer to a bowl, stir in ginger ale and apple juice, cover, and chill for 2 hours.

Calories Per Serving: 175	Carbohydrates: 45 g
Fat: 1 g	Dietary Fiber: 3 g
Cholesterol: 0 mg	Sodium: 147 mg
Protein: 1 g	

❋ *Melon Soup* ❋

PREPARATION TIME: *25 minutes plus 4 hours chilling time* • YIELD: *4 servings*

4 cups chopped cantaloupe
4 cups chopped honeydew melon
⅛ teaspoon cayenne pepper

½ teaspoon ground cinnamon
1 tablespoon sugar
2 tablespoons lime juice

1. Puree melon chunks, cayenne pepper, cinnamon, and sugar in a food processor or blender until smooth.

2. Place melon puree in a covered bowl and chill for 4 hours. Stir in lime juice, transfer soup to individual bowls, and serve.

Calories Per Serving: 127
Fat: 1 g
Cholesterol: 0 mg
Protein: 3 g

Carbohydrates: 31 g
Dietary Fiber: 2 g
Sodium: 29 mg

❆ *Blueberry Soup* ❆

PREPARATION TIME: *10 minutes plus 20 minutes cooling time and 2 hours chilling time* • COOKING TIME: *12 minutes* • YIELD: *3 servings*

3½ cups blueberries
2 tablespoons lemon juice
1 stick cinnamon
3 cups water

1½ tablespoons cornstarch
⅓ cup sugar
½ cup red wine
⅓ cup nonfat plain yogurt

1. Combine blueberries, lemon juice, cinnamon stick, and water in a saucepan. Simmer for 10 minutes.
2. In a separate bowl, mix 3 tablespoons soup with cornstarch and stir vigorously. Stir cornstarch mixture into soup. Add sugar and wine, and bring to a boil. Reduce heat and simmer, stirring constantly, until soup becomes clear, about 2 minutes. Remove cinnamon stick.
3. Allow soup to cool, then chill for 2 hours. Transfer to individual bowls, top with yogurt, and serve.

Calories Per Serving: 525
Fat: 1 g
Cholesterol: 1 mg
Protein: 3 g

Carbohydrates: 131 g
Dietary Fiber: 5 g
Sodium: 39 mg

SALADS

Shrimp-Asparagus Salad • Artichoke-Chicken Salad • Chicken
Salad with Bean Sprouts and Mushrooms • Chicken, Black Bean,
and Bell Pepper Salad • Chicken Salad with Broccoli, Orzo, and
Artichokes • Chicken-Cauliflower Salad • Chicken, Snow Pea,
and Spinach Salad • Chicken and Corn Salad • Fruited Chicken
Salad • Chicken and Papaya Salad • Chicken and Red
Pepper Salad • Tangy Chicken Salad with Scallion Dressing •
Pineapple-Chicken Salad • Polynesian Chicken Salad •
Moroccan Chicken Salad with Zucchini • Balsamic Zucchini-
Chicken Salad • Warm Vegetable Salad • Whole Supper
Vegetable-Chicken Salad • Tropical Crab Salad • Shrimp-
Vegetable Salad • Shrimp Salad Orientale • Pineapple-Shrimp
Salad • Chesapeake Bay Shrimp and Crab Salad • Crab-Broccoli
Salad with Pasta Shells and Citrus Dressing • Southwestern Fish
Salad • Tuna and Spinach Salad with Cannellini Beans • Tuna-
Macaroni Salad with Orange • Ocean City Tuna-Pasta Salad •
Apple-Pineapple-Pepper Salad • Pasta Salad with Broccoli, Bell
Pepper, and Zucchini • Peasant Pasta Salad • San Juan Fruited

Rice Salad • Rice and Vegetable Salad with Yogurt-Lemon
Dressing • Black Bean and Corn Salad • Lentil-Tomato Salad •
Easy Broccoli-Stuffed Tomatoes • Spinach-Lime Salad • Garden
Vegetable Salad with Pasta Shells • Pineapple-Carrot Salad with
Cinnamon Yogurt • Hearty Steamer Salad

❊ *Shrimp-Asparagus Salad* ❊

PREPARATION TIME: *20 minutes* • YIELD: *6 servings*

*2 cups chopped fresh asparagus spears
(1-inch lengths)*
1 medium onion, sliced
2 cups diced zucchini
1 medium cucumber, peeled and sliced
*1 medium green bell pepper, cored
and cut into thin strips*
1 cup chopped fresh parsley
*2 cups fresh medium shrimp, cooked,
peeled, deveined, and halved
lengthwise*
¾ cup orange juice
1 teaspoon prepared horseradish
½ teaspoon ground black pepper

1. In a large bowl, combine asparagus, onion, zucchini, cucumber, bell pepper, parsley, and shrimp.
2. In a separate bowl, mix orange juice, horseradish, and black pepper, and pour over salad. Toss well and serve.

Calories Per Serving: 101
Fat: 1 g
Cholesterol: 83 mg
Protein: 12 g

Carbohydrates: 13 g
Dietary Fiber: 1 g
Sodium: 143 mg

❊ *Artichoke-Chicken Salad* ❊

PREPARATION TIME: *15 minutes plus 2 hours chilling time* • YIELD: *6 servings*

3 cups cooked rice
*2 skinless boneless chicken breast ten-
derloins, about 4 ounces each,
cooked and chopped*
*1 medium green bell pepper, cored
and chopped*
*1 medium red bell pepper, cored and
chopped*
3 medium tomatoes, chopped
*1 cup water-packed canned artichoke
hearts, drained and chopped*
1 tablespoon olive oil
2½ tablespoons white wine vinegar
½ teaspoon ground black pepper
4 scallions, sliced
2 tablespoons minced pimientos

1. Combine rice, chicken, bell peppers, tomatoes, and artichoke hearts in a large bowl.
2. In a separate bowl, mix olive oil, vinegar, and black pepper, and pour over salad. Toss well and chill for 2 hours.
3. Serve topped with scallions and pimientos.

Calories Per Serving: 219
Fat: 3 g
Cholesterol: 23 mg
Protein: 13 g

Carbohydrates: 35 g
Dietary Fiber: 3 g
Sodium: 51 mg

❊ Chicken Salad with Bean Sprouts ❊ and Mushrooms

PREPARATION TIME: *15 minutes plus 1 hour chilling time* • YIELD: *4 servings*

6 cups shredded fresh spinach
2 cups bean sprouts
1½ cups sliced mushrooms
2 skinless boneless chicken breast ten-
    derloins, about 4 ounces each,
    cooked and chopped
1 cup sliced, canned water chestnuts,
    drained

4 scallions, sliced
6 tablespoons rice vinegar
¼ teaspoon ground black pepper
2 teaspoons reduced-sodium soy
    sauce
2 cloves garlic, minced

1. Combine spinach, bean sprouts, mushrooms, chicken, water chestnuts, and scallions in a large bowl.
2. In a separate bowl, mix vinegar, black pepper, soy sauce, and garlic. Pour dressing over salad and toss to coat all ingredients. Chill for 1 hour before serving.

Calories Per Serving: 127
Fat: 1 g
Cholesterol: 35 mg
Protein: 19 g

Carbohydrates: 14 g
Dietary Fiber: 3 g
Sodium: 185 mg

❊ Chicken, Black Bean, and Bell Pepper Salad ❊

PREPARATION TIME: *15 minutes plus 2 hours chilling time* • YIELD: *6 servings*

3 cups low-sodium canned black
    beans, rinsed and drained
2 medium green bell peppers, cored
    and chopped

1 medium red bell pepper, cored and
    chopped
1 medium red onion, chopped
¼ cup chopped fresh parsley

2 skinless boneless chicken breast tenderloins, about 4 ounces each,
   cooked and chopped
6 tablespoons rice vinegar

2 cloves garlic, minced
¼ teaspoon cayenne pepper
¼ teaspoon ground black pepper

1. Combine beans, bell peppers, onion, parsley, and chicken in a large bowl.
2. In a separate bowl, whisk together vinegar, garlic, cayenne pepper, and black pepper. Pour dressing over salad and toss to coat all ingredients.
3. Chill for 2 hours before serving.

Calories Per Serving: 192
Fat: 1 g
Cholesterol: 33 mg
Protein: 15 g

Carbohydrates: 27 g
Dietary Fiber: 3 g
Sodium: 28 mg

❊ Chicken Salad with Broccoli, Orzo, ❊ and Artichokes

PREPARATION TIME: *20 minutes* • COOKING TIME: *19 minutes* •
YIELD: *4 servings*

2 quarts water
1 cup uncooked orzo
4 cups chopped broccoli
½ cup water-packed canned artichoke
   hearts, drained and chopped
2 medium tomatoes, chopped
2 scallions, sliced

1 teaspoon olive oil
¼ cup red wine vinegar
2 cloves garlic, minced
¼ teaspoon ground black pepper
1 cup chopped cooked chicken breast
6 cups chopped fresh spinach

1. Bring water to a boil in a large saucepan. Add orzo and cook for 6 minutes. Stir in broccoli and simmer until broccoli is just tender, about 4 more minutes. Drain well and transfer to a large bowl.
2. Add artichoke hearts, tomatoes, scallions, olive oil, vinegar, garlic, black pepper, and chicken to the bowl. Add spinach, toss, and serve.

Calories Per Serving: 239
Fat: 3 g
Cholesterol: 35 mg
Protein: 23 g

Carbohydrates: 34 g
Dietary Fiber: 7 g
Sodium: 141 mg

❊ *Chicken-Cauliflower Salad* ❊

PREPARATION TIME: *20 minutes* ⋅ YIELD: *4 servings*

2 cups chopped cauliflower
1 medium red bell pepper, cored and
    chopped
1 cup diced zucchini
4 scallions, sliced
2 cups juice-packed canned pineapple
    chunks, juice reserved

1 cup chopped cooked chicken breast
2 tablespoons wine vinegar
1 teaspoon olive oil
¼ teaspoon ground black pepper
8 large spinach leaves

1. Combine cauliflower, bell pepper, zucchini, scallions, pineapple chunks, and chicken in a large bowl.
2. In a separate bowl, whisk together reserved pineapple juice, vinegar, olive oil, and black pepper, and pour over salad.
3. Serve salad over spinach on individual plates.

Calories Per Serving: 161
Fat: 2 g
Cholesterol: 26 mg
Protein: 13 g

Carbohydrates: 26 g
Dietary Fiber: 3 g
Sodium: 72 mg

❊ *Chicken, Snow Pea, and Spinach Salad* ❊

PREPARATION TIME: *15 minutes plus 2 hours chilling time* ⋅
COOKING TIME: *2 minutes* ⋅ YIELD: *4 servings*

6 cups water
3 cups snow peas
2 medium red bell peppers, cored and
    chopped
2 skinless boneless chicken breast ten-
    derloins, about 4 ounces each,
    cooked and chopped

5 cups torn spinach leaves
3 cloves garlic, minced
3 tablespoons balsamic vinegar
1 teaspoon sesame oil
2 tablespoons lemon juice
¼ teaspoon ground black pepper

1. Bring water to a boil in a large saucepan. Add snow peas and sauté until they are just tender, about 2 minutes. Rinse immediately in cold water.
2. Combine bell peppers, chicken, and spinach in a large bowl.
3. In a separate bowl, whisk together remaining ingredients and drizzle over salad. Chill for 2 hours before serving.

Calories Per Serving: 141
Fat: 2 g
Cholesterol: 35 mg
Protein: 19 g

Carbohydrates: 14 g
Dietary Fiber: 6 g
Sodium: 94 mg

❈ *Chicken and Corn Salad* ❈

PREPARATION TIME: *15 minutes plus 1 hour chilling time* • YIELD: *4 servings*

1 cup nonfat plain yogurt
1 tablespoon curry powder
2 tablespoons dry white wine
¼ teaspoon ground black pepper
2 skinless boneless chicken breast ten-
  derloins, about 4 ounces each,
  cooked and shredded

2 cups corn kernels
1 medium green bell pepper, cored
  and chopped
2 medium tomatoes, chopped
2 scallions, sliced
6 cups shredded fresh spinach

1. Combine yogurt, curry powder, wine, and black pepper in a large bowl. Mix well.
2. Stir in chicken, corn, bell pepper, tomatoes, and scallions. Chill for 1 hour.
3. Serve salad over spinach on individual plates.

Calories Per Serving: 221
Fat: 1 g
Cholesterol: 36 mg
Protein: 23 g

Carbohydrates: 35 g
Dietary Fiber: 6 g
Sodium: 145 mg

❈ *Fruited Chicken Salad* ❈

PREPARATION TIME: *20 minutes* • YIELD: *6 servings*

2 cups diced zucchini
2 medium apples, peeled, cored, and
  chopped
1 cup juice-packed canned pineapple
  chunks, drained
2 medium carrots, scraped and grated
1 medium green bell pepper, cored
  and cut into thin strips

1 medium onion, sliced
3 skinless boneless chicken breast ten-
  derloins, about 4 ounces each,
  cooked and chopped
½ cup chopped fresh parsley
¾ cup pineapple juice
1 teaspoon Dijon mustard
½ teaspoon ground black pepper

1. Combine zucchini, apples, pineapple chunks, carrots, bell pepper, onion, chicken, and parsley in a large bowl.
2. Mix remaining ingredients in a separate bowl. Toss well with salad and serve.

Calories Per Serving: 142   Carbohydrates: 26 g
Fat: 1 g   Dietary Fiber: 3 g
Cholesterol: 23 mg   Sodium: 50 mg
Protein: 11 g

❋ Chicken and Papaya Salad ❋

PREPARATION TIME: *15 minutes* • YIELD: *3 servings*

1 medium papaya, peeled, cored, and cubed
1 medium carrot, scraped and shredded
1 medium green bell pepper, cored and chopped
1 cup diced zucchini
¼ cup chopped red onion

1 cup chopped cooked chicken breast
¾ teaspoon dried basil
2 tablespoons wine vinegar
1 teaspoon olive oil
3 tablespoons lemon juice
⅛ teaspoon cayenne pepper
6 large spinach leaves

1. Combine papaya, carrot, bell pepper, zucchini, onion, and chicken in a large bowl.
2. In a separate bowl, mix together basil, vinegar, olive oil, lemon juice, and cayenne pepper, and pour over salad.
3. On individual plates, top spinach leaves with salad and serve.

Calories Per Serving: 201   Carbohydrates: 30 g
Fat: 3 g   Dietary Fiber: 6 g
Cholesterol: 35 mg   Sodium: 102 mg
Protein: 17 g

❋ Chicken and Red Pepper Salad ❋

PREPARATION TIME: *15 minutes* • YIELD: *4 servings*

6 tablespoons dry red wine

1 cup canned roasted red bell peppers, chopped, 3 tablespoons liquid reserved

½ teaspoon sugar

1 teaspoon dried basil

¼ teaspoon ground black pepper

2 skinless boneless chicken breast tenderloins, about 4 ounces each, cooked and shredded

3 ripe olives, sliced

6 cups shredded fresh spinach

1. In a large bowl, whisk together wine, roasted pepper liquid, sugar, basil, and black pepper.
2. Stir in chicken, roasted peppers, and olives. Toss to coat all ingredients.
3. Serve salad over spinach on individual plates.

Calories Per Serving: 123
Fat: 1 g
Cholesterol: 35 mg
Protein: 17 g

Carbohydrates: 13 g
Dietary Fiber: 4 g
Sodium: 148 mg

❀ *Tangy Chicken Salad with Scallion Dressing* ❀

PREPARATION TIME: *20 minutes* • YIELD: *6 servings*

3 skinless boneless chicken breast tenderloins, about 4 ounces each, cooked and chopped

2 cups sliced canned water chestnuts, drained

1 cup juice-packed canned pineapple chunks, drained

3 medium stalks celery, sliced

1 medium carrot, scraped and shredded

1 medium onion, chopped

1 medium green bell pepper, cored and cut into thin strips

2 cups nonfat plain yogurt

2 tablespoons dry white wine

2 cloves garlic, minced

1 scallion, minced

2 tablespoons lemon juice

¼ teaspoon ground black pepper

½ teaspoon curry powder

12 large lettuce leaves

1 cup sliced cucumber

1. Combine chicken, water chestnuts, pineapple chunks, celery, carrot, onion, and bell pepper in a large bowl.
2. In a separate bowl, mix together yogurt, wine, garlic, scallion, lemon juice, black pepper, and curry powder, and dress salad.
3. Serve salad over lettuce on individual plates, and top with cucumber slices.

Calories Per Serving: 176
Fat: 1 g
Cholesterol: 37 mg
Protein: 19 g

Carbohydrates: 24 g
Dietary Fiber: 2 g
Sodium: 99 mg

�֎ *Pineapple-Chicken Salad* �֎

PREPARATION TIME: *15 minutes* • YIELD: *4 servings*

2 scallions, sliced
1 cup juice-packed canned pineapple
　chunks, drained
1 cup sliced mushrooms
1 medium green bell pepper, cored
　and cut into thin strips
1 medium carrot, scraped and grated
1 cup diced zucchini

1 cup cubed, cooked chicken breast
8 large romaine lettuce leaves
1 medium tomato, cut into thin
　wedges
3 tablespoons lime juice
½ cup pineapple juice
¼ teaspoon ground black pepper

1. Combine scallions, pineapple chunks, mushrooms, bell pepper, carrot, zucchini, and chicken in a large bowl.
2. On individual plates, top two lettuce leaves with salad and tomato wedges.
3. In a separate bowl, combine lime juice, pineapple juice, and black pepper. Pour over salads and serve.

Calories Per Serving: 145
Fat: 1 g
Cholesterol: 26 mg
Protein: 13 g

Carbohydrates: 24 g
Dietary Fiber: 4 g
Sodium: 35 mg

✖ *Polynesian Chicken Salad* ✖

PREPARATION TIME: *15 minutes* • YIELD: *4 servings*

2 cups cooked rice
1 medium green bell pepper, cored
　and cut into thin strips
1 medium red bell pepper, cored and
　cut into thin strips

1 medium yellow bell pepper, cored
　and cut into thin strips
1 cup chopped fresh asparagus spears
　(1-inch lengths)
2 cups diced cooked chicken breast

3 scallions, sliced
1 cup sliced celery
¼ cup orange juice

2 teaspoons reduced-sodium soy
  sauce
1 tablespoon rice vinegar
¼ teaspoon ground black pepper

1. Combine rice, bell peppers, asparagus, chicken, scallions, and celery in a large bowl.
2. In a separate bowl, whisk together orange juice, soy sauce, vinegar, and black pepper. Toss well with salad and serve.

Calories Per Serving: 249
Fat: 1 g
Cholesterol: 53 mg
Protein: 24 g

Carbohydrates: 35 g
Dietary Fiber: 2 g
Sodium: 151 mg

❋ Moroccan Chicken Salad with Zucchini ❋

PREPARATION TIME: *25 minutes plus 1 hour chilling time* • YIELD: *6 servings*

3 cups shredded cooked chicken
  breast
1 medium red bell pepper, cored and
  cut into thin strips
1 medium green bell pepper, cored
  and cut into thin strips
2 cups diced zucchini
1 medium onion, sliced
1 tablespoon ground cumin
½ teaspoon cayenne pepper
1 teaspoon paprika

4 cloves garlic, minced
¼ cup lemon juice
¼ cup red wine vinegar
1 cup low-sodium nonfat chicken
  broth
1½ teaspoons olive oil
2 tablespoons dried cilantro
½ cup minced fresh parsley
½ cup ground black pepper
¼ cup sliced green olives

1. Combine chicken, bell peppers, zucchini, and onion in a large bowl. Cover and chill for 1 hour.
2. In a separate bowl, whisk together cumin, cayenne pepper, paprika, garlic, lemon juice, vinegar, broth, and olive oil, and pour over salad. Add cilantro and parsley, and toss well.
3. Sprinkle with black pepper and serve topped with olives.

Calories Per Serving: 115
Fat: 3 g
Cholesterol: 35 mg
Protein: 15 g

Carbohydrates: 8 g
Dietary Fiber: 1 g
Sodium: 228 mg

❋ *Balsamic Zucchini-Chicken Salad* ❋

Preparation Time: *15 minutes plus 2 hours chilling time* ▪ Yield: *6 servings*

6 cups chopped zucchini
4 medium tomatoes, chopped
1 medium carrot, scraped and thinly sliced
1 medium green bell pepper, cored and chopped
1 medium yellow bell pepper, cored and chopped
2 skinless boneless chicken breast tenderloins, about 4 ounces each, cooked and chopped
1 tablespoon olive oil
¼ cup lemon juice
¼ cup balsamic vinegar
1 teaspoon dried basil
1 teaspoon dried oregano
½ teaspoon ground black pepper
2 cloves garlic, minced

1. Combine zucchini, tomatoes, carrot, bell peppers, and chicken in a large bowl.
2. In a separate bowl, whisk together olive oil, lemon juice, vinegar, basil, oregano, black pepper, and garlic.
3. Toss dressing with salad and chill for 2 hours before serving.

Calories Per Serving: 114
Fat: 3 g
Cholesterol: 23 mg
Protein: 12 g
Carbohydrates: 13 g
Dietary Fiber: 3 g
Sodium: 32 mg

❋ *Warm Vegetable Salad* ❋

Preparation Time: *15 minutes* ▪ Cooking Time: *36 minutes* ▪
Yield: *4 servings*

¼ cup low-sodium nonfat chicken broth
1 cup uncooked white rice
2 cups water
2 cups fresh or thawed frozen corn kernels
1 medium carrot, scraped and sliced
½ cup fresh or thawed frozen green peas
1 medium green bell pepper, cored and chopped
1 medium red bell pepper, cored and chopped
3 scallions, sliced
⅓ cup red wine vinegar
2 cloves garlic, minced
¼ teaspoon ground black pepper
6 cups chopped fresh spinach

1. Heat broth in a large saucepan. Add rice and sauté for 5 minutes. Stir in water, bring to a boil, reduce heat, cover, and simmer for 15 minutes.
2. Add corn, carrot, peas, and bell peppers. Return to a boil, reduce heat, cover, and simmer until rice and vegetables are just tender, about 10 minutes.
3. Stir in scallions, vinegar, garlic, and black pepper.
4. Serve over spinach on individual plates.

Calories Per Serving: 305   Carbohydrates: 68 g
Fat: 1 g   Dietary Fiber: 6 g
Cholesterol: 0 mg   Sodium: 106 mg
Protein: 10 g

❊ *Whole Supper Vegetable-Chicken Salad* ❊

PREPARATION TIME: *20 minutes* • YIELD: *6 servings*

2 cups chopped broccoli
2 cups chopped cauliflower
2 cups diced zucchini
1 medium stalk celery, sliced
1 medium carrot, scraped and grated
1 medium onion, sliced
1 cup chopped fresh parsley

3 skinless boneless chicken breast tenderloins, about 4 ounces each, cooked and chopped
¼ cup shredded nonfat cheddar
¾ cup orange juice
1 teaspoon Dijon mustard
½ teaspoon ground black pepper

1. Combine broccoli, cauliflower, zucchini, celery, carrot, onion, parsley, chicken, and cheddar in a large bowl.
2. In a separate bowl, mix orange juice, mustard, and black pepper. Toss well with salad and serve.

Calories Per Serving: 96   Carbohydrates: 9 g
Fat: 1 g   Dietary Fiber: 2 g
Cholesterol: 25 mg   Sodium: 139 mg
Protein: 15 g

❊ *Tropical Crab Salad* ❊

PREPARATION TIME: *15 minutes plus 1 hour chilling time* • YIELD: *4 servings*

3 medium papayas, peeled, cored, and cut into 1-inch cubes
1½ cups fresh cooked or shredded canned crabmeat
3 scallions, sliced
¼ cup seedless raisins
¾ cup nonfat plain yogurt
1½ teaspoons curry powder
1 tablespoon lime juice
8 large lettuce leaves
¼ teaspoon ground black pepper

1. Combine papayas, crabmeat, scallions, raisins, yogurt, curry powder, and lime juice in a large bowl. Toss gently and chill for 1 hour.
2. Serve salad over lettuce leaves on individual plates, sprinkled with black pepper.

Calories Per Serving: 268
Fat: 1 g
Cholesterol: 46 mg
Protein: 15 g

Carbohydrates: 49 g
Dietary Fiber: 7 g
Sodium: 225 mg

✳ Shrimp-Vegetable Salad ✳

PREPARATION TIME: 15 minutes • COOKING TIME: 4 minutes •
YIELD: 4 servings

1 medium green bell pepper, cored and finely chopped
1 medium yellow bell pepper, cored and finely chopped
1 medium carrot, scraped and grated
¼ cup thinly sliced red onion
1 medium stalk celery, sliced
½ pound fresh medium shrimp, cooked, peeled, and deveined
3 tablespoons lime juice
2 tablespoons vinegar
½ teaspoon dried thyme
½ teaspoon dried basil
1 jalapeño pepper, seeded and minced
8 large romaine lettuce leaves
1 medium tomato, cut into thin wedges
2 scallions, sliced
¼ cup chopped fresh parsley
¼ teaspoon ground black pepper

1. Combine bell peppers, carrot, onion, celery, and shrimp in a large bowl.
2. In a separate bowl, mix lime juice, vinegar, thyme, basil, and jalapeño pepper, and dress salad.
3. Serve salad over lettuce and tomato on individual plates, garnished with scallions and parsley and sprinkled with black pepper.

Calories Per Serving: 111
Fat: 1 g
Cholesterol: 86 mg
Protein: 14 g

Carbohydrates: 12 g
Dietary Fiber: 3 g
Sodium: 214 mg

❊ *Shrimp Salad Orientale* ❊

PREPARATION TIME: *20 minutes* • YIELD: *6 servings*

¼ cup lemon juice
2 teaspoons chili powder
¼ cup low-sodium nonfat chicken
   broth
1 teaspoon sugar
1 teaspoon ground coriander
1 tablespoon oyster sauce

1 pound fresh medium shrimp,
   cooked, peeled, and deveined
1 cup crabmeat
1 medium red onion, chopped
1 medium tomato, chopped
1 medium cucumber, peeled and
   thinly sliced
6 cups shredded romaine lettuce

1. Combine lemon juice, chili powder, broth, sugar, coriander, and oyster sauce in a saucepan. Bring to a boil. Add shrimp and crabmeat, and remove from heat. Stir in onion.
2. Add tomato, cucumber, and lettuce, and toss well. Transfer to individual plates and serve.

Calories Per Serving: 140
Fat: 2 g
Cholesterol: 138 mg
Protein: 22 g

Carbohydrates: 9 g
Dietary Fiber: 2 g
Sodium: 302 mg

❊ *Pineapple-Shrimp Salad* ❊

PREPARATION TIME: *15 minutes plus 2 hours chilling time* • YIELD: *6 servings*

3 scallions, sliced
1 medium red bell pepper, cored and
   chopped
2 medium stalks celery, sliced
1 cup sliced canned water chestnuts,
   drained
2½ cups juice-packed canned
   pineapple chunks, drained

½ pound fresh medium shrimp,
   cooked, peeled, and deveined
½ cup nonfat plain yogurt
1 teaspoon curry powder
1 tablespoon lemon juice
6 cups torn spinach leaves

1. Combine scallions, bell pepper, celery, water chestnuts, pineapple chunks, and shrimp in a large bowl.
2. In a separate bowl, whisk together yogurt, curry powder, and lemon juice. Pour over salad and toss gently. Chill for 2 hours.
3. Arrange spinach on individual plates, top with salad, and serve.

Calories Per Serving: 147

Carbohydrates: 25 g

Fat: 1 g

Dietary Fiber: 3 g

Cholesterol: 58 mg

Sodium: 132 mg

Protein: 11 g

❀ *Chesapeake Bay Shrimp and Crab Salad* ❀

PREPARATION TIME: *20 minutes* • YIELD: *6 servings*

12 cups shredded lettuce
3 scallions, sliced
2 medium stalks celery, sliced
1 cup fresh cooked or shredded
 canned crabmeat
2 medium tomatoes, cut into thin
 wedges
½ pound fresh medium shrimp,
 cooked, peeled, and deveined

½ cup nonfat plain yogurt
5 cloves garlic, minced
3 tablespoons lemon juice
1 teaspoon ground black pepper
¼ teaspoon hot pepper sauce
1 teaspoon dried dill
2 tablespoons grated onion

1. Combine lettuce, scallions, celery, crabmeat, tomatoes, and shrimp in a large bowl.
2. In a separate bowl, mix together remaining ingredients and pour over salad. Toss well and serve.

Calories Per Serving: 112

Carbohydrates: 10 g

Fat: 1 g

Dietary Fiber: 2 g

Cholesterol: 78 mg

Sodium: 172 mg

Protein: 16 g

❀ *Crab-Broccoli Salad with Pasta Shells* ❀ *and Citrus Dressing*

PREPARATION TIME: *20 minutes* • COOKING TIME: *2 minutes* •
YIELD: *4 servings*

1 cup chopped broccoli
2 cups cooked small pasta shells
½ cup sliced radishes
1½ cups fresh cooked or shredded
 canned crabmeat

1 medium yellow bell pepper, cored
 and cut into thin strips
3 scallions, sliced
½ cup chopped fresh parsley
½ cup orange juice

1 *tablespoon honey*   2 *cloves garlic, minced*
¼ *teaspoon ground black pepper*

1. Steam broccoli until tender-crisp, about 2 minutes.
2. Combine broccoli, pasta shells, radishes, crabmeat, bell pepper, scallions, and parsley in a large bowl.
3. In a separate bowl, mix orange juice, honey, black pepper, and garlic. Dress salad, toss gently, and serve.

Calories Per Serving: 194   Carbohydrates: 30 g
Fat: 2 g   Dietary Fiber: 3 g
Cholesterol: 51 mg   Sodium: 155 mg
Protein: 15 g

❋ *Southwestern Fish Salad* ❋

PREPARATION TIME: *15 minutes plus 1 hour marinating time* • YIELD: *4 servings*

1 *cup cubed cooked cod fillet*   ½ *teaspoon dried thyme*
¼ *cup lime juice*   8 *large romaine lettuce leaves*
¼ *cup chopped fresh parsley*   1 *medium tomato, cut into thin*
1 *medium green bell pepper, cored*   *wedges*
   and finely chopped   1 *medium cucumber, peeled and*
1 *medium carrot, scraped and grated*   *thinly sliced*
1 *cup thinly sliced mushrooms*   1 *tablespoon vinegar*
1 *medium stalk celery, sliced*   ¼ *teaspoon ground black pepper*
½ *teaspoon dried oregano*   2 *scallions, sliced*

1. Place cod in a small bowl, pour 3 tablespoons lime juice over fish, and marinate, refrigerated, for 1 hour.
2. In a separate bowl, combine parsley, bell pepper, carrot, mushrooms, celery, oregano, and thyme. Toss well. Stir in fish cubes.
3. Divide fish salad over lettuce leaves, tomato, and cucumber on individual plates.
4. In a separate bowl, combine remaining lime juice, vinegar, and black pepper. Sprinkle over salads, top with scallions, and serve.

Calories Per Serving: 120   Carbohydrates: 11 g
Fat: 1 g   Dietary Fiber: 3 g
Cholesterol: 36 mg   Sodium: 78 mg
Protein: 18 g

❋ *Tuna and Spinach Salad* ❋ *with Cannellini Beans*

PREPARATION TIME: *15 minutes* • YIELD: *4 servings*

2 medium tomatoes, chopped
1 3½-ounce can water-packed solid
    white albacore tuna, drained and
    crumbled
2 scallions, sliced
¼ cup chopped fresh parsley

¼ cup rice vinegar
2 cloves garlic, minced
¼ teaspoon ground black pepper
6 cups low-sodium canned cannellini
    beans, rinsed and drained
4 cups torn spinach leaves

1. Combine tomatoes, tuna, scallions, and parsley in a large bowl.
2. In a separate bowl, whisk together rice vinegar, garlic, and black pepper, and dress salad. Gently mix in beans.
3. Serve salad over spinach on individual plates.

Calories Per Serving: 254
Fat: 2 g
Cholesterol: 13 mg
Protein: 23 g

Carbohydrates: 39 g
Dietary Fiber: 12 g
Sodium: 207 mg

❋ *Tuna-Macaroni Salad with Orange* ❋

PREPARATION TIME: *15 minutes plus 1 hour chilling time* • YIELD: *4 servings*

1 6-ounce can water-packed solid
    white albacore tuna, drained and
    crumbled
2 cups cooked elbow macaroni
1 medium carrot, scraped and grated
1 cup chopped orange

2 medium stalks celery, sliced
2 scallions, sliced
2 tablespoons lemon juice
½ cup nonfat plain yogurt
¼ teaspoon ground black pepper
8 large lettuce leaves

1. Combine all ingredients except lettuce. Toss gently and chill for 1 hour.
2. Arrange lettuce on individual plates, top with salad, and serve.

Calories Per Serving: 199
Fat: 1 g
Cholesterol: 15 mg
Protein: 18 g

Carbohydrates: 29 g
Dietary Fiber: 3 g
Sodium: 212 mg

❈ *Ocean City Tuna-Pasta Salad* ❈

PREPARATION TIME: *20 minutes*   •   YIELD: *6 servings*

3 cups cooked bow-tie pasta
1 6-ounce can water-packed solid
    white albacore tuna, drained and
    crumbled
¼ cup sliced olives
1 medium onion, chopped
1 medium red bell pepper, cored and
    chopped

1 medium green bell pepper, cored
    and chopped
3 medium stalks celery, sliced
¼ cup chopped fresh parsley
½ teaspoon paprika
1 cup nonfat plain yogurt
¼ cup lemon juice
1 teaspoon Dijon mustard
2 tablespoons wine vinegar

1. Combine pasta, tuna, olives, onion, bell peppers, celery, and parsley in a
   large bowl.
2. In a separate bowl, mix together paprika, yogurt, lemon juice, mustard,
   and vinegar. Toss well with salad, and serve.

Calories Per Serving: 178
Fat: 1 g
Cholesterol: 13 mg
Protein: 14 g

Carbohydrates: 26 g
Dietary Fiber: 2 g
Sodium: 326 mg

❈ *Apple-Pineapple-Pepper Salad* ❈

PREPARATION TIME: *20 minutes*   •   YIELD: *4 servings*

1 cup chopped apples
1 cup juice-packed canned pineapple
    chunks, drained
1 cup seedless raisins
1 medium red bell pepper, cored and
    cut into thin strips
1 cup chopped fresh parsley
2 cups cooked rice

1 scallion, minced
3 tablespoons sugar
¼ teaspoon dry mustard
2 tablespoons white wine vinegar
½ cup orange juice
½ cup nonfat plain yogurt
¼ teaspoon ground black pepper

1. Combine apple, pineapple, raisins, and bell pepper in a large bowl.
2. In a separate bowl, mix parsley, rice, and scallion, and blend with fruit
   mixture.

3. In a separate bowl, whisk together sugar, dry mustard, vinegar, orange juice, yogurt, and black pepper. Toss well with salad, and serve.

Calories Per Serving: 359   Carbohydrates: 87 g
Fat: 1 g   Dietary Fiber: 3 g
Cholesterol: 1 mg   Sodium: 31 mg
Protein: 6 g

❁ Pasta Salad with Broccoli, Bell Pepper, ❁ and Zucchini

PREPARATION TIME: *20 minutes plus 1 hour chilling time* • YIELD: *4 servings*

¼ cup diced nonfat cheddar   *1 cup diced zucchini*
2 medium tomatoes, diced   *3 cups cooked penne*
¼ cup sliced green olives   *¾ cup orange juice*
1 medium red bell pepper, cored and   *2 cloves garlic, minced*
  chopped   *½ teaspoon ground black pepper*
1 cup chopped broccoli   *½ cup chopped fresh parsley*

1. Toss together cheddar, tomatoes, olives, bell pepper, broccoli, zucchini, and pasta in a large salad bowl.
2. In a separate bowl, combine orange juice, garlic, black pepper, and parsley, and toss well with salad. Chill for 1 hour before serving.

Calories Per Serving: 216   Carbohydrates: 39 g
Fat: 2 g   Dietary Fiber: 4 g
Cholesterol: 3 mg   Sodium: 340 mg
Protein: 12 g

❁ Peasant Pasta Salad ❁

PREPARATION TIME: *15 minutes plus 1 hour chilling time* • YIELD: *2 servings*

2 cups cooked farfalle pasta   *1 jalapeño pepper, seeded and minced*
3 scallions, sliced   *½ cup nonfat plain yogurt*
2 cloves garlic, minced   *1½ tablespoons Dijon mustard*
4 medium tomatoes, chopped   *¼ teaspoon ground black pepper*

1. Combine pasta, scallions, garlic, tomatoes, and jalapeño pepper in a large bowl.
2. In a separate bowl, mix yogurt, mustard, and black pepper, and stir into salad. Chill for 1 hour before serving.

Calories Per Serving: 251
Fat: 1 g
Cholesterol: 1 mg
Protein: 8 g

Carbohydrates: 32 g
Dietary Fiber: 4 g
Sodium: 349 mg

❀ *San Juan Fruited Rice Salad* ❀

PREPARATION TIME: *20 minutes* • YIELD: *4 servings*

1 cup chopped orange
1 cup juice-packed canned pineapple chunks, drained
1 cup fresh blueberries
1 medium banana, sliced
1 cup chopped fresh parsley
2 cups cooked rice

1 scallion, minced
3 tablespoons sugar
¼ teaspoon dry mustard
2 tablespoons white wine vinegar
½ cup orange juice
¼ teaspoon ground black pepper

1. Combine orange, pineapple chunks, blueberries, and banana in a large bowl.
2. In a separate bowl, mix parsley, rice, and scallion, and combine with fruit.
3. In a separate bowl, whisk together sugar, dry mustard, vinegar, orange juice, and black pepper. Toss well with salad, and serve.

Calories Per Serving: 296
Fat: 1 g
Cholesterol: 0 mg
Protein: 4 g

Carbohydrates: 70 g
Dietary Fiber: 4 g
Sodium: 9 mg

❀ *Rice and Vegetable Salad with* ❀ *Yogurt-Lemon Dressing*

PREPARATION TIME: *15 minutes* • YIELD: *4 servings*

1 scallion, minced
1 medium cucumber, peeled and
    chopped
1 medium red bell pepper, cored and
    diced
½ cup chopped fresh parsley
2 cups cooked green peas

1 cup seedless raisins
1½ cups cooked rice
3 cups nonfat plain yogurt
2 tablespoons lemon juice
¼ teaspoon ground black pepper
4 large romaine lettuce leaves

1. Combine scallion, cucumber, bell pepper, parsley, peas, raisins, and rice in
   a large bowl.
2. Stir in yogurt and lemon juice, sprinkle with black pepper, and toss well.
3. Serve salad over lettuce on individual plates.

Calories Per Serving: 366
Fat: 1 g
Cholesterol: 4 mg
Protein: 17 g

Carbohydrates: 77 g
Dietary Fiber: 4 g
Sodium: 135 mg

✿ Black Bean and Corn Salad ✿

PREPARATION TIME: *20 minutes plus 2 hours chilling time* ▪ YIELD: *4 servings*

1 medium orange, peeled, sectioned,
    and coarsely chopped
2 cups low-sodium canned black
    beans, rinsed and drained
1 cup fresh, drained canned, or
    thawed frozen corn kernels

4 scallions, chopped
½ teaspoon ground cumin
2 teaspoons dried cilantro
2 tablespoons balsamic vinegar
¼ teaspoon ground black pepper

1. Combine orange, beans, corn, scallions, cumin, cilantro, vinegar, and
   black pepper in a large bowl.
2. Toss gently and chill for 2 hours before serving.

Calories Per Serving: 181
Fat: 1 g
Cholesterol: 0 mg
Protein: 9 g

Carbohydrates: 37 g
Dietary Fiber: 10 g
Sodium: 11 mg

❋ *Lentil-Tomato Salad* ❋

PREPARATION TIME: *20 minutes plus 1 hour chilling time* •
COOKING TIME: *30 minutes* • YIELD: *6 servings*

1½ cups dried lentils, rinsed and
    drained
4 cups water
2 medium onions, sliced
8 whole cloves
2 bay leaves
2 cloves garlic, minced
¼ teaspoon ground black pepper
1 teaspoon hot pepper sauce

2 teaspoons olive oil
½ cup red wine vinegar
3 medium stalks celery, sliced
½ cup chopped fresh parsley
¼ cup chopped onion
12 large lettuce leaves
2 medium tomatoes, cut into thin
    wedges

1. Combine lentils, water, sliced onions, cloves, bay leaves, garlic, black pepper, and ½ teaspoon hot pepper sauce in a large saucepan. Bring to a boil, reduce heat, cover, and simmer until lentils are tender, about 30 minutes. Drain. Remove bay leaves.
2. Stir in olive oil, vinegar, and remaining hot pepper sauce. Mix well and chill for 1 hour.
3. Add celery, parsley, and chopped onion. Mix well.
4. Arrange lettuce leaves on individual plates, top with salad and tomato wedges, and serve.

Calories Per Serving: 78
Fat: 2 g
Cholesterol: 0 mg
Protein: 4 g

Carbohydrates: 14 g
Dietary Fiber: 4 g
Sodium: 40 mg

❋ *Easy Broccoli-Stuffed Tomatoes* ❋

PREPARATION TIME: *10 minutes* • YIELD: *6 servings*

4 cups finely chopped broccoli
2 cloves garlic, minced
1 cup nonfat cottage cheese
6 large tomatoes, cut in half length-
    wise and cored

¼ teaspoon ground black pepper
½ cup nonfat plain yogurt

1. Blend broccoli, garlic, and cottage cheese briefly in a blender or food processor.
2. Stuff tomato halves with broccoli mixture. Top with black pepper and a dollop of yogurt, and serve.

Calories Per Serving: 77
Fat: 1 g
Cholesterol: 2 mg
Protein: 7 g

Carbohydrates: 13 g
Dietary Fiber: 4 g
Sodium: 108 mg

❋ Spinach-Lime Salad ❋

PREPARATION TIME: *15 minutes* • YIELD: *4 servings*

1 medium red bell pepper, cored and cut into thin strips
2 medium apples, peeled, cored, and chopped
6 cups chopped fresh spinach

1 cup diced zucchini
3 tablespoons orange juice
1 tablespoon lime juice
¼ teaspoon ground black pepper

1. Combine bell pepper, apples, spinach, and zucchini in a large bowl.
2. In a separate bowl, whisk together orange juice, lime juice, and black pepper. Toss well with salad, and serve.

Calories Per Serving: 67
Fat: 1 g
Cholesterol: 0 mg
Protein: 3 g

Carbohydrates: 15 g
Dietary Fiber: 4 g
Sodium: 68 mg

❋ Garden Vegetable Salad with Pasta Shells ❋

PREPARATION TIME: *20 minutes plus 1 hour chilling time* • YIELD: *4 servings*

¼ cup diced nonfat mozzarella
2 medium tomatoes, diced
¼ cup sliced green olives
1 medium green bell pepper, cored and chopped
1 medium onion, sliced

1 medium carrot, scraped and sliced
3 cups cooked small pasta shells
¾ cup orange juice
2 cloves garlic, minced
½ teaspoon ground black pepper
½ cup chopped fresh parsley

1. Toss together mozzarella, tomatoes, olives, bell pepper, onion, carrot, and pasta shells in a large salad bowl.
2. In a separate bowl, combine orange juice, garlic, black pepper, and parsley, and toss well with salad. Chill for 1 hour before serving.

Calories Per Serving: 221   Carbohydrates: 40 g
Fat: 2 g   Dietary Fiber: 4 g
Cholesterol: 3 mg   Sodium: 340 mg
Protein: 11 g

❋ *Pineapple-Carrot Salad with* ❋ *Cinnamon Yogurt*

PREPARATION TIME: *20 minutes* • YIELD: *4 servings*

2 medium green bell peppers, cored and chopped
1 cup diced zucchini
1 medium carrot, scraped and sliced
2 medium apples, peeled, cored, and chopped

1 cup juice-packed canned pineapple chunks, drained
1 cup nonfat plain yogurt
3 tablespoons orange juice
1 tablespoon lime juice
⅛ teaspoon ground black pepper
½ teaspoon ground cinnamon

1. Combine bell peppers, zucchini, carrot, apples, and pineapple chunks in a large bowl.
2. In a separate bowl, whisk together yogurt, orange juice, lime juice, and black pepper, and drizzle over salad. Sprinkle with cinnamon and serve.

Calories Per Serving: 141   Carbohydrates: 33 g
Fat: 0 g   Dietary Fiber: 3 g
Cholesterol: 1 mg   Sodium: 55 mg
Protein: 5 g

❋ *Hearty Steamer Salad* ❋

PREPARATION TIME: *10 minutes plus 1 hour chilling time* •
COOKING TIME: *1½ minutes* • YIELD: *4 servings*

1 cup chopped broccoli
1 cup chopped cauliflower
1 cup scraped and sliced carrot
1 cup chopped green beans (1-inch
   lengths)

1 cup sliced canned beets, drained
4 cups shredded lettuce
¼ cup balsamic vinegar
½ teaspoon black pepper

1. Steam broccoli, cauliflower, carrot, and green beans until tender-crisp, about 1½ minutes. Transfer to a large bowl and chill for 1 hour.
2. Combine steamed vegetables, beets, and lettuce. Dress with balsamic vinegar, sprinkle with black pepper, toss well, and serve.

Calories Per Serving: 59
Fat: 0 g
Cholesterol: 0 mg
Protein: 3 g

Carbohydrates: 13 g
Dietary Fiber: 2 g
Sodium: 188 mg

INDEX